marriage and family assessment

marriage and family assessment

A Sourcebook for Family Therapy

edited by
ERIK E. FILSINGER

SAGE PUBLICATIONS
Beverly Hills / London / New Delhi

To my parents,
John and Marjorie Filsinger,
for their love and
support during my youth

For information address:

SAGE Publications, Inc.
275 South Beverly Drive
Beverly Hills, California 90212

SAGE Publications India Pvt. Ltd. SAGE Publications Ltd
C-236 Defence Colony 28 Banner Street
New Delhi 110 024, India London EC1Y 8QE, England

Printed in the United States of America

Library of Congress Cataloging in Publication Data

Main entry under title:

Marriage and family assessment.

1. Family social work. 2. Family therapy. 3. Marriage
counseling. I. Filsinger, Erik E. [DNLM: 1. Family
therapy—Methods. 2. Marital therapy—Methods. WM
430.5.F2 M359]
HV697.M37   1983   362.8'2   83-11087
ISBN 0-8039-2028-8

FIRST PRINTING

Contents

Preface

This volume is based on an assumption: Practitioners and researchers have not done a good job of communicating with one another. A bridge is necessary between the two. Practitioners must be able to understand the contributions of researchers and researchers must be able to make their efforts meaningful for practitioners.

Unfortunately, it is possible, although there are notable exceptions, to talk about practitioners and researchers as belonging to separate camps. Part of the reason for this bifurcation is the self-selection of individuals as being more committed to "helping people" or interested in "science." In fact, the two should not be separate. The destinies of the two are intertwined. As graduate schools place more emphasis on training practitioners in basic research skills so that they can keep up with the latest techniques being presented in scholarly journals, and as researchers become more attuned to doing research on issues applicable to practical settings, the two will move closer together. In order to facilitate the process, this volume represents an attempt by researchers to bridge the gap. It is intended to offer assessment techniques that have been used primarily in research settings in a way in which those same techniques can be used by the practitioner.

The book is not about research settings. Rather, it is about ways in which the practitioner can use formal assessment to improve the results of the therapy process. Presumably, the higher the quality of the information the therapist uses, the better will be his or her judgments and treatments. At least the user has some documentation to make the therapy process more accountable for its success or failure.

The contributers to this volume are researchers, many of whom also have their own therapy practices. Most of their publications over the years can be found in research journals. In this volume, however, they have agreed to make an attempt to present their material so that it is maximally useful for the practitioner. Each of the methods they describe can be applied to a single case, whether an individual, a marriage, or a family.

While different schools of thought are represented, both in terms of theoretical and therapeutic orientations, the contributers share the belief that the therapy process can be furthered by gathering the highest-quality information. Arguments as to the possible clinical utility of assessment are contained throughout. Suggestions for the use of the contributors' techniques in therapeutic settings, including guidelines for administration, scoring, and interpretation, are also highlighted.

The authors were given a common outline and asked to follow it, as much as possible, in developing their contributions. As might be imagined, there was some diversity in the ways the authors fulfilled the outline, yet each contribution shares some structural similarity that should aid comparison of assessment techniques. Most of all, this is intended to be a user-oriented volume.

The chapters have been arranged into four sections. Part I is an introduction to formal assessment. Parts II-IV reflect two distinctions. One is between outsider and insider reports of family activity. In this case, outsider reports reflect observations made of family interaction, usually by disinterested third parties. Part II contains chapters that reflect the latest in observational methodologies. Insider reports are self-reports by family members that reflect the perceptions they have of family activity. While both Parts III and IV contain examples of insider and outsider reports, Part III focuses on the marital dyad, whereas Part IV focuses on the whole family system. It is hoped that this structure will facilitate the reader's location of materials that best fit his or her assessment needs.

As editor, I must give my thanks to all of the authors for submitting their materials in time to meet publication deadlines. My thanks must also be extended to the critical readers who reviewed parts of the manuscript. These individuals included Donald Baucom, Alan Gurman, Sandy Mazen, and Eileen Schofield. A special thanks must be offered to Philip McAvoy for his assistance in the final stages of the preparation of this volume and to Bonnie Muzio for clerical assistance throughout the project.

—*Erik Filsinger*
Tempe, Arizona

PART *I*

INTRODUCTION

If it is true that assessment is often an undervalued part of marriage and family therapy, then the case must be made as to why it should be more formally utilized. In Chapter 1, I have attempted to pull together part of this argument under the title "Assessment: What It Is and Why It Is Important." Some general guidelines for selecting a technique are offered, though the subsequent chapters also address rationales for selecting assessment techniques. In Chapter 2, Haynes and Chavez present an overview of the clinical usage of the interview. They assert that "the interview is one of the most frequently used, but least investigated, methods of assessing marital [and family] distress." Of particular interest to therapists will be their discussion of therapeutic goals and their suggested outline of an assessment interview. Because of the importance of these issues, which lay the groundwork for subsequent formal assessment techniques, Chapter 2 also serves as introductory material for this volume.

CHAPTER 1

Assessment:
What It Is and
Why It Is Important

ERIK E. FILSINGER
Arizona State University

When a client comes into an office or clinic, an evaluation process begins that does not end until the patient is not seen again. This evaluation includes judgments as to the nature of the client's problem, the client's strengths and weaknesses, the appropriate interventions, the progress of the therapy, its effectiveness, and its completion. Whether done formally or informally, that process is assessment. The position taken herein is that marriage and family therapy can benefit from closer attention to the role of assessment in therapy.

While it is true that many marriage and family therapists have been concerned with assessment for some time (see Bodin, 1968; Cromwell, Olson, & Fournier, 1976; Filsinger & Lewis, 1981; Riskin & Faunce, 1972; Snyder, 1981; Weiss & Margolin, 1977), the concern has not become a significant part of the regular routine of practicing marriage and family therapists. Cromwell and his colleagues (1976, p. 2) state that "to date, it appears that therapy continued to be practiced and evaluated as if it were an art rather than a science. It is our view that therapy is a science demanding more systematic and rigorous evaluations. . . . Therapists do in fact both diagnose and evaluate their own clinical work. However, this is often done in a highly selective, unsystematic, and subjective manner."

As evidenced in the state-of-the-art *Handbook of Family Therapy* (Gurman & Kniskern, 1981a), representatives of the major schools of therapy are able to elucidate the specific components of their therapy process as it relates to some very specific issues. When the therapy pro-

Author's Note: This chapter is based on a paper presented at the Conference on Family Competence, Center for Family Studies, Arizona State University, Tempe, February 1983.

cess can be dissected and communicated in specific, analytic terms to the next generation of therapists, and when those components can be tested for their effectiveness, marriage and family therapy has taken on some of the characteristics of a science. Its worth is to be judged more by objective standards and less by subjectivity.

While it is true that some therapeutic orientations are relatively more inherently tied to formal assessment than are others, members of the various schools of thought can indeed focus on the assessment procedures they use (Gurman & Kniskern, 1981a). A few examples can be cited. One of the hallmarks of the behavioral approaches is their emphasis on systematic assessment procedures throughout therapy (Jacobson, 1981). The McMaster model of family functioning is based on assessment procedures that identify the problems to be dealt with (Epstein & Bishop, 1981). Even therapists who deal less formally with assessment recognize the place it takes in their therapy process (Framo, 1981; Skynner, 1981; Whitaker & Keith, 1981).

Marital and family therapy is still quite young compared to the older disciplines in the behavioral sciences. This "youth" can be associated with much of its vitality. But, as Olson (1970, pp. 501-502) states, "Not unlike youth, however, the professions of marital and family therapy have proceeded with a great amount of vigor but without a sufficient amount of rigor. As a result, many of the visionary ideas have not been carefully enough developed or tested and are, therefore, in need of critical evaluation." Part of the maturation process of a discipline is the formalization of its procedures. Assessment is one such procedure in therapy.

Larger issues concerning attitudes toward the nature of therapy and its growth are involved. Gurman and Kniskern (1981b, p. 764) state that "most leaders of the family field are still addicted to proselytizing, with the result that more allegiance is paid to charismatic personalities than to a common goal of empirical scrutiny." However, there is a growing recognition of what the clinician and the researcher have to gain from a closer appreciation of each other's perspective. Gurman and Kniskern (1981b, p. 744) state that "clinical concerns and empirical concerns are not antagonistic, but are, in fact, synergistic and should be indistinguishable." In a series of publications, Olson (1970, 1981) has chided both researchers and therapists for going their separate ways with minimal knowledge of what the other is doing. He outlines a variety of ways that bridging that gap could be beneficial to the researcher as well as to the therapist. Among the contributions therapists can make to researchers is the broadening of their perspective on the complexity of family dynamics. Too often researchers are wedded to the narrow perspective of generating hypotheses out of a line of previous research published in the scholarly journals (see Olson, 1970). These studies tend to be methodologically sound, but are frequently insignificant or irrelevant for those professionals working with families.

The other side of the coin is that therapists have not taken advantage of the strengths that researchers can offer them. Among Olson's (1981) list of researcher contributions are helping therapists clarify concepts and goals, helping them diagnose problems and evaluate treatments, and providing normative data on nonclinic as well as clinic populations.

Part of the problem in the lack of clinician interest in assessment has been the relative inaccessibility of the assessment techniques. For the most part, the techniques have appeared in research journals or other publications written by researchers primarily for researchers. They have not been geared to the practitioner who has undergone training mostly focused on therapy technique and who is often unfamiliar with research methodology and terminology. The purpose of the present volume is to take some of those assessment techniques that have seemed remote and unresponsive to clinical needs and to present them in such a way that they are useful and responsive for the practitioner.

Reflecting the general developments in marriage and family therapy of the last two decades, the focus of this volume is on assessment techniques aimed at the couple or family. This is not to say that the individual is not important. The individual is important. Gurman (1978) has suggested that the argument over the individual versus the dyadic levels of analysis is misguided because those phenomena are inextricably linked. Moreover, "with regard to outcome assessment per se, it seems unfortunate that less than one-quarter of these (outcome) studies have evaluated change in spouses both as individuals and as a dyadic (social) unit. Clearly, the assessment alone of either of these parameters of change in couples therapy is inadequate" (Gurman, 1973, p. 149).

Two points can be made in this regard. Many of the instruments contained herein can be interpreted as saying something about the individual as well as about the dyad or the family. While the strictly individual assessment instruments are not included in the present volume, the therapist is advised to use them for telling something about individual pathology. Individual pathology can cause family disturbance as well as vice versa (Gurman, 1978).

Assessment: The Logic

In preparing their handbook, Gurman and Kniskern (1981a) gave their authors an outline that included a section on assessment. The purpose of the section was "to describe the methods, whether formal or informal, used to gain an understanding of a particular marriage's or family's style or pattern of interaction, symptomatology and adaptive resources" (p. xv). The questions listed under the topic of assessment included concern with the unit of analysis (for example, individual, couple, family), psychological levels, formal assessment instruments, relationship of assessment to treatment, and the role of verbal interviews versus more structured tasks.

Assessment can vary a great deal in terms of its formality. At the more informal end, it can be based on the therapist's observation of the couple during the course of therapy. Somewhat more formally, therapists can set aside the initial sessions with the couple in order to gain insight into their problem. A distinct therapy process then follows. Still more formal are assessment techniques that use specialized procedures to generate data to be examined for telltale patterns of dysfunction. The most formal are those that measure family characteristics with tools other than the therapist's own eyes.

Any one person's perspective is to some extent limited by its own subjectivity. The fundamental reason for increasing the objectivity of assessment procedures is that a therapist cannot help but let his or her perspective and biases enter into assessment judgments. Moreover, the therapist and the client develop a unique system of interaction and begin to elicit certain behaviors that would not be there if a different therapist or client were present. If errors enters into the judgment of the client's problem and/or progress, the therapist may not do as good a job in helping the client as he or she might if a different, more objective view were offered for consideration. Assessment by formal means should not replace the therapist's personal judgment. Rather, each should supplement the other in order to triangulate in on the truth.

As identified by Platt (1964), the sciences that seem to be developing the fastest have a common method of conducting their activities. Platt labels this investigative procedure "strong inference." It consists of devising alternative hypotheses, devising a crucial experiment that will exclude one or more of the hypotheses, carrying out the experiment, and devising new hypotheses that refine the original procedure. In the area of family therapy, the rival hypotheses could relate to alternative therapy techniques. An experiment that demonstrates the superiority of one approach should lead to the rejection of the other, at least under similar conditions with similar subjects. The superior technique could then be subjected to further scrutiny and a comparison of slight modifications.

This notion of falsifiability, the systematic exclusion of inferior hypotheses, is the basis of scientific progress (Pap, 1962). Falsifiability requires measurement strategies that are public and verifiable. The data must be reliable and valid, and the procedures must be replicable.

Part of the reason that therapists and researchers have not shared efforts previously is the general value orientation of some therapists who feel that formal assessment is cold, detached, and inhuman. Objectivity does not preclude humanity; rather, it informs humanity. It is better to use available techniques in order to double-check ourselves than to indulge our senses in an often imagined empathy based on a projection of our own life history and biases. The task for therapists is to select an assessment package that will provide them with information relevant to their treatment methods.

Assessment Components

At its core, assessment is the careful analysis of clients so that the appropriate strategy of helping them can be undertaken. Several writers have suggested that assessment involves diagnosis, treatment selection, and treatment evaluation (Ciminero, 1977; Cromwell et al., 1976). Keefe, Kopel, and Gordon (1978, p. 16) further dissect the assessment process: "Behavioral assessment involves five general stages: (1) problem identification; (2) measurement and functional analysis; (3) matching treatment to client; (4) assessment of ongoing therapy; and (5) evaluation of therapy."

During diagnosis the therapist uses the clinical interview (see Haynes and Chavez, Chapter 2) to arrive at a conclusion about the problem the couple or family is facing. A variety of techniques are available to add independent information as to the nature of the problem (for example, the Spouse Observation Checklist, Chapter 4; the Marital Communication Inventory, Chapter 10; the Family Environment Scale, Chapter 13; the Family Stress Measure, Chapter 14; and the Family Adaptability and Cohesion Scales, Chapter 15) or the behaviors within the family unit that support the dysfunction. This latter point is what Keefe et al. (1978) label a "functional analysis." A variety of assessment procedures are especially helpful in a detailed analysis of the family system (for example, the Couples Interaction Scoring System, Chapter 6; the Inventory of Marital Conflicts, Chapter 3; the Marital Interaction Coding System, Chapter 5; the Marital Agendas Protocol, Chapter 11; and the Family Environment Scale, Chapter 13).

Margolin and Fernandez (Chapter 16) make two points about the benefits to be obtained from formal diagnosis. First, it may be cost-beneficial to have a quick and complete overview of the couple's or family's relationship. Arriving at the same information through interviews takes a lot of time—time that could be used for therapy if formal assessment were used. In addition, the clinician can make good use of his or her private knowledge of where family members agree or disagree, selecting those issues for discussion at appropriate times.

Formal evaluation can also be an integral part of therapy. Going through an assessment procedure can be a good learning experience for clients. By having to fill out a questionnaire, for example, the spouses may be forced to look at their relationship along dimensions that are new to them. Couples are generally very poor at objectification, that is, at making objective observations about the specific dynamics of their relationship (Filsinger, Note 1; Weiss, 1978). The Spouse Observation Checklist (Chapter 4) involves daily recording by each spouse of behaviors emitted that day by the other, rating the behaviors as pleasers and displeasers. While some therapies include tracking skills, merely filling out a questionnaire may help the spouses begin to try to put cognitions with their emotions. If the assessment instruments benefit the therapy process, those cognitions will be functional ones.

Treatment strategies should be selected on the basis of the diagnosis. Very few informed therapists, if any, advocate a universal treatment for all problems. Instead, the family's characteristics, problems, and resources are taken into account and a treatment is stylized for that family. In reviewing the marital and family therapy literature of the 1970s, Olson, Russell, and Sprenkle (1980, p. 979) state, "The trend in the family therapy field appears to be toward specifying which mode of therapy is most effective for which group of clients presenting which sorts of problems." Unfortunately, not enough is known about the relative effectiveness of different types of treatments for different types of clients to be able to do the proper matching. This is definitely an area in which more clinical research is needed.

Treatment evaluation consists of both an assessment of the ongoing therapy process and an assessment of the eventual effectiveness of the treatment. The progress the couple is making in response to treatment or components of treatment is a great concern to therapists. Frequently an evaluation of this progress is a rather subjective judgment as to what seems to be working or what does not seem to be having the desired effect. Assessment could be used to monitor the progress the client is making from session to session. Improvement in one area of family functioning can be a cue to move to other issues. In addition, information obtained from assessment of the therapy process could be used to select the next appropriate intervention.

Assessment during the course of therapy may be very useful in catching deterioration, both in the family subsystem being treated and in other levels of the family system. Amelioration of father-son difficulties may give rise to marital problems, but assessment can help identify when such deterioration takes place. It may be necessary to devote part of the therapy process toward bringing the marriage back up to at least its baseline level.

Toward the end of the therapy process, assessment can be used to provide another source of information as to whether or not sufficient progress has been made to discontinue therapy. This could be indicated by the client obtaining some designated score on a standardized instrument. However, this score should be used to supplement rather than supplant the therapist's own judgment. Nevertheless, the outside information may be useful in guarding against the perceptual constancy of the therapist not recognizing that the change in fact has taken place.

Outcome assessment refers to the evaluation of treatment effectiveness. Outcome research has received a number of reviews (Gurman, 1973; Gurman & Kniskern, 1981b; Olson, 1970; Olson et al., 1980). Frequently the effectiveness of therapy is judged by the subjective report of satisfaction in the family unit. The Dyadic Adjustment Scale (Chapter 8) is one such example, as are the Marital Satisfaction Inventory (Chapter 9) and the Marital Communication Inventory (Chapter 10). Positive changes in the pre- to posttreatment scores on these assessment techniques indicate progress for distressed relationships.

Outcome measures most frequently reflect change that has occurred with regard to the problem for which the family had entered therapy; however, the nature of the problem may change or a new problem may be uncovered during the course of therapy. Improvement might occur in the original problem and the new one, but it might also occur in either one separately.

Because there may be some sleeper effects—that is, improvement may not show immediately but may emerge later—it is important to have multiple occasions of outcome evaluation spaced over a long enough period for the seeds that have been sown in therapy to grow. Possible deterioration in one or more systems of the family being treated necessitate both the ongoing evaluation mentioned above and the multiple-occasion outcome assessment. It may be that what is recorded as deterioration at one point is a necessary phase. However, it is very dangerous to assume that any deterioration is really a step toward progress. Therapy can and does do damage (Gurman & Kniskern, 1978).

Selecting an Assessment Technique

A number of questions should be asked in order to guide the assessment technique. (1) What aspects of the relationship do we want to measure? (2) At what level of analysis is the measurement appropriate (individual, couple, family)? (3) How much time and energy is required? And, of course, (4) to what use is the information gathered going to be put? The following points may help in choosing a package.

The use of multimethod procedures is advisable. This gives a perspective on the family from a number of different vantage points. In addition, different aspects of the family's life should be investigated, such as interaction, values, and satisfactions. Another way of approaching the choice of multimethods is to consider that the relationship can be seen from the inside by the couple or from the outside by observers. Olson (1981) has suggested that four types of research methods can be discerned: (1) Self-report methods have the insider's frame of reference and are subjective in nature; (2) behavioral self-reports are also from the insider's perspective but are more objective in nature; (3) observer subjective reports are outside and subjective; and (4) behavioral methods are outside and objective. Traditional questionnaires are an example of the self-report approach. The therapist's informal assessment is an observer subjective report. Behavioral self-reports include self and spouse behavior checklists, frequently filled out on a daily basis over a period of time. Observational coding systems represent the behavioral methods in Olson's scheme. It would be a good idea to have at least one technique that represents the insider's perspective and one technique that represents the outsider's perspective.

One of the problems with an observer's outside perspective is that the family tends to develop a private meaning system. Each behavior is loaded with meaning that only the husband or wife can understand. An assessment from the insider's viewpoint taps that perspective. On the other hand, there are frequently objective factors about the couple's interaction of which they are not aware, but that stand in the way of their adjustment. These processes must be picked up from the outsider's perspective.

A second aspect of multimethod assessment relevant here is the choice of the level of analysis. In any marital and family therapy, it is likely to have the individual, the dyad, and possibly the family involved. In addition, there is the possibility of the intergenerational system being involved. Cromwell and Peterson (1981) have suggested that assessment techniques should be chosen to represent each system level of analysis. That is, assessment should take place at the level of the individual, the dyad, and the family. They further caution that the assessment technique should fit that level of analysis. To support their contention they cite the family power literature, which for years explored power in the family at the level of the individual without ever taking family or couple measures. Personality tests of individual family members did little to add to the prediction of power in the marital relationship. Instead, measures of the couple's relationship were necessary. Therefore, an eye should be kept on fitting the measure to the conceptual level of interest.

Gurman and Kniskern (1981b) provide another systematic scheme for assessing change in marital and family therapy. One important difference is that they do not see the therapist as an outsider. Rather, they suggest that, at least during therapy, the therapist becomes part of the family system and is an insider. They also suggest that the difference between mediating and ultimate goals of therapy should be kept in mind. Mediating goals are those that are achieved in order to provide the means for improvement in the relationship, such as self-disclosure or change in communication patterns. Ultimate goals refer to the desired outcome for the relationship, for instance, alleviation of distress, sexual satisfaction, or amicable divorce.

Gurman and Kniskern (1981b) mention that for outcome criteria it may be useful to include some measures not directly derived from one's own theoretical orientation. They suggest, for example, that if problem-solving skills are a major component of the therapy, it may also be useful to see if differentiation of self occurs.

Unresolved Issues

Less clearly defined choices surround other issues. If the therapist wishes to use a measure of marital adjustment and is interested in the dyadic level of analysis, do responses to scales such as the Dyadic Adjustment Scale (Spanier and Filsinger, Chapter 8) meet the need? It is a moot point whether such scales measure the adjustment of the marriage or whether they represent individual adjustment to marriage. To date there are no universally accepted procedures for deriving couple scores from the separate responses of the spouses (though averages, differences, and total scores have been suggested). Interactional data would appear to be the clearest case of dyadic-level analysis (see Filsinger, Lewis, & McAvoy, 1981).

Perhaps a greater problem for the everyday practitioner relates to the scarcity of really good measures for some of the most central therapeutic concepts. Gurman and Kniskern (1981b, p. 764) state that "measures need to be used that are not only conceptually sound, but are also meaningful to clinicians and families, lest family therapy researchers evolve a 'system' unto themselves that is divorced from clinical application." On the other hand, therapists have shown a tenacity in holding on to concepts that either have not been shown to hold up when carefully investigated or are too abstract to measure. Olson (1970) suggests that the concept of the "double-bind" is one such example. Others might be the "superiority of co-therapists" and the necessity of including all members of the family in every case. On the former point, Gurman and Kniskern (1981b) suggest that evidence is lacking, and on the latter Weiss (1978) suggests that there are some issues of marital distress that do not necessitate going outside the dyad.

Related to the lack of good measures for some therapeutically interesting phenomena, it should be kept in mind that most assessment techniques are indeed linked, to some degree, to specific theoretical orientations and may do a better job of measuring some concepts than others.

Filsinger (Note 2) substantively compared five different marital observational coding systems and concluded that they do indeed emphasize different behaviors. These emphases are predictable from the theoretical orientations of their originators.

The theoretical biases underlying assessment techniques are a bane and a blessing. Because they are derived from different sources, the consumer has a variety of techniques from which to choose. Unfortunately, each technique is somewhat limited by the theoretical biases that underlie its development.

Perhaps the biggest unresolved issue for the area of assessment surrounds the question, "So what?" Techniques with demonstrated reliability and validity have been offered, but their practical significance has not yet been documented. It needs to be shown that a therapist who uses formal assessment does a better job of helping his or her clients than does a therapist who does not use formal assessment.

At the present time the assessment techniques are not used widely enough to offer evidence as to their clinical utility. Margolin and Fernandez (Chapter 16) argue on rational grounds that formal assessment provides superior diagnostic information; however, the empirical issues remain. Perhaps their suggestions can serve researchers as a series of evaluation questions. They bear repeating: (1) Does the instrument give us perspective on the intensity of the problem? (2) Does the instrument help us plan an intervention? (3) Is the instrument a cost-efficient way to collect information? and (4) Does the use of self-report questionnaires (the topic Margolin and Fernandez address) provide a safe medium for disclosing important information? It is hoped that research in the near future will begin to provide affirmative answers to these questions. Without the empirical basis for choosing formal assessment, many therapists will remain unconvinced. Conger (Chapter 7) offers a strong case for the contribution observational techniques can make to therapy by citing a couple of studies that indicate that self-reports by themselves would have missed some important features of family functioning. It is a start in gathering the necessary evidence.

Two additional areas of assessment interest are not dealt with in this volume. To date there are relatively few assessment techniques for one of the most important aspects of therapy—the therapist-client interaction. That area of investigation is quite understudied. Pinsof (1981) found only a handful of relevant studies in his review of the area. As a result, little is known about the best ways to assess this process. It is an important question that should be addressed in order to help the therapist fine tune his or her techniques for maximum effectiveness. In addition, the question of the costs versus the benefits of various types of treatments has not been fully investigated (Gurman & Kniskern, 1981b).

Conclusion

Assessment is a necessary part of therapy that is involved in diagnosis of patient problems, selection of treatment procedures, evaluation of these procedures during the course of therapy, and judgment as to the outcome of therapy. Greater objectivity in assessment procedures is a desirable goal and can be obtained in a way that is beneficial to the therapy process. Assessment can lead to better choices of treatment strategies and a refinement of therapy strategies. Attention to issues of assessment is a necessary step in the development of a reflexive and critical evaluation of the profession. That reflexivity is an integral part of its growth.

Reference Notes

1. Filsinger, E. E. *A behavioral-systems conceptualization of relationship accomplishment.* Paper presented at the Theory Construction and Research Methodology Workshop, National Council on Family Relations, Washington, D.C., October 1982.
2. Filsinger, E. E. *Implications in the choice of a marital observation coding systems: A user's guide.* Paper presented at the Theory Construction and Research Methodology Workshop, National Council on Family Relations, Milwaukee, October 1981.

References

Bodin, A. M. Conjoint family assessment: An evolving field. In P. M. Reynolds (Ed.), *Advances in psychological assessment* (Vol. 1). Palo Alto, CA: Science and Behavior, 1968.

Ciminero, A. R. Behavioral assessment: An overview. In A. R. Ciminero, K. S. Calhoun, & H. E. Adams (Eds.), *Handbook of behavioral assessment.* New York: John Wiley, 1977.

Cromwell, R. E., Olson, D. H. L., & Fournier, D. G. Tools and techniques for diagnosis and evaluation in marital and family therapy. *Family Process,* 1976, *15,* 1-49.

Cromwell, R. E., & Peterson, G. W. Multisystem-multimethod assessment: A framework. In E. E. Filsinger & R. A. Lewis (Eds.), *Assessing marriage: New behavioral approaches.* Beverly Hills, CA: Sage, 1981.

Epstein, N. B., & Bishop, D. S. Problem-centered systems therapy of the family. In A. S. Gurman & D. P. Kniskern (Eds.), *Handbook of family therapy.* New York: Brunner/Mazel, 1981.

Filsinger, E. E., & Lewis, R. A. (Eds.). *Assessing marriage: New behavioral approaches.* Beverly Hills, CA: Sage, 1981.

Filsinger, E. E., Lewis, R. A., & McAvoy, P. Trends and prospects for observing marriage. In E. E. Filsinger & R. A. Lewis (Eds.), *Assessing marriage: New behavioral approaches.* Beverly Hills, CA: Sage, 1981.

Framo, J. L. The integration of marital therapy with sessions with family of origin. In A. S. Gurman & D. P. Kniskern (Eds.), *Handbook of family therapy.* New York: Brunner/Mazel, 1981.

Gurman, A. S. The effects and effectiveness of marital therapy: A review of outcome research. *Family Process,* 1973, *12,* 145-170.

Gurman, A. S. Contemporary marital therapies: A critique and comparative analysis of psychoanalytic, behavioral and systems theory approaches. In T. J. Paolino & B. S. McCrady (Eds.), *Marriage and marital therapy: Psychoanalytic, behavioral and systems theory perspectives.* New York: Brunner/Mazel, 1978.

Gurman, A. S., & Kniskern, D. P. Deterioration in marital and family therapy: Empirical, clinical, and conceptual issues. *Family Process,* 1978, *17,* 3-20.

Gurman, A. S., & Kniskern, D. P. (Eds.). *Handbook of family therapy.* New York: Brunner/ Mazel, 1981.(a)

Gurman, A. S., & Kniskern, D. P. Family therapy outcome research: Knowns and unknowns. In A. S. Gurman & D. P. Kniskern (Eds.), *Handbook of family therapy.* New York: Brunner/Mazel, 1981. (b)

Jacobson, N. S. Behavioral marital therapy. In A. S. Gurman & D. P. Kniskern (Eds.), *Handbook of family therapy.* New York: Brunner/Mazel, 1981.

Keefe, F. J., Kopel, S. A., & Gordon, S. B. *A practical guide to behavioral assessment.* New York: Springer, 1978.

Olson, D. H. Marital and family therapy: Integrative review and critique. *Journal of Marriage and the Family,* 1970, *32,* 501-538.

Olson, D. H. Family typologies: Bridging family research and family therapy. In E. E. Filsinger & R. A. Lewis (Eds.), *Assessing marriage: New behavioral approaches.* Beverly Hills, CA: Sage, 1981.

Olson, D. H., Russell, C. S., & Sprenkle, D. H. Marriage and family therapy: A decade review. *Journal of Marriage and the Family,* 1980, *42,* 973-993.

Pap, A. *An introduction to the philosophy of science.* New York: Free Press, 1962.

Pinsof, W. M. Family therapy process research. In A. S. Gurman & D. P. Kniskern (Eds.), *Handbook of family therapy.* New York: Brunner/Mazel, 1981.

Platt, J. R. Strong inference. *Science,* 1964, *146,* 347-353.

Riskin, J., & Faunce, E. E. An evaluative review of family interaction research. *Family Process,* 1972, *11,* 365-455.

Skynner, A. C. R. An open-systems, group-analytic approach to family therapy. In A. S. Gurman & D. P. Kniskern (Eds.), *Handbook of family therapy.* New York: Brunner/ Mazel, 1981.

Snyder, D. K. Advances in marital assessment. In C. D. Spielberger & J. N. Butcher (Eds.), *Advances in personality assessment* (Vol. 1). Hillsdale, NJ: Erlbaum, 1981.

Weiss, R. L. The conceptualization of marriage from a behavioral perspective. In T. J. Paolino & B. S. McCrady (Eds.), *Marriage and marital therapy: Psychoanalytic, behavioral and systems theory perspectives.* New York: Brunner/Mazel, 1978.

Weiss, R. L., & Margolin, G. Assessment of marital conflict and accord. In A. R. Ciminero, K. D. Calhoun, & H. E. Adams (Eds.), *Handbook of behavioral assessment.* New York: John Wiley, 1977.

Whitaker, C. A., & Keith, D. V. Symbolic-experiential family therapy. In A. S. Gurman & D. P. Kniskern (Eds.), *Handbook of family therapy.* New York: Brunner/Mazel, 1981.

CHAPTER *2*

The Interview in the Assessment of Marital Distress

STEPHEN N. HAYNES
RALPH E. CHAVEZ
Southern Illinois University—Carbondale

The interview is one of the most frequently used, but least investigated, methods of assessing marital distress (Haynes, Jensen, Wise, & Sherman, 1981). Although other marital assessment instruments have been subjected to empirical analysis (Filsinger & Lewis, 1981; Jacob, 1976; Jacobson & Margolin, 1979; Stuart, 1978), the interview has remained relatively free of such scrutiny. Out of several hundred articles involving marital assessment reviewed for this chapter, psychometric issues of the marital assessment interview were addressed in fewer than a handful. The assessment interview has also been used for a variety of other purposes without regard to its psychometric characteristics (Cormier & Cormier, 1979; Haynes, 1978; Haynes & Jensen, 1979; Haynes & Wilson, 1979; Kerlinger, 1973; Korchin, 1976; Linehan, 1977; Morganstern, 1976; Sanson-Fisher & Martin, 1981).

The goal of this chapter is to present an overview of methodological and clinical aspects of the marital assessment interview. Although the interview is used for a variety of purposes in marital assessment (such as demographic research and adoption decisions), the comments in this chapter are confined to its use in the assessment of maritally distressed clients in clinical settings. The inferences presented should be interpreted cautiously because of the paucity of relevant research. This presentation is based on findings from studies on the use of the assessment interview with nonmarital problem behaviors, nonempirically based discussions of the marital assessment interview, and our clinical experiences in marital assessment. We recognize the tentative nature of the following inferences

Authors' Note: Support for the completion of this chapter was provided, in part, by the Clinical Center at Southern Illinois University—Carbondale. The authors would like to express their appreciation to Linda Gannon for her helpful comments on an earlier draft.

23

and recommendations, but hope that they will serve as a stimulus for generating interest in the empirical validation of assessment interviews in general and marital assessment interviews in particular.

This chapter focuses on the assessment of distressed marital relationships. Although a formal marital relationship differs from other dyadic relationships, the concepts and methods presented are applicable to the assessment of any dyadic intimate relationship, such as homosexual, nonmarital but cohabiting, and parent-adolescent relationships.

The chapter is divided into several sections. First, the goals of the marital assessment interview are presented. Subsequent sections address psychometric considerations and sources of error. The structure and conduct of the marital assessment interview is then discussed. Finally, the applicability of computer interviews is briefly considered.

Goals

The general functions or goals of the marital assessment interview are to design, facilitate, and evaluate intervention strategies. These can be divided into a number of more specific and *interrelated* goals, which are outlined below.

Screening Clients for Marital Therapy

One of the initial tasks of the marital assessor is to decide if marital therapy is appropriate or inappropriate for a particular client (individual or couple) (Baublitz, 1978). This judgment is based on several considerations: (1) the degree to which personal problems of one or both spouses are the major source of distress and not amenable to modification through marital therapy (Jacobson, 1977); (2) the degree of commitment or willingness to participate in the marital intervention process (Addario & Rodgers, 1974; Keefe, Kopel, & Gordon, 1978); (3) the impact of other mediational variables (such as intellectual development) that can significantly affect the probability of effective intervention; and (4) the degree to which marital interaction may be maintaining other behavior problems.

Two considerations are particularly relevant when deciding on the appropriateness of marital therapy for a particular client. First, marital therapy frequently can be an effective intervention strategy for individual behavior problems. A wide range of behavior problems (such as depression, ingestive disorders, or anxiety) can sometimes be partially attributed to spouse-controlled social contingencies or eliciting factors (Ciminero, Calhoun, & Adams, 1977; Haynes & Gannon, 1981; Rimm & Masters, 1979). In these cases, marital intervention can be an important treatment component. Second, many client mediational variables that affect the decision about the appropriateness of therapy are modifiable. Discussions with the client, readings by the client, alterations of the treatment program design, or time-limited contracts can increase the potential impact of marital therapy.

Identifying Interactional Determinants of Marital Distress

There are many determinants of marital distress (such as financial problems or social upheaval), but assessment efforts are most profitably directed at those that are modifiable in a clinical setting. Behavioral exchanges or interactions between spouses constitute one of the most powerful and modifiable determinants of marital distress and, therefore, one of the most important foci of the assessment interview.

There are a number of possible interactional determinants of marital distress (Jacobson & Margolin, 1979). These include high rates of aversive behavior exchange, low rates of positive behavior exchange, high levels of negative reciprocity, low levels of positive reciprocity, changes in social contingency schedules, lack of or inappropriate verbal communication, and lack of negotiation and contracting skills.

The interview assessment of behavioral exchanges is guided by four important concepts: (1) Identified interactions should be specific and minimally inferential; (2) complex behavioral interrelationships such as behavioral chains, stimulus-response chains, response hierarchies, and response classes frequently have important controlling functions (Gottman, 1979; Haynes, in press; Voeltz & Evans, 1982); (3) behavioral exchange determinants can be situation specific (Kazdin, 1979); and (4) behavioral exchange determinants may be noncontiguous with their effects (Margolin, 1981).

Identifying Situational Aspects of Marital Distress

Most determinants of marital distress occur neither randomly nor continually. Because of its flexibility, the interview is the most useful assessment procedure for detecting situational specificity of determinants (Haynes, 1978; Haynes & Jensen, 1979; Kazdin, 1982; Plaum, 1981; Shapiro, 1979). For example, distressing verbal exchanges may occur during discussion of some problem areas but not others; the expression of affection may be an area of conflict in some situations but not in others.

Specific *areas* of conflict or desired change must also be identified (Ayers, 1976; Framo, 1976; Peterson, 1977; Tearnan & Lutzker, 1980; Williams, 1974). These can include raising children, interaction with in laws or friends, health, religious or moral values, and others.

Assessing Cognitive and
Other Subjective Variables

Couples infrequently report that they are seeking marital therapy because of high rates of aversive interchanges or low rates of positive behavior exchanges. They more frequently report that they are seeking help because they *feel* unloved, neglected, rejected, frustrated, or hurt. These subjective variables are important determinants of marital distress and, therefore, they, as well as their behavior exchange covariates, must be the focus of assessment.

Cognitive variables are assessment targets because they can function as dependent, controlling, or mediating variables (Ayers, 1976; Addario & Rodgers, 1974). For example, marital therapy usually requires some degree of between-spouse reciprocity of behavior change. Attributions in which one spouse is blamed for marital problems can hinder program effectiveness. Cognitive factors such as attitudes toward and perceptions of the spouse, casual attributions, expectations about the therapy process, and concepts of the ideal marital relationship can affect levels of marital distress.

Assessing Mediating Variables

Successful intervention with distressed marital couples requires that each spouse emit prescribed behaviors, such as attending sessions, completing assessment procedures, role playing new interaction patterns, and practicing new communication patterns at home. Spouses vary in their likelihood of emitting these *behavioral prescriptions* and, therefore, in their probability of favorable response to intervention efforts.

A number of factors influence a client's participation in the intervention process. These include: (1) *expected losses or gains* associated with a change in the marital relationship, (2) level of *insight* into the social interaction determinants of distress and the intervention process, (3) intellectual and cognitive *resources*, (4) the presence or absence of personal *behavior problems* (such as alcoholism or psychosis), (5) *social validity* (perceived credibility or appropriateness) of the assessment-intervention process, and (6) *attributions* of causality or blame.

Expected gains or losses associated with marital intervention constitute a particularly powerful determinant of intervention outcome. For example, some clients are fairly satisfied in a stereotypical marital relationship in which they have few household responsibilities and many sources of extramarital interests and make most of the decisions in the marriage. The gains and losses potentially associated with marital therapy should be carefully considered with the client, because marital intervention might result in a more equitable distribution of decision making and household chores and an increase in the extramarital activities of the spouse. Participation of the client in the intervention process would be limited unless expected losses were outweighed by expected gains.

Because these mediating variables affect the probability that a client will follow the behavioral prescriptions that are part of every intervention program, they must be addressed prior to initiating intervention. Failure to address or, when necessary, modify mediating variables is a major reason for intervention failure.

Providing a Sample of Marital Interaction

Because of the *Social laboratory* nature of the interview process (Bell, 1967), the interviewer is frequently provided with an opportunity to observe the verbal and nonverbal aspects of marital interaction. Although this is not a primary goal of the assessment interview, it provides an informal means of evaluating one of the most important sources of distress: *communication problems* (Haynes, Follingstad, & Sullivan, 1979; Margolin, 1981). Despite being a rich source of hypotheses concerning communication patterns and determinants of distress, such a qualitative analysis cannot substitute for a more systematic assessment of communication patterns (Gottman, 1979).

Facilitating Program Evaluation

Because the marital assessment interview is usually applied in an unsystematic manner, it is seldom suitable as a measure of program effects. However, when appropriately administered, it can provide both qualitative and quantitative indices of such effects (Boyd & Bolen, 1970). It is particularly suited to the application of rating scales and can be used to measure self-reported frequencies and conditional probabilities of specific marital exchanges (Haynes, in press).

There are several considerations that will increase the utility and validity of the interview for program evaluation. First, items should be carefully and consistently delivered with maximum behavioral and situational specificity in order to minimize inferential errors. Quantitative indices should be derived whenever possible and should target intervention generalization and side effects in addition to effects on the main target variables. Finally, program evaluation should continue in a systematic manner throughout and following intervention (Martin, 1976) and should include the intervention process as well as outcome.

Identifying Positive Aspects of the Marital Relationship

Because intervention programs most often focus on areas of dissatisfaction and their presumed determinants, positive aspects of marital relationships are frequently ignored. However, their assessment can contribute to the design and success of intervention. Preintervention assessment of relationship strengths can help motivate couples to participate in the intervention process (Stuart, 1978; Peterson, 1977) by enhancing the expected benefits associated with intervention. This information can also be useful in designing intervention programs because positive events and interactions can serve as contingencies in contracting components of intervention programs (Stuart, 1978) and an increase in their frequency and range can sometimes enhance marital satisfaction.

Facilitating Client-Assessor Interaction

The goals outlined above are primarily relevant to the data acquisition functions of the interview. An equally important function of the marital assessment interview is to establish a facilitative relationship between client and assessor (Belson, 1975; Wieman, Shoulders, & Farr, 1974; Guerney, 1977; Haynes, 1978; Williams, 1974) to ensure cooperative participation in the intervention process. The interaction between assessor and client can have a significant impact upon the probability of intervention success. Maintaining a positive client-assessor relationship is particularly challenging in structured, empirically oriented interviews focusing on specific behavior-environment interactions. Methods of maintaining such a relationship are discussed briefly later in this chapter.

Another component of preintervention assessment involves informing clients about the assessment and intervention process (Keefe et al., 1978; Guerney, 1977). The assessor must explicitly communicate with clients about their responsibilities and rights, contingencies (such as charges for missed sessions), and additional assessment procedures (Addario & Rodgers, 1974; Baublitz, 1978; Belson, 1975; Follingstad & Haynes, 1981). Clients have the right to make informed decisions about their participation in the assessment-intervention process, including the right to seek other forms of intervention or other therapists.

Selecting Additional Assessment Strategies

A variety of strategies are available for the assessment of marital distress and interaction, including self- and participant monitoring, questionnaires, analogue and naturalistic observation, and critical event sampling. Except in prespecified intervention programs (Jacobson, 1977), decisions about the use of particular assessment instruments are made on the basis of information derived from the assessment interview (Nelson & Barlow, 1980). Assessment procedures are differentially applicable as a function of the specific areas of distress, problematic interactions, and environmental constraints idiosyncratic to a particular couple (Haynes, 1983).

Developing a Functional Analysis

One supraordinate goal of the marital assessment interview is to contribute to the development of an etiological conceptualization, or functional analysis, of marital distress for a particular marital couple. This functional analysis is an integration of the specific areas of satisfaction and dissatisfaction, the determinants of dissatisfaction, cognitive and subjective factors, environmental supports, and situational factors (Haynes, in press). On the basis of this conceptualization, the assessor develops an intervention strategy that is adapted to the unique determinants and characteristics of each distressed couple. Its significance derives from the fact that faulty integration or conceptualization of assessment data will lead to unsuccessful intervention strategies.

Additional Goals

Two other frequent goals of the marital assessment interview have been intentionally omitted from the preceding delineation: (1) gathering historical information (Addario & Rodgers, 1974; Belson, 1975; Framo, 1976; Jacobson, 1977; Martin, 1976; Strauss, Carpenter, & Nasrallan, 1978) and (2) evaluating the "personalities" of the spouses (Martin, 1976; Platt, Weyman, Hirsch, & Hewitt, 1980; Seeman & Edwardes-Evans, 1979). Their exclusion is based primarily on the social-learning orientation of the interview model presented in this chapter and a need for parsimony in the assessment process.

While historical information can sometimes identify developmental aspects of marital distress, interview time can be spent more heuristically by concentrating on more contemporaneous determinants. However, the assessor should realize that information on the development of marital dissatisfaction can sometimes be very useful for identifying important etiological factors and for developing prevention programs.

Assessment of the "personality" of each spouse is a frequent focus of more psychodynamically oriented marital therapists and is based on the assumption that marital distress is frequently a result of individual behavior problems or psychopathology. There is little doubt that individual behavior problems can cause and exacerbate marital distress and, as noted previously, can have a significant impact upon the probability of successful intervention. However, individual behavior problems are frequently manifested in and sometimes controlled by marital interaction. As a consequence, they can often be modified through marital intervention. Attention to the interaction between spouses, rather than the independent behavior of each spouse, is a parsimonious method of identifying the relevant controlling variables of marital distress and personal behavior problems.

Psychometric Considerations

Of the several sources of information in the interview (such as observation of marital interaction), the clients' verbal reports have the greatest impact on the etiological conceptualization and intervention design. Therefore, the validity of these reports is of utmost importance and is addressed in the following sections.

Reliability and Validity

"Reliability" is a generic term referring to the stability of measures derived from an assessment instrument. In most cases the reliability of an assessment instrument sets the upper limit on the validity of derived data. The reliability of a marital assessment interview can be measured through reference to its administration or client responses. Reliability of *interview administration* is the degree to which one interviewer presents interview items in a consistent fashion or the degree of similarity in administration between interviewers and between an interviewer and a "criterion" interviewer. Reliability of an assessment interview can also be evaluated in terms of the stability of *client responses* to the same or similar interview items within the interview or across separate interviews.

Despite the frequent use of the marital assessment interview, we located only one article (Crowe, 1978) that directly examined the reliability of the marital assessment interview. However, there have been a number of studies on the reliability of interviews that contained some maritally relevant items (Annis, 1979; Berg & Fielding, 1979; Caetano, Edwards, Oppeineim, & Taylor, 1978; Clare & Cairns, 1978; Hay, Hay, Angle, & Nelson, 1979; Herjanic & Campbell, 1977; Hesselbrock, Stabenau, Hesselbrock, Mirkin, & Meyer, 1982; Mazure & Gershon, 1979; Muto, 1979; Pai & Kapur, 1981; Perri, Richards, & Schultheis, 1977; Platt et al., 1980; Sloman & Webster, 1978; Strauss et al., 1978; see also reviews by Haynes, 1978; Haynes & Jensen, 1979; Haynes & Wilson, 1979; Linehan, 1977; Morganstern, 1976; Sanson-Fisher & Martin, 1981).

The vast majority of these studies found that the assessment interview elicited satisfactorily reliable data, but taken together they suggest significant variance in reliability across stimulus items. These studies indicate that the interview *can* provide reliable data on clinically significant issues. However, reliability is not a consistent attribute of an interview (Sanson-Fisher & Martin, 1981) and must be consistently monitored within and across assessment interviews.

Interpretation of reliability coefficients is further complicated by the fact that many of the constructs targeted for assessment are unstable. Unlike traits such as "intelligence," daily or weekly variance in self-reported marital satisfaction or in the rates of specific interactive behaviors would not be unexpected. Therefore, *true variability* in the behavior must be separated from *error variability* attributable to the assessment instrument. Methods of partialing true from error variability are discussed in Haynes (1978).

Validity refers to the degree to which measures derived from an assessment instrument accurately reflect the constructs they are intended to measure. There are a number of ways to measure validity of the marital assessment interview. The primary method involves *criterion-related validity* (comparing interview-derived data with data from other assessment instruments such as questionnaires or comparing reports between spouses). Criterion-related validity may involve *predictive validity* (the degree to which interview-derived data predicts future measures of behavior), *concurrent validity* (the degree of association between data derived from the interview and a concurrently administered assessment instrument), and *discriminant validity* (the degree to which interview-derived data can discriminate between known groups such as those seeking and those not seeking divorce).

One particularly important and frequently neglected form of validity of the marital assessment interview is *content validity*—the degree to which the items in the interview adequately sample relevant aspects of the marital relationship and marital distress. Content validity is a subjectively measured attribute of an assessment instrument and is tied to the construct system from which it is derived. Because construct systems evolve, the content validity of marital assessment interviews must also evolve to reflect these conceptual advances.

Only one study (Haynes et al., 1981) has systematically examined the validity of the marital assessment interview. However, a number of studies have examined the validity of the interview when used in the assessment of nonmarital target behaviors (Dirk & Kuldau, 1974; Herjanic and Campbell, 1977; Kolb & Gunderson, 1980; Perri et al., 1977; Remington & Tyrer, 1979). The majority of these studies found that the assessment interview resulted in data with a satisfactory degree of validity, although variance across populations and targeted constructs was apparent.

In the only systematic evaluation of the validity of the marital assessment interview, Haynes et al. (1981) exposed twelve dissatisfied and sixteen satisfied couples to a multimethod assessment procedure involving an interview, questionnaires, and an analogue communication situation. Spouses were interviewed either together or separately. The interview contained items relating to satisfaction with various aspects of marriage (such as sex or expressing affection) and other marital interactions (such as who is more positive during discussions), as well as items not specifically related to marital satisfaction (such as self-reported assertion). The questionnaires and behavioral observation assessments served as criterion measures for validation of the marital assessment interview. The results suggested (1) a high level of discriminant validity for the marital interview; (2) higher coefficients of criterion-related validity for separate than for joint interviews; (3) that the presence of the spouse had a significantly greater impact on responses to the "high-sensitive" items (such as satisfaction with sex) than "low-sensitive" items (such as demographic information); (4) higher between-spouse agreement for joint than for separate interviews; and (5) greater validity for separate than for joint interviews in predicting verbal communication patterns.

This study supported the criterion-related validity of a representative marital assessment interview, but, more importantly, suggested that validity is influenced by the content and characteristics of the interview process. In particular, the presence or absence of the spouse during the interview significantly affected between-spouse agreement and coefficients of criterion-related validity. This effect was particularly evident with items judged to be "sensitive" in a marital relationship.

Inferential reliability and *validity* are also important psychometric considerations. Inferential reliability is the degree to which information derived from an assessment process results in similar conceptualizations or interpretations within or across assessors. Inferential validity is the degree to which the inferences drawn from the resulting data are valid. Different assessment instruments may provide reliable and valid data but may vary in the degree to which those data lead to valid conceptualizations. In addition, valid data from an assessment instrument may be interpreted idiosyncratically across assessors (Emmelkamp, 1981; Haynes, in press). Inferential validity is influenced by, but not totally determined by, criterion validity and content validity of the assessment instruments.

Additional Psychometric Considerations

The previous discussion of the psychometric qualities of the assessment interview was limited to only one of its functions—the acquisition of information necessary for a valid etiological conceptualization and intervention design. However, psychometric characteristics of an assessment instrument are not generalizable beyond the particular function addressed, and an interview that validly acquires information on etiology may be ineffective in meeting other assessment goals (such as assessing mediational variables). Therefore, the psychometric evaluation of the marital assessment interview should include evaluation of all functions for which it is used. Furthermore, assessment instruments should be evaluated on dimensions other than reliability and validity, such as *sensitivity* to intervention effects, *cost-efficiency, applicability,* and *utility.*

Sources of Error

The utility of the marital assessment interview is dependent on the degree to which the resultant measures are representative of the constructs they are designed to measure. Interpretative problems arise because these data are influenced by many sources of variance and are only approximations of the targeted phenomena. Historically, the interview has been assumed to be more sensitive than other assessment instruments to sources of error. However, it is probably more accurate to state that the sources of error for the interview differ, but may not be more extensive than, those affecting other assessment instruments.

There are several classes of error variance in the marital assessment interview. These include the structure and focus of the interview, the characteristics and behavior of the interviewer and client, and the reactive effects associated with the interview process.

The Structure and Focus of the Interview

The validity of the data derived from the marital assessment interview and its interpretation are affected by its content, the degree of specificity and sensitivity of the stimulus items, the retrospective nature of some of the acquired data, and the preliminary instructions to clients. In addition to the inferential errors associated with inadequate content validity discussed previously, the validity and utility of client responses are affected by their behavioral and situational *specificity* (Mischel, 1968). Interview stimulus items that are more behaviorally and situationally specific tend to elicit information with a greater degree of generalizability and predictive validity and to decrease the probability of interpretative errors by the client and assessor.

As noted in the study by Haynes et al. (1981), validity can also vary with the *sensitivity* of the items. Because of the social laboratory nature of the interview situation, items with a high valence, compared to those with a low valence, may be more sensitive to biases associated with the social interaction process of the interview (Annis, 1979; Zanes & Matsoukas, 1979).

Initial instructions can also affect the degree of error associated with the marital assessment interview. As demonstrated by Schiederer (1977), instructions to clients about how to behave in the interview and the focus and purpose of the interview can have a positive effect on the information obtained and the reactions by both the interviewer and client to the interview process.

Characteristics and Behavior
of the Interviewer

The effects of the *characteristics of the interviewer* (such as social class, age, sex, or race) on obtained data have been the subject of a number of studies (Campbell, 1981; Cleary, Mechanic, & Weiss, 1981; Epstein & Jayne, 1981; Krauskopf, Baumgardner, & Mandracchi, 1981; Weeks & Moore, 1981), the results of which are conflicting and difficult to interpret (Abramowitz & Dokecki, 1977). Certainly, clients bring to the assessment interview an array of social experiences that affect their responses and interaction with the interviewer. However, the degree of impact of this source of error variance has not been determined. Furthermore, that impact is likely to be mediated by the structure and focus of the interview situation and the behavior of the interviewer.

There is little doubt that the *behavior of the interviewer* can have a significant impact upon the behavior of the client (Cox, Rutter, & Holbrook, 1981; Gillis & Patrick, 1980; Hopkinson, Cox, & Rutter, 1981; Iwata, Wong, Riordan, Dorsey, & Lau, 1982; Price & Cuellar, 1981; *see* also reviews by Haynes, 1978; Linehan, 1977; Matarazzo & Wiens, 1972; Sanson-Fisher & Martin, 1981; Wiens, 1976). The marital assessment interview involves a social influence process in which the interviewer selectively reinforces and shapes the client's behavior and provides cues and prompts to the client about appropriate and inappropriate interview behaviors. These cues and contingencies can significantly affect the type of information provided by the client as well as the client's perception of the interview process. Because of this powerful social influence process, the data derived are particularly sensitive to the *interviewer's biases* or *expectancies* (Shapiro, 1979).

Characteristics and Behavior
of the Client

Error variance in interview-derived data cannot be attributed solely to the interview structure or the interviewer. Assuming stability along the dimensions, differences in reliability and validity between clients and within clients would still be observed (Bell, 1967; Platt et al., 1980; Rosenberger & Lowine, 1982). This source of error is most closely tied to the subjective and historical nature of the data acquired in the interview and the social interaction process of this situation previously discussed.

A significant proportion of most marital assessment interviews are conducted with both spouses present. As noted by Haynes et al. (1981), the presence or absence of a spouse can affect the client's response to various interview items, particularly items that have a high valence to the marital relationship. Although the mechanisms of social control responsible for these effects have not been studied, the social laboratory paradigm suggests that a client's responses may be affected by their expected impact on the spouse (the operant nature of the client's response) and by the expected contingencies delivered by the spouse (such as later verbal punishment). The assessor must continually be cognizant that verbal reports have both reflective and operant qualities. They can reflect marital perceptions and behaviors, but can also be emitted because of their expected impact on the spouse or interviewer.

Reactivity

A threat to the predictive validity of the interview is attributable to its potential reactive effects. Client reports may accurately reflect the targeted phenomena at the time of their acquisition, but the interview process may result in a modification of those phenomena (Haynes & Wilson, 1979). Reactive effects may occur because clients continue interview-initiated discussions at home, modify their interaction patterns, gain an increased awareness of spouse perceptions, or change their expectancies or attitudes.

Summary

The marital assessment interview can be conceptualized as a social laboratory. The data acquired are significantly affected by the social interaction among the participants as well as sources of error variance idiosyncratic to self-report measures. These are all potential threats to the validity of the marital assessment interview because they can decrease the degree to which obtained data are representative of the targeted behaviors. It should be emphasized that these sources of error are interactive and controllable. For example, the impact of interviewer biases can be minimized through the use of behaviorally specific questions delivered in a reliable fashion within a structured format. Therefore, sources of error are *potential* rather than static characteristics of an assessment instrument and can be minimized with a carefully constructed interview process.

The potential for error underscores the importance of reliability and validity evaluation and the use of multimethod assessment procedures. Embedding reliability checks in the interview, readministering some items, and comparing interview-derived data with data derived from other assessment instruments can suggest a range of confidence within which the obtained data can be viewed.

Structure and Conduct

The structure of the marital assessment interview—its content, temporal aspects, and specific foci—and the behavior of the interviewer are functions of the goals of the interview and the particular construct system within which it occurs. The recommendations for structure and conduct presented below are for an initial clinical assessment interview and are based primarily upon a social learning framework. We do not present these as validated procedures, nor do we presume that other assessors have not developed equally valid and useful marital assessment interview procedures. The outline presented is necessarily brief; more comprehensive treatments of this topic have been presented by Cormier and Cormier (1979), Haynes (1978), and Matarazzo and Wiens (1972).

Organizational and Temporal Structure

Many published articles have employed *structured interviews* in the assessment of both marital distress (Ayers, 1976; Haynes et al., 1981; Hiebert & Gillespie, 1977; Jacobson & Margolin, 1979; Stuart, 1978; Williams, 1974) and nonmarital problem behaviors (Cox et al., 1981; Herjanic & Campbell, 1977; Hesselbrock et al., 1982; Heizer, Clayton, Pambakian, & Woodruff, 1978; Mazure & Gershon, 1979; Rosenberger & Lowine, 1982; Siegel, Matthews, & Leitch, 1981; Spence, 1981; Tsuang, Woolson, & Simpson, 1980; see also the review by Sanson-Fisher & Martin, 1981). Guidelines for the use of structured interviews have also been provided by Burke and DeMers (1979), Haynes (1978), Holland (1970), Sanson-Fisher and Martin (1981), and others.

There are numerous benefits associated with the use of a structured rather than an unstructured marital assessment interview: Such an interview (1) facilitates the specification and quantification of target behaviors and situational determinants, (2) reduces between-interviewer variance and the impact of interviewer errors and biases, and (3) reduces the ambiguity of the interview situation for the client.

Although nonmarital structured interviews have undergone considerable development and psychometric analysis, we could locate no study that evaluated the charactertistics or psychometric properties of a structured marital assessment interview. The study by Haynes et al. (1981) involved an *analogue* interview because it contained only samples of items commonly found in a marital assessment interview.

The *temporal aspects* of the marital assessment interview are also important. The assessment interview is but one of several assessment procedures that typically precede intervention, and it is important that the assessment process not unnecessarily retard the beginning of intervention. For this reason, we attempt to conduct the assessment interview in a single session of 2-2½ hours' duration. We have found that such an intensive initial marital assessment interview is well received by clients, increases their motivation for marital enhancement, increases the credibility of the assessment-intervention process, and speeds the initiation of intervention.

A Sample Semistructured Interview Outline

Presented below are an outline and examples of initial stimuli for a conjoint marital assessment interview that we have found to be parsimonious and effective in eliciting the information necessary for an etiological conceptualization and intervention design. A structured assessment interview, such as the one described below, is necessarily limited in focus and sometimes less flexible in identifying idiosyncratic issues or problem areas. For this reason, we use a two-staged interview process involving an initial short unstructured phase followed by a longer structured phase (Keefe et al., 1978). In the first 10-15 minutes we assume a nondirective, reflective, supportive but probing interaction style. This helps us gain an overall understanding of the types and degree of the clients' concerns, goals, and motivations, and also functions as a screening phase to ensure that marital intervention is appropriate.

I. *Initial instructions* (purpose of interview, its structure, appropriate client behaviors) 2-3 minutes: "First, I would like to explain about the purpose of this session, how it is organized, and what you can do to make it most profitable."

II. *Open-ended phase,* 10-15 minutes: "Would you tell me more about why you came to the clinic?"

III. *Marital history and demography,* 3-5 minutes: "That was helpful in letting me know some of your concerns. Would you now briefly tell me a little about the history of your relationship, how you met, and so on?"

IV. *Identification of problem behaviors:* "What things does your husband (wife) do that you wish he (she) would do less often or not at all?"

V. *Identification of behavioral deficits:* "What things does your husband (wife) do that you wish he (she) would do more frequently? What are some things that your husband (wife) never does that you wish he (she) would do?"

VI. *Identification of strengths:* "Can you tell me some things that your husband (wife) does that you like and appreciate?"

VII. *Identification of client's perceived responsibility:* "What do you do that causes difficulties in your relationship? What do you currently do that contributes in a positive way to the marriage? What could you do to increase the enjoyment of the marriage for both of you?"

VIII. *Final open-ended phase:* "In addition to those issues we have discussed, are there any other changes that would make the marriage more enjoyable for you or are there other issues we have overlooked?"

IX. *Brief feedback and establishment of a contract:* "There are several factors that seem to be contributing to your marital difficulties. Here is what I think would be most helpful in terms of additional assessment and the start of therapy."

Interviewer Behaviors

The most important aspect of the interview is not its overall structure, but the behavior of the interviewer. Interviewer behaviors that we have found to be most effective in parsimoniously achieving the goals of the marital assessment interview are drawn from client-centered and social learning frameworks. We try to develop positive client-assessor interactions through the use of reflections, paraphrases, and empathic statements. However, we realize that these serve both as discriminative stimuli about the kinds of information wanted and as powerful discriminative reinforcers for the client—we use them judiciously. The need for specific and quantifiable information for a functional analysis and basis for program evaluation requires the use of behavioral reflections, probes, and specific questions. Behavioral reflections are paraphrases of social-environmental interactions, such as, "So, you are less likely to compliment or be physically affectionate with Linda after work if you have had some uncomfortable run-ins with your boss that day."

The success of this recommended interview format in achieving the assessment goals outlined earlier in this chapter is a function of several factors in addition to the interviewer behaviors outlined above: (1) probes are delivered to one spouse at a time in alternating fashion, and the interviewer focuses on that spouse until all available information in that category is obtained; (2) interruptions or comments by the nonparticipating spouse are constructively punished; (3) arguments between spouses during the interview session are not allowed, although we frequently do not interfere with the initial argument in order to evaluate the couple's style of negative interaction; (4) avoidance behaviors (such as "I don't know" or "I can't think of anything") are not reinforced; (5) the interviewer maintains a reinforcing interaction with the client while probing for behavioral and situational referents; (6) tangential or historical comments are not reinforced; (7) the client is explicitly informed about and reinforced for desirable interview behaviors; (8) cognitions and subjective perceptions are evaluated; and (9) there is a strong emphasis on deriving clear, specific, minimally inferential, and quantifiable information.

Toward a Computer-Mediated Interview

The interview is used more frequently and for more purposes than any other marital assessment instrument. Its functions go beyond data acquisition and it has an important role in establishing and facilitating the intervention process. However, it has been subjected to little empirical scrutiny. There are several psychometric aspects of the interview that need to be addressed, including internal and external reliability, criterion-related validity, utility, content validity, inferential validity, and cost-efficiency. Perhaps most important, the multiple and interacting sources of error variance in the data derived from the marital assessment interview require examination.

Psychometric characteristics and error variance should not be considered stable properties of an assessment instrument, nor should they be considered unmodifiable. Therefore, marital assessment interviews should (1) be carefully constructed, (2) be conducted by well-trained interviewers, (3) contain internal reliability checks, and (4) be administered within a multimethod assessment program.

Because marital assessment interviews are costly in professional staff time, advances in *computer interviewing* are particularly exciting (Angle, 1981; Angle, Ellinwood, Hay, Johnsen, & Hay, 1977; Angle, Hay, Hay, & Ellinwood, 1977; Kleinmuntz, 1972). Computer interviews typically involve a cathode-ray monitor and a keyboard connected to a small computer. The client sits in front of the screen, which projects stimulus items, and enters his or her responses on the keyboard. Computer interview systems are interactive in that the client's responses indicate which branches of a stimulus tree are followed. Although in early stages of development, research on computer interviews has suggested that they can gather and integrate a tremendous amount of information and are well received by clients. In addition, several sources of error, such as interviewer fatigue, biases, and between- and within-interviewer variance, are reduced. However, the computer interview may not meet all the goals associated with the assessment interview; additional research on its psychometric properties is needed.

One asset of the computer interview is that it can facilitate the standardization of marital assessment interviews. Currently, there are no widely accepted standardized marital assessment interview formats, nor is there any standardization of probes, content, focus, or other stylistic issues.

Conclusion

We have briefly presented a recommended outline for a semistructured marital interview, along with recommended interview behaviors, However, these are based upon clinical experiences with minimal empirical basis. The development and psychometric evaluation of a standardized marital assessment interview, as well as evaluation of the impact of various assessor behaviors, would be important steps in establishing the interview as a valid marital assessment strategy.

References

Abramowitz, C. V., & Dokecki, P. R. The politics of clinical judgement: Early empirical returns. *Psychological Bulletin,* 1977, *84,* 460-476.

Addario, D., & Rodgers, T. A. Some techniques for the initial interview in couples therapy. *Hospital and Community Psychiatry,* 1974, *25,* 799-800.

Angle, H. V. The interviewing computer: A technology for gathering comprehensive treatment information. *Behavior Research Methods & Instrumentation,* 1981, *13,* 607-612.

Angle, H. V., Ellinwood, E. H., Hay, W. M., Johnsen, T., & Hay, L. R. Computer-aided interviewing in comprehensive behavioral assessment. *Behavior Therapy,* 1977, *8,* 747-754.

Angle, H. V., Hay, L. R., Hay, W. M., & Ellinwood, E. H. Computer assisted behavioral assessment. In J. D. Cone & R. P. Hawkins (Eds.), *Behavioral assessment: New directions in clinical psychology.* New York: Brunner/Mazel, 1977.

Annis, H. M. Self-report reliability of skid-row alcoholics. *British Journal of Psychiatry,* 1979, *134,* 459-465.

Ayers, G. W. A time-limited approach to marital therapy. *Psychiatric Forum,* 1976, *5,* 24-30.

Baublitz, J. I. Transitional treatment of hostile married couples. *Social Work,* 1978, *23,* 321-323.

Bell, J. E. Contrasting approaches in marital counseling. *Family Process,* 1967, *6,* 16-26.

Belson, R. The importance of the second interview in marriage counseling. *Counseling Psychologist,* 1975, *5,* 27-31.

Berg, I., & Fielding, D. An interview with a child to assess psychiatric disturbance: A note on its reliability and validity. *Journal of Abnormal Child Psychology,* 1979, *7,* 83-89.

Boyd, W., & Bolen, D. The compulsive gambler and spouse in group psychotherapy. *International Journal of Group Psychotherapy,* 1970, *20,* 77-90.

Burke, J. P., & DeMers, S. T. A paradigm for evaluating assessment interviewing techniques. *Psychology in the Schools,* 1979, *16,* 51-60.

Caetano, R., Edwards, G., Oppeineim, A. N., & Taylor, C. Building a standardized alcoholism interview schedule. *Drug and Alcohol Dependence,* 1978, *3,* 185-197.

Campbell, B. A. Race-of-interviewer effects among Southern adolescents. *Public Opinion Quarterly,* 1981, *45,* 221-240.

Ciminero, A. R., Calhoun, K. S., & Adams, H. E. (Eds.). *Handbook of behavioral assessment.* New York: John Wiley, 1977.

Clare, A. W., & Cairns, V. E. Design, development and use of a standardized interview to assess social maladjustment and dysfunction in community studies. *Psychological Medicine,* 1978, *8,* 589-604.

Cleary, P. D., Mechanic, D., & Weiss, N. The effect of interviewer characteristics on responses to a mental health interview. *Journal of Health and Social Behavior,* 1981, *22,* 183-193.

Cormier, W. H., & Cormier, L. S. *Interviewing strategies for helpers: A guide to assessment, treatment, and evaluation.* Monterey, CA: Brooks/Cole, 1979.

Cox, A., Rutter, M., & Holbrook, D. Psychiatric interviewing techniques: V. Experimental study: Eliciting factual information. *British Journal of Psychiatry,* 1981, *139,* 29-37.

Crowe, M. J. Conjoint marital therapy: A controlled outcome study. *Psychological Medicine,* 1978, *8,* 623-636.

Dirk, S. J., & Kuldau, J. M. Validity of self-report by psychiatry patients of employment earnings and hospitalization. *Journal of Consulting and Clinical Psychology,* 1974, *42,* 738-746.

Emmelkamp, P. M. G. The current and future status of clinical research. *Behavioral Assessment,* 1981, *3,* 249-253.

Epstein, N., & Jayne, C. Perceptions of cotherapists as a function of therapist sex roles and observer sex roles. *Sex Roles,* 1981, *7,* 497-509.

Filsinger, E. E., & Lewis, R. A. (Eds.). *Assessing marriage: New behavioral approaches.* Beverly Hills, CA: Sage, 1981.

Follingstad, D. R., & Haynes, S. N. Naturalistic observation in assessment of behavioral marital therapy. *Psychological Reports,* 1981, *49,* 471-479.

Framo, J. L. Family of origin as a therapeutic resource for adults in marital and family therapy: You can and should go home again. *Family Process*, 1976, *15*, 193-210.

Gillis, J. S., & Patrick, S. W. A comparative study of competitive and social reinforcement models of interview behavior. *Journal of Clinical Psychology*, 1980, *36*, 277-282.

Gottman, J. M. *Marital interaction: Experimental investigations.* New York: Academic, 1979.

Guerney, B. G. *Relationship enhancement.* San Francisco: Jossey-Bass, 1977.

Hay, W. M., Hay, L. R., Angle, H. V., & Nelson, R. O. The reliability of problem identification in the behavioral interview. *Behavioral Assessment*, 1979, *1*, 107-118.

Haynes, S. N. *Principles of behavioral assessment.* New York: Gardner, 1978.

Haynes, S. N. Behavioral assessment. In M. Hersen, A. Kazdin, & A. Bellack (Eds.), *The clinical psychology handbook.* New York: Pergamon, 1983.

Haynes, S. N. Behavioral assessment in the design of intervention programs. In R. O. Nelson & S. Hayes (Eds.), *Conceptual foundations of behavioral assessment.* New York: Guilford, in press.

Haynes, S. N., Follingstad, D. R., & Sullivan, J. Assessment of marital satisfaction and interaction. *Journal of Consulting and Clinical Psychology*, 1979, *47*, 789-791.

Haynes, S. N., & Gannon, L. R. *Psychosomatic disorders: A psychophysiological approach to etiology and treatment.* New York: Praeger, 1981.

Haynes, S. N., & Jensen, B. J. The interview as a behavioral assessment instrument. *Behavioral Assessment*, 1979, *1*, 97-106.

Haynes, S. N., Jensen, B. J., Wise, E. J., & Sherman, D. The marital intake interview: A multimethod criterion validity assessment. *Journal of Consulting and Clinical Psychology*, 1981, *43*, 379-387.

Haynes, S. N., & Wilson, C. C. *Behavioral assessment: Recent advances in methods and concepts.* San Francisco: Jossey-Bass, 1979.

Heizer, J. E., Clayton, P. J., Pambakian, R., & Woodruff, R. A. Concurrent diagnostic validity of a structured psychiatric interview. *Archives of General Psychiatry*, 1978, *35*, 849-853.

Herjanic, B., & Campbell, W. Differentiating psychiatrically disturbed children on the basis of a structured interview. *Journal of Abnormal Child Psychology*, 1977, *5*, 127-134.

Hesselbrock, V., Stabenau, J., Hesselbrock, M., Mirkin, P., & Meyer, M. D. A comparison of two interview schedules. *Archives of General Psychiatry*, 1982, *39*, 674-677.

Hiebert, W., & Gillespie, J. The initial interview. In R. F. Stahmann & W. F. Hiebert (Eds.), *Klemer's counseling in marital and sexual problems.* Baltimore: Williams & Wilkins, 1977.

Holland, C. H. An interview guide for behavioral counseling with parents. *Behavior Therapy*, 1970, *1*, 70-79.

Hopkinson, K., Cox, A., & Rutter, M. Psychiatric interviewing techniques: III. Naturalistic study: Eliciting feelings. *British Journal of Psychiatry*, 1981, *138*, 406-415.

Iwata, B. A., Wong, S. E., Riordan, M. M., Dorsey, M. F., & Lau, M. M. Assessment and training of clinical interviewing skills: Analogue analysis and field replication. *Journal of Applied Behavior Analysis*, 1982, *15*, 191-203.

Jacob, T. Assessment of marital dysfunction. In M. Hersen & A. S. Bellack (Eds.), *Behavioral assessment: A practical handbook.* New York: Pergamon, 1976.

Jacobson, N. S. Problem solving and contingency contracting in the treatment of marital discord. *Journal of Consulting and Clinical Psychology*, 1977, *45*, 92-100.

Jacobson, N. S., & Margolin, G. *Marital therapy: Strategies based on social learning and behavior exchange principles.* New York: Brunner/Mazel, 1979.

Kazdin, A. E. Situation specificity: The two edged sword of behavioral assessment. *Behavioral Assessment*, 1979, *1*, 57-75.

Kazdin, A. E. Symptom substitution, generalization, and response covariation: Implications for psychotherapy outcome. *Psychological Bulletin*, 1982, *91*, 349-365.

Keefe, F. J., Kopel, S. A., & Gordon, S. B. *A practical guide to behavioral assessment.* New York: Springer, 1978.

Kerlinger, F. N. *Foundations of behavioral research* (2nd ed.). New York: Holt, Rinehart & Winston, 1973.

Kleinmuntz, B. *Computers in personality assessment.* Morristown, NJ: General Learning, 1972.

Korchin, S. J. *Modern clinical psychology.* New York: Basic Books, 1976.

Kolb, J., & Gunderson, J. G. Diagnosing borderline patients with a semistructured interview. *Archives of General Psychiatry,* 1980, *37,* 37-41.

Krauskopf, C. J., Baumgardner, A., & Mandracchi, S. Return rate following intake revisited. *Journal of Counseling Psychology,* 1981, *28,* 519-521.

Linehan, M. M. Issues in behavioral interviewing. In J. D. Cone & R. P. Hawkins (Eds.), *Behavioral assessment: New directions in clinical psychology.* New York: Brunner/Mazel, 1977.

Margolin, G. Practical applications of behavioral marital assessment. In E. E. Filsinger & R. A. Lewis (Eds.), *Assessing marriage: New behavioral approaches.* Beverly Hills, CA: Sage, 1981.

Martin, P. A. *The marital therapy manual.* New York: Brunner/Mazel, 1976.

Matarazzo, J. D., & Wiens, A. N. *The interview: Research on its anatomy and structure.* Chicago: Aldine, 1972.

Mazure, C., & Gershon, E. S. Blindness and reliability in lifetime psychiatric diagnosis. *Archives of General Psychiatry,* 1979, *36,* 521-525.

Mischel, W. *Personality and assessment.* New York: John Wiley, 1968.

Morganstern, K. P. Behavioral interviewing: The initial stages of assessment. In M. Hersen & A. S. Bellack (Eds.), *Behavioral assessment: A practical handbook.* New York: Pergamon, 1976.

Muto, K. Modification and development of ego identity status interview and ego identity of Japanese university students. *Japanese Journal of Educational Psychology,* 1979, *27,* 178-187.

Nelson, R. O., & Barlow, D. H. Behavioral assessment: Basic strategies and initial procedures. In D. H. Barlow (Ed.), *Behavioral assessment of adult disorders.* New York: Guilford, 1980.

Pai, S., & Kapur, R. L. The burden on the family of a psychiatric patient: Development of an interview schedule. *British Journal of Psychiatry,* 1981, *138,* 332-335.

Perri, M. G., Richards, C. S., & Schultheis, K. R. Behavioral self-control and smoking reduction: A study of self-initiated attempts to reduce smoking. *Behavior Therapy,* 1977, *8,* 360-365.

Peterson, D. K. A functional approach to the study of person-person interactions. In S. Magnusson & N. Endler (Eds.), *Personality at the crossroads: Current issues in transactional psychology.* New York: John Wiley, 1977.

Platt, S., Wehman, A., Hirsch, S., & Hewitt, S. The social behavior assessment schedule: Rationale, contents, scoring and reliability of a new interview schedule. *Social Psychiatry,* 1980, *15,* 43-55.

Plaum, E. Methodological problems of diagnosis based on interaction theory. *Psychologie und Praxis,* 1981, *25,* 91-98.

Price, C., & Cuellar, I. Effects of language and related variables on the expression of psychopathology in Mexican American psychiatric patients. *Hispanic Journal of Behavioral Sciences,* 1981, *3,* 145-160.

Remington, M., & Tyrer, P. The social functioning schedule: A brief semi-structured interview. *Social Psychiatry,* 1979, *14,* 151-157.

Rimm, D. C., & Masters, J. C. *Behavior therapy: Techniques and empirical findings.* New York: Academic, 1979.

Rosenberger, P., & Lowine, R. Conceptual issues in the choice of a structured psychiatric interview. *Comprehensive Psychiatry,* 1982, *23,* 116-121.

Sanson-Fisher, R. W., & Martin, C. J. Standardized interviews in psychiatry: Issues of reliability. *British Journal of Psychiatry,* 1981, *139,* 138-143.

Schiederer, E. G. Effects of instructions and modeling in producing self-disclosure in the initial clinical interview. *Journal of Consulting and Clinical Psychology,* 1977, *45,* 378-384.

Seeman, M. V., & Edwardes-Evans, B. Marital therapy with borderline patients: Is it beneficial? *Journal of Clinical Psychiatry,* 1979, *40,* 308-312.

Shapiro, M. B. Assessment interviewing in clinical psychology. *British Journal of Social and Clinical Psychology,* 1979, *18,* 211-218.

Siegel, J. M., Matthews, D. A., & Leitch, C. J. Validation of the Type A interview assessment of adolescents: A multidimensional approach. *Psychosomatic Medicine,* 1981, *43,* 311-321.

Sloman, L., & Webster, C. D. Assessing the parents of the learning disabled child: A semi-structured interview procedure. *Journal of Learning Disabilities,* 1978, *11,* 73-79.

Spence, S. H. Validation of social skills of adolescent males in an interview conversation with a previously unknown adult. *Journal of Applied Behavior Analysis,* 1981, *14,* 159-168.

Strauss, J. S., Carpenter, W. T., & Nasrallan, A. T. How reliable is the psychiatric history? *Comprehensive Psychiatry,* 1978, *19,* 213-219.

Stuart, R. B. *Helping couples change.* New York: Guilford, 1978.

Tearnan, B., & Lutzker, J. R. A contracting package in the treatment of marital problems: A case study. *American Journal of Family Therapy,* 1980, *8,* 24-31.

Tsuang, M. T., Woolson, R. F., & Simpson, J. C. The Iowa structured psychiatric interview: Rationale, reliability, and validity. *Acta Psychiatrica Scandinavica,* 1980, *62,* 1-38.

Voeltz, L. M., & Evans, I. M. The assessment of behavioral inter-relationships in child behavior therapy. *Behavioral Assessment,* 1982, *4,* 131-165.

Weeks, M. F., & Moore, R. P. Ethnicity-of-interviewer effects on ethnic respondents. *Public Opinion Quarterly,* 1981, *45,* 245-249.

Wieman, R. J., Shoulders, D. I., & Farr, J. Reciprocal reinforcement in marital therapy. *Journal of Behavior Therapy and Experimental Psychiatry,* 1974, *5,* 291-295.

Wiens, A. N. The assessment interview. In I. B. Weiner (Ed.), *Clinical psychology.* New York: John Wiley, 1976.

Williams, A. R. The initial conjoint marital interview: One procedure. *Family Coordinator,* 1974, *23,* 391-395.

Zanes, A., & Matsoukas, E. Different settings, different results? A comparison of school and home responses. *Public Opinion Quarterly,* 1979, *43,* 550-557.

PART *II*

OBSERVATIONAL TECHNIQUES

As Wynne (1981, p. vii) has stated, "Nearly all family therapists claim to give detailed attention to observable behavior and interaction." Assessment involving the observation of family interaction has a long history in marriage and family therapy (Filsinger, Note 1). The practice is based on the belief that there is no substitute for the direct observation of the family process (Notarius, Markman, and Gottman, Chapter 6). In contrast, traditional self-reports of marriage and family characteristics are felt to be distorted by a number of within-family biases and are felt to be essentially tapping the satisfaction of the family members, as opposed to their actual behaviors.

In this part of the book, chapters are devoted to assessment techniques based on observation of family behavior. Chapter 3, by Hudgens, Portner, and Kearney, provides an overview of the clinical usage of one of the oldest observational techniques still in use, the Inventory of Marital Conflicts (IMC). The IMC is a structured situation designed to produce conflict between spouses. As a structured situation for observing conflict, it has been widely employed. It also comes with a set of rules for coding the couple's interaction style.

The Spouse Observation Checklist (SOC), discussed in Chapter 4 by Weiss and Perry, uses direct observations of the couple concerning each other's behavior on a given day. Behaviors are noted as occurring and are rated as pleasers or displeasers. The SOC provides an informative map of the specific behaviors spouses use and of the way in which they affect the other spouse.

Chapter 5 presents one of the classic modern-day observational techniques, the Marital Interaction Coding System (MICS). Fitting with the rapid development in the field, the specific technique discussed is the third generation of the MICS, the MICS-III. The evolution of the MICS-III is discussed by Weiss and Summers in some detail. As opposed to the other chapters in this volume, this chapter offers the unique opportunity to see the more formal concerns in the development of an observational coding system. Less research-oriented readers may wish to skim some of the more detailed portions of the chapter, but they will not want to miss the substantive issues.

45

Notarius, Markman, and Gottman discuss clinical applications of the Couples Interaction Scoring System (CISS) in Chapter 6. The CISS has been used in some of the most rigorous investigations of marital interaction. It is a tribute to the authors' writing ability that they make the discussion of extremely complex issues so intuitive. Their discussion carries beyond observation to inferences concerning such topics as hidden agendas couples bring with them and specific suggestions on how to identify sequences of marital interaction in clinical settings.

In the last chapter of the section, Conger discusses the potential contribution formal observation can make to the therapeutic enterprise. Conger focuses on what observational systems have told us about the nature of family distress and ways in which the therapist could use that information. It should be highlighted that two of the techniques he discusses, the Social Interaction Scoring System (SISS) and the Dyadic Interaction Scoring Code (DISC), are both designed for use with portable data collectors, a fact that greatly facilitates data collection, storage, and analysis.

The reader should pay particular attention to what Conger has to say. While some writers in the area have suggested that observation of family interaction by trained observers is of little clinical value (Jacobson, Elwood, & Dallas, 1981), it may be that machine-aided data collection will tip the scales toward practicality. Much of the objection to observation by trained others is the cost of time and effort involved. Weiss and Summers (Chapter 5) state that training for the MICS involves 2 to 3 months. Notarius and his colleagues (Chapter 6) point to 24 hours of coding for each hour of interview. Knowledge of the behaviors coded in the MICS and CISS may be of value to the therapist as features of family interaction to look for without formal asssessment. Even the language involved in describing coding categories may constitute a useful language system in clinical discussions (Notarius et al., Chapter 6). However, it may be that machines will ultimately provide the ready access and quick turnaround necessary in clinical settings. In lieu of that development, the applications of observational techniques to therapeutic situations presented in this section should prove an invaluable addition to the therapist's bag of tricks.

Reference Notes

1. Filsinger, E. E. *Choices among marital observation coding systems.* Manuscript submitted for publication, 1982.

References

Jacobson, N. S., Elwood, R., & Dallas, M. The behavioral assessment of marital dysfunction. In D. Barlow (Ed.), *Behavioral assessment of adult dysfunction.* New York: Guilford, 1981.

Wynne, L. Preface. In A. S. Gurman & D. P. Kniskern (Eds.), *Handbook of family therapy.* New York: Brunner/Mazel, 1981.

CHAPTER 3

Capturing Marital Dynamics: Clinical Use of the Inventory of Marital Conflict

ALLETTA HUDGENS
Minnesota Human Development Consultants

JOYCE PORTNER
University of Minnesota

MICHAEL KEARNEY
Hennepin County Mental Health Center

Marriage counselors and researchers have used a variety of criteria to group couples into types. However, this tendency toward typing marriages is not solely the domain of the scholar and clinician. The "typing process" is often observed as people discuss their own marriages or those of others. For example, "He's so quiet and she's so talkative" is a common typing descriptor. Or, as was overheard by one of the authors: "She walks all over him" — "Yes, but he worships the ground she walks on."

Recently, marriage counselors have discussed the need for more precise, efficient, time-limited approaches for describing and typing relationships. The Inventory of Marital Conflict (IMC; Olson & Ryder, 1970) is useful toward this end. The IMC is one of a set of inventories developed to study the interaction process in couples and families at different stages

Authors' Note: The authors wish to thank Dr. David Olson for his very helpful comments and suggestions on earlier drafts of this chapter.

Instrument Source Note: The Inventory of Marital Conflict is one of a series of interaction inventories designed to assess marital and family dynamics at specific stages of the family life cycle. The other instruments include the Inventory of Pre-Marital Conflict (IPMC), the Inventory of Parent-Child Conflict (IPCC), and the Inventory of Parent-Adolescent Conflict (IPAC). Copies of these interaction instruments can be purchased by writing to Dr. David Olson, Family Social Science, 290 McNeal Hall, University of Minnesota, St. Paul, Minnesota 55108.

of the family life cycle. The other inventories deal with premarital, parent-child, and parent-adolescent conflict (see Instrument Source Note, at chapter opening).

Previous studies provide evidence that supports the IMC in its ability to discriminate between couples. The following studies used the IMC task as a stimulus situation, and each utilized a different coding system to describe the couple's interaction. Birchler, Weiss, and Vincent (1975) and Vincent, Weiss, and Birchler (1975) studied the impact of negative and positive reinforcers on couple interaction. The IMC discriminated between distressed and nondistressed couples on both positive and negative behavior. Distressed couples were significantly less positive and more negative than nondistressed couples. In a study by Gottman, Notarius, Markman, Banks, Voppi, and Rubin (Note 1), the IMC was able to discriminate between successful and unsuccessful couples. Miller (1975), using cluster analysis of data generated by the IMC procedure, was able to identify empirically nine couple types, each of which had high internal consistency.

Another study provided construct validity of the IMC. Clinical ratings produced similar results to empirical typologies (Olson, Kearney, & Doyle, Note 2). In a multitrait, multimethod study, clinicians' qualitative methods (ratings) were compared with systematic coding of the interaction using the Marital and Family Interaction Coding System (MFICS) developed by Olson and Ryder (Note 3). The three factors that resulted from these codes were *task leadership, conflict,* and *affect.* These three factors were used to develop empirically *nine* types of couples. The results indicated a high level of congruence between the clinical ratings and the empirical codes. The results lend empirical support to the validity of using the IMC in the applied fashion described in this chapter.

This discussion presents information and suggestions for clinicians based on the use of the IMC during the initial stages of therapy with 25 couples. The couples were seen in two settings. One was a family treatment center in a suburban area and the other was a student counseling bureau at a large university.

The IMC has been used frequently in research settings. However, its use in clinical settings has not been explicitly described previously. The authors found that the IMC provided a useful diagnostic and treatment planning tool for examining patterns of *communication, problem-solving* behaviors, areas of *conflict,* and use of *leadership* and *affect* behaviors.

It is intended that the discussion presented here will enable other therapists to develop expertise quickly in using this interaction instrument. The treatment planning and therapy with one couple is described to provide an overall perspective on the use of the IMC.

Description of the
Inventory of Marital Conflict

The Inventory of Marital Conflict (IMC) was developed by Olson and Ryder (1970). It is a structured revealed-difference exercise for observing and recording couple interaction patterns.

The IMC consists of two sets (Part A and Part B) of nine vignettes (paragraph-length case studies) drawn from common problem areas identified by young married couples. Representative vignette issues include relations with family and friends, jealousy, use of leisure time, division of labor, and work/family tensions. Husbands and wives receive slightly different information on two-thirds of these vignettes, thereby building in inherent disagreement and the necessity for conflict resolution.

The following is a representative vignette from the IMC:

> *Husband's version:* When Don finally gets home from work he takes off his jacket, tie and shoes, and makes himself comfortable with a can of beer. After dinner Don has a little more energy, so he goes back and puts away the various articles of clothing he has taken off. One day Francine tells Don he is sloppy and lazy and demands that he not leave clothes lying around, even for a short period of time. Two days later, Don forgets to do as his wife demanded, and she angrily repeats her complaint. An argument develops.

> *Wife's version:* When Don finally arrives home from work he immediately sits down and makes himself comfortable with a can of beer and scatters his jacket, tie and shoes on the furniture and/or floor, where they stay until sometime after dinner. After putting up with this sloppiness for a while, Francine asks Don to stop tossing his clothes around the apartment, even if he does eventually pick them up. Two days later, Don repeats his usual performance as if Francine had said nothing. When she mentions it again, an argument develops.

Husbands and wives are asked individually to determine a possible problem solution, relevancy of the vignette issue, and who is more responsible for the problem. Couples are then asked to discuss the nine vignettes jointly and arrive at a joint decision on who is more responsible and which of the problem solutions is better.

The joint discussion is tape-recorded, at office or at home, and used as the basis of the clinical assessment. The IMC procedure generally requires 15 minutes to complete the self-report portion and 15-30 minutes for the discussion. Use of the tape recording in the clinical assessment and treatment planning is the focus of this chapter.

Usefulness of the IMC
in Clinical Situations

There are a number of advantages in using the IMC with couples in the clinical setting.

(1) It provides an objective view of the couple's interaction. The therapist and couple can quickly and easily observe the communication style, problems with communication, problem solving, and decision making, and specific issues that cause difficulty. Couples can participate directly in the diagnostic and treatment process. They can step back and listen to their own interaction, making it more likely that they will take responsibility for their treatment along with the therapist.

(2) It is easy to use and requires only minimal materials. The only equipment needed is the inexpensive IMC forms, pencils, and a tape recorder. A clerical person can administer the inventory. The whole procedure takes only 30 to 45 minutes. It is easy for the couple to do and gives them a sense of doing something specific about their problem.

(3) It is relatively nonthreatening and enjoyable. Couples can quickly drop their "front-stage" behavior and decrease their anxiety about discussing their marital relationship, since they are discussing stories about other people. Couples usually become quite involved in the vignettes and like the process of discussion.

(4) It is relevant to life situations. The situations presented in the stories are common to young married couples. The couples tend to reveal their own issues and controversies in the discussion, giving a focus for treatment planning.

(5) It minimizes interactive effects of the therapist's presence. Since the IMC is administered without the therapist present, couples may be less likely to suppress or exaggerate certain behaviors that the therapists' presence might elicit. The therapist can then compare the tape-recorded behavior with the therapy session behavior.

(6) It allows the therapist and the couple to examine couple behavior when not immersed in it. The therapist can stand back and develop alternative hypotheses regarding the couple's problems and interaction patterns. Diagnosis and treatment planning may be shortened by using this systematic procedure. The process helps the couple develop a working model for objectively examining their interaction.

(7) It is useful as an evaluation tool. Parts of the tape can be relayed to illustrate strengths or dysfunctional behavior as therapy proceeds. An alternative form of the IMC can be given at the end of treatment to illustrate and validate the couple's progress. It may be given in a later, follow-up visit to determine the long-lasting effects of therapy.

Limitations to Using the IMC

Several limitations in using the IMC became apparent to the authors in using it with the 25 couples, although none of them were seen as deterrents to its use.

(1) Time necessary to become oriented to the IMC. The IMC requires the therapist to spend time becoming familiar with administering and interpreting the couple interaction generated by the IMC.

(2) Required investment of time to use the IMC. Once the therapist is acclimated to the IMC, it still requires 15-30 minutes per couple of analysis time outside of clinical sessions to listen to the tape and develop interpretations about the couple's behavior.

(3) Particular relevance to young, married couples. The IMC was originally developed with a population of young married couples. At times, couples further along in the marital cycle have difficulty relating to the vignette issues. It might be more appropriate for these couples to take the Inventory of Parent-Child Conflict (IPCC) or the Inventory of Parent-Adolescent Conflict (IPAC).

These limitations are not meant to discourage therapists from using the IMC. Rather, the intent is to point out the realities that limit the use of interaction-generated clinical information from the IMC.

Use of the IMC Tape by the Couple

Generally, the couple completed the IMC questionnaire and discussion/tape recording at the counseling agency. After this, the therapist discussed with the couple their reaction the the experience.

The couple was requested to listen to the tape before the next session, first individually and then together, to see what they would learn about their style of interacting with each other. The way the couple used or did not use the tape was instructive in itself.

It is useful to give the couple a handout that lists and allows space for responding to the following questions:

(1) Did you like what you did in the tape? Why or why not?
(2) What do you wish you had done differently?
(3) What did you like about your partner's behavior? Be specific.
(4) What did you *not* like about your partner's behavior? Be specific.
(5) Were there any surprises? What were they?
(6) What kinds of issues were problematic to deal with?
(7) What feelings do you hear expressed in your and your partner's interaction?
(8) What other observations, thoughts, feelings, intentions, or actions do you have as a consequence of listening to your interaction?

The couple's task is to listen to the tape in a general way. The therapist will be listening for specific areas.

Use of the IMC Tape
by the Therapist:
What to Watch for

When beginning to use the IMC, the therapist generally needs to listen to the tape recording twice, first for a general sense of the couple and the IMC process, and second to pick up and record specific issues to discuss with the couple. With experience, one listening is usually sufficient.

Previous research using the IMC has frequently utilized the Marital and Family Interaction Coding System (MFICS; Olson & Ryder, Note 3). Several factor analyses have demonstrated that the twenty codes represent three consistent factors: task leadership, conflict, and affect. The clinical guidelines presented here are derived from the empirical factors underlying the IMC. The therapist may make interpretations based on the previous theoretical work and empirical factors of task leadership, conflict, and affect related to the IMC. Other therapists might pay attention to other aspects of behavior, depending on their own theoretical frameworks.

The following suggestions alert the therapist to specific behaviors and interactions in four areas: *task leadership/dominance, conflict, affect,* and *communication styles.* Specific case examples from the 25 couples illustrate these areas.

Task Leadership/Dominance

Task leadership/dominance consists of statements and behaviors that move the discussion along toward making a decision. Questions such as these may be helpful in observing task leadership/dominance behaviors: Which spouse tends to initiate the discussion on vignettes? Who does most of the talking? Are there struggles over who has control of the decision? Who moves the discussion on to complete the task? Does one partner defer to the other continually? Which partner documents opinions in order to influence the other?

Task leadership/dominance styles tend to be consistent within any one couple's interaction. A variety of styles were observed. Bob and Dolly could not make any decisions at all. Dolly got distracted by irrelevant issues and Bob refused to take a stand on anything, so nothing else got done as they danced gingerly around each other. With another couple, Elaine initiated more interaction than Dick, who became increasingly silent on the tape. They were able to see how powerful the silence was and how Elaine was pressing for reaction from him and more closeness. Dick felt more and more pressured and withdrew even more. With Carol and Fred, there was a lot of comfortable give and take, shared initiation of topics, and asking for and stating consensus.

The task leadership dimension provides information as to how leadership styles and relationship roles form and are negotiated. Spouses' desires regarding expectations and roles may be discussed. Maintenance of undesirable authority patterns may be examined. Role negotiation may be practiced within the structured therapy setting.

Type and Level of Conflict

Couples discussing the IMC are expected to exhibit conflict, as the instrument is specifically designed to elicit it. Questions such as these may be helpful in observing the couple's conflict type and level: What aids or hinders the couple from making a joint decision? Does the agreement occur in an open, firm, friendly manner? Over what issues does a couple disagree (money, time, task assignment, sex, friendships, values)? How repetitious or drawn out are discussions involving disagreement? Does either partner belittle, discount, or make cutting remarks while discussing an issue? Does either partner use personal experience or information to support his or her argument?

Patterns in resolving conflict vary considerably. During Mary and Tom's interaction, Mary never gave an opinion on anything, but Tom displayed a lot of anger in what he later identified as an attempt to force Mary to interact with him. Joe and Nancy were dully repetitious in discussing issues and always ended with indecision or a deadlock. With Bill and Betty, she brought in new information and suggestions, while he used a sense of humor to lighten things when tension was high. They agreed to swap giving in on joint decisions, or they would defer decision on a difficult item and come back to it later.

When these couples could step back and listen to their process, they had a springboard from which to begin to understand their behavior and to initiate some changes. With the therapist's assistance, couples may identify their own tendencies toward passive, aggressive, or assertive styles. They may practice unfamiliar styles, gaining a sense of how it feels both to give and to receive messages in these three styles.

Passivity (avoidance) or aggressiveness (attack) are often used when compromising skills are absent. Conflict-resolution skills may be clarified and practiced in the structured counseling setting. These include such skills as determining the issue, considering alternative solutions, establishing priorities, developing an action plan, and evaluating progress. Couples with effective conflict-resolution skills should be reinforced for this ability.

Affect

Affect may be signaled by both verbal and nonverbal cues. Inflection of the voice, tonal quality, laughter, and silence may indicate tension, distance, warmth, hostility, anger, sadness, excitement, and so on.

These questions may be helpful in observing extent and type of affect: Does the couple seem very involved emotionally or is their approach intellectual? Is affect similar or dissimilar between spouses? How frequently does either partner encourage or support the other? How frequently does either partner criticize, blame, or make negative remarks about the other? How frequently are partners supportive or critical of themselves? Is humor used to lighten the task and dissipate tension? How frequently do couples laugh? Who laughs the most? What does it denote, such as tension, good humor, or self-doubt? Are there frequent silences? Are silences natural, thoughtful? Are they strained, angry, embarrassed? When and where do they occur? How likely are partners to raise their voices during discussion? Who is most likely to do this? Does the raised voice appear to be negative, positive, or neutral in tone?

Affect was exhibited by our 25 couples in various ways. In one couple, Ken muttered a lot under his breath and was hard to hear on the tape. Lil reacted by talking less and making inconsequential remarks. Silences became more frequent and protracted. There was an aura of fear and withdrawal accompanying the tense silence. Listening to their tape, the couple was surprised to discover this behavior and wanted to work with the therapist to learn what the fear was about and to get more closely involved with each other.

In another couple, Jane consistently put Don down in discussion. In an angry manner, she would say, "That's just like the time we went on the trip. You were never prepared and on time." Don would break out of his usual passivity to say, loudly and and defensively, "Well, how can I be prepared when you're always changing your mind about what you want?" Strength in the relationship was seen where there were supportive comments, such as "Yes, I like that idea," or "Now that you put it that way, I agree," or "That's an interesting point. Let's talk some more."

Often part of a treatment plan involves identifying and communicating feelings. For example, in one couple, Muriel laughed nervously every time Ed disagreed with her and every time she asked for permission to express an opinion. Ed responded by disagreeing with her more often and more loudly. Listening to the tapes helped the couple become aware of some of their feeling responses.

Communication Style

These questions may be helpful in observing communication styles: Does each partner speak for him- or herself? How often do they say "I" compared to "you" or "we"? Is the couple talking *with* or *at* each other? Does each partner truly *listen* to the other? Do they respect each other and draw each other out? Do they reflect back and answer with related statements, or do they ignore the other, change the subject, and so on? How rigid or flexible is the communication? Are interruptions permitted in an easy, comfortable manner? Do the interruptions indicate creativity and spontaneity, or rudeness and hostility? Is the pattern of discussion always the same for each vignette? What interaction rules do you discover? Is it important to be polite? Is one partner supposed to take care of the other? Is it okay to express anger? How frequently is a person's tone of voice congruent with the message delivered? Was this more the case with one spouse than the other?

The 25 couples used some of the following communication patterns. Dave refused to take a stand on anything, saying, "Well, I'm not sure. You can look at it both ways. You should be able to see that." Margaret responded with "Can't you ever make up your mind?" They would enter a vicious cycle of mutual blame, unable to state their own opinions clearly.

Bob had been meek and mild in the first session with Alice and the therapist. On the IMC tape, he demonstrated that he could speak up and defend himself well, showing more flexibility than he had dared expose in front of the therapist. Alice reacted to him by raising her voice and pouting, saying, "Well, go ahead and do what you want." Bob would then say, "Well, I'd like you to approve of what I decide." The couple and therapist used the tape to examine their capacity for flexibility and creativity along with their paradoxical and rigid belief that marriage meant decisions had to be joint and that good communication meant always agreeing on everything.

George often apologized for his opinions and ideas and Harriet would jump in to take care of him, working very hard to bolster his ideas. George would ask, "Can we put down my choice for this item? I know it isn't a very good idea, but . . ." or "Well, I guess you're right. You usually are."

While communicating over the IMC vignettes, some spouses may be very aggressive, others passive, and still others assertive. The aggressive style is relatively easy to pick out. The goal is to have one's own choice selected by the spouse as the joint decision. Claims of better memory, accusations of misreading, lack of understanding, laughter, put-downs, interruptions, and constant repetitions are just some of the tactics used. When both spouses adopt this style, the discussions are likely to be long, often ending in deadlock. One partner gives in or does a quid pro quo, "I'll give in on this one, but you have to give in on the next one." The passive style is also readily detectable. Often one partner will just go along with the decision without participating at all in the discussion.

Two additional aspects of the communication process are who speaks *to* whom and who speaks *for* whom. Sometimes one spouse acts as the communication switchboard, relaying messages for the other. In other cases, one spouse may speak for the other, assuming there is agreement when that may not be true.

Since the directions for the discussion phase of the IMC are very specific, the ability to remain focused on the task is one of the easiest to assess. Couples have commented that this experience provides them the opportunity to work at identifying *common ground* during disputes and has made them more aware of the many different ways of perceiving any one situation. Both of these are necessities for successful communication.

Diagnostic and Treatment Planning Session

Prior to the diagnostic and treatment planning session, the therapist has usually seen the couple for the first interview, administered the inventory or had the couple do it at home, and analyzed the couple interaction tape.

In the diagnosis and treatment planning session, the couple is first asked to discuss what they learned about their own interaction from listening to and thinking about the taped interaction. Then the therapist shares what has been learned, stating first any strengths noticed.

Observations stated about the interaction can be illustrated/documented by playing that portion of the tape. For instance, it might seem that the woman acts as a teacher and the man plays dumb in the discussion. The couple is generally better able to view that taped behavior objectively than if they were stopped right in the middle of such an interaction. They can then more rationally decide whether that behavior is acceptable or whether they wish to change it in some way. It is thought that systems change when perceptions that the couple brought with them to counseling are challenged.

After examining the tape with the couple, the therapist can give a summary of the problems recognized from the tape and other observations. The therapist and couple can proceed to set realistic and specific goals for therapy. These might include working on communication skills, decision-making skills, the recognition and use of anger, assertiveness and autonomy issues, sexual issues, fair fighting, intimacy issues, value differences, and male-female role issues.

Treatment Planning and Therapy with a Couple:
A Specific Example

Dan and Marie had come to counseling concerned about their escalating arguments. The issues that continually surfaced were difficulties in renovating a house, differing opinions as to when to have a child, and career and lifestyle decisions. Dan would get defensive; Marie would get angry. Frightening feelings would arise, and the issues would go underground, never to be resolved.

The couple had taken a couples' communication course several years before and knew the basic skills of speaking for self and listening. However, they still had trouble using these skills effectively rather than manipulating during problem solving. They had a strong commitment to each other and to the marriage and were eager to find a way to deal with their intense feelings to improve their marital relationship. They and the therapist were puzzled about why things were not going better.

After an initial session with the couple, the therapist began to map a strategy for assessing their relationship. She suggested that she see each of them individually one time to explore their family backgrounds and their individual issues. The couple would then take the IMC, after which the couple-therapist team would listen to the tape separately and meet again. They would then discuss all the information and hunches gathered, define and focus the problems, and map a strategy of action.

The therapist decided to give the IMC because, even though the couple had good basic communication skills, they were not doing well with problem solving. The IMC would give a clearer picture of their behavior in conflict-resolution situations.

When asked by the therapist to say what they had learned from the tape, both spouses identified behaviors they did not like. Marie noted that although she stated definite opinions, she sounded too sweet and afraid of displeasing her husband. She also recalled that in discussing problems at home with Dan she either behaved in a similar fashion or came on stronger than she intended.

Dan noted his halting, ambiguous manner, and his inability to take a stand on issues. He thought that was his usual style in interacting with Marie, but sometimes when she expressed great anger, he got defensive and attacked her. She would then withdraw to reasonableness, leaving him feeling foolish and at fault.

The therapist began her input into the planning session by noting the strengths of the couple. Dan and Marie participated equally in the discussion and indicated a willingness to compromise. The therapist also noted Dan's tentative manner and lack of firm stands on issues. She noted Marie's self-conscious tense laughter, which she thought indicated anger when Marie was trying to be polite and agreeable. Marie's affect was greater throughout than was Dan's. In the stories discussed, both Marie and Dan thought the husband was at fault twice as often as the wife.

The couple and therapist team decided to spend six sessions working on conflict resolution. They began by looking at the basis for the anger and fear they suspected was underneath their inability to accept and/or resolve their differences. During the following weeks, they examined the arguments that occurred. Considering their family background information, the therapist asked them if they had interacted in this way with anyone before. What evolved was the discovery that the basis for some of the anger and fear that blocked them was old, unresolved issues from their families of origin.

The therapist decided that a family of origin approach would be most effective with this couple. The same therapist might have focused on other approaches with other couples. Dan became aware of the low self-esteem he had felt in his original family. This was reflected in his feeling that he could never be good enough for Marie. Therefore, he often played victim and then felt manipulated.

Marie became aware of the anger she had never resolved toward her father. She saw that she often projected this anger onto Dan. She also became aware of her tendency to want to control Dan and to have things perfect in her own behavior as well as in that of her partner. They both learned to identify these processes in the middle of an issue, and to talk about the communication itself at the point it occurred.

At the end of the contracted six sessions, the therapist and couple thought that Dan and Marie had new insights and skills in conflict resolution, were being more supportive of each other, and enjoyed their relationship more. Dan and Marie elected to work on their own as a couple for two months. They would then return to do a posttest on the other form of the IMC. They had bought a tape recorder and were using it when they had problem-solving discussions. They found they could listen more objectively to a tape and analyze their real-life conversations as they had done with the IMC tape.

Summary

The Inventory of Marital Conflict is a useful tool for clinicians to increase specificity and efficiency in diagnosis, goal setting, strategy planning, and evaluation in couple therapy. It can be used with a variety of theoretical orientations and elicits involvement from the couple in the process of diagnosis and treatment. It is especially useful in the initial assessment along with clinical interviews with the couple, individually and together.

The focus on interaction style of the couple is conducive to the therapeutic goals of increasing communication skills, conflict resolution, problem solution, and mutual reinforcement of supportive behavior. As this discussion has shown, the IMC is inexpensive and fairly easy to use with a minimum of time and effort. It can be adapted in creative ways to the individual orientation and style of the therapist.

APPENDIX

INVENTORY OF MARITAL CONFLICT

**by
David H. Olson
and
Robert G. Ryder**

IMC PROCEDURE MANUAL

Family Social Science
University of Minnesota
218 North Hall
St. Paul, Minnesota 55108

Revised June 1977

(continued)

APPENDIX   Continued

INVENTORY OF MARITAL CONFLICT (IMC)
CASE DESCRIPTIONS

FORM A   HUSBAND

1. Bob and Frank are good friends. Janis, Bob's wife, likes Frank but is becoming increasingly annoyed with his unannounced and excessively long visits to their apartment, especially at mealtimes. She has suggested to Bob that he ask Frank to please phone before visiting, but her husband feels this would be insulting to his friend. Janis suggests that she might ask Frank to please phone before visiting, but this only makes her husband angry. After accusing his wife of interfering with his friendship, he refuses to discuss the matter further.

2. Nina has been looking for a pair of shoes to wear with her favorite dress. Upon finding a pair of shoes on sale, Nina just cannot resist and purchases them. Later that evening she shows her new purchase to Peter. He remembers that she already has many pairs of shoes and asks about the necessity of such a purchase at this time. Nina becomes outraged and accuses him of being cheap and inconsiderate.

3. A conflict has arisen between Jack and Colleen following a party with friends. During the party, Jack talked to another woman, resulting in his wife becoming very angry. Following the party, Colleen angrily accuses Jack of intentionally ignoring her for the entire evening and becomes argumentative.

4. Mark and Elaine have both been working since their marriage in order to live at a level which they feel to be comfortable. Occasionally, Elaine becomes depressed because she wants to have a child but knows that on Mark's salary alone this would be extremely difficult. Elaine's emotions get the best of her and she accuses Mark of not being aggressive enough, implying that he is an inadequate provider. Mark was advised not to go to college because of scholastic difficulties and has done as well as could reasonably be expected, but his wife continually compares him unfavorable to his college-educated friends. Mark's self-esteem is injured and an argument begins.

5. Linda and Steve plan to take a weekend trip by car. While Linda is driving Steve to work on Friday morning, Steve hears a "pinging" noise and realizes that the spark plugs should be changed along with other minor adjustments. Since they plan to leave Friday evening and Steve has to work, he has to ask his wife to take the car to the garage. Linda complains about the other preparations she says she has to make for them and their two children but says she will have time to take the car to the garage, and agrees to do so. During the trip, Steve hears the "pinging" noise and realizes the spark plugs have not been changed. It turns out that Linda took the car to the garage but did not bother to mention the spark plugs. Linda says that if Steve doesn't like the way she does things he can do them himself. Steve points out that he was unable to take the car to the garage and that when she agrees to do something she should do it.

6. Dick and Diane have been married for three years. Dick likes his job and is anxious to get ahead. For the past year he has been voluntarily spending a great deal of extra time at his work. Diane has repeatedly accused Dick of caring more about his job than he cares for her. Dick explains that his career is important to both of them and that it is necessary for him to work additional hours if he expects to get promoted. Diane refuses to listen to Dick's explanations and unreasonably demands that he substantially cut down his hours of over-time work.

7. When Jerry comes home from work in the evening he is tired and likes to relax over a pleasant meal. After dinner he prefers to be alone with his wife. Betty, however, does not understand Jerry's unwillingness to go out after a hard day's work, and she is after him to go out partying in the evenings. She tells Jerry he is a lazy do-nothing.

8. Tom is very concerned about his wife's smoking habits. Betty is a very heavy smoker and has a severe cough. Although Tom used to be a heavy smoker himself, he has now quit completely, so he is convinced that Betty could at least cut down. He has told her in detail about the health hazards involved in smoking, and he has asked her to stop or at least cut down, if not for herself then because of her love for him. Betty's usual reaction has been to get sarcastic. She says she is trying but doesn't change. As a result there has been a series of arguments.

9. Each night Larry promises Judy that he will throw the garbage out after they finish dinner. Invariably, Larry forgets and leaves the kitchen without doing what he has promised. Judy has felt that the best thing to do is to throw the garbage away by herself and has been doing this later in the evening. When he notices this, Larry becomes angry with Judy, stating that this is his job. As Larry continues to follow his old habits, Judy begins to do the chore herself, only to be angrily criticized by her husband.

APPENDIX Continued

INVENTORY OF MARITAL CONFLICT (IMC)
CASE DESCRIPTIONS

FORM A   WIFE

1. Bob and Frank are good friends. Janis, Bob's wife, likes Frank but is becoming increasingly annoyed with his unannounced and excessively long visits to their apartment, usually at mealtimes. She has suggested to Bob that he ask Frank to please phone before visiting, but her husband feels this would be insulting to his friend. Janis suggests that she might ask Frank to please phone before visiting, but this only makes her husband angry. After accusing his wife of interfering with his friendship, he refuses to discuss the matter further.

2. Nina has been shopping around carefully for some time to find a pair of shoes she can afford that will go with her favorite dress. She finally finds a satisfactory pair of shoes and is happy to discover that they are on sale. She purchases the shoes and takes them home to show her husband, Peter. He does not care whether or not the shoes are satisfactory. He doubts that they are necessary at all and fails to understand their importance to her or how much trouble she has gone to in order to save money.

3. A conflict has arisen between Jack and Colleen following a party with friends. During the party, Jack was involved with another woman and ignores his wife. Colleen feels hurt and attempts to discuss her feelings of being neglected but feels like she is not understood.

4. Mark and Elaine have both been working since their marriage in order to live at a level which they feel to be comfortable. Occasionally, Elaine becomes depressed because she wants to have a child but knows that on Mark's salary alone this would be extremely difficult. Elaine's emotions get the best of her, and she accuses Mark of not being aggressive enough, implying that he is an inadequate provider. Mark was advised not to go to college because of scholastic difficulties and has done as well as could reasonably be expected, but his wife continually compares him unfavorably to his college-educated friends. Mark's self esteem is injured and an argument begins.

5. Linda and Steve plan to take a weekend trip by car. While Linda is driving Steve to work on Friday morning, Steve decides that the spark plugs need changing and that other minor adjustments should be made. He tells his wife to get the work done in time for them to leave that evening. Linda also has all the other preparations to manage for them and their two children, but she manages to get the car to the garage and asks for a tuneup. On the trip, Steve hears a "pinging" noise, discovers that the spark plugs are the same ones he had been using, and blames his wife for the spark plugs not being changed. Linda feels that if he is going to be so picky about how things are going to be done, he should assume some responsibility for doing them himself. Steve tells her he was too busy.

6. Dick and Diane have been married for three years. Dick likes his job and is anxious to get ahead. For the past year he has been voluntarily spending a great deal of time at his work. Diane feels that their marital relationship is deteriorating due to the lack of time they are able to spend together. She attempts to explain to Dick that financial success will be meaningless if their marriage is destroyed in the process. Dick cooly tells his wife that her response is so immature that it is pointless to discuss the subject further.

7. Jerry regularly comes home from work, eats, and sits down in front of the television screen for the entire evening. Betty is cooped up in the house all day and feels that she will go crazy if she can't get out and have some sort of contact with other human beings. Jerry refuses to go out and so there is a disagreement between Betty and Jerry.

8. Tom claims to be worried about Betty's health because she smokes so much and has a cough. He gives her endless detailed lectures about health hazards and is always demanding that she stop or cut down. Betty realizes that she smokes too much and is trying to cut down, but Tom's continued badgering is no help. Tom apparently feels that because he stopped smoking without any difficulty, everybody else should quit too and should have no trouble doing so. He seems unable to understand that it is difficult for her to change her smoking habits, and he says that if she really loved him she would quit. Betty has tried to control herself and not get angry at Tom's continuous comments, but Tom goes right on lecturing to her, leading to a series of arguments.

9. Each night Larry promises Judy that he will throw the garbage out after they finish dinner. Invariably, Larry forgets and leaves the kitchen without doing what he has promised. Judy has felt that the best thing to do is to throw the garbage away by herself and has been doing this later in the evening. When he notices this, Larry becomes angry with Judy, stating that this is his job. As Larry continues to follow his old habits, Judy begins to do the chore herself, only to be angrily criticized by her husband.

(continued)

APPENDIX Continued

FORM **A**

Couple Number

DO NOT MARK IN THIS SPACE

SEX ⓜ ⓕ

UNIVERSITY OF MINNESOTA
Family Social Science
297 McNeal Hall
St. Paul, Minnesota 55108

INVENTORY OF MARITAL CONFLICT

by
David H. Olson and Robert G. Ryder

INDIVIDUAL ANSWER FORM

CASE DESCRIPTION	YOUR CHOICE — WHAT SHOULD THEY DO?	Who Is Most Responsible? Husb / Wife	Is This Situation Relevant To: Your Relationship? YES / NO	Other Relationships You Know? YES / NO	JOINT DECISION Who Is Most Responsible? Husb / Wife	What Should They Do? A / B
1A Conflict over frequent visits by husband's friend and wife's annoyance.	Should Bob ask Frank to phone before visiting?					
	Should Janis stop interfering in her husband's friendship?	ⓗ ⓦ	ⓨ ⓝ	ⓨ ⓝ	ⓗ ⓦ	ⓐ ⓑ
2A Conflict about wife's purchase of a pair of shoes to wear with new dress.	Is it reasonable for Peter to question the necessity of Nina's purchase?					
	Should Peter try to understand Nina's well-planned purchase of these particular shoes?	ⓗ ⓦ	ⓨ ⓝ	ⓨ ⓝ	ⓗ ⓦ	ⓐ ⓑ
3A Conflict caused by wife feeling ignored by husband while at a party.	Should Jack be permitted to talk to another woman at a party without Colleen becoming upset?					
	Should Jack be more attentive to his wife at parties?	ⓗ ⓦ	ⓨ ⓝ	ⓨ ⓝ	ⓗ ⓦ	ⓐ ⓑ
4A Conflict between Mark and Elaine stemming from their desire to have a child but recognizing the financial burden.	Is Elaine justified in accusing Mark of being an inadequate provider?					
	Should Elaine be more understanding concerning Mark's ability and achievements?	ⓗ ⓦ	ⓨ ⓝ	ⓨ ⓝ	ⓗ ⓦ	ⓐ ⓑ
5A Conflict over car breakdown while taking a short weekend trip.	Is Steve being unreasonable in blaming his wife for the work not getting done?					
	Should Linda thoroughly carry out her responsibilities once she has accepted them?	ⓗ ⓦ	ⓨ ⓝ	ⓨ ⓝ	ⓗ ⓦ	ⓐ ⓑ
6A Conflict over husband spending time at the office.	Should Dick continue to devote the time that he knows is necessary to obtain advancement in his career?					
	Should Dick spend more time with his wife?	ⓗ ⓦ	ⓨ ⓝ	ⓨ ⓝ	ⓗ ⓦ	ⓐ ⓑ
7A Conflict regarding evening entertainment.	After working hard all day should Jerry be allowed to spend a quiet evening at home with his wife?					
	Should Jerry understand and respond to Betty's boredom by going out in the evening?	ⓗ ⓦ	ⓨ ⓝ	ⓨ ⓝ	ⓗ ⓦ	ⓐ ⓑ
8A Conflict over wife's smoking.	Should Tom feel he has the right to concern himself with his wife's health?					
	Should Tom leave Betty alone and quit pressuring her?	ⓗ ⓦ	ⓨ ⓝ	ⓨ ⓝ	ⓗ ⓦ	ⓐ ⓑ
9A Conflict about the responsibility for throwing the garbage away.	Is Larry neglecting his responsibility by not carrying out the garbage?					
	Is Judy expecting too much by asking her husband to carry out the garbage?	ⓗ ⓦ	ⓨ ⓝ	ⓨ ⓝ	ⓗ ⓦ	ⓐ ⓑ

STOP HERE

62

APPENDIX Continued

	DATE	COUPLE NUMBER
POST DISCUSSION FORM		(☐) Male
CHECK ONE ☑		(☐) Female

1. How much did you enjoy discussing these cases?	4. How satisfied were you about the final decisions that were made in these cases?
1 ☐ Very enjoyable 2 ☐ Somewhat enjoyable 3 ☐ Slightly enjoyable 4 ☐ Not enjoyable	1 ☐ Very satisfied 2 ☐ Somewhat satisfied 3 ☐ Slightly satisfied 4 ☐ Not satisfied
2. How personally involved did you feel in discussing the cases that were somewhat relevant or similar to your life?	5. Did your spouse react pretty much as you expected he/she would in resolving your differences?

SIMILAR	NOT SIMILAR	5 (continued)
1 ☐ Very involved	1 ☐ Very involved	1 ☐ Very similar to usual
2 ☐ Somewhat involved	2 ☐ Somewhat involved	2 ☐ Somewhat similar
3 ☐ Slightly involved	3 ☐ Slightly involved	3 ☐ Slightly similar
4 ☐ Not involved	4 ☐ Not involved	4 ☐ Not very similar

3. Did you feel the cases described situations that are real problems for families?	6. Did you feel that this technique is useful (helpful) for a couple to participate in?
1 ☐ All seemed real 2 ☐ Most seemed real 3 ☐ Some seemed real 4 ☐ Few seemed real 5 ☐ None seemed real	1 ☐ Very useful 2 ☐ Somewhat useful 3 ☐ Slightly useful 4 ☐ Not very useful

7. What do you think was the major purpose of your discussing these cases?

8. Feel free to add any other comments about the general procedure.

Reference Notes

1. Gottman, J., Notarius, C., Markman, H., Banks, S., Voppi, B., & Rubin, M. *Phenomenological behavior exchange models of marital success*. Unpublished manuscript, Department of Psychology, Indiana University, 1974.

2. Olson, D., Kearney, M., & Doyle, P. *Multi-trait, multi-method analysis of the Inventory of Marital Conflict*. Unpublished manuscript, Department of Family Social Science, University of Minnesota, 1980.

3. Olson, D., & Ryder, R. *Marital and Family Interaction Coding System (MFICS)*. Unpublished manuscript, Department of Family Social Science, University of Minnesota, 1975.

References

Birchler, G. R., Weiss, R. L., & Vincent, J. D. A multimethod analysis of social reinforcement exchange between maritally distressed and non-distressed spouse and stranger dyads. *Journal of Personality and Social Psychology*, 1975, *31*, 349-360.

Miller, B. *Types of marriage interaction and their relation to contextual characteristics in a sample of young married couples*. Unpublished doctoral dissertation, University of Minnesota, 1975.

Olson, D., & Ryder, R. Inventory of Marital Conflict (IMC): An experimental interaction procedure. *Journal of Marriage and the Family*, 1970, *32*(3), 443-448.

Vincent, J., Weiss, R., & Birchler, G. A behavioral analysis of problem solving in distressed and non-distressed married and stranger dyads. *Behavior Therapy*, 1975, *6*, 475-487.

CHAPTER 4

The Spouse Observation Checklist: Development and Clinical Applications

ROBERT L. WEISS
BARBARA ANN PERRY
University of Oregon

The Spouse Observation Checklist (SOC) grew out of a clinical research need to make available to therapists the daily exchanges of goods and services that characterize a sustained intimate relationship. Not only were such exchanges fundamental to the concept of behavioral marital therapy (BMT), but being able to assess movement in the quality of exchanges was necessary for therapeutic planning with couples. Since it first appeared formally (Weiss, Hops, & Patterson, 1973; Wills, Weiss, & Patterson, 1974), the SOC has been used extensively with couples in the United States and other countries in both clinical and research settings. At this writing there are some eighteen presentations and articles available in the English language that deal with the SOC in its various forms. Over the years the Oregon Marital Studies Program has received numerous requests from practitioners and researchers alike for information on scoring and interpretation of the SOC, and for references to published articles. Until now there has been no attempt to bring clinically relevant research materials on the SOC together in a systematic fashion. One of the aims of this chapter is to present a clinically focused accounting of the SOC.

Additionally, we will review the development of the SOC and some of the relevant literature, to understand better its potential clinical usefulness. Applications of the SOC are best understood within a clinical re-

Instrument Source Note: Individual copies of the SOC suitable for clinical use may be purchased from the Oregon Marital Studies Program, Department of Psychology, Straub Hall, University of Oregon, Eugene, Oregon 97403. The SOC and other related marital assessment devices are available in a therapist's guide, *Assessment and Treatment of Marital Dysfunction*, by R. L. Weiss and B. A. Perry, available from the Oregon Marital Studies Program.

search context. We will consider some of the methodological issues that might govern its clinical uses, so that clinicians and researchers will be in a better position to decide whether and how to utilize information from spouse observation.

Developmental Background

The SOC was born of a collaborative effort begun in the late 1960s among Gerald R. Patterson, Robert L. Weiss, and Robert C. Ziller at the University of Oregon Psychology Clinic and the original Oregon Research Institute (Gottman, 1979; Weiss & Wieder, 1982). These investigators, with their graduate students and research assistants, studied problems of small group conflict (focused on marital dyads) within the context of behavioral and social psychological theory.

From the earliest efforts to work with couples in marital distress, data were necessary on spouses' exchanges of daily benefits. It was often easy for couples to report graphically what their partners had failed to do, but, with remarkably few exceptions, they would fail to mention their partners' pleasing behaviors. The developing view of therapy emphasized that beneficial exchanges had to be foremost if the partners were to succeed. Spouses were taught pinpointing skills as a method for increasing the likelihood of their gaining desired goods and services, rather than allowed to rely on more typical coercive methods of evoking responses. Marital distress consisted in part of a rate of positive exchange that was too low and exchange of aversive behaviors at a rate that was too high. It was the clinical necessity of keeping track of these exchanges that first led to the SOC, or, as it was called earlier, the Pleasing-Displeasing tracking technology.

There was another facet to the development of the SOC. The technology of the infamous "golf counter" was used with couples as a method for inducing them to exchange positive affectional behaviors. Ogden Lindsley and Eric Haughton were major innovators in applying operant technology to clinical problems. Accurate recording of small events (such as smoking urges) could be easily recorded *in situ* on the Golf Pal, a wristwatchlike counter that could be used to record two or more classes of events. It was a short step from counting smoking urges to having couples track their exchange of affectional "pleases" (Ps) and "displeases" (Ds) by means of the wrist counters. Since it was not possible to count more than a very few high-rate behaviors with the wrist counters, a natural division arose between affectional (small, readily consumable) behaviors and instrumental (larger, less frequent) behaviors such as carrying out a chore or doing something special for one's partner. The latter were recorded on specially gridded 3 × 5 cards that could be carried throughout the day. Dissatisfaction with the cumbersome task of recording events on cards and counters led to a change in procedure: instrumental events were recorded in time zones, specific periods during the day when such records were made. Initially spouses were required to make continuous tracking records of Ps and Ds.

Although issues of what to record and how best to record it have been a concern, one thing was clear: Focusing couples' attention on acts and behaviors that each found either pleasing or displeasing became an important part of assessment and intervention in BMT.

The domain of pleasing and displeasing behaviors was defined by project personnel, each contributing to a pool immodestly called the "universal list of Ps and Ds." This method fell considerably short of the now more acceptable methods for establishing content validity, such as the behavioral analytic method, by which the criterion behavior evolves from careful study of successful and unsuccessful coping with some well-defined situation (Goldfried & D'Zurilla, 1969). A very large list (almost 500 unclassified items) of affectional and instrumental behaviors resulted, for example: "Spouse hugged and kissed me," "Spouse yelled at children," "Spouse put gas in car," "Spouse helped me reach orgasm."

To provide therapists with a method for individualizing items for their clients by selecting only those of concern to a given couple, all items were typed onto IBM computer cards. For each client couple the therapist had only to select the relevant items, submit the cards for computerized listing, and, presto, an individualized listing! Unfortunately, the therapist spent much time picking through the items and the resulting printout was not always of good quality. (With current word-processing equipment the task could be greatly simplified.)

Two changes in the Ps and Ds approach, particularly relevant to current usages, were made in the ensuing years. In the first published study by Wills et al. (1974), the SOC items were viewed as atoms that made up the larger molecule called "daily marital satisfaction." The thinking of the investigators was that daily satisfaction ratings (DSRs) must in some fashion be composed of events that transpire within the relationship, that is what the partners do to and for one another. The aim was to determine how such events (as defined by Ps and Ds) combined to account for variance in DSR scores. How do instrumental and affectional events, subdivided into Ps and Ds, contribute to DSR scores? This particular study was the model for many replication studies reported in the ensuing years. (Table 4.1 lists the relevant literature.) The main point was that behavioral events, actually spouse reports of what their partners may have provided, were sought as predictors of DSR.

TABLE 4.1

Author	Purpose	Couples	SOC Validity	Satisfaction Measure
Barnett and Nietzel, 1979	correlating instrumental and affectional behaviors to short- and long-term marital satisfaction	11D/11ND	r's between instrumental Ds, marital satisfaction, and sexual activity; affectional Ds and DSR	DSR, L-W
Birchler et al., 1975	interaction differences between D/ND; multilevel assessment	12D/12ND	P:D ratio differences; D 4:1, ND 38:1	NA
Christensen et al., in press	methodological study: quality of behavioral reports of interpersonal behavior; accuracy of recording; systematic bias	50ND 50 dating	greater tendency to blame partner as length of relationship increases	24 hr. L-W
Christensen and Nies, 1980	representativeness of SOC items; can couples reliably report events?	50ND	r's between Ps, Ds, and DSR; in general, original P/D designation confirmed	24 hr.
Elwood and Jacobson, 1982	Do clinical couples agree more than nonclinical couples on SOC items?	10D (pretherapy)	no greater SOC agreement for clinical than for nonclinical couples	NA
Jacobson, 1979	effectiveness of problem-solving training with severely distressed couples (single-subject design)	6D (therapy)	Ps, Ds used to track effects of Rx on specific target issues	NA
Jacobson et al., 1981	determine reliability of spouses as observers of events in their own relationship	160/20ND	generally low levels of between-spouse agreement; ND agree more than D; agreement improved over time	NA

Jacobson et al., 1982	test of reactivity hypothesis: D > ND in DSR reactivity to Ps and Ds	20D/21ND	high reactivity of D group to Ps/Ds; significant mean differences in D/ND labeling of positive, negative, and neutral	DSR
Jacobson et al., 1980	reactivity of D and ND couples to Ps and Ds	17D/6ND	D more reactive to Ds than ND	DSR
Margolin, 1981	test differences in patterns of exchanges of Ps/Ds at four stages of family life cycle	24D/26ND	P:D ratio differences for D/ND and stages of family life cycle; reciprocity data for the D/ND distinction	DSR; L-W
Margolin and Wampold, 1981	microanalysis of interactional patterns in D/ND differences related to satisfaction	22D/17ND	construct validity; sequential analyses of communication related to Ps and Ds	L-W
Margolin and Weiss, 1978	components of therapy comparison; Ps and Ds one of many measures	27D	response to Rx in one condition: increase Ps, decrease Ds	NA
Paige, 1978	patterns of Ps/Ds at three stages of family life cycle	121ND	normative data	DSR
Robinson and Price, 1980	compare home-observed and self-reported rates of Ps	4D/4ND	differences between D/ND in reported Ps; Ds underestimate rate of Ps	MHS
Vincent et al., 1980	predict effects of first baby on husband/wife marital satisfaction; used specific P/D related behaviors	32ND	complex patterns, e.g., wives who completed study reported significantly more Ps than those who terminated	DSR

(continued)

69

TABLE 4.1 Continued

Author	Purpose	Couples	SOC Validity	Satisfaction Measure
Volkin and Jacob, 1981	possible reactive effects of spouse monitoring	11D/25ND (wives)	no reactive effects of spouse monitoring: replicated Ps to DSR correlation	DSR
Weiss et al., (1973)	demonstrate effects of Rx on new assessment measures, including SOC	5D (therapy)	significant improvement in P:D ratios pre- to posttherapy (no control group)	NA
Wills et al., 1974	establish behavioral determinants of DSR	7ND	original P/D to DSR findings; wives' reporting of husbands' Ps sensitive to instructions given secretly to husbands	DSR

Both as an attempt to organize further the large number of SOC items and to provide a method for studying the relationship between cognitive and behavioral representations of interactional (dis)satisfactions, Weiss and Isaac (Note 1) had a group of 24 clinical judges sort the approximately 480 items of the SOC into 12 categories suggested by Azrin, Naster, and Jones (1973) as categories of the Marital Happiness Scale. Category names included for example, Affection, Sex, Consideration, and Household Management. These names were thought to represent familiar concerns to couples. Items were assigned to categories only if 20 percent or more of the judges agreed in their placement of each item. The resulting SOC form had 408 items classified into 12 categories; for 10 of these categories, items were further subdivided into groups of Pleases and Displeases. In this format items had to be responded to as a priori defined Ps or Ds. Thus the item "Spouse kissed me" was placed as an Affectional P, although one might have reacted negatively to that kiss. Because of this limitation, the form was changed so that every item can now be recorded as either P or D, and recordings are made for a 7-day period on a single form, along with a DSR rating.

Administration and Scoring
of the SOC

An abbreviated form of the SOC is presented in Table 4.2 as an illustration of the types of items in each of the 12 categories. As can be seen from the examples, the items refer to fairly specific behaviors that can be responded to as either pleasing or displeasing events received from (performed by) one's spouse. An item is recorded only if it occurred during the recording period; if an item occurs as a pleasing or displeasing event more than once, each occurrence is recorded separately, for example, 3 Pleases and 1 Displease.

The SOC can be introduced at any time during contact with a couple, but it is usually begun during an explicit baseline or assessment phase, that is, a two-week period when the therapist is collecting assessment information rather than commencing formal therapy. It is initially presented as a two-week assignment, and couples are instructed to return their completed forms weekly. During the initial two weeks couples are asked not to share their responses with one another. The SOC is usually completed nightly, at a fixed time set aside for this purpose. (Couples should allow at least one-half hour for the task.) They are instructed to read through the 400 items each time to ensure that they do not miss a behavior or only scan for obvious behaviors. Events that occur after they have completed that day's forms should be entered the following morning in the appropriate day's column. We do not insist that couples bound out of bed to record some end-of-the-day event.

TABLE 4.2   Twelve SOC Categories and Sample Items

Affection: physical closeness; pleasuring
- Spouse hugged or kissed me.
- Spouse greeted me affectionately when I came home.

Companionship: shared projects, recreational events, and leisure time
- We listened to music on the radio or stereo.
- We went jogging or bicycle riding.

Consideration: regard, acceptance, approval, personal favors and services, compliments, love talk, comforting
- Spouse acted patient when I was cross.
- Spouse did something for me instead of showing me how.

Sex: fulfillment, initiation-foreplay, responsiveness, menu of behaviors, attractiveness
- We tried some new sexual behaviors that we liked.
- Spouse rejected my sexual advances.

Communication Process: feelings other than those regarding spouse, information exchange, long-range planning, decision making, problem solving
- Spouse consulted me about an important decision.
- Spouse brought up bad times from past.

Coupling Activities: Mutual friendship, entertaining, relationship with relatives
- We invited a couple of our friends over to visit.
- Spouse made a bad impression on my friends.

Child Care and Parenting: caretaking, teaching, discipline, enjoyable activities
- Spouse comforted baby, made him/her stop crying.
- Spouse contradicted me in front of child.

Household Management: meals and shopping, chores and cleaning, auto and transportation
- Spouse did household repairs or arranged to have them done.
- Spouse nagged or became angry about chores I hadn't completed.

Financial Decision Making: budgeting, spending, income, and investments
- Spouse got a "good buy" on something.
- Spouse bought something important without consulting me.

Employment-Education: job satisfaction, job planning, demands of job
- We discussed future employment opportunities.
- Spouse talked too much about work.

Personal Habits and Appearance: expressions of creativity, self-improvement, personal attractiveness, territoriality, regard for belongings and living quarters, annoying mannerisms
- Spouse hung up his/her clothes in the closet.
- Spouse hogged the covers.

Self and Spouse Independence: friendships outside of relationship
- Spouse supported an independent activity of mine.
- Spouse spoke positively about an experience from which I was excluded.

Definition of time together is sometimes a problem: The rule is that this is time in which they could have interacted had they chosen to do so. Time spent together in the same room, although engaged in separate activities, counts as time together; time spent sleeping is not counted as time together—time spent cuddling would be; one person working in the front yard and one in the backyard is not time together. Sometimes unique definitions are necessary to fit the style of a couple; flexibility is often the handmaiden of useful data.

DSRs are made on a 9-point Likert scale ranging from 1 (extremely dissatisfied) to 9 (extremely satisfied). The rating is made daily and is restricted to how satisfied one was with the relationship, not life itself, that day. It is important to stress this discrimination, that is, one's spouse is a source of pleasure independently of how the world has treated you that day!

Making it reasonable for couples to go to this much effort is part of the context of administration: This is not a chore that couples relish doing nightly, nor do therapists look forward to scoring all the paperwork that results from two weeks of SOCs. Since there is no single set of instructions that would be best for all couples, we present a typical sample of instructions that we use, with the understanding that the clinician would change these to fit a particular couple:

> One of our concerns together will be how much benefit you derive from each other on a day-to-day basis. Obviously, there are few daily big payoffs, like trips to Hawaii, or new cars. Yet, as a couple, you are in a position to provide small favors, goods and services for one another. Therefore, it would be a good idea if we found out what you two do for one another that is pleasing and displeasing. What are some of the small things that you really like and those that you find annoying or displeasing? Couples are often pretty good at picking out what they don't like their partners to do, but they have difficulty knowing what their partners do that they like. So, to find out in your particular case I am going to ask you to be my eyes and ears: Record on these special sheets the things that happen that you find pleasing or displeasing. Do this each day, at the same time of day. I suggest we agree on a time when you will do this. [Agree on time, definitions of time together, and so on.]
>
> As you look over these pages you will notice items that will make you think, "Hey, we used to do that! How come we don't anymore?" Good question. For now don't change anything, just keep a record of what does happen. (You may be surprised that more things happen than you thought!)

The instructions go on to describe the DSR format, the importance of daily marital satisfaction rather than global satisfaction, and the difficulty in separating out feeling good at work and with one's spouse. The instructions are interactive: As the couple pages through the forms they ask questions and the therapist couches information in a way that fits each particular couple, increasing their interest in the task. The aim is to make the task inherently reasonable given the couple, their problems, and the therapist's inventiveness.

Scoring the SOC is done in part by the couples. First, they bring the daily totals to a summary page, a Ps and Ds entry for each of the 12 categories, together with their DSRs and time together ratings. These data (when checked for accuracy) can be used either to graph the relationship between DSR and frequencies of Ps and Ds or for correlations between daily totals and DSRs using the 14 days as bivariates. One could also use the individual category totals (for example, Consideration Ps) as a correlate of DSR, again using the days as data points. The aim is to discern patterns between behaviors and DSRs, either graphically or in correlational formats. The advantage of the correlational approach is that it makes it possible to suggest that when Ps are low (or Ds are high) during a particular week, satisfaction suffers. That is, if we obtain a high correlation between a category and DSR, we can say that the couple should view low satisfaction as a symptom of the rate of Ps or Ds, and not as the result of some mysterious outside factor.

The SOC can be given during intervention to facilitate joint pleases, and as a means of setting goals and testing whether relationship production goals are being met. These options will be considered below.

Clinical Interpretation of the SOC During Assessment

During the two-week assessment phase of therapy, the SOC provides the clinician with three types of data: (1) a sample of the couple's ability to comply with therapeutic instructions, (2) "hard data" detailing what contributes to relationship satisfaction, and (3) clinical "soft," impressionistic data.

Compliance Data

Couples who successfully complete their assignments are behaviorally involved in the therapy process. If couples do not complete the SOCs, if they have trouble returning them on time or if they are leaving out data, the clinician needs to assess whether this is a simple problem of lack of information or a problem of "resistance" requiring intervention at other than a level of skills training.

Not understanding the instructions or having unexpected emergencies occur at home, such as a child requiring emergency hospitalization, are examples of informational problems. By instructing the clients to call within two days if any questions arise about completing the forms, the therapist can avoid receiving incomplete data. This may also be accomplished by instructing the partners to note any unusual life events that make particular days atypical. The therapist needs to distinguish between couples' verbal and behavioral compliance: saying they will complete the forms but not doing so versus bitching about the forms but doing them anyway. What couples *do* is informative, not what they *say*. The therapist can ignore bitching about how abominable the forms are if the couple complies behaviorally. Compliance with the assessment tasks early on in therapy gives the best indicator of the couple's future compliance with assignments.

As with any therapeutic task, the therapist should make completing the SOC worth the client's while. This brings us to a second type of noncompliance. Often behavioral techniques do not work because they are "dumped" on the clients in a heavy-handed manner that suggests "there's only one way to do it." All of us like to feel special, different from others. The therapist can customize the assignment and prevent the couple from feeling as though they are being "trained" or "behavior modified" by the manner in which the assignment is made.

The quality of the data collected is an important issue. Did the couple wait two or three days before filling out the forms, rather than doing them daily? Did they fake the data? Did they (as one couple did) use the forms as one more weapon in their arsenal by throwing the forms in the fire (not once, but twice!) after arguing about how to complete them? Many problems can be avoided if the clinician anticipates problems couples will have in filling out the forms. Partners who wait two or three days and catch up by trying to recall what happened tend to remember only the negative behaviors and to forget what positives occurred. The result is an inaccurate picture of their relationship, presented not only to the therapist but to themselves as well. Asking partners what might happen during the upcoming week to hinder the data collection helps avoid problems by putting the couple on notice that they are in control of the data collection, that things cannot "just happen" and go unexplained. Often the process, what is done with the forms, is more informative than the content, the data on the sheets. In refusing to complete the SOC, or by subtly sabotaging the data, the client is sending a direct message to the therapist, a message that can range from "I don't think you really understood my position while we were talking so I'm doing this to let you know how upset/frustrated/hurt I am" to "I'll be damned if I'm going to do *any*thing that will help this marriage stay afloat."

If one partner does not fill out the forms, the therapist first determines if this is an informational problem and whether there is something he or she can do to facilitate the partner's completing the forms. If the problem is an issue of the "meaning" of the assignment (or of therapy), the therapist then structures the next session specifically around the nature of the therapeutic contract. During that session the couple and therapist deal only with that issue—no more relationship content until the therapeutic contract is firmly reestablished.

By structuring the SOC assignment and anticipating problems, the therapist eliminates much dysfunctional and "resistant" behavior. It is more beneficial to provide the couple with this structure in the beginning and to develop a solid therapeutic contract than to continually have to troubleshoot problems stemming from partners' hidden agendas.

Hard Data

The SOC provides "hard data" by illustrating what contributes to couple satisfaction and to relationship problems. Thus the number of Ps and Ds each partner had, in what categories, and the amount of time spent together can all be quantified. The relationship, if any, between daily marital satisfaction and Ps and Ds and specific areas of exchange are especially important. (We have already alluded to these methods above.)

One can also illustrate the nature of the exchange in a relationship by making a relatively simple graphic display showing the relationship between increasing level of DSR (X axis) and frequency of Ps and Ds (separately) on the Y axis. Simply collect all days with ratings of 1, 2, . . . 9 and average the corresponding frequencies of Ps (Ds) for each. Thus, if there were three days with DSRs of 5, one would first add the frequencies of Ps on those particular days, divide by three, and plot the mean against the DSR point = 5. What one frequently obtains is a graph line that meanders for Ps but shows a clear negative function for Ds, that is, as DSR increases, the associated values of Ds decrease. The interpretation of this dual result is that good days for the couple are associated with few Ds, but not necessarily with more Ps. This means that the best they can expect is a "not bad day," rather than a "good day." For many, this simple demonstration with their own data convinces them of the no-win situation they have created for themselves.

Clinical Soft Impressions

With experience clinicians find that the SOC provides useful information about the quality of how particular couples interact—something of the texture of their life together outside the therapy room, such as the novelty or lack of novelty in their relationship. There is considerable similarity in the lives of couples; all distressed couples show similar problems of communication and erosion of benefits. One can formulate appropriate treatment options based on whether the couple's problems are due to the commission of displeasing events, the omission of pleasing behaviors, or two few joint activities.

The SOC is more informative than the "cassette" (or cognitive theories) a couple has constructed to explain their hurts and disappointments, which the couple brings with them. This cassette usually focuses on all that is wrong with the relationship, how their personalities are so different, and why the other person will have to be the one to change. The clinician continually looks for behavioral signs of togetherness. If there are none, have they considered divorce? The clinician asks this question not because he or she wants them to be divorced, but because the couple should convince him or her that there is some reason to work on maintaining an intimate relationship. This challenge from the outside often makes it possible for the partners to draw their protective line closer about them, and the content of the Ps and Ds items help focus intervention targets for the couple. Some evidence for the behavioral glue of a relationship should be apparent from the SOC data.

Defining Treatment Goals

Defining treatment objectives for a couple requires integrating hard and soft data into a three-dimensional picture of the relationship, for instance, identifying dominant recurring patterns or themes, a sense of what is omitted from the relationship as well as areas of considerable benefit and displeasure, and a sense of what is preventing the couple from attaining their goals. The quality of items checked daily is as important as the number; one can generate high frequencies of very mundane goods and services. The SOC should confirm impressions derived from interviews and other sources: A couple who indicates that sex and affection are "no problem" for them yet fail to report such Ps on their checklists may be reluctant to talk about such a sensitive area. Severely distressed couples who report no Ds on their SOCs may be avoiding conflict out of fear of causing an avalanche of upset. Teaching them how to label displeases without fear of retaliation is an important target.

When Ps and Ds are not tied to relationship satisfaction (DSRs), as in higher DSR on days with high Ps, the problem may be (1) satisfaction that is tied to time together rather than quantity of Ps or Ds, (2) one or both partners taking the data, (3) relationship resources being diverted to other sources, such as an affair with another person, a computer, or work. If the husband's DSRs are higher when the wife is at home taking care of child and household, but she reports wanting to return to work or school, the therapist intervenes at the level of the implicit rules of their relationship, rather than emphasizing increasing the total number of Ps. To sidestep this system issue in favor of force-feeding Ps (including "love days") is risky because the unresolved resentment will become associated with the procedures themselves.

In sum, the Ps and Ds provide many opportunities to use what the couple has experienced recently as a springboard for defining targets of intervention. Since the SOC calls attention to specific behaviors (not philosophical issues), the couple may protest that these are trivial compared to their (unique) issues. This may be true, but even philosophers must eat, sleep, and enjoy the palpable events of the relationship day. For others, the SOC items make possible discussions that were not otherwise possible. Therapists can model their matter-of-fact acceptance of the necessity for human exchanges of affection, sex, consideration, and the like between spouses, and thereby lend authority to the individuals gaining benefits from the relationship. The message is, "How can we make this happen for you?"

Uses of the SOC in
Therapeutic Intervention

The SOC is also used during intervention, but less as an assessment-planning measure than as a vehicle for instigating and tracking behavioral changes. Within our model of marital therapy four areas of accomplishment are defined: objectification, support/understanding, problem solving, and behavior change (Weiss, 1978, 1980). Specific intervention techniques are organized under each of these headings as relationship treatment goals, and the goals are sequentially arranged (one works with objectification skills before attacking support/understanding, and so on). As an illustration of the SOC used during intervention, we will briefly mention its possibilities in the first two of the four areas of accomplishment, objectification and support/understanding.

Objectification. All techniques that facilitate behavioral discriminations, in the sense of clarifying denotative meaning, fall under the accomplishment of objectification. We objectify benefits by helping couples track daily pleasing and displeasing relationship events. Situations can be objectified by tracking the behaviors that seem to occur in which situations. Time and place are treated as controlling elements of our actions. When applied to the communication process, objectification involves pinpointing skills; a pinpointed statement focuses on behaviors, in specific situations, and refers to the desired rate of the behaviors. Pinpointing supplants mind reading and focuses attention on behaviors, not traits, of the other person. A partner is not lazy, he or she simply does not provide certain behaviors at a rate the other person desires.

Learning that marital satisfaction, rather than job or colleague satisfaction, is tied to the number and kind of events in the relationship is the first step in objectification of benefits. Because the couple has already used the SOC for baseline assessment, they can now think in terms of specific behavioral exchanges rather than in terms of personalities or traits. The specificity of SOC items allows partners to "complain" in an acceptable manner. That is, pinpointed complaints focus on something that partners can do or change; the complaint is limited in scope; it is not an attack on the personality or worth of the other. Complaints can be assigned priorities based on which ones are most important to address. A partner is not suffering from frigidity; the issue is, did sex occur? What do you want to have happen? Frigidity implies a state that cannot be altered; wanting sex twice a week implies a changeable state of affairs. At this level the focus can be directed toward what situations are conducive to allowing sex to occur, such as better time together, joint activities, and time to be alone without the children.

Finally, assessment is ongoing in the sense of providing the therapist with information about whether the couple can move ahead in the program as planned. One need not wait until months later to conclude that the couple is not changing.

Support/Understanding. The affectional, companionship, supportive functions in a relationship fall under this heading. The SOC is useful in helping couples define a menu of behaviors that for them are exemplars of closeness and caring. Starting with the behaviors provided on the SOC, the therapist can help them generate, for example, a list of what would be highly valued examples of being supportive. Therapists often assign "love days," which grew out of the Wills et al. (1974) study. Spouses agree individually to provide the other with a love day, defined as a specified day during which the partner provides as many Ps to the other as possible. Ignoring the fact that the suggestion was the therapist's, couples are often surprised to learn how pleasant it is to receive so many good things. The SOC is used to monitor changes in DSR when love days (and associated increases in Ps) occur.

Clearly, when the SOC is used to target support/understanding functions, it is not necessary to collect data on all the categories, unless, of course one is using some sort of a multiple-baseline approach. Similarly, the SOC can be used to establish bilateral change agreements, that is, couples identify supportive/understanding items (for them) from the SOC. These are highlighted with yellow highlighter, and the couple work as a team to increase those behaviors, meeting "production quotas" assigned by the therapist or by what they now see as reasonable goals to attain.

The range of applications is limited only by style and imagination. The points remain simple: The items must be customized to the individual couple, the behaviors can be objectified and tracked, and the relationship between goals and DSR is established. The use of the SOC during intervention is not an end in itself; the aim is only to facilitate movement and then fade out this type of prop completely.

Case Illustration

The following brief case illustrates a possible unexpected use of the SOC with a couple in distress.

Jerry, 34, and Marie, 32, were professionals in the same field, and had been living together for four years before seeking counseling. Their major complaints focused on his depression and drastic mood changes and an ongoing power struggle in which each viewed him- or herself as being manipulated. Both had had affairs in the past several months. They had been withdrawing from each other rather than risk any kind of confrontation and were continually shocked when they exploded at each other over seemingly small problems. They had seen another counselor for individual therapy and one or two joint sessions. They shared many outdoor activities, friendships, and political views. The couple expressed wanting more "consistency in our relationship," to not feel manipulated, improved communication, and that he should be less grumpy and not have uncontrolled mood swings.

On four of the measures included in the precounseling battery, the scores for husband and wife, respectively, were as follows: DAS (Dyadic Adjustment Scale) 97 and 104; MSI (Marital Status Inventory) 5 and 5; CES-D (Depression Screening) 42 and 7; ACQ (Areas of Change Questionnaire) total 13. Although the DAS and ACQ were not markedly distressed, both MSI and CES-D scores were deviant, especially the husband's depression score. On the MSI they had indicated talking with outside professionals about ending their relationship, an item that occurs much closer to divorce than their total scores would indicate.

When the two weeks of SOC data were displayed graphically, three features stood out immediately: (1) DSRs varied only between 4 and 7.5, indicating that at worst they were only slightly below uneventful satisfaction days; (2) in both husband and wife there was a marked parallelism between Ps and Ds, for example, the separate Ps and Ds curves rose and fell in unison; and (3) the relationship between DSR level and frequencies of Ps and Ds showed a strong correlation between high DSR and high Ps, that is, on the days with the highest DSR their Ps were also at the highest. Ds, on the other hand, were at a fairly low level (averaging about 2.4 per day), and there was virtually no rise and fall associated with magnitude of DSRs.

The therapist used the graphic display to conclude that, as a couple, they were focusing on their verbal representation of how bad they felt with one another, ignoring on a behavioral level just how tied into one another they were; that positive events, not negative events, were driving their satisfaction with each other. It was as though they had agreed to filter out what was happening behaviorally in favor of an idea, that is, I (we) are hurting.

Based on this new frame of reference, calling attention to their relationship strengths, they were then able to state requests as accelerates and not decelerates; that is, what each wanted positively, rather than what each wanted the other to stop. The focus was shifted from "how bad we are" to "how good we could be." The husband was helped to see that he wanted to express his feelings without the added responsibility of the wife having to do something about them—that is, he wanted to ventilate without her problem solving. Once she was freed of this responsibility, it was possible for her to separate her accepting him sexually from having to change his mood swings. These outcomes were accomplished in a total of five sessions, two of which were assessment sessions. Two years later, on followup, they reported being together and quite satisfied with their relationship. Again, this case is not typical, yet it does illustrate how the SOC provides information not otherwise immediately apparent and how that information is used to develop a target of intervention. In this instance, the action occurred within objectification and support/understanding targets.

Critique:
Strengths and Weaknesses

The SOC is designed for continuous self-tracking by spouses of their partners. It is a high-cost test to use because of its length, the daily demands it places on clients, and the ease with which clients can seemingly comply, yet provide useless data. From a psychometric point of view the usual reliability claims cannot be made for the SOC, and interobserver agreement tends to be quite low (Christensen & Nies, 1980; Elwood & Jacobson, 1982; Jacobson, Waldron, & Moore. 1980). Concepts of reliability are difficult to apply to the SOC because repeated daily observations are likely to generate autocorrelations that would have to be eliminated before day-to-day correlations of frequencies would be meaningful. (In the Wills et at., 1974, study, autocorrelations were negligible for Affectional Ps and Ds, but this would have to be determined for each new data set.) Day-to-day stability might not be desirable from a clinical standpoint, since intervention would be expected to change certain behaviors. Finally, as Christensen and Nies (1980) have shown, specific items occur with such low frequencies that reliable measurement seems highly unlikely. Aside from the poor interspouse agreement statistics, we must question whether the SOC is a behavioral assessment measure at all or whether it is a self-report measure.

In light of the criticisms one can level against the SOC on psychometric grounds, we may well ask, "How then is the SOC useful?" A large number of studies (Table 4.1) have shown that the SOC (and its variants) share common variance with DSR scores. Clinically, the SOC provides a wealth of information and is useful for planning. Our case illustration was selected to show this. The SDC must be used actively to justify the effort required of spouses and therapists alike; that is, it cannot be put aside after data collection. It is extremely useful in tracking specific intervention assignments—whether a couple is meeting production goals, as it were.

On a somewhat different level of clinical utility is the issue raised conceptually (Weiss, 1978, 1980) and experimentally (Jacobson et al., 1980; Jacobson, Follette, & Waggoner McDonald, 1982) regarding reactivity, namely, that distressed couples' satisfaction is more affected by daily changes in Ps and Ds than is that of nondistressed couples. This tit-for-tat accountability in marital exchanges may be problematic in its own right. To foster such accountability with SOC-like measures therefore may be ill advised.

Currently there are no data to address this concern. It is not logically correct to assume that if distressed couples engage in a certain type of behavior it would necessarily make others worse off if they were taught those same behaviors. It is probably the case that a relationship that fosters daily accountability does not contribute to noncontingent trust. It is analogous to the concept of self-esteem: If every behavior is evaluated for its potential contribution to self-worth, a person would be living under psychological siege! One needs to be grounded independent of moment-to-moment feedback.

The issues with distressed couples is somewhat different: We suspect that such persons track behaviors to support the claim that one is disadvantaged, although this need not always be the case. We also track to discriminate better what it is we want and enjoy. Therefore the SOC can be used to bolster potential benefits on a skills level. Learning what is desirable does not lead necessarily to a reduction of its value. However, there is no evidence for our claims at this point, yet some evidence to suggest that distressed couples pin their daily marital satisfaction on the vicissitudes of pleases and displeases (Jacobson et al., 1982).

Our next step with the SOC is a form devoted totally to pleasing behaviors, called the Cost-Benefit (C-B) Exchange (see Instrument Source Note, at chapter opening). Partners first rate the costs to themselves of providing all behaviors listed (essentially all the P items) as well as the benefits they would derive if their spouse provided the behaviors to them. By comparing one person's cost of giving items desired by the other we obtain an interesting profile of who can give what and at what cost. The C-B is still another illustration of how benefits and costs in a relationship can be quantified and related to other aspects of relationship functioning.

In sum, the SOC is a complex means of obtaining data relevant to spouse interaction. Currently it appears to be more useful heuristically for clinical work than as a standardized assessment device. It has a reasonable research pedigree, but it is to be viewed as the one marital assessment that can be administered routinely and by someone other than the therapist. As one gains experience with the SOC, one finds that, as in a viable marriage, there are surprises and disappointments, but it is always a challenge.

Reference Note

1. Weiss, R. L., & Isaac, J. *Behavior versus cognitive measures as predictors of marital satisfaction.* Paper presented at the meeting of the Western Psychological Association, Los Angeles, April 1976.

References

Azrin, N., Naster, B., & Jones, R. Reciprocity counseling: A rapid learning-based procedure for marital counseling. *Behavior Research and Therapy,* 1973, *11,* 365-382.

Barnett, L. R., & Nietzel, M. T. Relationship of instrumental and affectional behaviors and self-esteem to marital satisfaction in distressed and nondistressed couples. *Journal of Consulting and Clinical Psychology,* 1979, *47,* 946-957.

Birchler, G. R., Weiss, R. L., & Vincent, J. P. A multimethod analysis of social reinforcement exchange between maritally distressed and nondistressed spouse and stranger dyads. *Journal of Personality and Social Psychology,* 1975, *31,* 349-360.

Christensen, A., & Nies, D. C. The Spouse Observation Checklist: Empirical analysis and critique. *American Journal of Family Therapy,* 1980, *8,* 69-79.

Christensen, A., Sullaway, M., & King, C. E. Systematic error in behavioral reports of dyadic interaction: Egocentric bias and content effects. *Behavioral Assessment,* in press.

Elwood, R. W., & Jacobson, N. S. Spouses' agreement in reporting their behavioral interactions: A clinical replication. *Journal of Consulting and Clinical Psychology,* 1982, *50,* 783-784.

Goldfried, M. R., & D'Zurilla, T. J. A behavioral analytic model for assessing competence. In C. D. Spielberger (Ed.), *Current topics in clinical and community psychology* (Vol. 1). New York: Academic, 1969.

Gottman, J. M. *Marital interaction: Experimental investigations.* New York: Academic, 1979.

Jacobson, N. S. Increasing positive behavior in severely distressed marital relationships: The effects of problem solving training. *Behavior Therapy,* 1979, *10,* 311-326.

Jacobson, N. S., Elwood, R. W., & Dallas, M. Assessment of marital dysfunction. In D. Barlow (Ed.), *Behavioral assessment of adult disorders.* New York: Guilford, 1981.

Jacobson, N. S., Follette, W. C., & Waggoner McDonald, D. Reactivity to positive and negative behavior in distressed and nondistressed married couples. *Journal of Consulting and Clinical Psychology,* 1982, *50,* 706-714.

Jacobson, N. S., & Margolin, G. *Marital therapy; Strategies based on social learning and behavior exchange principles.* New York: Brunner/Mazel, 1979.

Jacobson, N. S., & Moore, D. Spouses as observers of the events in their relationship. *Journal of Consulting and Clinical Psychology,* 1981, *49,* 269-277.

Jacobson, N. S., Waldron, H., & Moore, D. Toward a behavioral profile of marital distress. *Journal of Consulting and Clinical Psychology,* 1980, *48,* 696-703.

Margolin, G. Behavioral exchange in happy and unhappy marriages: A family life cycle perspective. *Behavior Therapy,* 1981, *12,* 329-343.

Margolin, G. & Wampold, B. E. Sequential analysis of conflict and accord in distressed and nondistressed marital partners. *Journal of Consulting and Clinical Psychology,* 1981, *49,* 554-567.

Margolin, G., & Weiss, R. L. Communication training and assessment: A case of behavioral marital enrichment. *Behavior Therapy,* 1978, *9,* 508-520.

Paige, R. V. *Behavioral correlates of marital satisfaction during three stages of the marital life cycle.* Unpublished doctoral dissertation, University of Oregon, 1978.

Robinson, E. A., & Price, M. G. Pleasurable behavior in marital interaction: An observational study. *Journal of Consulting and Clinical Psychology,* 1980, *48,* 117-118.

Vincent, J. P., Cook, N. I., & Messerly, L. A social learning analysis of couples during the second post-natal month. *American Journal of Family Therapy,* 1980, *8,* 49-68.

Volkin, J. I., & Jacob, T. The impact of spouse monitoring on target behavior and recorder satisfaction. *Journal of Behavioral Assessment,* 1981, *3,* 99-109.

Weiss, R. L. The conceptualization of marriage and marriage disorders from a behavioral perspective. In T. J. Paolino & B. S. McCrady (Eds.), *Marriage and marital therapy: Psychoanalytic, behavioral, and systems theory perspectives.* New York: Brunner/Mazel, 1978.

Weiss, R. L. Strategic behavioral marital therapy: Toward a model for assessment and intervention. In J. P. Vincent (Ed.), *Advances in family intervention* (Vol. 1). Greenwich, CT: JAI, 1980.

Weiss, R. L., Hops, H., & Patterson, G. R. A framework for conceptualizing marital conflict, a technology for altering it, some data for evaluating it. In F. W. Clark and L. A. Hamerlynck (Eds.), *Critical issues in research and practice: Proceedings of the Fourth Banff International Conference of Behavior Modification.* Champaign, IL: Research Press, 1973.

Weiss, R. L., & Margolin, G. Marital conflict and accord. In A. R. Ciminero, K. S. Calhoun, & H. E. Adams (Eds.), *Handbook of behavioral assessment.* New York: John Wiley, 1977.

Weiss, R. L., & Wieder, G. Marital distress. In A. Bellack, M. Hersen, & A. Kazdin (Eds.), *International handbook of behavior modification and therapy.* New York: Plenum, 1982.

Wills, T. A., Weiss, R. L., & Patterson, G. R. A behavioral analysis of the determinants of marital satisfaction. *Journal of Consulting and Clinical Psychology,* 1974, *42,* 802-811.

CHAPTER 5

Marital Interaction Coding System-III

ROBERT L. WEISS
KENDRA J. SUMMERS

University of Oregon

This chapter reviews the development, past, and current usage of the Marital Interaction Coding System (MICS). As a technique for assessing marital interactions, the MICS occupies a unique place in the history of marital assessment. Not only has it served as the prototype for other interactional coding systems (for example, see Gottman, 1979; Filsinger, 1981), it has been used as a major outcome measure in studies of behavioral marital therapy (Weiss & Wieder, 1982). Its inclusion in this volume—oriented as it is to the clinical practitioner—requires further explanation. The MICS is one assessment technique that is not readily adaptable to professional practice, that is, by marital therapists working outside of a laboratory setting. The sheer technical expertise required to support on-line use of the MICS is one reason for its limited accessability. Just as with any behavioral observation system, the MICS requires trained coders who code behavior based on complex code definitions. In spite of this practical limitation, its inclusion is justified on the grounds that it represents an important assessment technique of concern to therapists and researchers alike. Our aim is to introduce the MICS in the hope that, despite the loss of immediate applicability to clinical practice, the information will broaden understanding of this approach to marital assessment.

In the following sections we will present the development and past usage of the MICS, highlighting both strengths and weaknesses inherent in this technique for assessing marital interaction. The technique will be presented, and with the aid of a clinical example we will introduce the latest revision of the MICS (MICS-III), one that incorporates important conceptual and methodological changes. We hope to anticipate future, more technical expositions of the MICS-III by focusing here on its clinical

Instrument Source Note: Copies of the MICS-III Manual and supporting materials may be purchased from the Oregon Marital Studies Program, Department of Psychology, Straub Hall, University of Oregon, Eugene, Oregon 97403.

applications; we will use the larger context of earlier MICS applications to illustrate the utility of the MICS.

Development and Overview

The MICS was designed to capture interaction behaviors germane to problem-solving attempts of couples. A method for describing couples' interactions objectively, not based on self-report, was needed. The first public document describing the MICS was authored by Hops, Wills, Weiss, and Patterson (Note 1). The MICS was one of many assessment techniques that grew out of the collaborative efforts of G. R. Patterson, R. L. Weiss, and R. C. Ziller in the late 1960s (see Gottman, 1979; Weiss & Wieder, 1982) and was patterned after the Family Interaction Coding System developed by Patterson and his associates. The MICS was developed with graduate students and research assistants working with the project. (Those making the major contribution to the development of the MICS were Marion Forgatch, Hyman Hops, and Thomas Wills.) As part of an integrated approach to the assessment and treatment of distressed relationships (see Weiss, Hops, & Patterson, 1973), the MICS described pre- to postintervention changes as well as interaction skills. The purpose was to describe the topography of behaviors, what the couples did as defined by 30 codes (see Table 5.1), independently of whether a particular behavior, say Positive Solution (PS), was in fact a workable or otherwise meritorious solution. A statement that met the definition of a PS was recorded even though in the coder's judgment the suggestion was unlikely to be carried out. The validity of such coded behaviors is an empirical question. For a discussion of the validity of the MICS, see Jacobson, Elwood, and Dallas (1981) or Markman, Notarius, Stephen, and Smith (1981) for their discussion of validity of coding systems.

Assessment Stages

The MICS technique actually consists of three separate assessment stages: (1) videotaping a couple's interaction, (2) observing and coding the videotaped interaction, and (3) scoring the coded interactions.

Videotaping. For the most part, the interactions to be coded are of partners' attempts to resolve either a relationship problem of their own or one instigated by a standardized revealed-difference method. Typically, the therapist or interviewer is absent during the couple's interaction. Although the setting is artificial (usually a room equipped with a one-way mirror and TV camera), couples readily become involved in the interaction and often show realistic emotion. The situation is somewhat artificial for many couples because (as they report) they usually do not discuss issues of relationship importance. (Some have requested that one-way mirrors be installed

TABLE 5.1   MICS-III Abbreviated Code Definitions

Code	Definition

AG: Agree
response that indicates agreement with spouse's opinion

AP: Approve
statement that favors spouse's attributes, actions, or statements

AR: Accept Responsibility
statement that conveys "I" or "we" are responsible for the problem

AS: Assent
head nods, "yeahs," and the like, that indicate listening or facilitate conversation

AT: Attention
listener maintains eye contact for at least 3 seconds

CM: Command
direct request for immediate action (for example, "Listen to me")

CO: Compliance
fulfills command within 30 seconds or command

CP: Complain
whining or bitter expression of one's own suffering without explicitly blaming
spouse

CR: Critize
statement expressing dislike or dislike or disapproval of specific spouse behavior
stated in a hostile or irritated tone of voice

CS: Compromise
proposal for mutual exchange of behavior

DG: Disagree
response that indicates disagreement with spouses

DR: Deny Responsibility
statement that conveys "I" or "we" are not responsible for the problem

EX: Excuse
denial of personal responsibility, based on implausible or weak rationale

HM: Humor
lighthearted statement intended to be humorous; not sarcasm

IN: Interrupt
spouse breaks in or attempts to break in while other is speaking

MR: Mindread
statement that implies or assumes an attitude or feeling on the part of the other

[MR+: Positive Mindread; implies favorable qualities]

[MR−: Negative Mindread; implies dislike or disapproval]

NC: Noncompliance
failure to fulfill command within 30 seconds of command

(continued)

TABLE 5.1 Continued

Code	Definition

NO: Normative
   any nonverbal behavior that is appropriate to the task or social requirements of
   the situation (for example, lighting a cigarette)

NR: No Response
   situation requires a response is given within 3 seconds (for example, failure to
   answer a question)

NS: Negative Solution
   proposal for the termination or, or a decrease in the frequency of, some behavior

NT: Not Tracking
   listener does not make eye contact for at least 3 seconds

PD: Problem Description
   statement describing a problem, stated in a neutral or friendly tone of voice

[PD-IN: Internal Problem Description; problems stated as within relationship]

[PD-EX: External Problem Description; problems stated as nonrelationship
   problems, such as problems at work, school, and so on]

PP: Positive Physical Contact
   affectionate touch, hug, or the like

PR: Paraphrase/Reflection
   statement that mirrors or restates an immediately preceding statement of
   the other

PS: Positive Solution
   proposal for the initiation of, or an increase in the frequency of, some behavior

PU: Put Down
   statement intended to hurt, demean or embarrass spouse

QU: Question
   any interrogative statement

SL: Smile/Laugh
   smile or laugh

TA: Talk
   irrevelant statements, inaudible speech, noninformational statements, and
   the like

TO: Turn Off
   nonverbal gestures that communicate displeasure, disgust, disapproval (for
   example, sighing, turning head away)

NOTE: Codes in brackets are new codes created in MICS-III revision.

in their homes.) We have found also that an audio reproduction of the interaction can substitute for video (Wieder & Weiss, 1980).

Coding. The coding of records is accomplished by trained coders. Training typically requires from two to three months of weekly instruction and practice. Coders must learn a set of complex definitions spanning some 30 codes, developing the hand-eye coordination necessary for viewing a fast-moving videotaped interaction and accurately recording appropriate code symbols on paper.

The basic unit of coding is the behavioral unit defined as behavior of homogeneous content, irrespective of duration or formal grammatical accuracy, emitted by a single partner. Every change in behavior is coded and every behavioral unit is bounded by a different behavior. This system does not record duration of behavior, and code frequency is defined as changes from one behavior to another. For example, one partner may assent (AS), break into a laugh (SL), and then assent (AS) while the other partner is describing a problem (PD). This would result in recording three separate behaviors for the first partner (in this case, AS, SL, AS) and one behavior for the latter partner (in this case, PD). Both persons are coded simultaneously and all behaviors are coded sequentially along an artificial time line of 30 seconds; a signal is presented to the coders every 30 seconds instructing them to go to the next line on the recording sheet. (The time lines are used primarily to facilitate agreement checks.) Each code is also designated as either a speaker or listener behavior. Speaker status is assigned to the partner who has the floor, that is, has control of the content of the interaction. Concurrent listening behavior of the other partner (the person not having the floor) defines the listener mode. Thus each instance of interaction behavior is described on two dimensions: (1) the specific MICS code and (2) its status as either speaker or listener behavior. Finally, two or more codes may be used to encode fully a single behavior, for example, a speaker may smile while describing a problem (PD/SL) or interrupt his or her partner with a problem solution (IN/PS). Double coding is necessary to capture fully what behaviors have occurred. These and other issues of coding are dealt with more fully in the coding manuals. A coding example is provided in Figure 5.1.

The MICS coding manuals have undergone three revisions since the MICS was developed, including the addition and deletion of codes, minor changes in code definitions, and changes in usage within the Oregon Marital Studies Program (OMSP). Prior to the first public document describing the MICS (Hops et al., Note 1), in-house versions added or eliminated some codes (the codes Smile and Solution Past were deleted and the code Negative Solution was added). The first revision, in 1976 (Re-

Husband Behavior	MICS-II Code	Wife Behavior	MICS-II Code
Ls: (attending)	|AT|	Sp: I think you should start listening to me. (hostile voice)	|CR|
Sp: I do listen. You don't say anything when you talk. (irritated voice) When you talk it is very hard to keep up with you because you talk in broken sentences. (neutral voice)	|DG| |CR| |PD|	Ls: (attending) (shakes head no) (not tracking) (attending)	|AT| |DG| |NT| |AT|
Ls: (attending)	|AT|	Sp: Because I'm trying to think when I talk. (neutral voice)	|PD|
Sp: I know I never do or I think while I'm talking. That is why I talk fast and why I talk hard. (neutral voice)	|AG| |PD|	Ls: (attending) (uh-huh while nodding head)	|AT| |AS|
Ls: (attending)	|AT|	Sp: The reason I talk slow is because I'm trying to figure out what I'm thinking and how to put it into words. (neutral voice)	|PD|
Sp: (interrupting) But you're never listening, you don't listen either. (neutral voice)	|IN/MR|	Ls: (attending)	|AT|
Ls: (attending)	|AT|	Sp: I do listen. You just don't think that I listen. (irritated voice)	|DG| |CR|

NOTE: Sp = speaker behavior; Ls = listener behavior.

MICS-II Record

H:	AT	DG	CR———	PD	AG	PD——	IN/MR	
W:	CR	AT	DG NT AT PD		AS PD		DG	CR

Figure 5.1   Coding Example: Negotiation Topic—Communication

vised MICS), created a 30-code system with the addition of 2 new codes: Paraphrase/Reflection and Mindread. The second revision, in 1979 (MICS-II), consisted of minor changes in code definitions (for example, Agree defined as verbal *and* nonverbal responses) and changes in usage. The third revision (MICS-III) created a 32-code system with the addition of 2 codes. MICS-III specifies two states of Problem Description and two valences of Mindread. These are "internal" or relationship-relevant problem description and "external" or nonrelationship problem description for the former, and both "positive" and "negative" mind-reading statements for the latter. (Tone of voice, whether the speaker is being helpful or sarcastic, figures in the positive/negative distinction.) The impetus for the new codes came largely from Gottman's (1979) Couples Interaction Scoring System (CISS).

Scoring. The analysis of MICS observation records provides a summary of interaction behaviors. The frequency (rate per minute) of codes was used as the original descriptive measure. As a means of reducing the number of individual codes to be reported, the codes were grouped into a priori categories describing (1) problem-solving functions, (2) both positive-verbal and -nonverbal behaviors, (3) both negative-verbal and -nonverbal behaviors, and (4) a problem-description category used to isolate various forms of talking about problems but not proposing solutions.

Gayla Margolin designed the first computer scoring program in our laboratory that listed data in their sequential patterns, that is, stimulus-response matrices showing one spouse's behaviors as stimuli for the responses of the other. Subsequent scoring programs were developed to include conditional probability analyses, sequences of floor switches, and content of successful/unsuccessful interrupts. These latter show which behaviors are effective in getting the floor from a speaker. A new computer scoring program was developed for use with the MICS-III by Darien Fenn, Karen Hudson, and Kendra Summers. The analyses provided by this scoring program will be presented in this chapter.

Historical Usage

The MICS has been used as a major assessment measure in numerous studies and to multiple ends. A total of 45 studies known to the authors have employed MICS codes to quantify couples' behaviors: 35 published studies and 10 unpublished papers. (Two additional studies have used the MICS to assess parent-child interactions: Blechman & Olson, 1976; Blechman, Olson, Schornagel, Halsdorf, & Turner, 1976.) Table 5.2 lists 39 of these studies. Unpublished studies are included only if the data were coded in our laboratory. The MICS literature can be categorized into four areas: (1) intervention/outcome; (2) discriminating distressed from non-distressed couples; (3) behavioral and self-report correlates of MICS; and (4) sensitivity and reliability of MICS.

Intervention/outcome. In 49 percent (19) of the studies, the MICS was used to assess pre- to postintervention changes in couples' behavior. In 42 percent (8) of these intervention/outcome studies, control groups, necessary to assess the effect of intervention on outcome, were included.

(text continues on page 101)

TABLE 5.2   Studies Using the MICS as a Dependent Measure

Author	Purpose	Couples	Task[a]	MICS Measures[b]	Results
Baucom, 1982	Evaluate treatment effectiveness of three 8-week interventions: problem-solving/communication (PS/C); contracting (CON); PS/C plus CON; waitlist control (WL).	D = 72	Real IMC	Summary categories[c] P and N (C-RPM)	Only PS/C + CON increased P. Both PS/C + Con and PS/C decreased N. WL increased N. No change in CON.
Birchler, Note 2	Assess D versus ND on Real and IMC tasks.	D = 30 ND = 30	Real IMC	Summary categories[d] Ps, Pv, Pnv, Nv, Nnv, Pd (RPM)	Real condition discriminated D versus ND on all measures except H-Nnv. IMC condition discriminated groups on Pnv and W-Nnv. D became more like ND on IMC task.
Birchler, Note 3	Assess D versus ND. Correlate MICS and partners' ratings of interaction behaviors.	D = 28 ND = 34	Real (Mj)	Summary categories[d] Ps, Pv, Pnv, Nv (RPM)	D versus ND higher Nv and lower Pv, Pnv, and W-Ps. 12/32 correlations were significant, 7 of these were for ratings of spouse Nv.
Birchler et al., 1975	Assess D versus ND interacting with spouse, D stranger, and ND stranger.	D = 12 ND = 12	FC IMC	Summary categories[e] P, N (RPM)	D versus ND higher N in FC and IMC conditions. D lower P in IMC only. Spouse versus average stranger interactions showed less P and more N.

Study	Purpose	N/D	Coding	Summary categories	Results
Boelens et al., 1980	Evaluate effectiveness of two 10-week interventions: reciprocity counseling; system-theoretic counseling; waitlist control.	D = 21	IMC	Summary categories[e] P, N, (Freq)	No significant pre- to posttherapy changes in P and N.
Burger and Jacobson, 1979	Correlate MICS with masculinity, femininity scores.	N = 43 (ND > D)	IPMC Real (Mj)	Individual codes AP, PR, PS, NR, CM, MR (Freq)	5/43 correlations were significant. Some tendency for femininity to be negatively correlated with negative codes (NR, CM).
Cohen and Christensen, 1980	Compare typical negotiations versus those instructed to display best and worst interactions. Evaluate effectiveness of one-day communication workshop.	N = 12 (ND > D)	Real (Mj)	Summary categories[f] Pv, Nv (NR)	No differences between best, worst, and typical conditions. Postworkshop increased Pv, no change in Nv.
Engle and Weiss, Note 4	Assess agreement between mental health professionals and MICS coding of helpful behaviors before and after a workshop on marital therapy.	D = 1 ND = 1	Real	Summary categories[c] P, Neut, N (C-Prop)	Judges' rates of identified helpful behaviors discriminated D versus ND; greater discrimination postworkshop. Pre to post changes coincided with P, Neut, and N MICS scores.
Hahlweg et al., 1979	Assess D versus ND.	D = 10 ND = 10	IMC	Summary categories[g] P, N (C-RPM)	D versus ND had higher N and lower P scores.
Harrell and Guerney, 1976	Evaluate effectiveness of 8-week intervention: negotiation skill training; no treatment control.	N = 60	MCNT	Summary categories[h] Pv, Nv (Freq)	Treatment group decreased both P and N.

(continued)

TABLE 5.2 Continued

Author	Purpose	Couples	Task[a]	MICS Measures[b]	Results
Haynes et al., 1979	Assess D versus ND and stability of codes across three sessions.	D = 7 ND = 6	Home	Individual codes[i] (NR)	D versus ND higher AT, AG, CR, IN, DG, and lower PP. High stability: SL, AT, AG, IN, and DG.
Haynes et al., 1981	Assess agreement between MICS and partners' verbal report in joint versus separate interviews.	D = 14 ND = 14	Real	Summary categories[j] P, N (Freq)	Partners' agreement with MICS was highest in the separate interview assessment situation.
Jacobson, 1977	Evaluate effectiveness of 8-week intervention: problem-solving and contracting; waitlist control.	D = 10	Real (Mj) Real (Mn)	Summary categories[k] Pv, Nv (C-Prop)	Treatment group increased Pv and decreased Nv. No changes in control.
Jacobson, 1978	Evaluate effectiveness of three 8-week interventions: good faith contracting (GF) quid pro quo contracting (QPQ); nonspecific (NS); waitlist control (WL).	D = 32	IMC Real (Mn)	Summary categories[l] Pv, Nv (C-RPM)	Both GF and QPQ increased Pv and decreased Nv. No changes in NS and WL.
Jacobson, 1979	Evaluate effectiveness of behavioral marital therapy (8 to 17 weeks).	D = 6	Real	Summary categories[l] Pv, Nv (C-RPM)	All couples increased Pv and decreased Nv.
Jacobson and Anderson, 1980	Evaluate effectiveness of four 3-week interventions to enhance problem-solving skills: instruction only (I); feedback plus I (FB) rehearsal plus I (BR); FB plus BR plus I; waitlist control.	D = 14 ND = 46	IPMC Real (Mn)	Summary category[k] Pv (C-RPM)	All treatment groups increased Pv. No change in control group.

94

Study	Purpose	Sample	Interaction	Coding	Results
Liberman et al., 1976	Evaluate effectiveness of two 8-week interventions: behavioral marital therapy; interaction-insight.	D = 9	Real (Mj)	Summary categories[m] Ps, Pv, Pnv, Nv, Nnv, Pd (C-Prop)	Behavioral group increased Pnv and decreased both Nv and Nnv. No change in insight group.
Lochman and Allen, 1979	Compare typical interactions with interactions in which one partner (elicitor) is instructed to either increase approval or disapproval.	N = 80[n]	IMC	Summary categories[o] Pv, Pnv, Nv, Nnv (Freq)	Both elicitors and receivers changed their behavior in expected directions except W receivers of increased H-Pv.
Margolin, 1978a	Correlate MICS with couple-based measures of marital satisfaction and behavior.	D = 27	Real	Summary categories[p] P, N (C-Freq)	No significant correlations between MICS scores and other measures.
Margolin, 1978b	Correlate MICS with partners' coding of helpful self and partner behaviors, and measure of marital satisfaction.	D = 27[q]	Real	Summary category[p] P (Freq)	All four correlations between partners' coding and MICS were moderately positive with only H coding of W significant. Only H-P correlated with H satisfaction.
Margolin et al., 1975	Evaluate 10-week intervention: behavioral marital therapy.	D = 1	Real (Mj) Real (Mn)	Summary categories[d] Ps, Pv + Pnv, Nv + Nnv, Pd (RPM)	Both partners increased Ps, and Pv + Pnv, and decreased Pd. For Nv + Nnv, W decreased and H increased.
Margolin and Wampold, 1981	Assess D versus ND; base-rate and lag sequential analyses. Correlate MICS with couple-based measures of marital satisfaction and behavior.	D = 22 ND = 17	Real	Summary categories[r] Ps, Pv, Pnv, Nv, Nnv, Neut (C-RPM)	D versus ND lower Ps, Pv, Pnv, and Neut. No difference for Nv and Nnv. Both D and ND evidenced positive reciprocity. D evidenced more negative reciprocity and negative reactivity. Only MICS P correlated with satisfaction.

(continued)

TABLE 5.2 Continued

Author	Purpose	Couples	Task[a]	MICS Measures[b]	Results
Margolin and Weiss, 1978a	Evaluate 2-week communication training program.	D = 1	Real	Individual codes that overlap with couple's goals (RPM)	Substantial increase in PS and decrease in AG that matched the couple's goals.
Margolin and Weiss, 1978b	Evaluate effectiveness of three 2-week interventions: nonspecific (NS); behavioral training (BT); attitudinal plus BT (AB).	D = 27	Real	Summary categories[p] P, N (C-Prop)	Only AB group increased P. All groups decreased N.
O'Farrell and Cutter, Note 5	Evaluate effectiveness of two 10-week interventions: behavioral marital therapy (BT); interactional (I); waitlist control (WL).	D = 36	Real	Summary categories[d] Ps, Pv + Pnv (C-Prop)	Only BT increased on both measures.
Patterson and Hops, 1972	Evaluate behavioral marital therapy (19 hours of professional time).	D = 1	Real	Summary categories[s] Ps, Pd, Nv (RPM)	Both partners increased Ps and decreased Nv.
Patterson et al., 1975	Evaluate effectiveness of behavioral marital therapy (average 6 weeks of therapy).	D = 10	Real (Mj) Real (Mn)	Summary categories[c] P, N (RPM)	Both partners in 8 couples increased P. Both partners in 7 couples decreased N. Rank-order correlations between partners increased for P and decreased for N from pre to post.
Peterson et al., 1981	Evaluate effectiveness of behavioral problem-solving intervention (3 and 5 weeks).	D = 2	FC Real	Individual codes (C-Freq)	Both couples increased the frequency of agreements and decreased negative statements (e.g., CP, CR, DR).

Revenstorf et al., 1980	Assess D versus ND; base rate and sequential analyses.	D = 10 ND = 10	IMC Real	Summary categories[t] Ps, P, N, Pd, Neut (Prop)	Both analyses of base rates and sequential patterns discriminated D versus ND.
Robinson and Price, 1980	Assess D versus ND. Correlate partners' MICS scores across 8 to 12 sessions. Correlate MICS with self-monitoring data.	D = 4 ND = 4	Home	Summary category[u] P (Freq)	No differences between D and ND rates of P. Significant positive correlation between partners' MICS scores. MICS significantly correlated with self-monitoring data.
Royce and Weiss, 1975	Identify behavioral cues that contributed to undergraduates' postvideo observation ratings of marital satisfaction, and couples' reported marital satisfaction.	D = 12 ND = 12	IMC	Summary categories[e] (P and N) and codes identified by judges (CP, SL, HM, PP, PS -> AG) (C-RPM)	Only MICS N and SL were associated with judges' ratings of satisfaction. PS followed by partner AG was positively associated with couples' reported marital satisfaction.
Schaap, 1982	Assess D versus ND versus CF (conflict couples in between D and ND status); base-rate and sequential analysis.	D = 9 ND = 9 CF = 9	Real (Mj)	Summary categories[v] P, Neut, N (C-Freq)	Base-rate analysis: D and CF versus D had more negative and fewer positive codes. Sequential analysis: D and CF versus ND more likely to engage in sequences of negative codes and less likely to engage in positive code sequences.
Stein, 1978	Evaluate effectiveness of three 5-week interventions: MCCP; contracting; MCCP-assessed 6 weeks after termination.	N = 24	Real (Mj)	Summary categories[x] P, N (C-RPM)	MCCP decreased P whereas the contracting group increased P. WL showed no changes. Follow-up MCCP group decreased N.

(continued)

TABLE 5.2 Continued

Author	Purpose	Couples	Task[a]	MICS Measures[b]	Results
Vincent and Friedman, 1979	Compare D versus ND, typical negotiations with negotiations in which couples are instructed to interact as if most happy (FG) or most unhappy (FB) couple.	D = 20 ND = 20	IMC	Summary categories[d] Ps, Pv, Pnv, Nv, Nnv, Pd (C-Freq)	In the typical condition D versus ND displayed more Nv and Nnv, and less Ps, Pv, Pnv. D and ND changed their verbal behavior as expected in FG and FB; no change in nonverbal behavior.
Vincent et al., 1975	Assess D versus ND in spouse and stranger dyads.	D = 12 ND = 12	IMC	Summary categories[y] Ps, Nv (C-Prop)	D versus ND higher Nv and lower Ps scores with the spouse. Both D and ND more Nv with strangers compared to strangers; only D showed less Ps with spouses.
Weiss et al., 1973	Study 1: Evaluate effectiveness of behavioral marital therapy (average 6 weeks). Assess stability of codes across baseline sessions.	D = 5[z]	Real (Mn) Real (Mj)	Individual codes (RPM)	Partners increased CS, NO, TA, and decreased AR, DG, PD, PU; for CR and CP, H increased and W decreased. During baseline both AS and AT decreased and NR and PS increased.
	Study 2: Evaluate effectiveness of behavioral marital therapy (average 6 weeks). Compare minor versus major problem negotiations.	D = 5[z]	Real (Mn) Real (Mj)	Summary categories[m] Ps, Pv, Pnv, Nv, Nnv, Pd (Prop)	Both partners increased Ps, Pv, Pnv, and decreased Pd, Nv, Nnv. Relative to minor problems partners displayed more Pd, and W-Nnv in major problem negotiations and less Pv and Pnv.

98

Weiss et al., Note 6	Assess interface between MICS and couple-based measures of spouse and stranger behaviors during problem-solving negotiations.	N = 25	Real (Mn) Real (Mj)	Weighted mean based on codes within 15 second intervals	Marital satisfaction was positively correlated with the MICS weighted mean and couple-based measures of spouse behavior but not stranger behavior. Holding satisfaction constant there was little association between couple-based measures of spouse and MICS; partners were more like MICS coders when rating strangers.
Wieder and Weiss, 1980	Assess the representativeness of MICS coding by isolating components of variance for couples, coders, and occasions in video and audio samples.	N = 14	Real	Summary categories[x] Ps, Pv, Pnv, Nv, Nnv (C-RPM)	For video samples 61 percent to 82 percent of the variance was accounted for by differences between couples and cross-situational changes within couples (for audio only, 63 percent to 85 percent). No evidence of observer drift, bias, or reactivity.
Witkin and Rose, 1978	Evaluate 6-week workshop on communication skills with two samples of couples.	Group 1 N = 6 Group 2 N = 8	Real (Mj)	Summary categories[d] Ps, Pv, Pnv, Nv, Nnv (C-RPM)	At termination Group 1 increased Pv; Group 2 increased Pv, Ps, and decreased Nnv. At 6-week follow-up Group 1 increased Pv and Ps and decreased Nnv; Group 2 increased PV and decreased Nv.

NOTE: H = husband; W = wife; C = couple; D = distressed couples; ND = nondistressed couples.

(See notes a through z on next page.)

TABLE 5.2 NOTES (a through z):

a. Task: type of interaction instructions; Real = attempt to resolve a current marital problem (Mj = major problem, Mn = minor problem); Home = home observation session with no specific task; IMC = vignettes from Inventory of Marital Conflict (Olson and Ryder, 1970); IPMC = vignettes from Inventory of Premarital Conflict (Olson, Note 7); FC = free conversation.

b. Type of measure in parentheses: C = couple scores = husband plus wife scores; RPM = rate per minute; Freq = frequency; Prop = proportion of total behavior; NR = not reported.

c. P = positive behavior = PS + PP + CS + AP + SL + AG + AR (AR is keyed negative); N = negative behavior = CP + CR + DR + EX + PU + DG + IN + NT; Neut = neutral behavior = PD + QU + NO + TA.

d. Ps = problem-solving = PS + AR + CS; Pv = positive verbal = AG + AP + HM; Pnv = positive nonverbal = AS + AT + SL + PP; Nv = negative verbal = CP + CR + DR + EX + PU; Nnv = negative nonverbal = NR + NT + TO; Pd = problem description = PD + NS.

e. P = positive behavior = AG + AP + HM + AS + SL + PP; N = negative behavior = CP + CR + DR + EX + PU + IN + DG + NR + NT + TO.

f. Only audiotapes coded for modified MICS that includes 12 verbal behavior codes; Pv = positive verbal = AP + AR + PR + PS; N = negative verbal = DG + negative blame + negative response.

g. Same as note e except P does not include AS code.

h. Pv = positive verbal = AG + AP; Nv = negative verbal = IN + PU.

i. Codes derived from the MICS: SL, PP, AG, CR, AT, IN, DG, NR, suggestion, compliment.

j. P = positive behavior = AG + AR + HM + PS; N = negative behavior = DR + CR + DG + TO.

k. Modified MICS; Pv = positive verbal = PS + PC + AR + request for change; Nv = negative verbal = CM + CR + DG + CP + PU + IN +DR + PD + EX.

l. Modified MICS that includes 12 verbal codes, code content of categories not reported.

m. Same as note d except Pd also includes SP code, and Pnv does not include AT code.

n. Couples were dating couples.

o. Code content of summary categories are not reported.

p. Same as note d except P = positive behavior = Ps + Pv + Pnv; and N = negative behavior = Nv + Nnv.

q. Same cases reported on in Margolin (1978a), Margolin and Weiss (1978b).

r. Same as note d except Pnv does not include AT, and the Pd category is replaced with Neut; Neut = neutral behavior = CM + CO + DG + IN + NC + NS + PD + QU + TA.

s. Same as note d except Pd = PD + SP.

t. Ps = problem solution = PS + CS + AR; P = positive reaction = AP + AG + SL + AT + CO + AS + PP + HM; N = negative reaction = CM + CP + CR + NC + DR + EX + NS + DG + PU + NR + NT + TO + IN; Pd = problem description = PD + QU; Neut = neutral = TA + NO.

Table 5.2 Notes (Continued)

u. Modified MICS; P = positive behavior = AT + AG + PP + HM + CO + CS + SL + concern.

v. P = positive behavior = SL + HM + AG + AP + AR + AS + CO; Neut = neutral behavior = NO + PD + GU + PS + NS + CS + TA; N = negative behavior = DG + DR + CM + NC + CR + CP + PU + EX + IN + NR.

w. MCCP = Minnesota Couples Communication Program (Miller, Nunally, and Wackman, 1976).

x. Same as note d except Ps includes PR code and Nv includes MR code.

y. Ps = problem-solving = PS + AR + CS; Nv = negative verbal = CP + CR + DR + EX + PU + IN + DG.

z. Same couples reported on in Patterson et al. (1975).

In all but one study (Boelens, Emmelkamp, MacGillavry, & Markvoort, 1980), the MICS was used to assess effects of communication and/or problem-solving skills training.

Discriminating distressed from nondistressed couples. Behavioral differences between distressed and nondistressed couples have been examined in 12 of the 39 studies. Distressed couples have been compared to nondistressed couples on both individual MICS codes and on summary scores. Two forms of analysis, base-rate and sequential analysis, have been reported. The issues are: (1) whether distressed, relative to nondistressed, couples display overall higher rates of "negative" behaviors and overall lower rates of "positive" behaviors, and (2) whether the two groups of couples differ in the sequential patterning of their behaviors, that is, whether the behavior of one partner constrains the occurrence of behavior of the other.

Behavioral and self-report correlates. At issue here is the degree of association between various MICS scores and measures of marital satisfaction or some other skill-related behaviors; these are studies that establish the concurrent validity of the MICS. Correlational analyses have been used to address several issues: (1) whether descriptions of laboratory interactions by couples and outside observers agree with MICS coding of interactions (Margolin, 1978b; Weiss, Wasserman, Wieder, & Summers, 1981; Royce & Weiss, 1975; Birchler, Note 2); (2) to what extent couples' cognitions and/or sentiments about their relationship agree with MICS scores (Haynes, Follingstad, & Sullivan, 1979; Margolin, 1978b; Margolin & Wampold, 1981; Weiss et al., 1981); and (3) to what extent MICS codes are representative of couples' home interactions (Margolin, 1978a; Margolin & Wampold, 1981; Patterson, Hops & Weiss, 1975).

Sensitivity and reliability of MICS. Studies have focused on: (1) whether the MICS is sensitive to instructional manipulation, that is, whether couples can appear more or less distressed (Cohen & Christensen, 1980; Vincent & Friedman, 1979; Lochman & Allen, 1979); (2) the ability of the MICS to discriminate between distressed and nondistressed couples in various settings, that is, at home (Haynes et al., 1979; Robinson & Price, 1980) and with strangers (Birchler, Weiss, & Vincent, 1975; Vincent, Weiss, & Birchler, 1975); and (3) the effect of differing instructions or degree of task structure on couples' behaviors (Birchler et al., 1975; Weiss et al., 1973; Vincent et al., 1975). Related to reliability are issues of generalizability (Wieder & Weiss, 1980) and stability of MICS scores (Haynes et al., 1979; Robinson & Price, 1980; Weiss et al., 1973). Generalizability refers to the ability of the MICS to account for sources of variance, as in different occasions of testing, different settings (topics), and differences among coders. One would predict specific sources of variance to be significant, that is, coders should not be a significant source of variance, whereas occasions (pre- to posttherapy) would be significant. Stability refers to results from repeated testings or stability across settings (lab versus home).

Limitations of MICS-II

The complexity and richness of the MICS have made generalized usage rather difficult, as noted above, yet these limitations are inherent to the MICS approach. However, there are a number of problems associated with MICS-II, mostly of a technical nature, a consideration of which will clarify changes made in MICS-III.

(1) An important feature of MICS coding requires that behaviors be coded conjointly, for example, as speaker speaks, listener listens. At minimum, the listener may simply attend (AT) while the speaker is speaking. When lag sequential analyses are desired, the rule is that one person's behavior is the antecedent of the other person's behavior. Concomitance violates the rule of sequence. Earlier versions of the MICS imposed a lag sequential analysis upon data that are essentially a combination of concomitant and sequential patterns. The result was that behaviors were said to *follow* other behaviors when in fact some of these were not sequential. The result was an ambiguously defined lag sequential analysis. An important innovation in MICS-III is the definition of contextual or concomitant speaker-listener patterns, called Dyadic Behavior Units (DBUs).

(2) Again, if one were to use MICS data for sequential analyses, there would be some 30 × 30 or 900 possible sequences of single codes. Even if it were possible to comprehend such a vast array of data, there would be

so many zero entries that the matrix would be statistically uninterpretable. (A vast number of codes would be needed to ensure proper representation of behavior sequences.) If one were to adopt the solution of using summary, rather than individual, codes (as mentioned above), there is the problem that nine MICS codes are omitted from the previously defined categories, and the categories themselves may not represent functional units. The summary categories provided by MICS-III are based on functional units, such as Blame, Validation, and Facilitation.

(3) Typically, the unit of behavior is defined in terms of homogeneous content. However, MICS allows for double and triple coding of behavior samples (for example, IN/QU/PD/SL) to describe the behavior more fully. Such a fuller description, however, no longer provides a single code to define the unit of behavior. In the example, the PD (problem description) is the basic homogeneous unit, but it was conveyed as an interrupt, in the form of a question and while smiling. Since there is no single code unit that describes this complex behavior (interrupt, question, and so on), we are left with the options of either ignoring the qualifiers (IN, QU, SL) or counting them as additional new behaviors. In the latter case the result would be to inflate the frequency of the respective behavior units. Even more important is the problem this causes for sequential analyses. As already noted, sequential analyses cannot be carried out on individual codes when there are as many as 30 codes. Therefore, if we resort to some system for categorizing the codes into functional units, we have no basis for defining a category based on double and triple code combinations. For example, is the category to be defined on the basis of the IN, the PD, or the SL? MICS-III defines explicit rules for these cases; the category is defined in terms of the verbal behavior (PD in the example).

(4) Two MICS codes, AT and NT, define listener attending behaviors. AT and NT differ from other MICS codes in that the coding of behavior is a function of listener status; attending behavior is coded only for listeners and not for speakers. Thus AT and NT do not represent discrete behavioral events; rather, they define states of listener attention. The two codes represent the very minimum level of MICS behavior, that is, when partners are not speaking they are at least either attending or not attending. Previous analyses did not distinguish AT and NT as representing states of listener attention. AT and NT were treated like other codes, and the frequency of occurrence was counted. However, each instance of AT and NT was not recorded; instead, they were recorded when they first occurred within each 30-second interval and only recorded again when listener attention state changed. As a result of these procedures, analyses were ambiguous with regard to both the frequency of listener AT and NT behaviors and sequences of behavior. MICS-III defines AT and NT as

states of listener attention and analyses are based on the separate status assigned to these codes.

(5) In MICS, behaviors that continue into the next 30-second interval are recoded. This recoding procedure artificially inflates behavior frequencies in subsequent analyses. Code frequencies partly reflect the recoding procedure, rather than the actual number of couple behaviors emitted. The recoding procedure also complicates sequential analyses. The real sequence of behavior is often obscured by the addition of codes as a function of line changes. The MICS-III eliminates the recoding procedure to provide frequency statements and sequential analyses that are based on the actual couple behaviors.

Overview of MICS-III

Development and Description of Technique

There are two salient features of MICS-III compared to previous editions of the MICS: (1) The status assigned to codes is greatly clarified over previous usage and, as a result, (2) codes are grouped more clearly according to function. The result of these changes is a much more coherent sequential analysis.

Status of codes. The objective in any coding system is to define unambiguously the unit of behavior. Whenever multiple codes are required to capture ongoing behavioral acts, the question arises as to definition of the behavioral unit. Of the 32 MICS codes, 28 define specific verbal and nonverbal behaviors as relatively homogeneous acts. For the moment we can refer to these 28 as *Behavior* codes. These codes also embody such usual distinctions as verbal versus nonverbal, positive versus negative affect, and speaker versus listener behavior.

Of the 28 Behavior codes, 8 occupy dual status: IN, CO, NC, PP, SL, AS, NO, and TO can either be Behavior codes or they can qualify verbal behavior. Thus a PD can be qualified by other actions, such as an SL, a PP, or an IN, as examples. A further distinction can be made for 3 of the 8 dual-status codes, IN, CO, and NC. These are truly conditional codes in that they can be coded only in response to speaker behaviors. One can only interrupt ongoing speech, and comply (not comply) with a previously issued request. The other 5 of the 8 dual-status codes (PP, SL, AS, NO, and TO) are homogeneous with regard to affect or affect-related behaviors.

Table 5.3 illustrates the results of applying a series of decision rules that were used to group codes for subsequent analyses of behavior units. The first rule asserts that behavioral units will be defined by the verbal content of the behavior; that is, when one partner engages in two or more behaviors simultaneously, the unit is defined by the content of the verbal behav-

TABLE 5.3   MICS-III Code Classifications

Status of Codes		Codes
Behavior		
	Functional Category	
	Problem Description	PD-IN, PD-EX
	Blame	CP, CR, MR−, PU
	Proposal for Change	PS, CS, NS
	Validation	AG, AP, AR, CO
	Invalidation	DG, DR, EX, IN, NR, NC, TO
	Facilitation	PR, MR+, HM, PP, SL, AS
	Irrelevant	TA, NO
Modifier		IN, CO, NC, QU, CM
Nonverbal Affect Carrier		PP, SL, AS, NO, TO
State		AT, NT

ior. The 8 dual-status codes are assigned a separate status when they occur with verbal behavior; they function either as Modifier or as Nonverbal Affect Carrier codes.

There are four codes not yet accounted for—AT, NT, QU, and CM. The first two, AT and NT, define states of listener attention rather than discrete behavioral acts. AT and NT are distinguished from other codes and are labeled State codes. As noted above, State codes represent the lowest level of codable behavior. In subsequent analyses, the rule used to define concurrent listener behavior is that any other listener behavior takes precedence over AT and NT. Both QU and CM define the grammatical form of verbal behavior, that is, questions and commands are styles of verbal interaction. Thus QU and CM never appear on records without some verbal content code. QU and CM are like Modifier codes in that they qualify verbal behaviors and are classified as such. Again, in subsequent analyses, the decision rule for defining behavior units is that the verbal content codes are given precedence over QU and CM.

The decision rules give rise to a schema for categorizing the MICS codes as illustrated in Table 5.3. The Behavior codes are grouped into functionally defined categories, such as Problem Description, Blame, Proposal for Change, Validation, Invalidation, Facilitation, and Irrelevant. (As noted above, four codes do not occupy dual status; that is, QU,

CM, AT, and NT can never be coded as Behavior codes.) In an important sense the Behavior codes capture what content is being displayed. Modifier codes are used to qualify these contents. Certainly interrupting, questioning, commanding, complying (noncomplying) are also forms of behavior, but they do not reflect content; they represent acts that either qualify how content occurred or responses to prior behaviors (comply/noncomply). If a speaker commands, "Stop talking about that!" and the listener does stop, the compliance is recorded as a CO act.

The designation of Nonverbal Affect Carrier codes is used to capture affect-related nonverbal behaviors. When a person does any of these behaviors they can be coded as single behaviors (for example, SL) or they can modify other behavior codes. Finally, State codes, AT and NT, reflect the state of listener attention, that is, whether the listener is attending or not. Although this may be seen as an important behavior in its own right, State codes are examples of minimal behavior and coders attempt to define what the listener is doing beyond mere attention.

Figure 5.2 gives a second coding example, which illustrates the usage of MICS-III using the dialogue in Figure 5.1.

Administration and Coding Procedures

The MICS can be administered in many contexts, all of which require that couples make an attempt to resolve a conflict, either one of their own or one induced by various revealed-difference procedures. The focus is on problem solving with regard to an issue of importance to them. Topics can be generated from precounseling forms, self-report devices that allow the therapist to rank order the significance of marital problems by content. In our own program we provide couples with a listing of common marital problems (child discipline, finances, sexual compatibility, and so on) and they are asked to select topics from the list that are germane to their relationship. From these, it is possible to select rather troublesome and not so troublesome topics for discussion.

Videotaped (or audiotaped) discussions are carried on for ten minutes with the therapist absent from the room. On a prearranged signal, couples begin and end each topic. Usually two topics are recorded in any given session. The instructions to couples emphasize the following points: (1) attempt to resolve the issue at hand as best you can; (2) we expect that it will not necessarily result in a solution, but try; and (3) be as natural as you can by giving us a sample of how you would approach such a resolution at home.

Coding procedures are standardized in our laboratory setting. Sessions are assigned to pairs of coders at random, restricted only by availability. The session is reviewed in a single pass to establish the style of a

MICS-III Record

H:	DG	CR———	PD-IN		AG	PD-IN——		IN/MR	
W:	CR	DG	NT	AT	PD-IN		AS	PD-IN	DG CR

Figure 5.2   Coding Example

given couple, that is, range of voice loudness and the like, to provide a basis for judging that a speaker is talking more forcefully than usual. Coders then formally code the session, reviewing the tape and replaying any difficult segments. A comparison is made, code for code, between coders' protocols; this comparison is used to determine coding agreement. Differences are recorded and conferenced and a master code sheet is prepared, which is then used to enter code data into the computer. Each session entered is scanned by the computer program for errors (illegal code sequences) and corrections made. A session is stored on disk under a control number; couples' names never appear on these records. A number of precautions are taken to maintain fidelity of the coding. Coder pairs are rotated among coders, coders are not informed as to the conditions of the session, for example, whether pre- or posttherapy. Records are checked at random by a master coder to determine whether coder drift has occurred (Johnson & Bolstad, 1973); coders could, over time, emphasize certain codes that are easier, thereby avoiding more difficult discriminations. Issues of reliability are considered below, but it should be mentioned here that coder agreement is determined before protocols are conferenced and records for each coder are kept over time. Coders who fall below 70 percent agreement are scheduled for retraining.

Coder training. Given the responsibility placed on coders, it is necessary to have a systematic coder training program. We do this by conducting regular coder training classes with students at the University of Oregon. The class includes memorization of a training manual, scheduled lecture/demonstration sessions, examinations on the system, and graded practice on training tapes. All of this culminates in each coder establishing his or her agreement with standard tapes that have been coded by master coders. Thus it is possible to pinpoint a coder's weaknesses and to institute remedial training. Newly trained (reliable) coders work in pairs with experienced coders and all coders participate in regular tutorial sessions to help discriminate difficult codes encountered by the group. In this way the coders all share in code definitions.

Scoring Procedures

Scoring is accomplished with a new computer scoring program developed in our own lab. The MICS-III computer scoring program differs from previous MICS scoring procedures in that a new conceptualization of MICS codes is adopted, and more analysis options are provided. One major difference between MICS-III scoring and previous scoring procedures is incorporation of the new code classification schema (Table 5.3). The MICS-III code classifications provide a method for clarifying the meaning and function of codes in the system. The use of the new code classification also provides a method for categorizing behaviors for subsequent sequential analyses; as previously mentioned, when double coding occurs, the behavior unit is classified on the basis of the Behavior codes.

A second major difference between MICS-III and previous analyses is the use of a second data set termed Dyadic Behavior Units (DBUs). A sequence of DBUs is created by the computer from the original stream of codes stored on disk. This new data set is created for sequential analyses. DBUs are constructed to represent interactions as sequences of concurrent husband and wife, speaker and listener, behavior. DBUs define partners' concurrent and sequential behaviors. The original code sequence is inappropriate for sequential analyses of MICS data in that it represents interactions as sequences of individual behaviors; that is, sequences in which Partner A behaves, then Partner B, then A, and so on. Sequences of DBUs recognize that both partners are always behaving in one form or another—that at any point in time the interaction is described by both partners' behavior. For example, consider a segment of the interaction shown in Figure 5.2:

H:	AT	DG	CR------
W:	CR	AT	DG

The sequence of individual behaviors from the original data set is:

$$W{:}CR \rightarrow H{:}AT \rightarrow H{:}DG \rightarrow W{:}AT \rightarrow H{:}CR \rightarrow W{:}DG$$
$$\quad\;\; \text{lag 1} \quad\;\; \text{lag 2} \quad\;\; \text{lag 3} \quad\;\; \text{lag 4} \quad\;\; \text{lag 5}$$

A sequential analysis of the above behaviors would result in specifying the H:AT as immediately following the W:CR when in fact the H:AT occurred at the same time as W:CR and the H:DG immediately followed the W:CR. In contrast, the sequence of DBUs created from the data is:

$$\begin{array}{ccc} \text{H:AT} & \text{H:DG} & \text{H:CR} \\ \text{W:CR} & \text{W:AT} & \text{W:DG} \end{array}$$
$$\qquad\quad \text{lag 1} \quad\;\; \text{lag 2}$$

The sequence of DBUs appropriately represents the H:AT as concurrent behavior of W:CR, which is followed by H:DG and W:AT at lag 1. In this example it is obvious that the method of defining behavior units is crucial to the results.

The construction of DBU sequences follows specific rules: (1) each DBU contains both a husband and wife code describing concurrent behavior homogeneous in content; (2) only Behavior and State codes are used; (3) Behavior codes take precedence over State codes (State codes are used only when no concurrent Behavior code is listed); and (4) a new DBU is created whenever one partner's behavior changes. The fourth rule allows either speaker or listener behavior to provide new inputs into the couple's system. For example, if the husband offered a Compromise (CS) and at the same time the wife first Assented (AS) and then Disagreed (DG), the sequence of DBUs would be:

H:CS   H:CS
W:AS   W:DG

Two DBUs are created to reflect the change as the dyadic transaction. Thus for DBUs the basic unit is dyadic behavior homogeneous in content; individual behavior units do not necessarily overlap with units of dyadic behavior.

To summarize, MICS-III analyses provide a summary of behavior for both individual partners and their behavior as a dyad. Two different data sets are utilized in analyses. Analyses of individual partners' behavior utilize the original set of data recorded by coders, whereas sequential analyses utilize the transformed data set of DBUs. The specific analyses for each data set are briefly summarized below to indicate the type of data that may be extracted from the MICS. A more detailed and technical summary of the scoring procedures in MICS-III may be obtained from the authors.

Analyses of individual behavior units. The MICS-III computer scoring program provides four summary tables using the original data set. Each of these tables lists scores for husband and wife separately. The scores may be used to assess differences between base rates of husbands and wives or between various types of couples (for example, distressed versus nondistressed), occasions (such as pre- versus postintervention), or settings (such as lab versus home).

The Raw Code Frequencies Table lists frequency, rate per minute, and proportion of total behavior for each individual code. The State/Behavior Tables list the frequency with which each specific speaker and listener behavior occurred by the listener's concurrent attention state (AT and NT). For example, the Speaker Table would list the frequency with which the listener either attended or did not attend to criticisms by the partner.

A dual purpose is served by these tables; they list the frequency of both (1) speaker versus listener behaviors, and (2) AT versus NT behavior. Double Code Matrices record the frequency of double-code pairs. These data are useful in detecting style differences between partners or various couple groups. Category Frequency Distribution Histograms display minute-by-minute frequencies of each Behavior code category (Blame, Validation, and so on) in the form of a histogram. These histograms display the patterning of behaviors across time and provide a global picture of the sequencing of behavior.

Analyses of Dyadic Behavior Units. Two computer printouts are provided of the DBUs. Both analyses list DBU frequencies by summary categories; that is, Problem Description, Proposals for Change, Blame, Irrelevant, Validation, Invalidation, Facilitation, Attention, and Inattention. This procedure reduces the number of potential DBUs to 81; any of the 9 husband behaviors may occur with any of the 9 wife behaviors. The first analysis, the Dyadic Behavior Units Matrix, displays the frequency with which each DBU occurred in the interaction. A 9×9 matrix displays the wife behaviors that occurred with husband behaviors. The Sequential Contingency Tables list the frequency of behavior sequences. Four sequential patterns are analyzed: husband-to-wife, wife-to-husband, husband-to-husband, and wife-to-wife behaviors. The behavior pairs are depicted below:

$$H \rightarrow H$$
$$W \rightarrow W$$

These four pairs of behavior sequences are displayed in separate 8×8 matrices (the Irrelevant category is not presented). Entries in each table cell represent the frequency with which each pair occurred. Each cell separately lists five frequencies for pairs at lags 1 to 5. For example, consider the following sequence of DBUs:

$$\begin{array}{cccc} \text{H:PD} & \text{H:DR} & \text{H:AT} & \text{H:IN} \\ \text{W:AS} \rightarrow & \text{W:NT} \rightarrow & \text{W:CR} \rightarrow & \text{W:CR} \\ & \text{lag 1} & \text{lag 2} & \text{lag 3} \end{array}$$

Taking the H:PD as the criterion behavior, the husband-to-wife pairs are: H:PD → W:NT at lag 1; H:PD → W:CR at lag 2; and H:PD → W:CR at lag 3. Taking the W:AS as the criterion behavior, the wife-to-husband pairs are: W:AS → H:DR at lag 1; W:AS → H:AT at lag 2; W:AS → H:IN at lag 3. The tables list total frequency of pairs for the entire interaction, taking each successive DBU as the criterion behavior and summing frequencies for the entire interaction. In addition to frequencies, a test for lagged dependence is conducted on each behavior pair. The z statistic suggested by Allison and Liker (1982) is used to test the dependence of a partner's behavior at time $t + k$ ($k = 1, 2, .. 5$) on behavior at time t. This statistic compares the conditional probability of the behavior at time $t + k$ against its unconditional probability. No significant difference between probabilities indicates that the two behaviors are independent—that the behavior at time $t + k$ is not influenced by the previous behavior. Significant differences between probabilities indicates that the behavior at time $t + k$ is influenced by the previous behavior.

Reliability

Reliability of coding is assessed by calculating observer agreement. Total number of code-for-code agreements are divided by the number of agreements plus disagreements. Disadvantages associated with these percentage agreement scores are discussed elsewhere by Jacobson et al. (1981). A second approach to assessing reliability is analysis of generalizability. An example of generalizability analysis with MICS coded observations is provided by Wieder and Weiss (1980), who assessed representativeness of scores across facets of couples, observers, and occasions. Most of the variance in coded observations was attributable to differences among couples and the interaction of couples and occasions. Neither coders nor occasions were significant sources of variance, which indicates that there was no coder drift, coder bias, or couple reactivity.

Interpretation

There are two levels at which MICS data may be interpreted: At the first level base-rate data may be used to identify behavioral deficits and excesses by focusing on problems in individual partners' behaviors and the skill components of problem solving. At the second level, sequential analyses may be used to identify behavior patterns. Rather than focusing on problems with individual partners' behavior, sequential analyses identify problems in transactions between partners.

Together, base-rate and sequential analyses are necessary to assess individual competencies and dyadic patterns of behavior. This dual approach to assessment has discriminated interaction behaviors of distressed and nondistressed couples (Gottman, 1979; Margolin & Wampold, 1981; Revenstorf, Vogel, Wegner, Hahlweg, & Schindler, 1980). For example, Margolin and Wampold (1981) assessed patterns of positive and negative reciprocity in MICS coded interactions of distressed and nondistressed couples. They found that both distressed and nondistressed couples were equally likely to reciprocate positive behaviors, although nondistressed couples had higher base rates of positive behaviors. In contrast, distressed couples were more likely than nondistressed couples to reciprocate negative behaviors, although the couple groups showed no differences in base-rate levels of negative behaviors. Both analyses together provided a richer description of group differences than either measure alone.

Issues in Clinical Applications:
Utility and Alternatives

A major drawback to wide clinical use of the MICS is the large investment of time and money in video equipment, coding, and data analysis. Procedures employed for research purposes prove too costly for most clinical applications outside research settings, although observational procedures may be readily adapted by private practitioners. Audio recording may be substituted for video, which, in addition, may provide a more portable method of obtaining home interaction samples. Clinicians may learn to do their own coding, perhaps employing summary categories as the basic coding unit.

A second issue in clinical applications is whether videotaped interactions provide a representative sample of behavior. Some couples do report that interactions in the lab are not typical of interactions at home for various reasons, such as stage fright, the constraint of sitting in chairs, and having a scheduled talk with no interruptions. To enhance representativeness we leave the room while couples discuss current marital problems rather than contrived problem topics. Partners' perceptions of their interactions and of representativeness provide important assessment information and should be solicited.

Summary

This chapter presented past and present usage of the MICS. As a technique for assessing marital interaction, the major strength of the MICS is its reliance on direct observation and objective records of behavior rather than self-report. The MICS is a complex coding system comprising some 30 codes designed to record partners' behaviors in conflict-resolving discussions. The major strength of the MICS is also the major block to its wide clinical usage. The MICS requires a considerable investment of resources in equipment, administration and coding, and scoring. The MICS has been used primarily as an objective measure of therapy outcome and to discriminate between distressed and nondistressed couple groups. We provide a listing of these studies. As part of an integrated approach to assessment, the MICS also provides information from which to explore the interface between couples' cognitions and behaviors. MICS-III provides a more comprehensive assessment of marital interactions than previous versions in its dual approach to assessment. The development of

MICS-III was prompted by the need to assess sequential behavior patterns as well as behavior frequencies. MICS-III analyses provide information to assess both interaction skillfulness and functional relationships between partners' behaviors. Although the MICS is not immediately applicable, it is hoped that its presentation in this chapter has broadened understanding of the MICS as one approach to marital assessment.

Reference Notes

1. Hops, H., Wills, T. A., Weiss, R. L., & Patterson, G. R. *Marital Interaction Coding System.* Eugene: University of Oregon and Oregon Research Institute, 1972.

2. Birchler, G. R. *Perceptual biases of distressed and nondistressed marital partners concerning conflict resolution.* Paper presented at the meeting of the Western Psychological Association, San Diego, April 1979.

3. Birchler, G. R. *A multimethod analysis of distressed and nondistressed marital interaction: A social learning approach.* Paper presented at the meeting of the Western Psychological Association, Seattle, 1977.

4. Engle, K., & Weiss, R. L. *Behavioral cues used by marital therapists in discriminating distress.* Paper presented at the meeting of the Western Psychological Association, Los Angeles, April 1976.

5. O'Farrell, T. J., & Cutter, H. S. *Evaluating behavioral marital therapy for alcoholics: Procedures and preliminary report.* Paper presented at Banff International Conference on Essentials of Behavioral Treatment of Families, March 1981.

6. Weiss, R. L., Wasserman, D. A., Wieder, G. R., & Summers, K. J. *Subjective and objective evaluation of marital conflict: Couples vs. the establishment.* Paper presented at the annual meeting of the American Association for the Advancement of Behavior Therapy, Toronto, November 1981.

7. Olson, D. H. Inventory of Premarital Conflict. Unpublished inventory, 1977.

References

Allison, P. D., & Liker, J. K. Analyzing sequential categorical data on dyadic interaction: A comment on Gottman. *Psychological Bulletin,* 1982, *91,* 393-403.

Baucom, D. H. A comparison of behavioral contracting and problem-solving/communications training in behavioral marital therapy. *Behavior Therapy,* 1982, *13,* 162-174.

Birchler, G. R., Weiss, R. L., & Vincent, J. P. A multimethod analysis of social reinforcement exchange between maritally distressed and nondistressed spouse and stranger dyads. *Journal of Personality and Social Psychology,* 1975, *31,* 349-360.

Blechman, E. A., & Olson, D. H. Family Contract Game: Description and effectiveness. In D. H. Olson (Ed.), *Treating relationships.* Lake Mills, IA: Graphic Publishing, 1976.

Blechman, E. A., Olson, D. H., Schornagel, C. Y., Halsdorf, M., & Turner, A. J. The Family Contract Game: Technique and case study. *Journal of Consulting and Clinical Psychology,* 1976, *44,* 449-455.

Boelens, W., Emmelkamp, P., MacGillavry, D., & Markvoort, M. A clinical evaluation of marital treatment: Reciprocity counseling vs. system-theoretic counseling. *Behavioral Analysis and Modification,* 1980, *4,* 85-96.

Burger, A. L., & Jacobson, N. S. The relationship between sex role characteristics, couple satisfaction, and couple problem-solving skills. *American Journal of Family Therapy,* 1979, *7,* 52-60.

Cohen, R. S., & Christensen, A. Further examination of demand characteristics in marital interaction. *Journal of Consulting and Clinical Psychology,* 1980, *48,* 121-123.

Filsinger, E. E. The Dyadic Interaction Scoring Code. In E. E. Filsinger & R. A. Lewis (Eds.), *Assessing marriage: New behavioral approaches.* Beverly Hills, CA: Sage, 1981.

Gottman, J. M. *Marital interaction: Experimental investigations.* New York: Academic, 1979.

Hahlweg, K., Helmes, B., Steffen, G., Schindler, L., Revenstorf, D., & Kunert, H. Beobachtungssystem für partnerschaftliche interaktion. *Diagnostica,* 1979, *25,* 191-207.

Harrell, J., & Guerney, B. G. Training married couples in conflict negotiation skills. In D. H. Olson (Ed.), *Treating relationships.* Lake Mills, IA: Graphic Publishing, 1976.

Haynes, S. N., Follingstad, D. R., & Sullivan, J. C. Assessment of marital satisfaction and interaction. *Journal of Consulting and Clinical Psychology,* 1979, *47,* 789-791.

Haynes, S. N., Jensen, B. J., Wise, E., & Sherman, D. The marital intake interview: A multimethod criterion validity assessment. *Journal of Consulting and Clinical Psychology,* 1981, *49,* 379-387.

Jacobson, N. S. Problem solving and contingency contracting in the treatment of marital discord. *Journal of Consulting and Clinical Psychology,* 1977, *45,* 92-100.

Jacobson, N. S. Specific and nonspecific factors in the effectiveness of a behavioral approach to the treatment of marital discord. *Journal of Consulting and Clinical Psychology,* 1978, *46,* 442-452.

Jacobson, N. S. Increasing positive behavior in severely distressed marital relationships: The effects of problem-solving training. *Behavior Therapy,* 1979, *10,* 311-326.

Jacobson, N. S., & Anderson, E. A. The effects of behavior rehearsal and feedback on the acquisition of problem-solving skills in distressed and nondistressed couples. *Behavior Research and Therapy,* 1980, *18,* 25-36.

Jacobson, N. S., Elwood, R. W., & Dallas, M. Assessment of marital dysfunction. In E. H. Barlow (Ed.), *Behavioral assessment of adult disorders.* New York: Guilford, 1981.

Johnson, S. M., & Bolstad, O. D. Methodological issues in naturalistic observation: Some problems and solutions for field research. In L. A. Hamerlynck, L. C. Handy, & E. J. Mash (Eds.), *Behavior change: Methodology, concepts, and practice.* Champaign, IL: Research Press, 1973.

Liberman, R. P., Levine, J., Wheeler, E., Sanders, N., & Wallace, C. J. Marital therapy in groups: A comparative evaluation of behavioral and interactional formats. *Acta Psychiatrica Scandinavica,* Supplementum 266. Munksgaard, Copenhagen, 1976.

Lochman, J. E., & Allen, G. Elicited effects of approval and disapproval: An examination of parameters having implications for counseling couples in conflict. *Journal of Consulting and Clinical Psychology,* 1979, *47,* 634-636.

Margolin, G. Relationships among marital assessment procedures: A correlational study. *Journal of Consulting and Clinical Psychology,* 1978, *46,* 1556-1558. (a)

Margolin, G. A multilevel approach to the assessment of communication positiveness in distressed marital couples. *International Journal of Family Counseling,* 1978, *6,* 81-89. (b)

Margolin, G., Christensen, A., & Weiss, R. L. Contracts, cognition, and change: A behavioral approach to marriage therapy. *Counseling Psychologist,* 1975, *5,* 15-26.

Margolin, G., & Wampold, B. E. Sequential analysis of conflict and accord in distressed and nondistressed marital partners. *Journal of Consulting and Clinical Psychology,* 1981, *49,* 554-567.

Margolin, G., & Weiss, R. L. Communication training and assessment: A case of behavioral marital enrichment. *Behavior Therapy,* 1978, *9,* 508-520. (a)

Margolin, G., & Weiss, R. L. Comparative evaluation of therapeutic components associated with behavioral marital treatments. *Journal of Consulting and Clinical Psychology,* 1978, *46,* 1476-1486. (b)

Markman, H. J., Notarius, C. I., Stephen, T., & Smith, R. J. Behavioral observation systems for couples: The current status. In E. E. Filsinger & R. A. Lewis (Eds.), *Assessing marriage: New behavioral approaches.* Beverly Hills, CA: Sage, 1981.

Miller, S., Nunnally, E. W., & Wackman, D. B. Minnesota couples communication program [MCCP]: Premarital and marital groups. In D. H. Olson (Ed.), *Treating relationships.* Lake Mills, IA: Graphic Publishing, 1976.

Olson, D. H., & Ryder, R. G. Inventory of marital conflicts (IMC): An experimental interaction procedure. *Journal of Marriage and the Family,* 1970, *32,* 443-448.

Patterson, G. R., & Hops, H. Coercion, a game for two: Intervention techniques for marital conflict. In R. Ulrich & P. Mountjoy (Eds.), *The experimental analysis of social behavior.* New York: Appleton-Century-Crofts, 1972.

Patterson, G. R., Hops, H., & Weiss, R. L. Interpersonal skills training for couples in early stages of conflict. *Journal of Marriage and the Family,* 1975, *37,* 295-302.

Peterson, G. L., Fredericksen, L. W., & Rosenbaum, M. S. Developing behavioral competencies in distressed marital couples. *American Journal of Family Therapy,* 1981, *9,* 13-24.

Revenstorf, D., Vogel, B., Wegener, C., Hahlweg, K., & Schindler, L. Escalation phenomena in interaction sequences: An empirical comparison of distressed and non-distressed couples. *Behavioral Analysis and Modification,* 1980, *4,* 97-115.

Robinson, E. A., & Price, M. G. Pleasurable behavior in marital interaction: An observational study. *Journal of Consulting and Clinical Psychology,* 1980, *48,* 117-118.

Royce, W. S., & Weiss, R. L. Behavioral cues in the judgment of marital satisfaction: A linear regression analysis. *Journal of Consulting and Clinical Psychology,* 1975, *43,* 816-824.

Schaap, C. *Communication and adjustment in marriage.* Netherlands: Swets & Zeitlinger B. V., 1982.

Stein, S. J. *Effects of communication training and contracting on disturbed marital relationships.* Unpublished doctoral dissertation, University of Ottawa, 1978.

Vincent, J. P., & Friedman, L. C. Demand characteristics in observations of marital interaction. *Journal of Consulting and Clinical Psychology,* 1979, *47,* 557-566.

Vincent, J. P., Weiss, R. L., & Birchler, G. R. A behavioral analysis of problem-solving in distressed and nondistressed married and stranger dyads. *Behavior Therapy,* 1975, *6,* 475-487.

Weiss, R. L., & Birchler, G. R. Adults with marital dysfunction. In M. Hersen & A. Bellack (Eds.), *Behavior therapy in the psychiatric setting.* Baltimore: Williams & Wilkins, 1978.

Weiss, R. L., Hops, H., & Patterson, G. R. A framework for conceptualizing marital conflict: A technology for altering it, some data for evaluating it. In F. W. Clark & L. A. Hamerlynck (Eds.), *Critical issues in research and practice: Proceedings of the Fourth Banff International Conference on Behavior Modification.* Champaign, IL: Research Press, 1973.

Weiss, R. L., & Wieder, G. B. Marital and family distress. In A. S. Bellack, M. Hersen, & A. E. Kazdin (Eds.), *International handbook of behavior modification.* New York: Plenum, 1982.

Wieder, G. B., & Weiss, R. L. Generalizability theory and the coding of marital interactions. *Journal of Consulting and Clinical Psychology,* 1980, *48,* 469-477.

Witkin, S. L., & Rose, S. D. Group training in communication skills for couples: A preliminary report. *International Journal of Family Counseling,* 1978, *6,* 45-56.

CHAPTER 6

Couples Interaction Scoring System: Clinical Implications

CLIFFORD I. NOTARIUS
Catholic University of America

HOWARD J. MARKMAN
University of Denver

JOHN M. GOTTMAN
University of Illinois

Communication and Marriage

How shall we understand the dissatisfaction of a couple who comes to a marital therapist for help? Over the years, therapists, theorists, and researchers from varied disciplines have suggested we consider personality traits, level of emotional maturity, distribution of power in the relationship, commitment to the relationship and alternatives available to the marital partners, established patterns of rewards and punishments, attributional processes, exchange of pleasing and displeasing behaviors, communication skills, and the characteristics of interactional exchanges, to name but a few of the concepts and processes discussed in the literature. It is likely that at some time, each perspective has something to contribute to our understanding of the couple. The question that then emerges is: Given our state of knowledge about marriage, where shall we focus our attention in order to further our understanding of marital satisfaction and distress and to help couples improve their relationships? While not denying the potential importance of other areas, we have cho-

Instrument Source Note: Copies of the CISS Manual and supporting materials are available from Dr. John M. Gottman, Department of Psychology, University of Illinois, Urbana, Illinois 61801; Dr. Cliff Notarius, 4418 Renn Street, Rockville, Maryland 20853; or Dr. Howard Markman, Department of Psychology, University of Denver, Denver, Colorado 80208.

sen to focus our efforts on understanding the nature of communication exchanges between husbands and wives. Our work is based on the assumption that the study of marriage and marital therapy can best be advanced at this time through a better understanding of marital communication processes.

This assumption is grounded in a theoretical perspective developed by communication theorists (for example, Watzlawick, Beavin, & Jackson, 1967), and out of an epistemological model for advancing scientific knowledge in an area of inquiry. The communications theorists turned away from traditional intraindividual psychological models toward interactive systems models that emphasized the importance of context for understanding individuals and their relationships with others. What they meant by context was the reciprocal interaction of the person and the environment; in particular, they considered other persons the salient features of the environment. In a common example from this framework, a therapist discovers that the "successful" treatment of an individual often is associated with the outbreak of a related symptom pattern in the patient's untreated spouse. The person's social network is thus viewed as a system. It was believed to be impossible to understand an individual's symptoms of distress, including those classically defined as individual pathology, independent of the context of the person's intimate relationships. The implications of this perspective for the assessment and treatment of couples was captured by Watzlawick et al. (1967, p. 45): "Patterns of communication can eventually be identified that are diagnostically important and permit the planning of the most appropriate strategy for therapeutic intervention. This approach, then, is a search for pattern in the here and now rather than for symbolic meaning, past causes, or motivation."

This perspective defines the domain of study but not the method of investigation. We chose to develop and use observational methods because we were convinced that the best way to advance our knowledge of marriage and marital therapy was through careful descriptive analysis of marital interaction guided by the communication theorist's model of human interaction. Historically, psychology and other social sciences have focused on grand, comprehensive theories that often outstep the data available to support such work. In pursuing this course, researchers and clinicians have tended to bypass that all-important early step of scientific inquiry wherein attention is focused on a careful description of the phenomenon of interest. It is through detailed descriptive analyses that we are able to produce the replicable factual puzzles that justify explanatory theoretical efforts (Cook & Campbell, 1979). If we bypass the descriptive, phenomenon-oriented stage, our theories are unlikely to be based on reproducible facts and as such are likely to have little validity, are likely to be difficult to evaluate, and ultimately are unlikely to contribute to advancing our state of knowledge or to improving our clinical effectiveness.

Our attempts to describe marriage carefully began with our observations of distressed and nondistressed couples as they engaged in a variety of interactional tasks. In reviewing videotapes of couples interacting, it was apparent that the meaning and the impact of interpersonal messages were determined by both the nonverbal behaviors accompanying message delivery and the message content. This observation was consistent with the communications-oriented therapists who had proposed that every message was composed of two components, a "report" and a "command" (Watzlawick et al., 1967). The report component refers to the literal content of a message, while the command component is a comment on the relationship that exists between the interactants. The relationship component of a message implicitly communicates, "This is how I see myself. . . . This is how I see you. . . . This is how I see you seeing me. . . . " (Watzlawick et al., 1967, p. 52). In the interactional flow the relational message is carried by the complement of the nonverbal communication channels, including facial expression, voice tone, body posture, and gesture. As we observed couples interacting, it was quickly apparent that the relational component, the nonverbal aspects of message delivery, played an essential role in determining the pragmatic effects of a given message. For example, the message "Are we going to your mother's again?" might express a less-than-eager anticipation of the event if the content, the report, was delivered with a whining tone of voice and with stress on "again." Alternatively, it might be a statement of hopeful planning if the report was delivered with a caring tone of voice, a slight raise of the eyebrows, and a stress on "going."

Thus our search for the "facts of marriage" was guided by (1) an assumption concerning the importance of communication processes in marital functioning, (2) our clinical intuitions as we observed distressed and nondistressed couples interacting, and (3) recognition of the important role of nonverbal behavior in determining the meaning of interpersonal messages. Based on these principles and the need for using observational research strategies to advance the current state of knowledge, we developed a coding system capable of exhaustively categorizing communication between spouses.

The Couples Interaction Scoring System (CISS; pronounced "kiss") is the product of our efforts. The basic coding unit of CISS is called the "thought unit" and it is equivalent to the smallest semantic unit, such as, "That's a very good suggestion." Each thought unit receives three codes: a content or report code, and two affect or nonverbal behavior codes, one for speaker and one for listener. Thus a unique feature of CISS is that each thought unit is coded for both *content and observed affect.* There are 28 CISS content codes, which group into the following 8 summary codes: (1) expressing feelings or attitudes about a problem; (2) mind reading feelings, attitudes, opinions, or behaviors; (3) expressing agreement with partner; (4) expressing disagreement with partner; (5) problem solving or exchanging information; (6) talking about communication process; (7) summarizing other; and (8) summarizing self. The three CISS affect or nonverbal behavior codes that apply to both speaker's and listener's behavior are positive, negative, or neutral. The specific code is assigned on the basis of voice tone, facial expression, gestures, and body position. For additional information on CISS, see Gottman (1979) and Notarius and Markman (1981).

Communication in Couples: Distressed Patterns Revealed

In this section we will review what we have learned about communication processes in distressed and nondistressed couples through our investigations using CISS. The results we will summarize are based on several studies conducted in different laboratories over the last several years. The same basic paradigm was used in each study; the procedure involved videotaping the interactions of distressed and nondistressed couples as they discussed a salient interpersonal issue. The videotaped conversations, ranging from 20 to 60 minutes, were then coded using CISS by having one group of coders assign content codes to each thought unit and having a second group of coders assign affect codes to the speaker's and the listener's nonverbal behavior. As you read the following section, see how well the communication patterns identified by CISS apply to distressed couples you have worked with and assess whether or not these identified patterns help you to better understand the repetitive interactional cycles characterizing distressed and nondistressed marital interaction. The interactional patterns characterizing nondistressed relationships suggest outcome measures you may wish to consider for evaluating the effectiveness of your clinical work as well as potential intervention objectives.

Conflict-resolution patterns. Our findings on the way couples go about solving relationship problems are powerful and consistent from study to study. Furthermore, the differences are very subtle in form, although they have profound implications for how happy the marriage is.

We can arbitrarily divided the discussion of a marital issue into three phases: the *agenda-building phase,* the *disagreement phase,* and the *negotiation phase.* Each phase has its own objectives and characteristic good and bad maneuvers.

The objective of the agenda-building phase is to get the issues out as they are seen by each person. The bad maneuver is called *cross com-*

plaining and it means meeting a complaint by a spouse with a complaint of one's own. For example:

> W: I've got nobody to talk to all day, so when you come home I need you to listen to me.
> H: Well, I come home too tired to deal with another problem. I'm beat and just want to be left alone so I can relax.

This is cross complaining and it leaves both people feeling uncared for and victimized.

The good maneuver, amazingly enough, is not very different. It is called a *validation sequence,* and it goes like this:

> W: I've got nobody to talk to all day.
> H: Yeah.
> W: So, when you come home I need you . . .
> H: To listen to you.
> W: Yeah, to listen.
> H: Well, I come home too tired to deal with another problem.
> W: Umm. Had enough all day.
> H: I'm beat . . .
> W: Mm-hmm.
> H: . . . and just want to be left alone so I can relax . . .
> W: Uh huh, unwind for a while.
> H: Yeah.

What is different about cross complaining and validation? A critical role is played by nonverbal codes, such as "mm-hum," "yeah," "oh, I see," and "uh-huh," that show the speaker that the listener is tracking. They do not necessarily communicate that the listener agrees with the spouse's point of view, but that the listener thinks it could make sense to feel that way. Duncan and Fiske (1977) call these listener responses "back channeling" and suggest that these responses serve to regulate speaking turns. But they are much more than that in the agenda-building phase of a discussion of a marital issue. They communicate agreement not with a speaker's point of view or *content,* but with a speaker's *affect.* They thus communicate a great deal. They grease the wheels for affective expression.

In the *negotiation phase* the goal is compromise, or the coordination of both people toward a common end. The bad maneuver is the counterproposal, or meeting a proposal for a solution to a problem by one person with an alternative suggestion. An example of the good maneuver is the following:

> H: We spent all of Christmas at your mother's last year. Let's take a winter vacation alone this year. It'd be very romantic.

W: You're right. That vacation idea sounds good. But isn't it too late to change plans now? What if we don't stay as long at my mother's and take that vacation starting the 27th?

The nature of the agreement here is very different than it was in the agenda-building phase. Instead of the listener tracking response it is now necessary to actually modify one's own point of view and accept some of one's partner's idea.

What about the middle phase? It is called the *disagreement* or *arguing phase* and the objective of this phase is for both partners to argue energetically for their points of view and for each partner to understand the disagreement between them. The difference between satisfied and dissatisfied couples is subtle, in some ways, during this phase. Two differences are *mind-reading* sequences and *metacommunication* sequences. A mind-reading statement is an attribution of the spouse's actions, feelings, or motives, such as, "You get so tense in those situations." Almost all couples mind read in this way; they do not tend to ask questions about how their partners feel. But if a mind-reading statement is delivered with negative affect, such as anger or disgust, it is rightly taken as a criticism, and the partner will disagree and elaborate. For example:

H: I want to go to the party.
W: (Angry) You get so tense at those parties.
H: I don't get so tense. I'm a little uptight, it's true, but a lot of it's your fault.
W: My fault?

If the same statement were said with neutral or positive affect, it would probably be met with a different response. For example:

W: (Caring tone of voice) You get so tense at those parties.
H: Yeah, I know. But I really want to go to this one. Maybe I should have a drink before we go.
W: Okay. Then I'll drive.

Metacommunication is a comment about the process of communication itself. An example is, "You keep interrupting me." This kind of communication was considered of critical importance by early systems theorists such as Gregory Bateson. We found that satisfied and dissatisfied couples use metacommunication equally often. However, the *sequences* the two groups engage in are very different. For dissatisfied couples, metacommunication is an "absorbing state," that is, it is hard to exit once entered. For example, suppose a dissatisfied couple is discussing their budgetary problems. A common metacommunication sequence would be:

H: You're interrupting me.
W: I wouldn't have to if I could get a word in edgewise.
H: Oh, now I talk too much. Maybe you'd like me never to say anything.
W: Be nice for a change.
H: Then you'd never have to listen to me, which you never do anyway.
W: If you'd say something for a change maybe I would listen. You
   overelaborate with technical detail.
(And on and on)

The emotion has been transferred to the metacommunication content and it does not serve as a repair mechanism. For satisfied couples, meta-communicative chains are brief and contain agreements that lead rapidly back to the conversation. For example:

H: You're interrupting me.
W: Sorry, what were you saying?
H: I was saying let's go over our expenditures for the last few months so we
   can plan a realistic budget.

The negative affect has not transferred to the metacommunicative chain because agreement is interspersed. The critical roles played by the "climate of agreement" and by the reciprocation of negative affect are apparent.

The role of reciprocity in marriage has been a focus of investigation in its own right for some time, and we now turn to a review of CISS findings addressing reciprocity.

Reciprocity. Reciprocity is an interpersonal process that creates inter-actional structure. It is demonstrated by showing that a particular behavior of a spouse predictably follows similar behavior of the partner. For example, negative reciprocity would be demonstrated if when one spouse is negative (for example, angry, disgusted, contemptuous, fearful), the partner is then more likely than would ordinarily be the case to be negative in response. The presence of reciprocity suggests interactional chains that seem predetermined; once the chain starts, each person follows the other's behavior in kind until the cycle ends.

In all of our studies, we have found very strong evidence of negative reciprocity in distressed relationships. In fact, these negative affect chains are so powerful at discriminating distressed from nondistressed couples that we can use them as a discriminator when couples are not even trying to resolve a relationship issue, but are having what is supposed to be an enjoyable conversation. Examining the interactions of nondistressed couples, it appears that it is the satisfied *wife* who is most likely to break the negative affect chain, and not the satisfied husband. In some sense, you could say that wives in distressed marriages have stopped doing this

relationship work of deescalating negative affect. While our studies suggest that in high-conflict discussions it is the nondistressed wife who usually plays this vital role, it seems clear in any discussion that one partner in
the nondistressed relationship has more of a role in interrupting negative
cycles than the other.

Our work revealed some surprises about positive reciprocity. On the
basis of some cherished clinical beliefs, we expected to find greater patterning of positive acts between spouses in nondistressed relationships
than between partners in distressed relationships. For example, Lederer
and Jackson (1968) proposed the quid pro quo as the minimal basis for a
functioning marriage. If the quid pro quo hypothesis were correct, we
would expect to see evidence of positive reciprocity in the interactional
sequences of nondistressed relationships; for instance, if we knew that the
husband in a happy marriage had just been positive toward his wife, we
would have predicted that she would be more likely to be positive to him
than she would ordinarily be. We found scant support for positive reciprocity and the quid pro quo hypothesis.

This finding is important because the quid pro quo has been promoted
as a basic strategy for successful marital therapy. Typically, this approach
has distressed couples negotiating reciprocal positive contracts with a
therapist's aid. Given the results from our studies using CISS to code
marital interaction, positive reciprocity does not seem to be the major
working basis of a happy marriage. This is not inconsistent with our findings that interaction is more positive and less negative, overall, in satisfied
marriages; rather, it appears that positivity between partners in satisfied
couples is not *strongly linked temporally*. In fact, in a wide variety of research literature it seems to be the case that the presence of a great deal of
interaction structure itself tends to be characteristic of distress.

This may seem surprising when it comes to positive interaction, but it is
not surprising upon closer analysis. The presence of interaction structure
in an unhappy marriage means that interaction patterns are more predictable, which means that every message in an unhappy marriage conveys less information. The distressed interaction system is thus more
rigid, or has less newness in it and hence less potential for spontaneous
change. In a happy marriage, one is not positive because one's spouse
has just been positive. On the contrary, positiveness is much less conditional. One may do something nice because one wants to make one's
spouse feel better, because of an understanding of the stress one's partner
has been under. In fact, a study by Murstein, Cerreto, and MacDonald
(1977) showed that unhappily married couples were more likely than
happily married couples to hold that a quid pro quo was a good basis for a
marriage. The pattern was reversed for relationships between room-

mates. Roommates who got along subscribed to a quid pro quo belief. This suggests that such a pattern might be useful in some relationships. We suggest that it may also be important in marriages in certain situations in which closeness is being reestablished (for example, recuperation after a big fight).

Hidden agendas. Reviewing the reciprocity findings, we began to explore possible causes for the powerful *negative affect cycles* that characterized distressed relationships. We have suggested that one of the sources of negative reciprocity is that there are "hidden agendas" present when a couple discusses an issue that create very powerful feelings and lead to defensiveness. By a "hidden agenda," we mean an unresolved and undiscussed issue that functions as an affective filter through which a person sorts messages received. For example, consider the following problem-centered conversation:

W: You know we have to share this car to get to work but you resent it, you have to be at work an hour earlier, so you won't get out of bed in the morning. I have to keep waking you up.

H: (laughs)

W: (laughs) So you start getting mad at me telling me to leave you alone, you can get up by yourself.

H: No, see, what I mean is, um, that . . .

W: Well, I don't like having to do it, George.

H: I got up fine when I lived with Skip.

W: You were late every day.

H: It doesn't, hm, see, eh, it, I, it doesn't so much matter if I'm late for work like it does you, see.

W: You shouldn't be late.

H: Yeah, but Jim doesn't put up the work assignments till 9:20 or sometimes even till 9:30. So you just have to sit around anyway.

W: Well, I'm not going to be late.

H: Well, I sorta like being, ah, at work, getting to work early, ya know.

W: You sorta like it, you sorta like it.

H: Well, I'd like to make it a habit really.

W: You've got to learn to get up yourself.

H: I would rather wake up with an alarm, really, I would than . . .

W: Than my voice.

H: Than, okay, than your voice. (laughs) Cause my mother used to wake me when I was goin' to school, and, see . . .

W: And I remind you of your mother.

H: Sorta ya know. You could start sayin' once "George, get up," like that and set the alarm again, that'd be it.

W: No. You can do it yourself since you hate the sound of my voice.

H: I don't hate it actually.

W: How does that make me feel?

H: Sorta bad.

W: When you lived with Skip you were fine in the morning.

H: No, well, I'm usually . . . don't wake up in a good mood, an' he's, I
   always thought he was spaced out but I found myself talkin' to him in
   the mornin' cause he was quiet.
W: So, why did you marry me?
H: I don't know (laughs). But you know how it is in the morning (pause).
   No, cause I know how it feels tryin' to be on time, I really do.
W: You do? Do you know what it feels like?
H: Yeah, I know what it feels like.
W: Then why don't you have a little respect for me? You have no idea
   what it feels like to be me.
H: Well I will. I'll try. I'll try to get up in the morning. I wish I wasn't such a
   night owl. But, I'll try when the alarm goes off and you wake me up.
W: I'm not waking you up anymore. Get Skip to come over.

Of course, it's easy to see in this conversation that the issue is not entirely
getting to work on time. She feels lonely, not valued or understood, by her
husband. She tells him so, but he keeps returning to the issue of getting up
in the morning. He's trying to placate her by acting boyish and making a
joke out of it all, to no avail. He keeps putting his foot in his mouth. He says
innocently that he simply doesn't like the sound of her voice in the morning; he found it easier to talk to his old roommate. She's understandably
upset. Well, he doesn't mean it that way, he says. What do they both want?
He wants her to be more understanding of him in the morning. Well, that's
precisely what she wants. Yet both leave the discussion frustrated and un-
satisfied, despite the fact that they both care a lot. Why?

She feels he doesn't care about her and we later discover that he feels
she doesn't respect his separateness and autonomy (he is a night person
and not very responsive in the mornings). These are the two major hidden agendas—caring and respect.

As with all hidden agendas, they cannot be addressed in the context of
the issue itself, but must be dealt with themselves, because they have
manifestations throughout the marriage, not only for conflict resolution,
but also for other aspects of the marriage that involve closeness and
friendship. Without addressing these hidden agendas, the clinician will
never help the marriage fundamentally by a focus on social skill training
in conflict resolution.

Clinical Applications

The CISS, like other behavioral observation systems, is impractical for
use in typical assessment and therapeutic situations. Unlike self-report
measures and global behavioral observation procedures, micro-level interactional analysis provided by CISS codes is very time consuming. For
first-time users, we estimate that it can take 24 hours to code an hour of
videotape. Thus we do not recommend that the CISS be included as part

of a general couples' assessment package. However, the interactional patterns described above, which we have identified through our research, are central to the assessment, treatment, and prevention of marital and family distress. Thus the issue is how to identify these patterns without extensive coding. That is, how can these basic research results be translated into clinical assessment of marital interaction?

In this section, we present our initial answers to this question, based on our own clinical work with couples. Guided by our research findings, discussed above, we act as participant-observers during marital therapy sessions to identify the specific interactional patterns operative in our client couples. The study of interactional sequences with CISS has provided us with a language system necessary for identifying these sequences and for communication with couples about their interactional styles.

Clinical Observation
of Marital Interaction

The clinical assessment of couples is based on three principles: (1) The unit of analysis is the sequence itself, rather than the interaction components (specific CISS codes) that make up the sequence; (2) there are certain behaviors that tend to start sequences; and (3) interaction sequences, especially those that occur frequently, often hold the key to understanding a couple. The interaction sequences that we assess include negative cycles, cross complaining, positive cycles, and problem solving. In addition, we assess key interactional constructs that have emerged as indicators and possible determinants of marital distress. These constructs include hidden agendas, negativity screens (which transform "outsider" coded positive behavior into negatively received messages by spouse), and relationship tone (measured by positive and negative affect). Finally, we assess the couple's sense of mastery for solving relationship problems and the couple's level of intimacy (Markman, Jamieson, & Floyd, in press; Notarius & Vanzetti, see Chapter 11, this volume).

We have found this clinical observation strategy and orientation useful for most couples with whom we have worked. Although we use a broadly defined behavioral systems perspective to guide our work, the focus of interaction should be relevant regardless of a therapist's orientation. For many systems of marital therapy, understanding interaction patterns is a first step in assessing the marriage, and changing interaction is a primary focus of treatment.

Sex differences. We pay particular attention to sex differences in the interaction due to recent findings converging on the wife as the barometer of the marital relationship (Floyd & Markman, in press). We noted earlier that a major difference between distressed and nondistressed couples is that nondistressed wives tend to break negative cycles, whereas this does not tend to occur in distressed relationships. We hypothesized that distressed wives may have given up working on the relationship, perhaps due to years of trying to get their husbands to change. Similarly, Sabatelli, Buck, and Dreyer (1982) found that low levels of marital complaints were associated with wives using their communication skills to compensate for husbands' lack of skills. This pattern fits with those who have argued that relationships are more satisfying for men than for women (for example, see Bernard, 1973; Gove & Tudor, 1973) and perhaps is due to females possessing better intimacy skills. As discussed elsewhere (Markman, in press), perhaps wives in successful marriages have been able to train their husbands to become more intimate.

Sampling interactions. Interaction samples can be obtained as part of a formal assessment sequence and/or during the course of intervention. Obtaining structured interactional samples in marital and family assessment is not a new endeavor. Under the influence of the early family interaction researchers (for example, Strodtbeck, 1951), gathering interaction sequences has been implicitly or explicitly a part of many approaches. For example, Watzlawick (1966) published an influential paper on a structured family interview. The first part of the assessment was an unrevealed-differences task in which each family member was separately asked by an interviewer to provide an answer to the question, "What is the problem in your family?" Then the family was brought together and asked to reach a joint decision about how to answer this question about their family. The resulting interaction was seen as providing a prototypical example of family interaction patterns.

We have developed a task that we use in both research and clinical situations with couples to provide a sample of interaction. Spouses are asked to rate independently the intensity of ten common marital problem areas and then to agree jointly on the top three problems currently influencing their relationship. The interviewers than ask the couple to take one of the top problem areas, usually the top-ranking area, and work toward a mutually satisfying resolution for the selected problem. Interviewers then passively observe the couple as they discuss the problem area. Recently, one of us (JG) has begun to use a three-part interview in which the couple is asked to: (1) share the events of the day, (2) solve a salient relationship problem, and (3) have an enjoyable conversation. Observing couples in these three encounters allows assessment of: (1) escalation and deescalation during the events-of-the-day discussion, (2) problem-solving styles and escalation of negative affect (carried over from the events-of-the-day discussion) during problem solving, and (3) "rebound" during the enjoyable conversation segment. In the last section of the interview, it is important to note whether the couple is able to drop conflict and find something pleasurable to talk about or is unable to leave conflict and hurt behind.

Case example. Consider the following brief conversation that might be observed during a first assessment interview:

W: Maybe I can say this now that we are here. I'm really fed up with what happened last night. It's little, but it happens all the time. You always refuse to help with taking care of the house.

H: That's happened in the past, but it's not going on now. You think it is, but it's not.

W: It was going on last night . . .

H: (Interrupting) Last night I was tired, and I wanted to relax for a few minutes and watch the news, I . . .

W: (Interrupting) That's not what I'm talking about, you're . . .

H: (Interrupting and yelling) Let me finish!

This couple seems to be trapped in a negative cross-complaining cycle. As in this vignette, these cycles tend to be sparked by a description of a problem that is perceived negatively by the listener. This tends to be followed by a negative comment by the partner and the negative exchanges spiral. Note how quickly the couple got into this cycle and how difficult it is likely to be to exit from it once started. This process may be the inevitable outcome of problem discussions in couples who have accumulated a history of past problem-solving failures.

Also note that the beginning stage of the cycle is marked by mind reading ("You always refuse") and global, nonspecific complaints ("I'm fed up with things"). These statements, which can trigger defensiveness, can be used by couples as discriminative stimuli to engage functional interaction alternatives (for example, calling a "stop action") rather than as "unconscious" discriminative stimuli for deepening and extending the dysfunctional interactional exchanges. (For additional discussion of intervention strategies, see Gottman, Notarius, Gonso, & Markman, 1976.)

We often find that self-statements (that is, internal conversations), such as "Here we go again," "I'm getting angry," "She's not listening," or "He'll never change," often accompany the initial stages of negative cycles. These statements, once recognized, can also be used as cues to engage more functional alternative behaviors. These negative self-statements can be contrasted with more positive statements that are associated with a sense of mastery or efficacy about the relationship. For example, spouses who believe "We can work this out," "We can change," "I will try my best to understand what she is saying and feeling" may be one step ahead in resolving relationship conflicts.

Finally, the husband in our example is suggesting (through his statement, "That's in the past, it's not going on now") that his wife is viewing relationship events through a negative screen (Floyd & Markman, in press) or is allowing her negative sentiment to override an accurate perception of events (Weiss, 1980). Once identified, negative screens can be attacked through both cognitive and behavioral interventions. In some cases, these screens may be signs of hidden agendas. For example, the wife may be feeling that her husband does not love her enough to change and that she is tired of working on the relationship without perceived reciprocity.

Fit with Other Assessment Data

The hypotheses derived about the couple from the above procedures should be compared with other sources of information (such as interview and self-report data) to provide the basis for formulating and evaluating treatment plans for a couple. In our clinical work, we routinely assess multiple sources of information about the couple using multiple methods. Olson's (1977) assessment framework, crossing perspective (insider/participant-observer/outsider) with method (self-report/observational) provides a useful way of summarizing what we do. For example, global CISS coding by therapists is located in the participant-observer/observational cell, while interview data is located in the inside/self-report cell.

Margolin (1978) has found that complete agreement between assessment data should not be expected. This is due to both variance associated with different methods and the different information tapped by the different procedures. Thus CISS data may tell us a lot about interaction patterns, but relatively little about the couple's awareness of the impact of each other's communications. Awareness of impact is better assessed with a phenomenological procedure such as the Talk Table (Gottman, Notarius, Markman, Bank, Yoppi, & Rubin, 1976) or the Communication Box (Markman & Poltrock, 1982). For example, spouses might be instructed to hold up a "+", "−", or "0" card while they listen to their partners speak so as to indicate continuously the current impact of received messages. This easily used procedure (described as the Floor Exercise in Gottman, Notarius, Gonso, & Markman, 1976) provides the speaker with ongoing feedback on how his or her messages are being subjectively received by the listener.

Further research is needed to understand the predictive and discriminative validity of various patterns of intercorrelations between assessment procedures. Research with clinical populations and in clinical settings is particularly important given that most of the research data reflect group differences rather than predictions based on individual couples (see note of caution below).

In clinical situations, the therapist must compare the findings from the various assessment sources and develop a working conception of the couples based on the data. Different sources should be compared to rule out hypotheses rather than to confirm them. It's important to stress that self-report data cannot substitute for direct observation. Most self-report scales are highly correlated and seem to tap the same basic dimension of satisfaction. Since most distressed couples are *unaware* of their own contribution to creating and maintaining relationship problems, understanding of the couple's relationship is dependent on directly observing the couple's interactional exchange.

From Assessment to Intervention

The results of the interactional assessment, combined with other assessment data, provide the basis for formulating and evaluating therapeutic goals. In general, the goals of marital and family therapy are to bring about changes in the interaction of the couple or family so as to enable members to develop individually while at the same time experience a sense of belongingness or support (Minuchin & Fishman, 1981). We have described an assessment procedure for identifying the interaction patterns that need change. The major therapeutic task is to link these current interaction patterns to the present concerns, and then to implement interventions to change the negative interaction patterns.

It is well beyond the intention of this chapter to discuss in detail the intervention plan that is formulated on the basis of the assessment data we have presented (see Gottman, Notarius, Gonso, & Markman, 1976; Markman, Floyd, Stanley, & Jamieson, in press, for details). Briefly, we have found two procedures useful in improving couples interaction. First is the use of video- or audiotape feedback. We essentially teach couples the language of CISS and then have them learn to recognize the key sequences and/or issues that characterize their interaction. The couples then learn and practice alternative communication patterns and skills, for example, using "stop actions" to get out of negative cycles. Second, we teach couples a model of good communication that is simple yet powerful: Good communication occurs when speaker intent equals listener impact. This simple model can be dramatically implemented, as we mentioned above, by using the "floor exercise" discussed in *A Couples Guide to Communication* (Gottman, Notarius, Gonso, & Markman, 1976). Both interventions can be applied in multiple situations to help couples understand and solve their communication problems identified through the assessment phase of therapy.

A Note of Caution

The basic empirical research conducted with the CISS, described earlier, provides strong evidence for the reliability and validity of the CISS; however, there is a problem applying these results to the assessment and treatment of distressed couples. We have based most of our analysis of couples interaction on a between-group strategy, comparing groups of distressed couples to groups of nondistressed couples. For example, our sequential analyses considered the interaction of distressed couples as one large set of data, rather than as the data from individual couples that were then averaged. These results are valid for the types of generalizations about marriage made in this chapter. However, in doing clinical assessment the issue becomes within-subject analysis. Generalization on the basis of group data to a single case (that is, a couple in therapy) goes beyond the available empirical data base. Thus, for example, when a couple shows a pattern that is consistent with a distressed group, the evaluator can only speculate about the meaning of the couple's interaction for that one couple as opposed to concluding that this couple is like other distressed couples or that this couple is necessarily distressed. The one exception in our work up to now is the research based on the point graphs, which are essentially single case studies (Gottman et al., 1977; Gottman, 1979). The shapes of the point graphs are correlated with marital satisfaction and with specific sequences of interaction. Thus clinical assessment and treatment based on CISS results as described in this section should be done with these limitations in mind.

Economical Coding Systems

We have work in progress on several economical coding systems that may provide alternatives to both CISS coding and the clinical assessment procedures described above. In this section we offer six potentially useful alternatives. Three procedures fall under the domain of couples coding their own communication, and three under the domain of more global, construct-oriented observations.

Couples coding their own communication. Three procedures are available for an insider/subjective assessment of interaction. One involves having spouses rate each other after each set of statements using a set of buttons to rate their emotional reactions (Gottman et al., 1976; Markman & Poltrock, 1982; Notarius & Vanzetti, Note 1). The second involves the couple using this procedure to rate their reactions while they watch a videotape of their communication (Markman, Note 2). The third involves each spouse using a dial to rate his or her affect while watching a videotape of his or her own interaction (Levenson & Gottman, Note 3).

Global observational systems. Most research and clinical situations call for the assessment of a particular construct (such as communication skill or empathy). Behavioral observational systems in general may not be the best method (they are certainly not the most economical) to measure specific constructs (see Markman, Notarius, Stephens, & Smith, 1981, for a critique of the construct validity of behavioral observation systems). Global systems can be developed to code for levels of particular constructs. For example, Floyd and Markman (Note 4) developed a measure of communication skill based on CISS and MICS codes and trained coders to use a five-point scale to code a set of statements for skill level. This procedure maintains fidelity to the interaction sequence.

Alternatively, video- or audiotapes can be globally scored for levels of constructs by having coders use Likert scales to rate the interaction after listening to the entire tape (for example, see Guerney, Coufal, & Vogelsong, 1981). Of course, the possibility for sequential analysis is lost with this procedure. Finally, Gottman is working on two "rapid CISS" systems. One system will code for specific interactional sequences that have been found to discriminate between distressed and nondistressed couples. The second system will code for the extent to which ten specific affects are present in each speaking turn (such as interest, humor, affection, anger, disgust, sadness).

Future Directions —
Coding Affect

Gottman (1982) challenged the prevailing view of affective communication in social interaction, which may be called the "additive channel model," and by implication the current CISS affect coding procedures. At the present time the state of the art in studying affect is based on a metaphor borrowed from electronics, namely, that communication occurs in separate "channels": linguistic, paralinguistic, facial, gestural, and proxemic. Furthermore, the dominant view is that emotion resides in the so-called nonverbal channels. To study emotion in a purely scientific manner it thus becomes necessary to filter out the verbal content and focus on the nonverbal. This has led to a technology of electronic filtering, random splicing, spectral analysis of voices, and stop-frame video analysis.

These assumptions about affect are all pseudoscientific. These so-called channels of emotional communication cannot be isolated, separately investigated, and then later reintegrated. At issue here is the validity of the "additive channel model" of nonverbal communication that is currently dominant. According to this model, each nonverbal channel must be studied *separately* from *every* other channel and each channel must be *isolated* from verbal content. Failure to study the independent channels is hypothesized to contaminate one's results. This thinking has led to the development of an advanced technology through which nonverbal channels can be assessed separately and their contributions simply added together. A critical assumption of this model is that the channels, in fact, do combine additively and not interactively. This assumption is questionable.

Current research on the vocal channel guided by the additive model illustrates the weaknesses in the approach. Various strategies have been developed to remove the content from speech so as to isolate the vocal components of emotion. One strategy to accomplish this is by random splicing; another is by electronic filtering of high-frequency cycles. A problem with random splicing is the loss of temporal form, so that an angry moment, precisely defined by steadily rising volume, will be chopped up and randomly spliced together so that its temporal form is unrecognizable and the anger is lost. A problem with electronic filtering is that we may be filtering out precisely the emotional cues of interest. Rubenstein and Cameron (1968) have found emotional communication to occur in the high-frequency shifts of the voice that may be eliminated by electronic filtering. Leaving technology aside, consider a wife telling her husband, "I'd like to eat as soon as possible." If the wife stresses the word "soon" it would communicate impatience; if she stresses the word "possible" it would inform the husband that she is in no great hurry. If the wife's statement were content filtered, the interaction between paralinguistic cues and the words would be lost and so too would the emotional component of the message. If you listen carefully to conversation, the same argument can be extended to other paralinguistic cues, including pause, whine, and so on.

Gottman (1982, p. 949) summarizes:

> The point is that an additive model of communication is not tenable: *Emotion is communicated by a nonadditive gestalt of channels.*
>
> This is *not* to say that physical cues of nonverbal behavior do *not* provide reliable emotional information independent of language. On the contrary, the researcher of emotional communication must know all channels well [emphasis in original].

We found that when we analyzed a conversation with this "gestalt" approach to affect we were able to characterize a great deal of the conversation as affective. Furthermore, our various sources of data (self-report, physiological, behavioral) seemed to relate to one another. This new "gestalt approach" is not intended to reject the notion that specific physical cues are often useful indices of emotional expression, but to supplement this viewpoint. In the CISS affect is coded only when specific physical cues are detected, and only in the nonverbal channels. Current modifications of the CISS challenge the additive channel model and also challenge the notion that only specific cues should be employed to index affect. The alternative view is a "cultural informants" rather than a physical feature approach. Sensitive observers are employed to detect specific affects (such as anger), but not with reference only to specific features (such as increased volume and staccato rhythm). There are, for example, many ways of displaying anger in any given culture, and a competent informant can detect them. The cultural informants approach thus has abandoned the notion of the complete catalogue of physical features.

Also, the CISS affect codes were either positive, negative, or neutral. The new affect codes are highly specific affects (for example, sadness, contempt, anger, affection).

Summary

CISS was developed as an observational tool to study and to reveal the interaction patterns that characterize a marriage. A unique characteristic of the CISS system is that content and affect are coded separately. The findings reviewed illustrate some of the essential interactional differences between distressed and nondistressed couples. These identified patterns suggest an important clinical assessment agenda for marital therapists, and the "language" of CISS may help clinicians with this important therapeutic task. Finally, we discussed CISS in the context of other assessment devices and reviewed new developments in the coding of affect.

Reference Notes

1. Notarius, C., & Vanzetti, N. *Assessing expectations and outcomes in marital interaction.* Paper presented at the meeting of the Association for Advancement of Behavior Therapy, Toronto, November 1981.
2. Markman, H. *Couples assessment and observation of their own communication: Implications for the prevention and treatment of marital distress.* Manuscript submitted for publication, 1982.
3. Levenson, R., & Gottman, J. *Marital interaction: Physiological linkage and affective exchange.* Manuscript submitted for publication, 1982.
4. Floyd, F., & Markman, H. *An economical measure of couples communication skill.* Manuscript submitted for publication, 1982.

References

Bernard, J. *The future of marriage.* New York: World, 1973.
Cook, T. D., & Campbell, D. T. *Quasi-experimentation: Design and analysis for field settings.* Chicago: Rand McNally, 1979.
Duncan, S. & Fiske, D. W. *Face-to-face interaction: Research, methods, and theory.* Hillsdale, NJ: Lawrence Erlbaum, 1977.
Floyd, F., & Markman, H. Observational biases in spouse observation: Toward a cognitive / behavioral model of marriage. *Journal of Consulting and Clinical Psychology,* in press.
Gottman, J. *Marital interaction: Experimental investigation.* New York: Academic, 1979.
Gottman, J. Temporal form: Toward a new language for describing relationships. *Journal of Marriage and the Family,* 1982, *44,* 943-962.
Gottman, J., Markman, H., & Notarius, C. The topography of marital conflict: A sequential analysis of verbal and nonverbal behavior. *Journal of Marriage and the Family,* 1977, *39,* 461-477.
Gottman, J., Notarius, C., Gonso, J., & Markman, H. *A couples guide to communication.* Champaign, IL.: Research Press, 1976.
Gottman, J., Notarius, G., Markman, H., Bank, S., Yoppi, E., & Rubin, M. E. Behavior exchange theory and marital decision making. *Journal of Personality and Social Psychology,* 1976, *34,* 14-23.

Gove, W. R., & Tudor, J. Adult sex roles and mental illness. *American Journal of Sociology*, 1973, *77*, 812-835.

Guerney, B., Coufal, J., & Vogelsong, E. Relationship enhancement versus a traditional approach to therapeutic/preventative/enrichment parent-adolescent programs. *Journal of Consulting and Clinical Psychology*, 1981, *49*, 927-939.

Lederer, W., & Jackson, D. *The mirages of marriage*. New York: Norton, 1968.

Margolin, G. Relationships among marital assessment procedures: A correlational study. *Journal of Consulting and Clinical Psychology*, 1978, *46*, 1556-1558.

Markman, H. The longitudinal study of couples interaction: Implications for understanding and predicting the development of marital distress. In N. Jacobson & K. Hahlweg (Eds.), *Marital interaction: Analysis and modification*. New York: Guilford, in press.

Markman, H., Floyd, F., Stanley, S., & Jamieson, K. A cognitive/behavioral program for the prevention of marital and family distress: Issues in program development and delivery. In N. Jacobson & K. Hahlweg (Eds.), *Marital interaction: Analysis and modification*. New York: Guilford, in press.

Markman, H., Jamieson, K., & Floyd, F. The assessment and modification of premarital relationships: Implications for the etiology and prevention of marital distress. In J. Vincent (Ed.), *Advances in family interaction, assessment, and theory* (Vol. 3). Greenwich, CT: JAI, in press.

Markman, H., Notarius, C., Stephens, T., & Smith, R. Current status of behavioral observational systems for couples. In E. E. Filsinger & R. A. Lewis (Eds.), *Assessing marriage: New behavioral approaches*. Beverly Hills, CA: Sage, 1981.

Markman, H., & Poltrock, S. A computerized system for recording and analysis of self-observation of couples interaction. *Behavior Research Methods and Instrumentation*, 1982, *14*, 186-190.

Minuchin, S., & Fishman, H. *Family therapy techniques*. Cambridge, MA: Harvard University Press, 1981.

Murstein, B., Cerreto, M., & MacDonald, M. A theory and investigation of the effect of exchange-orientation on marriage and friendship. *Journal of Marriage and the Family*, 1977, *39*, 543-548.

Notarius, C., & Markman, H. Couples Interaction Scoring System. In E. E. Filsinger, & R. A. Lewis (Eds.), *Assessing marriage: New behavioral approaches*. Beverly Hills, CA: Sage, 1981.

Olson, D. Insiders' and outsiders' views of relationships: Research strategies. In G. Levinger & H. Raush (Eds.), *Close relationships: Perspectives on the meaning of intimacy*. Amherst: University of Massachusetts Press, 1977.

Rubenstein, L., & Cameron, D. Electronic analysis of nonverbal communication. *Comprehensive Psychiatry*, 1968, *9*, 200-208.

Sabatelli, R., Buck, R., & Dreyer, A. Nonverbal communication accuracy in married couples: Relationship with marital complaints. *Journal of Personality and Social Psychology*, 1982, *43*, 1088-1097.

Strodtbeck, F. Husband-wife interaction over revealed differences. *American Sociological Review*, 1951, *16*, 468-473.

Watzlawick, P. A structured family interview. *Family Process*, 1966, *5*, 256-271.

Watzlawick, P., Beavin, J., & Jackson, J. *Pragmatics of human communication: A study of interactional patterns, pathologies, and paradoxes*. New York: Norton, 1967.

Weiss, R. Strategic behavioral marital therapy: Toward a model for assessment and intervention. In J. Vincent (Ed.), *Advances in family intervention, assessment, and theory* (Vol. 1). Greenwich, CT: JAI, 1980.

CHAPTER 7

Behavioral Assessment for Practitioners: Some Reasons and Recommendations

RAND D. CONGER
University of Illinois

The present volume contains a host of procedures developed for the purpose of assessing the current state of marital and family relationships, whether the target of inquiry is a single distressed couple or a sample of research subjects. Of special importance for this particular chapter are those measurement techniques that deal with directly observed behavior exchange in families, such as those described in Chapters 5 and 6 of this book. Even a brief review of these materials, however, will indicate to the reader that there are several difficulties that may limit the usefulness of systematic observation of families as part of clinical practice. Observing social interaction is a time-consuming, labor-intensive enterprise that can add to the often burdensome demands already placed on a clinician's time. On the other hand, there are positive aspects to observational procedures that may, in a demonstrable fashion, improve the effectiveness of our attempts to prevent or remedy family difficulties.

The intent of this chapter is to assist practitioners who would like to use behavioral assessment as a diagnostic tool. The objective is to delineate a set of procedures that should alleviate some of the problems inherent in using these techniques in clinical settings. The purpose is not to advocate direct observation as a substitute for other questionnaire or self-report procedures. Rather, I suggest that directly observed interactions contain information not readily available from the results of paper-and-pencil techniques and that these data have unique clinical import. The chapter

Author's Note: I wish to acknowledge the support of NIMH Grant R01MH35682, which assisted the development and completion of this chapter.

will proceed in three stages, including: (1) consideration of some of the reasons for clinical use of behavioral assessment, (2) a description of those aspects of social exchange that appear to discriminate distressed from nondistressed families or couples, and (3) a review of some of the problems that inhibit the use of observational methods in clinical assessment and a proposed set of guidelines for ameliorating these difficulties.

The Importance of
Behavioral Assessment

For many years social and behavioral scientists have been aware of the fact that there is only a loose correspondence between what people say they do and their actual behaviors (Deutscher, 1973). Moreover, individuals are not very accurate in identifying the causes of their own actions (Wilson & Nisbett, 1978). Given the loose fit among attitudes, beliefs, rationales, and the things people do in their daily activities, many theorists have come to regard cognitions about one's environment or self as a separate channel of information that is important in its own right but is seldom a substitute for data concerning individual behavior. That is, the way a person describes or responds to questions concerning, for example, the actions or attitudes of self or other family members provides the clinician with important insights concerning family functioning. But the picture of couple or family relationships obtained in this fashion is incomplete and may even give a distorted picture of how individuals interact when they are together (see also Filsinger, Chapter 1, this volume).

An example of possible difficulties that may occur when only self-reports by individuals are available for family or couple assessment is suggested by the results of a series of studies reported by Gottman (1979). In this research couples were brought into a laboratory, where they were asked to discuss issues either likely or unlikely to lead to some conflict within the dyad. Spouses were seated face-to-face at an apparatus called a "talk table." Although they could see each other perfectly well, this table was slanted in such a way that their hands were not visible to one another. As each person spoke, he or she was able to trip a toggle switch on his or her side of the table to indicate whether the statement made to the partner was intended to be positive or negative in emotional affect. In turn, the listener activated a similar toggle switch indicating whether he or she perceived the same message as positive or negative.

The results of these studies indicated that couples having problems in their relationships were no more likely than nondistressed couples to speak to one another in a fashion that they intended to be aversive; nor were they less likely to expect their verbalizations to convey positive affect. Regardless of this equality of intent between types of couples, though, the distressed spouses interpreted the statements by their mates as more negative and less positive than did those who were not dissatisfied with their relationships. A clinician faced with such conflicting interpretations of verbal interaction within a marital dyad might have real difficulty deriving an accurate picture of communication patterns for a couple, especially if the members of the dyad were engaging in socially desirable behaviors in their meetings with the therapist.

In addition to the intended and perceived impact of verbal interactions, however, Gottman and his colleagues have also collected a great deal of information regarding observed interactions between husbands and wives. Those data provide objective support for the proposition that distressed couples, compared to nondistressed couples, are more negative and less positive in their interactions with one another. This second channel of information suggests, then, that the perception of distressed spouses that their mates are relatively more negative and less positive in their verbal behaviors has some merit. For a clinician attempting to determine whether one spouse is unable to interpret correctly the messages sent by his or her mate, or whether one spouse is inaccurately conveying intended information, objective behavioral assessment may provide the second channel of information that is needed to clarify which of these two situations is most correct.

One might reasonably assume, however, that a trained clinician would be able to determine the interactional dynamics that promote marital or family distress through the interview process that accompanies intervention. That is, a clinician normally spends a great deal of time observing a family as members relate and discuss their history and current circumstances. A recent study by Starr and Dietrich (Note 1), however, casts some doubt on the ability of practitioners to discriminate accurately the often subtle behavioral differences between dysfunctional and nondistressed family types.

In their study, Starr and Dietrich videotaped parent-child dyads from families in which physical child abuse had occurred and in carefully matched control families with no record of abuse. Parents and children were instructed to play or talk with one another as they normally would while, with their knowledge, a videotape was made. A total of 8 of these videotapes, 4 abuse and 4 control, were randomly selected from tapes made as part of a larger study of child abuse and drug addiction. Segments of these tapes were then viewed in abuse-control pairs by 23 mental health professionals who averaged almost 15 years each in experience with troubled individuals and families and by 45 university undergraduates. After each pair of tapes was shown, observers were asked to indicate which family was abusive.

The results of the study were illuminating. The overall accuracy of discriminating abusive from control families by observing these interaction sequences was what would be predicted by chance, about 50 percent. Indeed, the undergraduate students were slightly more accurate, scoring correct responses 52 percent of the time; the mental health professionals were correct 48 percent of the time. The only individual who guessed correctly in each instance was a blind student who relied only on the sound track of each tape. In addition, the researchers discovered that years of experience as a professional did not significantly improve the accuracy of the mental health workers.

In assessing the reasons given by these practitioners for their categorizations of dyads, Starr and Dietrich discovered an important fact. In all cases descriptions of interactional style were unsystematic. For example, in some instances observers developed global impressions of social exchange between parent and child, while at other times raters focused on specific behavioral events. As Starr and Dietrich (Note 1, p. 2) note, "Some emphasized the parent, others the child and a few commented on aspects of their interaction. Most stressed the affective climate. Some were specific, others provided global impressions and interpretations. Impressions by different professional observers of the same family often were remarkably different. Thus, one father was described by two different observers as 'in touch' and as 'not in touch' with his child." The authors found that such contradictory conclusions about these parent-child dyads were typical, and concluded that "unsystematic, global observations, even when made by experienced clinicians, tell us little about behavior" (p. 2).

Similar findings were reported by Burgess and Conger (1978), who found that experienced observers, when relying solely on global impressions, could not discriminate between abusive, neglectful parents and matched control parents even after spending several hours with them in their homes. They were able to discriminate between family types, however, through the data they produced using systematic observation based on a theoretically relevant behavioral code. The interactional differences between families were not apparent to observers, though, until the frequencies of behavior they had obtained were statistically summarized. Starr and Dietrich (Note 1) also found that they could discriminate between abusive and control families when observations were systematic, that is, anchored to a clear set of behavioral definitions that led to counts and durations of specific types of interaction.

To summarize, it appears that distressed and nondistressed families or couples do differ in terms of interactional style. Moreover, data concerning patterns of actual behavioral exchange can add significantly to the information a clinician can obtain about a family by only asking questions regarding their treatment and perceptions of one another. Some research not yet discussed has also demonstrated that modification of interactional style can lead to improvements in family functioning (see Conger, Lahey, & Smith, Note 2; Jacobson, 1978). This research suggests that differences in behavior exchange between distressed and nondistressed families are a contributing factor in the problems that lead to clinical intervention. Available evidence, then, indicates that clinicians should be able to improve: (1) their diagnosis of couple or family functioning, (2) their prescription for intervention, and (3) their assessment of family change through careful observation and description of behavioral interaction. Such descriptions, however, cannot rest on global impressions, but must be systematic and well anchored to carefully defined categories of behavior that are known to be most characteristic of troubled families. We now consider some of the more robust behavioral discriminators of differing family types.

Behavioral Interaction and Family Distress

From his review of behavioral assessment of problem families, Conger (1981, p. 238) concludes that troubled families or couples are behaviorally most distinct in terms of the mutual punishment family members inflict upon one another:

> If any one theme has characterized the phenomena reviewed herein, it is best captured by some notion of mutual pain. Whether knowingly or not, family members are shockingly callous of one another's emotional or physical well-being, especially those families in which spouses are unhappy with one another or in which a child or parent is out of control. The tendency toward aggression in families has led Gelles and Straus (1979) to characterize it as one of the most violent social entities in our society.

Perhaps no other single dimension of behavior will be more useful for clinicians than one that taps the sometimes relatively subtle aversive or noxious responses emitted by family members. These types of behaviors are especially robust in their power to discriminate clinical from nonclinical families. But there are other important interactional manifestations of distress as well. The following brief reviews of marital and parent-child difficulties provide the material needed for our set of recommendations regarding routine use of behavioral assessment in work with troubled families.

Marital/Dyadic Distress

Present data on marital interactions suggest that distressed couples, compared to nondistressed couples, are: (1) less positive toward one another, (2) more negative toward one another, (3) less capable problem solvers, and (4) more reciprocal in their exchange of noxious behaviors. For example, Vincent, Weiss, and Birchler (1975) studied 12 distressed and 12 nondistressed couples in a laboratory setting designed to create some degree of interpersonal conflict. Observers coded interaction from videotapes, which allowed regular reliability checks to assure that observer agreement met minimal levels of acceptability. Behaviors were coded in sequence within 30-second time periods. The results of the study showed that nondistressed dyads, compared to distressed couples, engaged in more positively reinforcing exchanges and were more capable problem solvers. Importantly, the distressed spouses demonstrated higher rates of problem-solving behavior in interactions with opposite-sex strangers, a finding that suggests that their deficits in this area were closely tied to problems in their marriages rather than a reflection of a general inability to solve problems with others. In another study, Birchler, Weiss, and Vincent (1975) examined the data for the same 24 couples studied by Vincent et al. (1975) and found that there was a higher rate of aversive interaction in the distressed than in the nondistressed group.

Gottman's (1979) work has extended this earlier research on couple interaction and has led to a structural model of marital interaction. Briefly, the model states that dysfunctional marital relationships, compared to satisfactory marriages, will be characterized by more rigidly patterned interaction, that is, a tendency by spouses to respond to one another in a stereotypical fashion. For example, according to Gottman, distressed couples, compared to nondistressed couples, are more likely to react aversively to one another's unpleasant behaviors (negative reciprocity). A corollary of rigidity in interaction is a generally lower rate of behavior exchange overall. In addition, distressed couples will be more negative in their interactions with one another and slightly less positive. Finally, unhappy couples will tend to have one partner who is more dominant than the other in the sense that actions of the more powerful mate predict his or her partner's behavior more adequately than the reverse. Dominance, for Gottman, is defined in terms of the asymmetry in predictability from one spouse's behavior to the other's.

Using several different samples of husbands and wives, all of whom were observed in a discussion setting wherein they were asked to resolve some problem(s) of import to them, Gottman marshals a great deal of support for his model. For example, he found that couples in one sample were discriminated on one measure of positiveness, the ratio of agreements to agreements plus disagreements. The proportion of agreements for distressed husbands was 0.46, compared to 0.66 ($p < 0.05$) for those in the nondistressed group. In addition, wives who were dissatisfied with their marriages had an average ratio of only 0.39, contrasted with 0.76 ($p < 0.001$) for nondistressed wives. Positive affect measured nonverbally did not distinguish one group from the other; however, 25 percent of all behavior by distressed couples was aversive, an amount many times higher than the 3 percent ($p < 0.001$) figure for satisfied couples.

The data concerning negative interactions are a prelude to the next component in the model, namely, that there should be greater reciprocity in aversive behaviors by couples who are experiencing marital problems than by those who are not. For Gottman, reciprocity is defined in terms of conditional and unconditional probabilities. When one partner's behavior increases the probability that his or her spouse will respond in kind, then the succeeding action is reciprocal. For example, if the base rate (unconditional probability) for the husband's negative behavior to his wife is 0.02, but that figure increases to 0.25 when she is first aversive to him, then the difference in probabilities between the two events is likely to be significant and the husband's behavior would be a contingent, reciprocal response. Consistent with his model, Gottman found that an initial negative behavior by either partner in distressed marriages increased the probability of aversive responses by the spouse to a greater extent than in nondistressed dyads. This result was true for up to six subsequent interactions following an initial negative response, the end point in his analysis. Interestingly, there was little difference between groups on the dimension of positive reciprocity.

In his presentation of patterns of interaction among other parts of his behavior code, Gottman conceptualized each couple's discussion as occurring in three stages. At the outset, each dyad tended to build an agenda of issues that would guide the remainder of their interaction during the session. This first third of each encounter found the clinic, or distressed, couples falling into seemingly endless loops of problem expression or attributions concerning one another's behavior or thoughts ("mindreading"). Indeed, the results are reminiscent of a "sidetracking" phenomenon described by Patterson, Hops, and Weiss (1975). The nonclinic couples, however, tended to display patterns of behavior that led to fairly rapid agreement on what the agenda should be. They stayed "on track" in their discussions.

The middle period of each session, what Gottman calls the "arguing phase," did not produce sequences of interaction that readily distinguished the two groups. But during the last third of each session (negotiation), nonclinic couples were more likely than clinic couples to reach agreement on some proposed solution to the issues under discussion. Gottman's data, then, are quite consistent with the findings from other studies that suggest that unhappy couples have trouble keeping their communication focused on the topic of interest. They are also inept at proposing solutions for their conflicts and at reaching some agreement about which proposed solution is most appropriate.

Although the above review is particularly brief, it does identify the major behavioral dimensions that have been shown to discriminate distressed from nondistressed couples. Our recommendations for clinical use of behavioral assessment with marital dyads, then, will be based on the above findings. To recapitulate, behavioral assessment of marital distress by clinicians will need to include the identification of positive and negative affective responses, problem-solving skills, and certain patterns of affective response.

Parent-Child Interactions

The study of distressed families in which the identified problem concerns parent-child relationships has primarily focused either on parents who are negligent or abusive or on children who are aggressive, behaviorally atypical, or noncompliant (Conger, 1981). Research in these areas has dealt more with the affective dimension of family interaction and less with problem-solving strategies typical of couples research. For example, in a study describing patterns of family interaction for 27 families referred for treatment because of an extremely aggressive boy in the family and 27 matched control families, Patterson (1976) used a 29-category behavioral code that included 14 possible coercive responses (for example, tease, whine, and yell). He found that deviant boys averaged 0.66 coercive behaviors per minute, compared to 0.28 per minute ($p < .01$) for the controls. In addition, the aggressive boys were more likely to follow one aversive behavior with yet another for 9 of the 14 aversive responses. In each instance, the mean rate of coercive behavior was higher in problem families, reaching conventional levels of statistical significance for the target child, older siblings, and mothers. In addition, family members in the clinic group were less likely to approve of one another's actions than controls. Finally, punitive responses to a child's hostility or aggression by control parents led to a decrease in the probability of further coerciveness. In the problem families, however, parental punishment actually led to an increase in the likelihood that one set of aversive behaviors would reoccur.

Other researchers have also found that clinic-referred children and adolescents are likely to come from families in which positive, nurturant, or supportive behaviors occur at depressed rates, but noxious, aversive, or negative interactions are relatively frequent (see Conger, 1981). The same qualities of interaction are descriptive of families with abusive or neglectful parents as well. One illustration of work in this area is the research by Burgess and Conger (1978), who predicted patterns of behavior exchange similar to those suggested by Gottman (1979). That is, they expected that members of abusive and neglectful families would interact at lower rates, would be less positive in their interactions, and would be more aversive than controls. To test these propositions, they developed a general code for assessing social behavior that discriminated verbal from physical contacts, assessed the emotional affect of each response (neutral, positive, or negative), and indicated whether or not a particular act involved a command or compliant response. The behavioral code was used to study in-home interactions in families where children had been physically abused (n = 17) or seriously neglected (n = 17), and in closely matched control families (n = 19) with no known history of abuse or neglect.

As expected, the findings were generally in accordance with the researchers' predictions—especially for the mothers in the distressed groups who were more negative and less positive than controls in their interactions with their children. Surprisingly, the lowest rates of positive behavior to children, and the highest rates of negative contacts, were found for mothers in the neglect group. Positive interactions normally would include compliments or displays of physical affection. On the other hand, aversive behaviors involve threats, disparaging remarks, or punitive physical behaviors. Other investigators have reported similar findings for families suffering from problems of abuse or neglect (see, for example, Reid, Taplin, & Lorber, in press; Aragona & Eyberg, 1981).

The above discussion suggests that distressed families with problems typically confronted by family practitioners tend to share some common interactional characteristics that discriminate them from nonclinic groups. Moreover, there is evidence that modification of these dysfunctional patterns of behavioral exchange is associated with reduced levels of family distress (Conger, 1981). Regardless of the problem area, the social exchange of affective behaviors and, especially in the case of marital difficulties, the inability to resolve significant conflicts appear to be the most salient behavioral dimensions of clinical concern. These categories of interaction form the basis for our recommendations concerning the use of behavioral assessment by practitioners.

Some Problems and Proposed Solutions

The most obvious problem in the application of behavioral assessment techniques to clinical practice is the level of expense involved in human and material resources. Researchers using observational methods typically employ a staff of trained coders and other assistants who help to refine behavioral codes, record interactions, store and analyze data, and report the results of each study (see Conger & Smith, 1981; Gottman, 1979). They may also use relatively expensive electronic equipment, such as behavioral event recorders, audiovisual equipment, or computer hardware, or need to develop at some cost the computer software necessary to do their analyses. All of these factors militate against the use of systematic behavioral observation by practitioners working either alone or in small groups.

At first glance, then, the usefulness of behavioral assessment to most family therapists appears limited. However, when one analyzes the differences between clinical and research needs, the situation changes dramatically. To begin with, enough work has now been done on the analysis of social interactions that practitioners do not need the personnel required to devise and test new coding systems. Rather, they need to make informed decisions about adapting existing behavioral taxonomies to their particular circumstances. The information contained in this volume and others like it provides the background needed to facilitate this decision-making process (for example, see Filsinger & Lewis, 1981). Moreover, software, equipment, and personnel needs are also simplified since the clinician does not have to study relatively large numbers of families for comparative purposes or report sophisticated statistical analyses such as those required by basic or applied research. Instead, the clinician needs only to get some idea of the current level of functioning in a family and then assess from time to time possible changes in initial levels of interaction. The following set of recommendations considers each of the above points.

Equipment and Settings

A first step in applying behavioral assessment to clinical practice does require investment in audiovisual equipment, that is, a camera, video-recorder, and microphone(s). Without such assistance it would be very difficult for a therapist to acquire and adequately employ observational methodology. However, these types of equipment are becoming relatively inexpensive and, for the private practitioner, are tax deductible. As will become clear in later discussion, though, it is not necessary to use behavioral event recorders, computer terminals, or other hardware/software to apply behavioral assessment to clinical environments. Nor is it required that special laboratories be used for family observation.

Indeed, the most appropriate setting for recording family interaction will be the office in which treatment is provided. Video equipment can be in clear view and the couple or entire family should be aware when it is being used. Videotaping sessions will reveal important information even when relatively short, say, 20 to 30 minutes in length (Cooper, Grotevant, & Condon, 1982). The major consideration for such tapings is the use of a task that will tend to elicit affective and problem-solving behaviors that are the primary discriminators of family distress (Conger, 1981; Weick, 1968). For example, Gottman (1979) recommends that couples be asked to attempt to resolve a problem about which they are in conflict. This technique should also be effective with parents and older children or adolescents. Conger, Lahey, and Smith (Note 2) have found that competitive games provide appropriate tasks for eliciting supportive or derogatory behaviors between parents and younger children. Although the therapist should be absent from the room while taping occurs, time should be allowed after a videotaping session to assure that the family or couple is not left in a state of conflict concerning the session before they leave the office. The observation setting should be the same for future tapings as the therapist attempts to assess changes in interaction across time.

In addition to videotapes, other new technological developments may be useful. Recently a number of hand-held portable data collectors have come onto the market (Holm, 1981). Although each has somewhat different configurations, they all share the feature of enabling the user-observer to enter coded behaviors on a keyboard, store the sequence of codes, and then output them for review. What results is an easily readable description of the interaction. Two existing coding systems, the Dyadic Interaction Scoring Code (Filsinger, 1981, in press) and the Social Interaction Scoring System (Conger, Note 3), were developed for use with portable data collectors.

Personnel

As with equipment, personnel needs are significantly reduced when one's objective is the provision of services rather than the accumulation of basic information about family processes. Statisticians, computer programmers, and even additional observers are not a necessary part of the clinical setting. Once the practitioner has decided upon an existing code that meets his or her needs and that has been shown to identify interactional characteristics most typical of distressed couples or families, a complete codebook of behavioral definitions and examples can be obtained from the appropriate researcher. These coding manuals are usually written for self-study and ambiguities can be clarified through communication with the author of the code. It is important to realize, though, that any scheme for describing human interaction will always contain some ambiguities.

Because the therapist will already have selected a code that has demonstrated validity, that is, that has been shown to discriminate distressed from nondistressed families, the primary methodological concern will be the reliability of the code as employed by the practitioner. Reliability has to do with the consistency of a measure (Kidder, 1981), or, given identical events, the capacity to produce the same results each time these events are measured. Typically, behavioral researchers assess reliability by having two observers view the same sequence of interactions to determine the extent to which they agree on what has occurred. However, a single observer could view, and then re-view, the same videotape on several different occasions to assure that the same actions are being coded in the same fashion each time. If the estimates for specific behaviors by specific individuals are approximately the same for repeated viewings of three or four practice tapes, the practitioner will be assured that he or she is using the code in a consistent or reliable manner. The therapist might ask some nondistressed families or couples to participate in identical videotaping as well to determine whether his or her use of the code will, in fact, identify differences between family types.

Although the above regime of self-instruction may take some time—I would estimate about six months to one year of study and practice for a limited time each week to gain confidence—the outcome should find the therapist in a much better position to assess family status and change meaningfully. Certainly the therapist will be in a position to go beyond global descriptions of behavior that were found earlier to be largely non-informative. Developing these skills by coordinating efforts with colleagues should accelerate the learning process. In effect the practitioner will have made progress in beginning to understand interactional dynamics within families in a far more subtle and accurate fashion than is usually the case in clinical settings.

In terms of analyses, simple checklists of behavioral events should more than suffice. For example, the therapist might simply count the number of supportive or positive verbalizations by each family member to the others. A given videotape may be played and replayed a number of times to determine the frequencies of these events, which will be defined in terms of the coding system employed. The relative frequency of positive verbalizations can be computed by dividing all positive speech events by total number of speech episodes. Simple frequencies or relative frequencies of behaviors require nothing more elaborate than counting and dividing, which can easily be accomplished without the aid of a computer or even a pocket calculator. If sequences of interaction are of special importance, the therapist might count the number of times an aversive behavior by one family member leads to immediate retaliation by a second, or the number of times a suggested resolution to a problem is met with outright rejection rather than acceptance or proposed modification. Because the purpose of analysis in these clinical situations is diagnosis rather than tests of theoretical propositions, simple descriptions of interaction are sufficient; in fact, they are preferable to more sophisticated statistical analyses.

An Illustration

The following discussion will serve to illustrate how the above recommendations can be applied with two specific coding systems: one developed for assessing dyadic interaction, the other for describing behavioral exchange between parents and children. An important point in these remarks is that the clinician is not constrained to use only one coding system or to use any particular code in its entirety. As long as the behavioral code employed, or those aspects of the code that are utilized, is appropriate to the clinical problem being addressed, the practitioner may be selective in his or her use of assessment techniques. For example, the most robust discriminator of distressed couples in Gottman's (1979) coding system (see Notarius, Gottman, and Markman, Chapter 6, this volume) is negative emotional affect coded nonverbally. For his or her particular purposes, a therapist may choose to use only that dimension of the Couple Interaction Scoring System.

As noted earlier, one aspect of interaction that is associated with marital distress is the inability to agree on significant issues for discussion during a conflict-resolution task. In addition, distressed couples are less capable of resolving conflicts once they are identified. To address these issues one might employ a code proposed by Filsinger (in press): the Dyadic Interaction Scoring Code (DISC). Among the DISC categories are "problem description, requesting information or clarification, agreement, disagreement, negative affect and positive affect." A clinician employing this code would expect to find that a distressed couple would engage in a great deal of problem description, but that these statements would often be followed by additional descriptions of problems, disagreements, or negative affect. Positive changes in the relationship should lead to problem descriptions that are more often followed by agreement, positive affect, or requesting information and clarification.

Another coding system that has proven useful for studying parent-child interactions is the Social Interaction Scoring System (SISS; Conger, Note 3). This behavioral code has demonstrated reliability and has been shown to discriminate between distressed and nondistressed families (Conger et al., Note 2; Weinrott & Jones, Note 4). Of special significance is the dimension of emotional affect, which is coded in terms of verbalizations, physical contacts, or physical gestures that communicate neutral, negative, or positive affect. For example, from a videotape of a family playing simple games together, the practitioner could determine the frequency of verbal interactions that are negative (for example, derogations, disagreements, expressions of dislike) or positive (for example, compliments, expressions of affection, agreements). As therapy progressed, it would be expected that the ratio of negative verbalizations to positive verbalizations would decrease if family functioning improved.

Conclusions

The present chapter has attempted to show that behavioral assessment is an important technique for obtaining a complete picture of family functioning. In addition, the systematic assessment of behavioral interaction provides data that are less prone to error and contradiction than the global impressions of families upon which practitioners are too often forced to rely. We have also argued that observational procedures can be simplified and reduced in cost to the point that they are employable by many professionals delivering services to families. Indeed, we would suggest that the study and acquisition of systematic observational skills will likely improve the diagnostic and treatment competence of professionals in the field.

Reference Notes

1. Starr, R. H., Jr., & Dietrich, K. N. *Child abuse prediction and parent-child interaction.* Paper presented at the biennial meeting of the Society for Research in Child Development, San Francisco, March 1979.

2. Conger, R. D., Lahey, B. B., & Smith, S. S. Paper presented at the National Conference of Family Violence Researchers, University of New Hampshire, Durham, 1981.

3. Conger, R. D. *Coding manual for the Social Interaction Scoring System.* Unpublished manuscript, University of Illinois, 1982.

4. Weinrott, M. R., & Jones, R. R. *Overt versus covert assessment of observer reliability.* Unpublished manuscript, Evaluation Research Group, Eugene, Oregon, 1982.

References

Aragona, J. A., & Eyberg, S. M. Neglected children: Mothers' report of child behavior problems and observed verbal behavior. *Child Development*, 1981, *52*, 596-602.

Birchler, G. R., Weiss, R. L., & Vincent, J. P. A multimethod analysis of social reinforcement exchange between maritally distressed and nondistressed spouse and stranger dyads. *Journal of Personality and Social Psychology*, 1975, *31*, 349-360.

Burgess, R. L., & Conger, R. D. Family interaction in abusive, neglectful and normal families. *Child Development*, 1978, *49*, 1163-1173.

Conger, R. D. The assessment of dysfunctional family systems. In B. Lahey & A. Kazdin (Eds.), *Advances in clinical child psychology* (Vol. 4). New York: Plenum, 1981.

Conger, R. D., & Smith, S. S. Equity in dyadic and family interaction: Is there any justice? In E. E. Filsinger & R. A. Lewis (Eds.), *Assessing marriage: New behavioral approaches.* Beverly Hills, CA: Sage, 1981.

Cooper, C. R., Grotevant, H. D., & Condon, S. M. Methodological challenges of selectivity in family interaction: Assessing temporal patterns of individuation. *Journal of Marriage and the Family*, 1982, *44*, 749-754.

Deutscher, I. *What we say/what we do: Sentiments and acts.* Glenview, IL: Scott, Foresman, 1973.

Filsinger, E. E. The Dyadic Interaction Scoring Code. In E. E. Filsinger & R. A. Lewis (Eds.), *Assessing marriage: New behavioral approaches.* Beverly Hills, CA: Sage, 1981.

Filsinger, E. E. A machine-aided marital observation technique: The Dyadic Interaction Scoring Code. *Journal of Marriage and the Family*, in press.

Filsinger, E. E., & Lewis, R. A. (Eds.). *Assessing marriage: New behavioral approaches.* Beverly Hills, CA: Sage, 1981.

Gelles, R., & Straus, M. A. Determinants of violence in the family: Toward a theoretical integration. In W. R. Burr, R. Hill, F. I. Nye, & I. L. Reiss (Eds.), *Contemporary theories about the family: Research-based theories* (Vol. 1). New York: Macmillan, 1979.

Gottman, J. M. *Marital interaction: Experimental investigations.* New York: Academic, 1979.

Holm, R. A. Using data logging equipment. In E. E. Filsinger & R. A. Lewis (Eds.), *Assessing marriage: New behavioral approaches.* Beverly Hills, CA: Sage, 1981.

Jacobson, N. S. Specific and nonspecific factors in the effectiveness of a behavioral approach to the treatment of marital discord. *Journal of Consulting and Clinical Psychology,* 1978, *46,* 442-452.

Kidder, L. H. *Research methods in social relations* (4th ed.). New York: Holt, Rinehart & Winston, 1981.

Patterson, G. R. The aggressive child: Victim and architect of a coercive system. In E. J. Mash, L. A. Hamerlynck, & L. C. Handy (Eds.), *Behavior modification and families.* New York: Brunner/Mazel, 1976.

Patterson, G. R., Hops, H., & Weiss, R. L. Interpersonal skills training for couples in early stages of conflict. *Journal of Marriage and the Family,* 1975, *37,* 295-302.

Reid, J. B., Taplin, P. S., & Lorber, R. A social interactional approach to the treatment of abusive families. *Proceedings of the 11th Banff International Conference on Behavior Modification,* in press.

Vincent, J. P., Weiss, R. L., & Bircher, G. R. Dyadic problem solving behavior as a function of marital distress and spousal vs. stranger interactions. *Behavior Therapy,* 1975, *6,* 475-487.

Weick, K. E. Systematic observational methods. In G. Lindzey & E. Aronson (Eds.), *The handbook of social psychology* (Vol. 2). Reading, MA: Addison-Wesley, 1968.

Wilson, T. D., & Nisbett, R. E. The accuracy of verbal reports about the effects of stimuli on evaluations and behavior. *Social Psychology,* 1978, *41,* 118-131.

MARITAL QUESTIONNAIRES

Self-reports of the nature of marital and family life provide what has come to be referred to as the "insider's" view of families. Self-reports offer several important advantages. They are relatively easy to administer and to score; they represent the most commonly employed techniques in research and in practice; and they are likely to continue to be used widely in the future. While self-reports may be subject to motivational distortion, the data reflect the perceptions of the individual reporting them. Those perceptions may be extremely important in understanding the dynamics of family life.

Part III deals with self-reports of marriage. Spainer and Filsinger (Chapter 8) present the Dyadic Adjustment Scale (DAS), a recent global assessment device in the tradition of the well-known Locke-Wallace Marital Adjustment Test (MAT). Because the DAS was developed specifically to overcome some of the problems associated with the MAT, the DAS is included in this volume rather than the MAT. The chapter presents a concise discussion of a relatively easy-to-use global assessment of marital adjustment. The DAS may be particularly useful in judging treatment effectiveness at the end of therapy and at follow-up.

Snyder (Chapter 9) discusses in somewhat more detail the clinical usage of the Marital Satisfaction Inventory (MSI). The MSI has impressive psychometric investigations behind it. It should be and is placed within the mainstream of traditional psychological testing. It comes with manuals, standard answer sheets, templates for scoring, and norms for interpretation.

While most of the recent research on marital communication has shifted to observational techniques, there are self-report instruments of that aspect of marital functioning. Schumm, Anderson, and Griffin (Chapter 10) provide an overview of the usage and application of Bienvenu's Marital Communication Inventory (MCI). Schumm has done much of the recent research on the MCI, and the reader should find the discussion of the MCI and its clinical application stimulating.

Another new technique, the Marital Agendas Protocol, is offered in Chapter 11 by Notarius and Vanzetti. It is a way of assessing couples' presenting complaints and of evaluating treatment effectiveness. An interesting feature of the Marital Agendas Protocol is that it is based in part on self-efficacy theory applied to couples. *Relational efficacy* is the perception by the spouses that they will be able to emit the responses necessary to improve the relationship. Resistance to the therapy process may involve low relational efficacy—the spouses do not think that they can change.

Chapter 12, by Fournier, Olson, and Druckman, involves a discussion of another significant issue: Can assessment serve to help premarital dyads sort out issues that might otherwise impede relationship development? It is the essence of primary prevention to seek to avoid marital distress by contacting couples before they marry and by attempting to identify potential problems to be worked out. Although PREPARE-ENRICH is not the only premarital package currently offered, it is a significant representative of that approach.

CHAPTER 8

The Dyadic Adjustment Scale

GRAHAM B. SPANIER
State University of New York—Stony Brook

ERIK E. FILSINGER
Arizona State University

This chapter describes the background, development, and use of the Dyadic Adjustment Scale (Spanier, 1976, 1979; Spanier & Thompson, 1982). The scale is designed to measure marital adjustment; it is also applicable to unmarried couples. Since researchers and practitioners see both married and unmarried couples, it is useful to have a standardized assessment of couples' relationships. The scores derived from the Dyadic Adjustment Scale (DAS) give a good overall look at the level of adjustment achieved by the couple. Although developed primarily out of the family sociological tradition, the DAS can be used meaningfully within a wide range of therapeutic orientations.

Background

Rationale

Marital adjustment has been one of the most widely used and researched concepts in family studies. Over the years, it has been measured by a variety of research instruments, most of them paper-and-pencil self-reports. The frequency of use of self-report methods over the years attests to their likely continued usage in the future. In perhaps the earliest study, Hamilton (1929) obtained a satisfaction score from 13 questions administered by cards but answered orally. Since that time, researchers have used anywhere from one question to several hundred to assess what they thought was marital adjustment.

During the years following the first marital adjustment research, the concept continued to be investigated. Bernard (1933), Burgess and Cot-

---

Instrument Source Note: The DAS is presented in Table 8.1. Permission is not required from the author to use the DAS for noncommercial, research, or educational purposes.

trell (1939), Burgess and Wallin (1953), and Terman (1938) all made contributions to the study of marital adjustment. Harvey Locke and his colleagues (Locke, 1947; Locke & Wallace, 1959; Locke & Williamson, 1958) made significant advances in the study of marital adjustment in the 1950s. Locke applied techniques for scale building and measurement, and was able to advance our ability to measure (or predict) marital adjustment. Probably the most widely used measure of marital adjustment in the last two decades has been the Locke-Wallace Marital Adjustment Scale. Locke and Wallace (1959) developed their 15-item scale based on previous scales. They found that those 15 items could be used for studying marital adjustment. The scale could be completed in only a minute or two. It was found to be reliable (split-half r = .90) and was able to discriminate between couples who, by other evidence, were known to be well adjusted and those known to be poorly adjusted.

While the substantive understanding of factors related to marital adjustment increased during the 1940s and 1950s, many early measures, including the Locke-Wallace Scale, were not carefully evaluated for validity or tested for reliability, at least according to today's standards. In addition, the field was flooded with many different terms that relate to aspects of marital adjustment (such as satisfaction, happiness, balance, integration, formation, crystallization, value consensus, cohesiveness, conflict, interaction, communication, and interpersonal competence). This confusing plethora of terms was often both ambiguous and overlapping. In fact, Lively (1969) suggested that all the terms should be discarded.

Spanier and his colleagues have attempted to bring the work on marital adjustment up to date both on conceptual and methodological levels. Spanier and Cole (1976) reviewed the literature on the conceptualization of marital adjustment. Based on their review, they offer the following definition: "Marital adjustment is a process, the outcome of which is determined by the degree of: (1) troublesome marital differences; (2) interspousal tensions and personal anxiety; (3) marital satisfaction; (4) dyadic cohesion; and (5) consensus on matters of important to marital functioning" (Spanier & Cole, 1976, pp. 127-128). Working within that conceptual model, Spanier (1976) developed the Dyadic Adjustment Scale.

Development and Psychometric Properties

The DAS was drawn from an initial pool of 300 items. These items were all the items ever used in any scale measuring marital adjustment or a related concept, plus several new items developed to tap new areas of adjustment ignored in previous measures. Duplicate items were eliminated. Three judges examined the items for content validity against the Spanier and Cole (1976) definition of marital adjustment. By consensus among the judges, items were either eliminated or retained. The 200 re-

maining items were modified where necessary to make them more complete, and 25 new items were included to check for effects of alternative
wording and fixed-choice response categories. All these items, along
with some demographic items, were used to create a questionnaire.

The questionnaire was administered to a purposive sample of 218 married persons in central Pennsylvania. The sample consisted primarily of
working- and middle-class residents of the area. In addition, questionnaires
were mailed to every person in Centre County, Pennsylvania, who obtained a divorce decree during the 12 months previous to the mailing.
These respondents were asked to answer the relationship questions on the
basis of the last month they spent with their spouses. Out of approximately
400 mailed questionnaires, 94 usable questionnaires were received. Also, a
small sample of never-married cohabiting couples was given the questionnaire to determine the applicability of the scale to nonmarital dyads; however, these data were not part of the scale construction analysis.

The frequency distributions of the items were analyzed and all items
with low variance and high skewness were eliminated. Where differences
in response variation were significant, items with the lesser variation were
excluded. Remaining variables were analyzed using a t test for significance of difference between means of the married and divorced samples.
After items that were not significantly different at the .001 level were eliminated, 52 items remained. The questions with alternative wording were
reexamined and items with the lowest t test values were excluded. The
remaining 40 variables were factor analyzed to determine the presence of
hypothesized components, and to make a final determination of items
that were to be included in the scale. After 8 were eliminated due to low
factor loadings (below .30), 32 items remained. These items are included
in Table 8.1.

The factor analysis produced four interrelated dimensions: Dyadic
Consensus (the degree to which the couple agrees on matters of importance to the relationship); Dyadic Cohesion (the degree to which the couple engages in activities together); Dyadic Satisfaction (the degree to
which the couple is satisfied with the present state of the relationship and
is committed to its continuance); and Affectional Expression (the degree
to which the couple is satisfied with the expression of affection and sex in
the relationship). The subscales are also indicated in Table 8.1.

The basic structure of the DAS and its subscales was supported in a
subsequent study by Spanier and Thompson (1982). They used a technique called maximum likelihood confirmatory factor analysis to test statistically whether or not the original factor study (Spanier, 1976) could be
replicated in a new data set. Their sample of 205 couples consisted of
recently separated or divorced couples from the same geographic region
as the original study. The hypothesized structure was found to fit the data

TABLE 8.1 The Dyadic Adjustment Scale and Subscales

Items	Responses[a]						Subscale
	Always agree	Almost always agree	Occasionally disagree	Frequently disagree	Almost always disagree	Always disagree	
Handling family finances	5	4	3	2	1	0	Dyadic Consensus
Matters of recreation	5	4	3	2	1	0	Dyadic Consensus
Religious matters	5	4	3	2	1	0	Dyadic Consensus
Demonstrations of affection	5	4	3	2	1	0	Affectional Expression
Friends	5	4	3	2	1	0	Dyadic Consensus
Sex relations	5	4	3	2	1	0	Affectional Expression
Conventionality (correct or proper behavior)	5	4	3	2	1	0	Dyadic Consensus
Philosophy of life	5	4	3	2	1	0	Dyadic Consensus
Ways of dealing with parents or in-laws	5	4	3	2	1	0	Dyadic Consensus
Aims, goals, and things believed important	5	4	3	2	1	0	Dyadic Consensus
Amount of time spent together	5	4	3	2	1	0	Dyadic Consensus
Making major decisions	5	4	3	2	1	0	Dyadic Consensus
Household tasks	5	4	3	2	1	0	Dyadic Consensus
Leisure-time interests and activities	5	4	3	2	1	0	Dyadic Consensus
Career decisions	5	4	3	2	1	0	Dyadic Consensus

	All the time	Most of the time	More often than not	Occasionally	Rarely	Never	
How often do you discuss or have you considered divorce, separation, or terminating your relationship?	0	1	2	3	4	5	Dyadic Satisfaction
How often do you or your mate leave the house after a fight?	0	1	2	3	4	5	Dyadic Satisfaction
In general, how often do you think that things between you and your partner are going well?	5	4	3	2	1	0	Dyadic Satisfaction
Do you confide in your mate?	5	4	3	2	1	0	Dyadic Satisfaction
Do you ever regret that you married? (or lived together)	0	1	2	3	4	5	Dyadic Satisfaction
How often do you and your partner quarrel?	0	1	2	3	4	5	Dyadic Satisfaction
How often do you and your mate "get on each other's nerves?"	0	1	2	3	4	5	Dyadic Satisfaction

	Every day	Almost every day	Occasionally	Rarely	Never	
Do you kiss your mate?	4	3	2	1	0	Dyadic Satisfaction

	All of them	Most of them	Some of them	Very few of them	None of them	
Do you and your mate engage in outside interests together?	4	3	2	1	0	Dyadic Cohesion

(continued)

159

TABLE 8.1 Continued

Items	Responses[a]						Subscale

How often would you say the following events occur between you and your mate?

	Never	Less than once a month	Once or twice a month	Once or twice a week	Once a day	More often	Subscale
Have a stimulating exchange of ideas	0	1	2	3	4	5	Dyadic Cohesion
Laugh together	0	1	2	3	4	5	Dyadic Cohesion
Calmly discuss something	0	1	2	3	4	5	Dyadic Cohesion
Work together on a project	0	1	2	3	4	5	Dyadic Cohesion

These are some things about which couples sometimes agree and sometimes disagree. Indicate if either item below caused differences of opinions or were problems in your relationship during the past few weeks. (check yes or no)

	Yes	No		Subscale
Being too tired for sex	0	1		Affectional Expression
Not showing love	0	1		Affectional Expression

The dots on the following line represent different degrees of happiness in your relationship. The middle point, "happy," represents the degree of happiness of most relationships. Please circle the dot which best describes the degree of happiness, all things considered, of your relationship.

Dyadic Satisfaction

160

Dyadic Satisfaction

0	1	2	3	4	5	6
Extremely unhappy	Fairly unhappy	A little unhappy	Happy	Very happy	Extremely happy	Perfect

Which of the following statements best describes how you feel about the future of your relationship?

___ 5   I want desperately for my relationship to succeed, and *would go to almost any length to see that it does.*

___ 4   I want very much for my relationship to succeed, and *will do all I can* to see that it does.

___ 3   I want very much for my relationship to succeed, and *will do my fair share* to see that it does.

___ 2   It would be nice if my relationship succeeded, *but I can't do much more than I am doing now* to keep the relationship going.

___ 1   It would be nice if my relationship succeeded, but *I refuse to do anymore than I am doing* now to keep the relationship going.

___ 0   My relationship can never succeed, and *there is no more that I can do* to keep the relationship going.

NOTE: This table is reproduced in modified form from Spanier (1976). Readers who wish to use the scale for noncommercial, research, or educational purposes may do so without permission from the author.
a. The numbers presented herein are for scoring and should not appear on the form the individual fills out. The individual places a checkmark to indicate the correct response.

set, providing additional evidence of the existence of the four basic dimensions of marital adjustment contained in the DAS.

The theoretical range of scores of the total DAS is 0-151. The ranges for the subscales are: Dyadic Consensus, 0-65; Dyadic Cohesion, 0-24; Dyadic Satisfaction, 0-50; and Affectional Expression, 0-12. The mean scale scores for the married and divorced samples in the original study (Spanier, 1976) were 114.8 and 70.7, respectively. Table 8.2 contains the means for the DAS and subscales in a selected cross section of other studies. Since its creation, the DAS has received widespread use. Spanier has received over 500 requests for permission to use it. While it would appear that Spanier's (1976) original mean of 114.8 (S.D. of 17.8) is fairly representative, it should be noted that the mean of 70.7 (S.D. of 23.8) for the divorced sample may be low, probably due to some extent to selecting items that significantly discriminated married and divorced groups in his sample.

The means in several studies for the subscales of the DAS are also presented in Table 8.2. Unfortunately, an insufficient number of studies have employed the DAS on currently distressed couples for us to be able to talk definitively about norms for distressed couples. More will be said about this under the discussion of interpretation.

The DAS and its subscales have been checked for internal consistency reliability. Spanier (1976) reported the following coefficient alphas: Dyadic Adjustment, .96; Dyadic Consensus, .90; Dyadic Cohesion, .86; Dyadic Satisfaction, .94; and Affectional Expression, .73. Similar coefficient alphas were reported by Filsinger and Wilson (in press) for husbands and wives, respectively: Dyadic Adjustment, .94, .93; Dyadic Consensus, .91, .88; Dyadic Cohesion, .85, .80; Dyadic Satisfaction, .82, .84; and Affectional Expression, .73, .73.

The validity of the DAS was established in three ways. First, judges determined content validity based on the theoretical dimensions. Second, the scale discriminated married and divorced samples, suggesting criterion-related validity (Spanier, 1976). In another study, Margolin (1981) found that distressed and nondistressed samples were discriminated by the items common to the DAS and the Locke-Wallace Marital Adjustment Scale. Third, the DAS has the construct validity of conforming to a theoretical structure (Spanier, 1976; Spanier & Thompson, 1982).

The issue of variable weighting was considered. After empirical comparisons were considered, using alternative weighting procedures and consideration of the scaling literature, a decision was made against weighting. There do not appear to be significant sex differences in the DAS or its subscales.

TABLE 8.2 Examples of Means for the Dyadic Adjustment Scales and Subscales from Selected Studies

Study	Sample	Dyadic Adjustment	Dyadic Consensus	Dyadic Cohesion	Dyadic Satisfaction	Affectional Expression
Burger and Jacobson, 1979	60 married and cohabiting	109.62 (110.12)[a]				
Cyr, 1979	200 Marriage Encounter participants, French Canada	114.68	51.38	15.15	39.43	8.91
Dailey, 1979	28 married	116.7	50.2	17.8	39.9	8.8
	24 cohabiting	115.5	48.4	18.5	39.8	8.8
	20 homosexual	109.5	46.5	17.3	37.4	8.3
Filsinger and Wilson, in press	190 married, church-based	117.04 (117.63)	49.22 (50.11)	16.32 (16.45)	40.83 (40.38)	10.66 (10.69)
Laurich, 1980	20 Marriage Encounter, pretest	95.55				
	14 married controls, pretest	115.71				
Maurer, Note 1	74 married, community	108.6 (107.7)	45.9 (47.5)	15.5 (15.5)	39.0 (35.8)	8.2 (8.7)
Romig, 1979	32 beginning seminary, married	121.41 (122.44)				
	27 returning seminary, married	116.19 (118.44)				
Spanier, 1976	218 married	114.18	51.9	13.4	40.5	9.0
	94 divorced	70.7	35.4	8.0	22.2	5.1

a. Scores in parentheses indicate wives' (females') scores. The scores that precede them are the husbands' (males') scores.

163

Description of the Technique

The DAS is a measure of the individual's adjustment to marriage, but has also been used to study the adjustment of the couple to marriage. The scale can be also used to measure the adjustment of persons in nonmarried dyads. It can be used in diagnosing relationships as distressed or not, in identifying potential problems in the relationship, and in evaluating the effectiveness of treatment by comparing intake scores with posttreatment scores. It also can be used for long-term follow-up. Unfortunately, there is no alternative form of the DAS. Effects of retesting are not completely known. However, Filsinger (in press) found that his posttest-only control group was not significantly different from his posttest study group, suggesting that there were no effects of retesting for the study group over the one-year period of the investigation.

Administration. The DAS can be given to the couple anytime; however, it probably would be useful to have them fill it out at intake or during an early session. The clients should fill the form out separately and should not discuss their answers with each other before completing the scale. It also should not be discussed with the therapist until he or she has the opportunity to examine and score it.

Scoring. The DAS is scored by assigning numbers to each response as indicated in Table 8.1. The score for the individual is the sum of the numbers for each item. The total scale score is the most meaningful indicator for both researchers and therapists, but the responses to the subscales and to individual items can also be examined for clues as to the origins of problems.

Couple scores can be derived in a number of ways, for example, by adding the individual scores, taking the difference between them, and/or averaging them, but this practice is not empirically or theoretically justified in previous studies. At this point in time there are no aids to interpreting couple scores as normal or distressed.

Interpretation. As with most testing (APA, 1974), it should be kept in mind that tests are just aids that help the clinicians make judgments. There are no absolutes. With the DAS, sufficient studies comparing currently distressed and nondistressed couples have not yet found their way into the published literature to suggest a cutoff point for marital distress. The retrospective self-reports of divorced individuals cannot be taken as norms for currently distressed couples. One guideline that has been used in diagnosis is to suggest that a couple is distressed when one partner has a DAS score under 100 (Burger & Jacobson, 1979). At this time that criterion must be considered arbitrary pending further investigation. Given the continuum of possible scores, it is inadvisable to recommend a fixed cutoff point. A statistical test could be whether or not the scores are significantly different from the apparent norms for all married couples. Criteria for the subscales have not been investigated.

In any event, the information from the DAS should be cross-referenced by the practitioner with other information he or she has gathered from the couple. The other sources of information could be additional assessment instruments, personal observation, or other information the spouses disclose. This form of triangulation may best benefit the evaluation of the couple's relationship.

Clinical Usage

The DAS can be an aid to individual, marital, and family therapy because it gives a quick and easy look at the marital subsystem that is compatible with most therapeutic frameworks. In individual therapy, it can indicate whether or not there are marital problems. In marital therapy, it can be used to judge the severity of the problem and the effectiveness of treatment. In family therapy, it can be used to see if there are problems within the marital subsystem. The two clinical examples that follow are hypothetical constructs designed to illustrate potential uses of the DAS.

Clinical Example 1

A young couple in their late twenties, Bob and Jan, entered marital therapy because "they just seemed to fight all the time." They both professed to want the relationship to work, but felt they needed help. They had what would be considered a traditional sex-role relationship, with Bob working as an accountant and Jan staying home and taking care of their three-year-old son. They had been married for five years after knowing each other for three years before getting married. When asked what they fought about, they said, "Everything," and that they always had verbal disagreements.

They were asked to complete the DAS. Bob had a total scale score of 104, with subscale scores as follows: Dyadic Consensus, 43; Dyadic Cohesion, 14; Dyadic Satisfaction, 39; and Affectional Expression, 8. Jan's total DAS score was 108, with the following subscale scores: Dyadic Consensus, 45; Dyadic Cohesion, 16; Dyadic Satisfaction, 39; and Affectional Expression, 8.

From these scores it was not clear that, compared to others, their relationship was very distressed. The total scale scores were a little low, but not very far from the norms. An examination of their subscale scores showed that for both of them Dyadic Cohesion, Dyadic Satisfaction, and Affectional Expression were close to the norms. However, Dyadic Consensus was definitely low. They were in agreement that they did not agree on many issues in their relationship. An examination of the individual items within that subscale showed that they both identified religious matters, friends, and ways of dealing with parents or in-laws as "almost al-ways disagree." When these results were reported back to them, they agreed that those topics were in fact the bases for most of their fights. This information was then used in working on those areas of their relationship.

Clinical Example 2

James and Anna had brought their 13-year-old son, Wayne, in for treat-ment. He had developed a history of emotional outbursts at school and school officials suggested some outside help. The family therapist detected that all might not be right between James and Anna in their marriage, but when the subject came up they made it very clear that the problem was Wayne and that nothing was wrong between them (though they did seem to disagree over whose version should be stated to the therapist).

As part of gaining background information on the case, the therapist had them fill out the DAS. Both of their total scale scores were under 100, with Dyadic Satisfaction being particularly low. The therapist decided that these results should be interpreted for the couple, along with the normative guidelines, as a basis for further discussion. When asked to explain why they thought they had received the low scores, both James and Anna immediately began to share with the therapist and each other some of the problems they were having in the relationship.

Critique

The DAS is connected to a large body of primarily self-report litera-ture. It is well known and has connections to many of the past measures of marital adjustment. To the extent that the position is taken that it is the individual's perception of the relationship that is important in telling whether the relationship is distressed or not, the DAS is an effective in-strument. In that sense it gives a good overall evaluation of the content-ment or discontentment in the relationship.

The DAS is perhaps not as strong in diagnosing which specific aspects of the relationship are causing the problem. It is also not known how well it may or may not correlate with behavioral indicators of problems in a relationship. However, with a few exceptions (Haynes, Follingstad, & Sullivan, 1979; Lewis, Filsinger, Conger, & McAvoy, 1981), global self-report measures have not generally been shown to be related to behav-ioral indicators (for example, see Margolin, 1978).

With that in mind, in clinical applications the DAS probably serves its most useful function as a criterion for marital adjustment, both at the onset and after therapy to evaluate the couple's adjustment and their re-sponse to treatment. Because it is brief and serves as a criterion, it can be used with almost any of the other diagnostic instruments. It is our suggestion that the DAS should be supplemented by behavioral observation and by some more specific diagnostic instruments, such as those presented in other chapters in this volume.

As discussed above, more work needs to be done to establish: (1) norms on the DAS for distressed couples; and/or (2) norms for different sub-populations, such as age group and length of marriage. It would also be helpful to have alternative forms available for those cases in which repeated testing is desired.

Reference Note

1. Maurer, J. W. *Rationality and marital adjustment.* Unpublished manuscript, 1979.

References

American Psychological Association (APA). *Standards for educational and psychological tests.* Washington, DC: Author, 1974.

Bernard, J. An instrument for measurement of success in marriage. *Publications of American Sociological Society,* 1933, *27,* 94-106.

Burger, A. L., & Jacobson, N. S. The relationship between sex role characteristics, couple satisfaction and problem-solving skills. *American Journal of Family Therapy,* 1979, *7,* 52-61.

Burgess, E. W., & Cottrell, L., Jr. *Predicting success or failure in marriage.* Englewood Cliffs, NJ: Prentice-Hall, 1939.

Burgess, E. W., & Wallin, P. *Engagement and marriage.* Philadelphia: J. B. Lippincott, 1953.

Cyr, Y. *The Marriage Encounter approach to marital enrichment and spouses' perception of their relationship.* Unpublished master's thesis, University of Ottawa, 1979.

Dailey, D. M. Adjustment of heterosexual and homosexual couples in pairing relationships: An exploratory study. *Journal of Sex Research,* 1979, *15,* 143-157.

Filsinger, E. E. Love, liking and individual marital adjustment: A pilot study of relationship changes within one year. *International Journal of Sociology of the Family,* in press.

Filsinger, E. E., & Wilson, M. R. Social anxiety and marital adjustment. *Family Relations,* in press.

Hamilton, G. A. *Research in marriage.* New York: Boni, 1929.

Haynes, S. N., Follingstad, D. R., & Sullivan, J. C. Assessment of marital satisfaction and interaction. *Journal of Consulting and Clinical Psychology,* 1979, *47,* 789-791.

Laurich, C. M. *Marital adjustment as a function of marriage enrichment.* Unpublished master's thesis, University of Calgary, 1980.

Lewis, R. A., Filsinger, E. E., Conger, R. A., & McAvoy, P. Love relationships among heroin-involved couples: Traditional self-report and behavioral assessment. In E. E. Filsinger & R. A. Lewis (Eds.), *Assessing marriage: New behavioral approaches.* Beverly Hills, CA: Sage, 1981.

Lively, E. Toward conceptual clarification: The case of marital interaction. *Journal of Marriage and the Family,* 1969, *31,* 108-114.

Locke, H. J. Predicting marital adjustment by comparing a divorced and happily married group. *American Sociological Review,* 1947, *12,* 187-191.

Locke, H. J., & Wallace, K. M. Short marital adjustment and prediction tests: Their reliability and validity. *Marriage and Family Living,* 1959, *21,* 251-255.

Locke, H. J., & Williamson, R. C. Marital adjustment: A factor analysis study. *American Sociological Review,* 1958, *23,* 562-569.

Margolin, G. Relationships among marital assessment procedures. *Journal of Consulting and Clinical Psychology,* 1978, *46,* 1556-1558.

Margolin, G. Behavior exchange in happy and unhappy marriages: A family life cycle perspective. *Behavior Therapy*, 1981, *12*, 329-343.

Romig, C. A. *The effects of seminary experience on marital adjustment: A cross-sectional study.* Unpublished master's thesis, Trinity Evangelical Divinity School, 1979.

Spanier, G. B. Measuring dyadic adjustment: New scales for assessing the quality of marriage and similar dyads. *Journal of Marriage and the Family*, 1976, *38*, 15-28.

Spanier, G. B. The measurement of marital quality. *Journal of Sex and Marital Therapy*, 1979, *5*, 288-300.

Spanier, G. B., & Cole, C. L. Toward clarification and investigation of marital adjustment. *International Journal of Sociology of the Family*, 1976, *6*, 121-146.

Spanier, G. B., & Thompson, L. A confirmatory analysis of the Dyadic Adjustment Scale. *Journal of Marriage and the Family*, 1982, *44*, 731-738.

Terman, L. *Psychological factors in marital happiness.* New York: McGraw-Hill, 1938.

CHAPTER 9

Clinical and Research Applications of the Marital Satisfaction Inventory

DOUGLAS K. SNYDER
University of Kentucky

The last decade has witnessed a dramatic increase in both the diversity and the sophistication of new techniques for assessing marital and family interaction. These developments have paralleled both theoretical and technological advances in marital and family therapy, observational analysis, and psychological measurement. At the same time that new assessment techniques have expanded potential resources for clinical and research applications, they have also challenged clinicians to tailor their interventions to the specific needs of their clients and to document therapeutic efficacy as part of an increasing emphasis on professional accountability. Unfortunately, many researchers continue to adopt measurement techniques that are poorly validated or inappropriate to their needs, and too many clinicians still avoid the objective evaluation of their clients altogether. In part this resistance to new assessment strategies persists because many instruments remain unpublished and are relatively inaccessible; still other techniques are inordinately complex or impractical for routine clinical or research adoption, while others are so theoretical in nature as to provide little descriptive or prescriptive utility in clinical settings.

The Marital Satisfaction Inventory (MSI; Snyder, 1979a) was developed to provide both clinicians and researchers with an objective self-report technique for assessing individuals' attitudes and beliefs regarding specific areas of their marital relationship as well as evaluating more global marital dimensions and individual response characteristics. Briefly, the MSI is a 280-item inventory including one validity scale (CNV), one

Instrument Source Note: Administration and scoring materials, profile forms, and user's manual for the MSI may be requested from Western Psychological Services, 12031 Wilshire Boulevard, Los Angeles, California 90025.

global satisfaction scale (GDS), and nine additional scales assessing the following specific dimensions of marital interaction: general affective communication (AFC), problem-solving communication (PSC), quality and quantity of leisure time together (TTO), disagreement about finances (FIN), sexual dissatisfaction (SEX), sex-role orientation (ROR), history of family and marital disruption (FAM), dissatisfaction with children (DSC), and conflict over child rearing (CCR). In addition, two factor scales have been developed to assess the broad-band dimensions of marital disharmony (DHR) and disaffection (DAF). The MSI is administered to individual spouses separately, and requires approximately 30 minutes to complete. Individuals' responses are scored along the 11 profile scales (and any additional supplemental scales) and are plotted on a standard profile sheet utilizing sex-specific norms. Interpretive guidelines for the MSI (Snyder, 1981) permit the user to distinguish among the extent and specific sources of marital distress for each spouse separately, and to evaluate objectively their interactive components. Group mean profiles for specific criterion groups identified in previous research enable the user to evaluate additional cognitive and behavioral features likely to characterize the individual respondent.

Background and Rationale

In evaluating the relative merits of the Marital Satisfaction Inventory within the broad spectrum of self-report techniques, it is useful to draw upon the distinction between *sign* and *sample* approaches to psychological assessment. The sample approach to assessment emphasizes the direct observation of specific behaviors that are assumed to be representative of more general behavioral difficulties expressed in other contexts. Such an approach is particularly well suited to behavioral therapy techniques emphasizing the functional analysis of problematic behaviors and their relationship to observable environmental antecedents and consequences within the marital or family system. However, as Jacobson and Margolin (1979) have noted, even behavioral self-report techniques are limited in the extent to which they meet the assumptions of the sample approach. As such measures lose their high level of response specificity, they become indistinguishable from more general nonbehavioral self-report methods and increasingly susceptible to social desirability and other response-set biases.

The sign approach to psychological assessment makes no assumptions regarding the representativeness of actual test behaviors; rather it posits that these responses may serve as useful signs or indicators of behavioral or emotional tendencies outside the testing situation. With regard to marital assessment, this approach may be considered to include any number of self-report measures purporting to assess thoughts, feelings, or behaviors characterizing the marital relationship.

Within this general framework, self-report measures of marital and family interaction can be evaluated according to the assumptions they require for their interpretation and the extent to which these assumptions are justified by empirical research. At the first and simplest level of interpretation, individuals' responses are assumed to describe external reality accurately. Numerous studies have challenged the validity of such assumptions since individuals' responses may be influenced by misinterpretation of item content, misperception of reality, social desirability response sets, or deliberate distortion of known facts. A second, more sophisticated level of interpretation regards individuals' test responses not as factual self-reports, but rather as potentially useful expressions of self-attitudes. It is at this second interpretive level that the vast majority of self-report measures of marital and family interaction function, including several more widely used and empirically founded measures such as the Locke-Wallace Marital Adjustment Test (Locke & Wallace, 1959) and the more recently developed Dyadic Adjustment Scale (Spanier, 1976; see also Spanier and Filsinger, Chapter 8, this volume).

However, there exists a third level of interpretation, which assumes that what is actually reflected in an individual's response to any given item is an open question to be answered by empirical research. This empirical approach "involves a shift from viewing the item replies as samples of self-attitude (which they may be for the person completing the test) to perceiving them as behavioral signs (which they can become for the psychodiagnostician)" (Dahlstrom, 1969, p. 8). For example, a husband's self-report of too infrequent intercourse, while likely expressing an attitude of sexual dissatisfaction, may be found empirically to be associated with atypical expectations regarding sexual activity, higher-than-average current rates of intercourse, and such seemingly unrelated criteria as dissatisfaction with children. And while some of these correlates may not have been predicted on an intuitive or a priori basis, their significance from an interpretive standpoint is their systematic covariation with self-reports of too infrequent intercourse.

Interpretation of self-report measures at this third level requires extensive validational research relating individual test scores to relevant external criteria. Once such relationships have been delineated on an empirical basis, additional analyses are necessary to determine the range or "elevation" at which individual scores predict these criteria at "clinically significant" rates. This is what is meant by an *actuarial* approach to test interpretation—probabilistic statements equating particular test scores or signs to the likelihood of observing specific nontest behaviors or attitudes in the respondent. Recent validational efforts with the Marital Satisfaction Inventory have generated a substantial amount of data facilitating this third interpretive level. While additional work in this area remains to be done, it is anticipated that the commitment to an actuarial interpretive approach will eventually yield the clinical and research power and utility characterizing more sophisticated psychometric techniques.

Initial Construction and Validation

The initial construction and validation of the Marital Satisfaction Inventory have been described elsewhere (Snyder, 1979b). Briefly, the MSI was developed using a rational approach to scale construction in which test items are initially combined on an intuitive basis and scales are subsequently refined using any number of item-analytic procedures to increase internal consistency and maximize power of discrimination (Darlington & Bishop, 1966). A total of 440 true-false items were collected and divided into the 11 nonoverlapping scales described earlier, each counterbalanced for scoring in the true and false directions. An initial pilot study using 42 couples from the general population and 13 couples in the therapy confirmed the internal consistency of scales and showed most scales to be highly predictive of global criteria of marital distress, with MSI profiles significantly discriminating between couples in therapy and the matched control group.

A second study entailed a revision of the MSI and administration of the revised instrument to new samples of 111 couples from the general population and 30 couples in therapy. Revision of the MSI was based primarily on item analyses of the first study and emphasized reduction of nonpredictive variance among items. As a result of the revision process, the MSI was reduced by 36 percent in overall length, from 440 to 280 items, while retaining the 11 original scales. Scale content, abbreviations, and sample items[1] are as follows:

(1) *Conventionalization (CNV)*: This validity scale, derived from earlier work by Edmonds (1967), assesses individuals' tendencies to distort the appraisal of their marriage in a socially desirable direction. Items reflect denial of minor, commonly occurring marital difficulties and describe the relationship in an unrealistically positive manner. ("There is never a moment that I do not feel 'head over heels' in love with my mate." "My mate completely understands and sympathizes with my every mood.")

(2) *Global Distress (GDS)*: This global measure assesses individuals' overall dissatisfaction with the marriage. Items reflect general marital discontent, chronic disharmony, desire for marital therapy, and consideration of separation or divorce. ("My marriage has been disappointing in several ways." "The future of our marriage is too uncertain to make any serious plans.")

(3) *Affective Communication (AFC)*: This scale focuses on the process of verbal and nonverbal communication rather than its content and is the best single index of the affective quality of the couple's relationship. Items reflect individuals' dissatisfaction with the amount of affection and understanding expressed by their spouses. ("My spouse doesn't take me seriously enough sometimes." "I'm not sure my spouse has ever really loved me.")

(4) *Problem-Solving Communication (PSC)*: This second communication scale assesses the couple's general ineffectiveness in resolving differences. Items measure overt disharmony, rather than underlying feelings of detachment or alienation. ("Minor disagreements with my spouse often end up in big arguments." "My spouse and I seem able to go for days sometimes without settling our differences.")

(5) *Time Together (TTO)*: Items on this scale reflect a lack of common interests and dissatisfaction with the quality and quantity of leisure time together. ("My spouse and I don't have much in common to talk about." "About the only time I'm with my spouse is at meals and bedtime.")

(6) *Disagreement About Finances (FIN)*: This scale assesses marital discord regarding the management of family finances. ("My spouse buys too many things without consulting with me first." "It is often hard for my spouse and me to discuss our finances without getting upset with each other.")

(7) *Sexual Dissatisfaction (SEX)*: Items on this scale reflect dissatisfaction with both the frequency and quality of intercourse and other sexual activity. ("My spouse sometimes shows too little enthusiasm for sex." "My spouse has too little regard for my sexual satisfaction.")

(8) *Role Orientation (ROR)*: This scale reflects the adoption of a traditional versus nontraditional orientation toward marital and parental sex roles. Items are scored in the nontraditional direction. ("There should be more day-care centers and nursery schools so that more mothers of young children could work." "A wife should not have to give up her job when it interferes with her husband's career.")

(9) *Family History of Distress (FAM)*: Items reflect the individuals' unhappy childhoods and disharmony in the marriages of the respondents' parents and extended families. ("I was very anxious as a young person to get away from my family." "My parents didn't communicate with each other as well as they should have.")

(10) *Dissatisfaction with Children (DSC)*: This scale assesses parental dissatisfaction or disappointment with children. Items reflect the parent-child relationship rather than the relationship between the spouses. ("Having children has not brought all of the satisfactions I had hoped it would." "My children rarely seem to care how I feel about things.")

(11) *Conflict over Child Rearing (CCR)*: Items assess the extent of conflict between spouses regarding child-rearing practices and parental responsibilities. ("My spouse and I seem to argue more frequently since having children." "My spouse doesn't assume his (her) fair share of taking care of the children.")

Except for CNV and ROR, all scales are scored in the positive direction so that high scores reflect high levels of distress in that area.

Results from this second study generally revealed a sharp improvement in the psychometric characteristics and the predictive and discriminatory power of the revised MSI. Analyses of internal consistency produced alpha coefficients for individual scales ranging from .80 to .97. Test-retest analyses for 37 couples from the general population over a six-week interval yielded reliability coefficients ranging from .84 to .94. Additional results showed all scales except Role Orientation to be strongly related to global criteria of marital distress. Profile analyses confirmed the overall ability of the revised MSI to discriminate between couples in therapy and matched controls.

Subsequent studies using the method of contrasting groups have provided additional support for the discriminant validity of the MSI. Berg and Snyder (1981) showed that the MSI significantly discriminated 45 couples entering brief directive sex therapy at a sexual dysfunctions specialty clinic from 45 matched control couples entering conjoint marital therapy at a marital research clinic. In general, couples entering sex therapy had peak elevations on the MSI scale assessing sexual dissatisfaction (SEX) and had lower overall profiles reflecting less generalized distress than couples entering marital therapy. In a related study, Snyder and Berg (Note 1) determined that pretreatment MSI scores for 26 couples entering sex therapy significantly predicted posttreatment criteria of marital and sexual functioning. Results confirmed previous implications of marital distress as a moderator of couples' responses to sexually focused interventions and documented the importance of evaluating nonsexual aspects of a couple's relationship prior to implementing brief directive sex therapy.

Snyder, Fruchtman, and Scheer (Note 2) found the MSI to discriminate significantly between 65 residents of a wife-abuse shelter and a control group of 50 wives entering marital therapy but not experiencing physical abuse. In general, abused women tended to have significantly higher scale elevations and less variability on these scales than wives entering marital therapy. In studies focusing on individual MSI scales, Snyder and Gdowski (Note 3) determined that elevations on both Dissatisfaction with Children (DSC) and Conflict over Child Rearing (CCR) were strongly related to a broad range of child and adolescent psychopathology as assessed by the Personality Inventory for Children (Wirt, Lachar, Klinedinst, & Seat, 1977). Hill, Raley, and Snyder (1982) found that parents of psychiatrically hospitalized children had significantly higher elevations on Dissatisfaction with Children (DSC) than parents from a nonclinical comparison group, but that scores on this measure for the clinical group decreased significantly following group interventions with the parents emphasizing both educative and supportive functions.

Although these studies collectively confirmed the internal consistency, temporal stability, and discriminant validity of the Marital Satisfaction Inventory, additional studies were needed to delineate specific MSI scale-to-external criterion relationships in order to facilitate more precise interpretation of scale elevations on an actuarial basis. The following studies were designed to address this need.

Empirical Validation from an Actuarial Approach

Snyder, Wills, and Keiser (1981) conducted a clinical study extending the discriminant and convergent validity of the MSI within a homogeneous sample of maritally distressed couples. Fifty couples entering marital therapy underwent an extensive conjoint interview as part of a comprehensive diagnostic evaluation. Following this interview, each husband and wife was rated separately on a 61-item checklist of relevant clinical criteria in the following six areas: (1) general presentation of self and the marriage, (2) specific areas of spousal interaction, (3) familial and role dispositions, (4) psychiatric and physical distress, (5) interaction regarding children, and (6) prognosis. For each item, the clinician rated the presence or absence of that criterion and, if present, whether to a moderate or an extensive degree.

Subsequent correlational analyses were conducted to identify those specific clinical criteria that related to individual MSI scales in a systematic fashion. Overall, 95 significant scale correlates were identified, including 56 correlates applicable to both sexes and cross-validated in independent mixed samples, 32 correlates specific to wives, and 7 correlates interpretable for husbands alone. The pattern of scale-by-criterion correlations offered strong support for the basic interpretive intent of the MSI scales. Individual scales correlated predominantly with those criteria that one would predict on an intuitive basis while not correlating with criteria unrelated to their clinical purpose. Criteria not relating to the MSI tended to assess nonmarital issues, including psychiatric disturbance, physical health, and work satisfaction.

Additional analyses involved determining for each scale correlate the MSI scale range at which that criterion becomes "clinically meaningful" (Meehl & Rosen, 1955). For example, 57 percent of the subjects in the clinical validation study were rated from their interview as being dissatisfied with the frequency of sexual activity, with 26 percent being extremely dissatisfied in this regard (see Snyder, 1981, p. 43). However, for those individuals in the total validation sample obtaining a low score (below 50T) on the MSI scale of sexual dissatisfaction (SEX), the probability of dissatisfaction with the frequency of sexual activity dropped to 30 percent. For individuals with high scores on SEX (above 65T), dissatisfaction with the frequency of sexual activity increased to 96 percent, with 70 percent of individuals expressing extreme discontent in this area. Additional analyses evaluating the joint probability of criterion presence with increasing scale elevations were conducted for each of the 95 external criteria identified in the clinical validation study. Results of these actuarial analyses provide the basis of extensive interpretive guidelines presented in the *Manual for the Marital Satisfaction Inventory* (Snyder, 1981).

Scheer (1982) replicated these findings in a similar study of 50 couples from the general population. Use of a nonclinic sample was intended to document the MSI's ability to discriminate among minimal, mild, and moderate levels of distress with couples not presenting themselves for marital therapy. In addition, couples from the general population differ markedly from clinic couples in the degree to which they exhibit certain criterion behaviors and in their variability on particular MSI scales, thereby affording the potential identification of additional scale correlates not delineated in the clinical validation study. Fifty couples not in therapy were sampled from the general population using a modified peer-nomination procedure. Couples underwent an extensive conjoint interview and subsequently were rated on the same checklist employed in the earlier study, with additional items designed to discriminate between mild and moderate levels of distress. Scale-by-criterion correlational analyses were conducted in a manner identical to that of the previous investigation.

Again, results supported both the convergent and discriminant validity of the Marital Satisfaction Inventory within a nonclinical sample. Overall, a total of 269 significant scale correlates were identified, including 203 correlates applicable to both sexes and cross-validated in independent mixed samples, 23 correlates specific to wives, and 43 correlates interpretable for husbands alone. Both the overall pattern and relative magnitude of significant scale-by-criterion correlations were consistent with the interpretive intent of individual MSI scales. Moreover, results supported the usefulness of the MSI as a screening instrument with couples from the general population experiencing mild distress who may benefit from "preventive" counseling, or in various clinical situations where marital distress is not the chief presenting complaint or the focus of initial therapeutic interventions but nevertheless remains a salient clinical concern.

Clinical and Research Applications

Various clinical and research applications of the Marital Satisfaction Inventory are suggested by the discussion thus far. Although the advantages of the MSI include its ability to identify particular sources of marital discord and the relative extent of distress in these areas on an actuarial basis, there are occasions when a diagnosis of *general* marital dysfunction may have primary importance. For example, in a general adult outpatient or inpatient setting, the MSI provides a rapid cost-effective means of determining the extent to which marital distress functions as a possible precipitant of, or reaction to, a more general psychiatric disturbance. Similarly, the inventory offers an objective way to assess problems in the families of emotionally distressed children and adolescents. In various research designs, the primary objective of the investigator may be to identify global marital discord without the need to delineate specific sources of distress.

Snyder and Regts (1982) developed two broad-band factor scales of marital distress as supplements to existing MSI profile scales. These two new scales, labeled Disaffection (DAF) and Disharmony (DHR), were derived from factor analysis of the 127 items constituting the global distress (GDS) and affective triad (AFC, PSC, and TTO) profile scales. The relative brevity of these two factor scales, made up of a total of 44 items, facilitates their use on those occasions when situational constraints preclude administration of the entire inventory. Snyder and Regts demonstrated distinct distributions for the two scales across normative and clinical samples, suggesting that for purposes of discriminating among couples within the general population the more useful dimension is one of overt discord or perceived disharmony (DHR), whereas for couples in marital therapy the discriminating factor involves the extent of alienation or affective withdrawal (DAF). In addition, the new factor scales provide several advantages over previous marital measures in that: (1) they can be scored simultaneously with narrow-band profile scales of marital interaction already available on the MSI, including controls for a social desirability response set; (2) they have documented test-retest reliability; and (3) they relate to external criteria of marital functioning on an actuarial basis—a distinguishing feature essential to the sign approach to marital assessment.

Despite the availability of these factor scales for specific research and limited clinical purposes, more useful diagnostic and differentiating data will be generated by administration of the entire Marital Satisfaction Inventory. In using the MSI in clinical assessment for the planning of therapeutic interventions, attainment of the complete MSI profile facilitates evaluation of specific sources of relationship distress and their relative contribution to marital discord.

Jacobson and Margolin (1979) have reviewed several distinct contributions of relevant self-report measures to marital assessment. They note that inventories: (1) present a low-cost, low-effort method of gathering information; (2) permit sensitive information to be collected early; (3) allow couples to communicate information that spouses are eager to transmit; and (4) can be used as objective outcome criteria at termination and follow-up (Jacobson & Margolin, 1979, p. 78). They further suggest that appropriate self-report measures may establish the basis for therapeutic rapport and enable the therapist to plan and conduct interventions that are meaningful to the couple. In a review of dependent measures for clinical use, Nelson (1981) notes that outcome criteria should include measures sufficiently specific to detect changes in clients' behaviors as well as more global measures to assess changes in overall presenting complaints. Weiss and Margolin (1977, p. 596) have urged marital therapists to adopt multiple-area assessment both before and after treatment, in which data are systematically gathered "on untreated behaviors in areas germane to but not included in the marital intervention."

As a multidimensional measure that delineates specific sources of marital distress, the MSI facilitates formulation of therapeutic interventions. Throughout therapy and at termination it serves as an objective criterion for evaluating changes in spousal interaction. Its relative ease of administration and scoring make it an unobtrusive and efficient method of marital assessment. Finally, various validational studies and resulting interpretive guidelines promote the systematic, objective appraisal of distressed relationships on an empirical basis.

Administration and Scoring

Detailed instructions for administration, scoring, and interpretation of the Marital Satisfaction Inventory are provided in the test manual (Snyder, 1981; see Instrument Source Note, at chapter opening). Briefly, MSI testing materials include the administration booklet and answer sheet. The administration booklet contains 280 statements regarding various aspects of marriage and family life, which the individual indicates as being either "true" or "false" as applied to his or her own relationship. Individuals are instructed not to mark in the administration booklet, but rather to indicate their responses directly on the answer sheet. The answer sheet contains space for identification and other demographic information as well as a list of item numbers with circles labeled T (true) and F (false) corresponding to the numbered items in the administration booklet. Individuals without children stop after answering item 239, as indicated in the test booklet. In most cases where both husband and wife are completing the MSI, the spouses are instructed to answer the questions separately and without collaboration.

The MSI answer sheet may be entirely hand scored in five minutes using individual scoring keys (transparent templates) for each scale. The score for a given scale is calculated simply by counting the number of items for that scale answered in the scorable direction. A single MSI profile form is used for displaying test results for the wife, husband, or both individuals (see Figure 9.1 for an example). Plotting both spouses' profiles on the same form facilitates a comparison of the two. Raw scores on each scale are converted into linear T scores (with a mean of 50 and standard deviation of 10) to facilitate comparison of distress levels across different areas. The profile form provides two sets of norms to be used separately for husbands and wives.

Special answer sheets have been developed for use with optical scanning devices and computerized scoring. In addition, an automated interpretive program is being developed that will provide computerized interpretation of MSI profiles on both individual and conjoint bases. As with automated interpretive programs for other assessment devices, the MSI program is designed to take advantage of validational studies documenting scales' relationships to relevant clinical criteria, while presenting behavioral and emotional components associated with particular scale elevations or profile configurations as a series of hypotheses to be explored more fully by the individual clinician. It is anticipated that both the computerized scoring service and the automated interpretive program will be available to MSI users on a routine basis soon after publication of this volume.

Interpreting and Using Results

The amount of information generated by the MSI profile is substantial and increases considerably when two profiles are assessed interactively. In assessing a given individual profile one potentially has 55 pairwise comparisons between scales to consider—231 comparisons if evaluating two profiles conjointly. Additional three-way and higher-order comparisons among scales further increase both the potential depth and complexity of profile analysis. The six-step procedure for interpretation of MSI profiles presented below attempts to bring some order and manageability to the interpretive task. It incorporates to varying degrees interpretation of test data at the level of the individual test item, scores on individual scales, two- and three-way configurations among scales, and overall profile elevation and shape. It is offered as a general interpretive strategy, with the assumption that individual users will adapt and modify this procedure to meet both their clinical or research needs and theoretical preferences.

The first step in profile analysis involves determining the extent of conventionalization or defensiveness present in the individual's responses by noting the elevation of the Conventionalization (CNV) scale. Is the individual defensive and overly conventionalized in his or her description of the marriage or, at the other extreme, excessively critical of the relationship? One should evaluate the implications of this response style in light of the clinical setting and purposes for which the MSI is being used in this particular case. For example, a couple completing the MSI as part of a comprehensive evaluation of their psychiatrically distressed child or adolescent may be expected to exhibit more defensiveness regarding their marriage than the typical couple entering marital therapy. In instances of the latter, are the spouses' descriptions likely to provide a realistic portrayal of their marriage not only during the initial evaluation, but also throughout the course of therapy?

The second step involves evaluating the overall level of marital distress. This can be determined by inspecting both the Global Distress (GDS) scale on the left side of the profile as well as the general elevation of remaining clinical scales to the right. What are the individual's basic feelings toward the relationship and his or her spouse, independent of other stress in the couple's lives? Do specific conflicts occur within an otherwise positive relationship, or are they related to general disillusion? To what extent is the subjective experience of marital distress shared equally by both spouses? Are both individuals likely to seek change in the existing relationship, or is one member submitting to therapy primarily upon the demands of the other? Is the intensity or generalization of marital distress so great as to preclude the establishment of a collaborative set essential to conjoint therapy?

Following appraisal of global distress, it is useful to assess the general quality of communication and leisure interaction by evaluating relative elevations on scales constituting the affective triad (Affective Communication [AFC], Problem-Solving Communication [PSC], and Time Together [TTO]). Although as a general rule individuals entering marital therapy typically have moderate to high scores on these scales, differing levels of distress across these areas can facilitate useful distinctions between the extent of overt disagreement and underlying emotional withdrawal. For example, does the individual describe primary deficits in problem solving within a context of relative affection and intimacy, or is the relationship characterized by a more pervasive atmosphere of isolation and alienation—perhaps with little overt discord?

The fourth stage of the interpretive process entails inspecting the profile for specific sources of marital distress using the Disagreement About Finances (FIN), Sexual Dissatisfaction (SEX), Dissatisfaction with Children (DSC), Conflict over Child Rearing (CCR), and Role Orientation (ROR) scales. What are the specific sources of marital conflict? Is discord restricted to an isolated area, as in some cases of specific sexual dysfunctions or deficits in child-rearing skills, or has distress generalized across a broad spectrum of marital interaction? What are the relative sources of greatest dissatisfaction for spouses separately? Do spouses concur in their appraisals of the marital relationship or do they perceive the sources of their difficulties quite differently? One can examine the interrelationships among scales to gain additional understanding of the marital relationship. For example, differences in role orientation may serve as a major source of conflict over child rearing or dissatisfaction with children, particularly for women. Problems in the sexual relationship may or may not be seen to evolve from more fundamental deficits in affiliative processes.

The Family History of Distress (FAM) scale facilitates appraisal of the historical context of marital and family disruption. To what extent might current relationship difficulties be related to emotional stress or ineffective role models in the original families of the clients? What attitudes does the individual have that may be related to family therapy?

Finally, at any time during profile analysis the clinician may wish to examine individual responses to MSI items. Inspection of the answer sheet in conjunction with the administration booklet frequently allows the therapist to identify quite specific sources of marital contention or prompts an extended inquiry into an area that might otherwise have been overlooked. In addition, the user may check the similarity of the individual's profile to the group mean profiles of specific clinical groups. To the extent that an individual's profile matches the group profile of some particular criterion sample, the individual might be expected to display behavioral or cognitive characteristics typical of that group.

In interpreting the MSI profiles of two spouses conjointly, it is useful to complete each step for the two profiles separately and then to consider their interactive implications before proceeding to the next step. For the second through fourth steps, in particular, one might consider both the absolute differences in spouses' scores along each scale as well as their differences in rank-order of scale elevations. High scores on particular scales for one spouse frequently contribute to an understanding of elevations on different scales for the other.

Various approaches exist for incorporating marital assessment using the MSI into the overall therapeutic regimen. One approach is to have both spouses complete the MSI independently either immediately before or after the initial interview, to score both answer sheets during the week, and to provide the couple with a description and interpretation of results conjointly during the second session. While affording advantages of brief assessment and immediate feedback, this approach sometimes limits the amount of interview material incorporated into planning of therapeutic interventions and may raise pragmatic concerns regarding time constraints in the text administration. An alternative approach extends the assessment and interpretive phase across four sessions. During the initial session, the couple are interviewed conjointly to solicit general background information and problem identification. On the second visit, one individual (usually the more distressed of the two) is interviewed individually while his or her spouse completes the MSI; on the third visit these roles are reversed. During the fourth session extensive feedback is provided to the couple conjointly, incorporating both interview material and test results to formulate an individualized treatment plan collaboratively.

Depending on the length and progress of therapy, the MSI may be administered again at three to six months following the initial evaluation. This is frequently a helpful procedure for documenting changes that have occurred and establishing new directions for therapeutic endeavor. Readministration of the MSI at termination facilitates a review and integration of gains the couple have acquired. Residual areas of marital distress may be discussed in terms of constructive alternatives the couple may adopt on their own or as potential areas for further exploration during additional treatment at a subsequent time.

A Case Example

Sample MSI profiles and their clinical interpretation have been provided elsewhere. The text manual (Snyder, 1981) presents six case studies of couples evaluated prior to conjoint marital therapy. These couples vary both in the extent of their overall marital distress and in the nature of their presenting complaints. For each case, relevant background information, clinical findings, and profile interpretation using the six-step interpretive procedure outlined above are presented. Wills and Snyder (1982) provide detailed analyses of intake, midtreatment, and termination profiles for two couples seen in conjoint marital therapy. Discussion emphasizes the contribution of MSI test results to the design, implementation, and subsequent evaluation of therapeutic interventions. The following case represents a somewhat different situation with a couple already divorced but contemplating remarriage at the time of the initial evaluation.

Mr. and Mrs. P requested marital evaluation at an outpatient psychological clinic where their 16-year-old son was already receiving individual psychotherapy. The couple had married 20 years earlier but, after 10 years, began experiencing serious difficulties in their relationship and twice separated for periods of 6 months each. The couple had finally divorced 4 years earlier, but had been living together for the previous 18 months. They stated that they were now considering remarriage, but did not want to "rush into anything." Motives for remarriage included companionship, affection, and financial security for both individuals. Both

Mr. and Mrs. P remained ambivalent about remarriage, particularly the wife. In addition to the volatile nature of their relationship over the previous 10 years, current reservations included acute behavioral management problems with their 16-year-old son. Additional difficulties with an older and a younger son were also present to a lesser degree.

MSI profiles for Mr. and Mrs. P obtained over an initial three-week evaluation are shown in Figure 9.1. Both spouses described moderate to severe relationship distress across a broad range of areas, with Mr. P consistently reporting greater distress than his wife on all but two scales. Despite the generalization of moderate or greater distress across a variety of specific areas, both individuals obtained somewhat lower scores on Global Distress (GDS) than one would anticipate from their chaotic marital history, suggesting a reluctance to terminate their relationship or to perceive its shortcomings as outweighing potential benefits. Neither spouse made any attempt to distort the appraisal of their relationship in either a favorable or unfavorable direction, as their scores on Conventionalization (CNV) were quite typical of couples entering marital therapy.

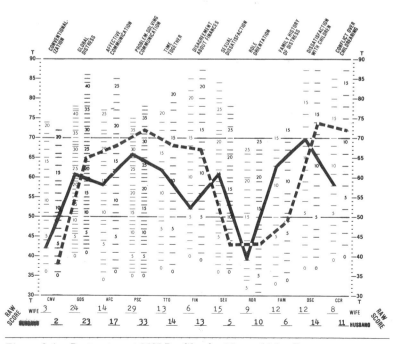

Figure 9.1   Pretreatment MSI Profiles for Mr. and Mrs. P

Mr. and Mrs. P obtained similar configurations on the affective triad, with both spouses reporting greater deficits in problem-solving communication (PSC) relative to difficulties in affective expression (AFC) and leisure time together (TTO). These results were consistent with reports from both individuals during the initial interview of a genuine caring for each other and a desire to spend more time together, but with severe stress in the affective relationship arising from a marked inability to resolve or contain even minor disagreements. Both spouses obtained higher scores on Dissatisfaction with Children (DSC) than on any other scale, indicating this area of family life as their most prominent source of marital discord. The markedly high score for Mr. P on Conflict over Child Rearing (CCR) reflected the extent to which difficulties with the children interfered with positive feelings toward his spouse, an experience not shared fully by his wife. The couple differed in their respective dissatisfaction in other areas as well. Mr. P reported extensive disagreement about finances (FIN), an area in which his wife described only moderate difficulties. In contrast, Mrs. P described significant dissatisfaction with the sexual relationship (SEX), whereas her husband apparently experienced very little discontent in this area.

Both Mr. and Mrs. P described highly traditional orientations toward marital and parental sex roles (ROR)—views consistent with their educational and cultural backgrounds. Both spouses reported distressed families of origin (FAM), with Mrs. P describing extensive disruption in her own family. It was likely that early family histories of both spouses contributed to this couple's current difficulties and hindered their successful resolution.

Additional information acquired from interviews further facilitated an understanding of Mr. and Mrs. P's marital difficulties. The couple had three sons by their marriage—ages 19, 16, and 12. The oldest son no longer lived at home but continued to be financially dependent on his parents. The 16-year-old son was in constant trouble with both school and legal authorities for repeated truancy, suspected drug abuse, and breaking and entering neighbors' homes for petty larceny. Mrs. P had two grown daughters from a previous marriage that had ended by her husband's death in a car accident. This first marriage had been a brief, severely distressed marriage that Mrs. P had entered as a teenager; she reported experiencing little grief when her first husband was killed. Both Mr. and Mrs. P reported that the first ten years of their marriage had been happy ones. However, as their children grew in number and in years, financial distress and child management difficulties became more acute. Mr. P assumed a second job to generate additional income, but was rarely home to provide his wife either emotional or physical support. As difficulties at home increased and his experiences there grew more aversive, Mr.

P withdrew from his family and began drinking heavily and gambling extensively. A destructive pattern quickly ensued whereby, in response to her husband's growing passivity and diminished parental effectiveness, Mrs. P became increasingly critical and berating, thereby exacerbating her husband's withdrawal.

As suggested by the MSI, family histories for both spouses contributed substantially to Mr. and Mrs. P's marital difficulties. Mrs. P's father died when she was five; her stepfather was an alcoholic who became physically abusive when intoxicated. In response to the extensive disruption in her family of origin, Mrs. P had learned to be as verbally aggressive as those around her. She had come to protect her own interests assertively, and had little tolerance for alcohol abuse of any degree. Mr. P had been adopted as a young child and knew little about his biological parents. His adoptive parents had a stable but unaffectionate marriage. Mr. P described his father as a quiet, uncaring man who yielded to his wife's authority in the home.

As with many couples entering marital therapy, administration of the MSI allowed Mr. and Mrs. P to indicate the specific sources of their discontent more precisely and to objectify what had previously been vague and diffuse feelings of anger and resentment. In this case, the relative similarity of spouses' profiles provided a common ground and collaborative set for establishing therapeutic priorities. In particular, MSI test results helped Mr. and Mrs. P to determine that, despite serious difficulties in specific areas of the marriage, each retained substantial desire to maintain and improve the relationship. MSI profiles led both spouses to identify child-rearing difficulties as a primary source of contention, and Mrs. P was helped to see how unresolved stress in this area strongly affected her husband's feelings toward her and toward the family in general. Test results also helped the couple to distinguish between deficits in problem solving and affective communication, and to identify improved means of resolving differences as an important therapeutic objective. In addition, test findings fostered discussion of both spouses' respective families and helped each to view current communication difficulties in part as an outgrowth of different sensitivities and contrasting approaches to the management of negative affect.

The couple were seen weekly in conjoint marital therapy over a six-month period. Initial interventions emphasized Mr. P's assuming greater responsibility for direction and discipline of the children at home; concurrently, Mrs. P was cautioned against undermining her husband's parental efforts by supplanting them with disciplinary measures of her own or blaming her husband when disciplinary efforts of both spouses failed to control the 16-year-old's rebellious behavior. Both spouses were taught more effective limit-setting techniques and were encouraged to resolve child-rearing differences during therapy sessions. This provided a means for addressing more general problem-solving deficits and rehearsing constructive alternatives in a highly structured and facilitative setting. In addition, specific interventions were employed to increase the amount of leisure time the couple spent together outside the home without the children. General results of these interventions included an increased intimacy in the marital relationship and a more appropriate and effective division of child-rearing responsibilities. The sexual relationship was not directly addressed since Mrs. P reported that distress in this area was a by-product of more general difficulties in the affective relationship. Similarly, Mr. P's gambling and excessive drinking abated almost immediately upon improving the home environment.

At termination, both spouses expressed renewed affection and commitment to their marriage, despite continuing difficulties with child rearing. MSI profiles obtained at termination reflected substantial reduction in distress for Mrs. P, in particular, across nearly all areas. Mr. P's profile reflected a marked increase in satisfaction with the quality and amount of leisure time spent with his wife, although he continued to experience considerable dissatisfaction with his children, with some generalization of this distress into the marital relationship.

Concluding Remarks

The Marital Satisfaction Inventory has been presented as an efficient, reliable, and empirically validated multidimensional measure of marital functioning for use in both clinical and research settings. A distinct advantage of this instrument is the inclusion of both broad- and narrow-band scales for assessing global distress and general response characteristics in addition to more specific sources of marital discord. Various studies have confirmed the MSI's ability to discriminate among clinically distressed groups, and to distinguish among various degrees and sources of relationship distress within relatively homogeneous samples of couples beginning marital therapy and nondistressed couples from the general population. The relative ease of test administration and scoring makes the MSI a cost-effective means of generating objective assessment data relevant to the initial planning and subsequent evaluation of therapeutic interventions. Explicit interpretive guidelines based on various validational studies facilitate the analysis and interpretation of test results on an actuarial basis.

The relatively atheoretical framework of the MSI facilitates its incorporation into various therapeutic contexts adopting different theoretical orientations. With its emphasis primarily on behavioral and attitudinal components of the marital relationship, the MSI neither assumes nor precludes higher-order inferences regarding either intrapsychic or broader systemic determinants of relationship distress. Nevertheless, marital therapists espousing a psychodynamic orientation will find that the MSI provides little information regarding unconscious conflicts or more general cognitive styles contributing to marital discord. Similarly, although various configurations on the MSI's affective triad, family, and child-related scales facilitate a tentative appraisal of the family's affective structure, a more systematic and complete evaluation of affective relationships incorporating self-reports from all family members might be obtained using an instrument such as the Inventory of Family Feelings (Lowman, 1980; see also Chapter 16, this volume). Nevertheless, clinicians adopting either psychodynamic or systems theory approaches may also desire some objective appraisal of specific marital complaints from spouses' perspectives and, as such, may find the MSI a useful tool in obtaining both initial and subsequent evaluations of the marital relationship. The MSI is likely to be most useful to therapists directing their interventions primarily at one or more of the specific areas of marital contention assessed by this measure. Such therapists may still find it useful to supplement the MSI with observational measures of the couple's communication or with additional behavioral techniques within areas designated by the MSI.

Expanded discussion of much of the material presented in this chapter can be found in other sources. Snyder (1979b) provides a more thorough review of historical developments in marital assessment from a self-report approach, and describes in greater detail the initial construction and validation of the MSI. Theoretical considerations underlying the psychometric approach to scale development are discussed at greater length in a general review of behavioral, communications, and psychometric approaches to marital assessment (Snyder, 1982). The MSI manual (Snyder, 1981) provides more detailed descriptions and interpretive guidelines for each of the 11 profile scales, and includes group mean profiles for various maritally distressed criterion samples. Actuarial analyses for specific scale criteria are provided for both distressed and nondistressed samples in Scheer (1982).

The delineation of interpretive criteria for the Marital Satisfaction Inventory should continue as users from a variety of professional and theoretical orientations incorporate the MSI into their research investigations and routine clinical practice. A validational study currently under way involves the attainment of a broad range of clinical correlates of the MSI from a national sample of couples entering marital therapy. Another study involves use of the MSI in identifying characteristics that predict couples' therapeutic responses to different treatment approaches. As I have noted elsewhere (Snyder, Note 4), once the field has developed comprehensive therapeutic models that address couples' unique strengths and vulnerabilities, clinicians can genuinely begin selectively to employ specific therapeutic techniques on an empirical basis having the maximum impact for any given couple. The objective assessment of couples' relationships from an actuarial approach should facilitate this therapeutic ideal.

Note

1. Sample items listed are all scored in the True direction. A complete listing of item composition for each scale, scoring direction, and response characteristics are provided in Snyder (1981).

Reference Notes

1. Snyder, D. K., & Berg, P. *Predicting couples' response to brief directive sex therapy.* Paper presented at the annual meeting of the American Psychological Association, Washington, D.C., August 1982.
2. Snyder, D. K., Fruchtman, L. A., & Scheer, N. S. *Relationships of physically abused women: Objective appraisal and clinical implications.* Unpublished manuscript, Wayne State University, 1981.
3. Snyder, D. K., & Gdowski, C. L. The relationship of marital dysfunction to psychiatric disturbance in children: An empirical analysis using the MSI and PIC. In D. K. Snyder (Chair), Gdowski, C. L., & Lowman, J. C., *New developments in the actuarial assessment of marital and family interaction.* Panel presented at the annual meeting of the National Council on Family Relations, Portland, October, 1980.
4. Snyder, D. K. Emerging trends in marital assessment: An overview. In K. D. O'Leary (Chair), *Assessing relevant dimensions for marital therapy.* Symposium presented at the annual meeting of the American Psychological Association, Washington, D.C., August, 1982.

References

Berg, P., & Snyder, D. K. Differential diagnosis of marital and sexual distress: A multidimensional approach. *Journal of Sex and Marital Therapy*, 1981, 7, 290-295.

Dahlstrom, W. G. Recurrent issues in the development of the MMPI. In J. N. Butcher (Ed.), *MMPI: Research developments and clinical applications.* New York: McGraw-Hill, 1969.

Darlington, R. B., & Bishop, C. H. Increasing test validity by considering interitem correlations. *Journal of Applied Psychology*, 1966, 50, 322-330.

Edmonds, V. H. Marital conventionalization: Definition and measurement. *Journal of Marriage and the Family*, 1967, 29, 681-688.

Hill, B. M., Raley, J. R., & Snyder, D. K. Group intervention with parents of psychiatrically hospitalized children. *Family Relations: Journal of Applied Family and Child Studies*, 1982, 31, 317-322.

Jacobson, N. S., & Margolin, G. *Marital therapy: Strategies based on social learning and behavior exchange principles.* New York: Brunner/Mazel, 1979.

Locke, H. J., & Wallace, K. M. Short marital adjustment prediction tests: Their reliability and validity. *Marriage and Family Living*, 1959, 21, 251-255.

Lowman, J. Measurement of family affective structure. *Journal of Personality Assessment*, 1980, 44, 130-141.

Meehl, P. E., & Rosen, A. Antecedent probability and the efficiency of psychometric signs, patterns, or cutting scores. *Psychological Bulletin*, 1955, *55*, 194-216.

Nelson, R. O. Realistic dependent measures for clinical use. *Journal of Consulting and Clinical Psychology*, 1981, *49*, 168-182.

Scheer, N. S. *Empirical validation of the Marital Satisfaction Inventory in a nonclinical sample.* Unpublished doctoral dissertation, Wayne State University, 1982.

Snyder, D. K. *Marital Satisfaction Inventory.* Los Angeles: Western Psychological Services, 1979. (a)

Snyder, D. K. Multidimensional assessment of marital satisfaction. *Journal of Marriage and the Family*, 1979, *41*, 8123-823. (b)

Snyder, D. K. *Manual for the Marital Satisfaction Inventory.* Los Angeles: Western Psychological Services, 1981.

Snyder, D. K. Advances in marital assessment: Behavioral, communications, and psychometric approaches. In C. D. Spielberger & J. N. Butcher (Eds.), *Advances in personality assessment* (Vol. 1). Hillsdale, NJ: Erlbaum, 1982.

Snyder, D. K., & Regts, J. M. Factor scales for assessing marital disharmony and disaffection. *Journal of Consulting and Clinical Psychology*, 1982, *50*, 736-743.

Snyder, D. K., Wills, R. M., & Keiser, T. W. Empirical validation of the Marital Satisfaction Inventory: An actuarial approach. *Journal of Consulting and Clinical Psychology*, 1981, *49*, 262-268.

Spanier, G. B. Measuring dyadic adjustment: New scales for assessing the quality of marriage and similar dyads. *Journal of Marriage and the Family*, 1976, *38*, 15-28.

Weiss, R. L., & Margolin, G. Assessment of marital conflict and accord. In A. R. Ciminero, K. S. Calhoun, & H. E. Adams (Eds.), *Handbook of behavioral assessment.* New York: John Wiley, 1977.

Wills, R. M., & Snyder, D. K. Clinical use of the Marital Satisfaction Inventory: Two case studies. *American Journal of Family Therapy*, 1982, *10*.

Wirt, R. D., Lachar, D., Klinedinst, J. K., & Seat, P. D. *Multidimensional description of child personality: A manual for the Personality Inventory for Children.* Los Angeles: Western Psychological Services, 1977.

CHAPTER 10

The Marital Communication Inventory

WALTER R. SCHUMM
Kansas State University

STEPHEN A. ANDERSON
University of Connecticut

CHARLES L. GRIFFIN
Kansas State University

One of the most frequently identified goals of treatment among marital and family therapists is improved *marital communication* (Beck, 1976; Gurman, 1975; Gurman & Kniskern, 1981; O'Leary & Turkewitz, 1978b).In spite of diverse theoretical viewpoints, marriage and family therapists have overwhelmingly recognized communication problems as having very damaging effects on the marital relationship (Geiss & O'Leary, 1981) and, accordingly, have cited communication goals as those most frequently guiding their therapeutic interventions (Sprenkle & Fisher, 1980). Those communication goals often include encouraging family members to listen attentively to each other, to express feelings openly and clearly, to speak for themselves, and to value the sender, the message, and themselves as important and worthwhile even in the midst of disagreement.

Many clinicians have adopted Bienvenu's (1978) Marital Communication Inventory (MCI) as a valid, unidimensional self-report measure of marital communication patterns and behaviors as perceived/reported by spouses themselves. Bienvenu (1978, p. 1) has indicated in his *Counselor's Guide* that the MCI was designed primarily to help counselors

Authors' Note: Preparation of this manuscript was supported in part by the Kansas Agricultural Experiment Station, Contribution 82-687-B. Appreciation is expressed to Family Life Publications, Inc., for their kindness in granting permission to reproduce items from the inventory here and in earlier studies.

Instrument Source Note: Forms of the MCI for husbands and wives are sold by Family Life Publications, Inc., P.O. Box 427, Saluda, North Carolina 28773.

assess the marital relationship, to be used clinically to assess and diagnose marital communication, and to serve as a research and teaching
tool in marriage and family life education. He has also suggested using
the MCI for marriage preparation (Bienvenu, 1970, p. 30), even though
later a separate premarital communication inventory became available
(Bienvenu, 1975). The MCI has been widely recognized in reviews of
therapy and program evaluation measures (Beck, 1976; Cromwell,
Olson, & Fournier, 1976; Montgomery, 1981; Murstein, 1978; O'Leary
& Turkewitz, 1978a; Powers & Hutchinson, 1979; Schiavi, Derogatis,
Kuriansky, O'Connor, & Sharpe, 1979; Straus & Brown, 1978). The MCI
has been used in no fewer than 21 professional articles and 43 doctoral
dissertations (involving at least 25 different universities) since 1971, the
majority of these reports concerning the evaluation of marital enrichment or therapy (Schumm, 1983; Schumm, Anderson, Race, Morris,
Griffin, McCutchen, & Benigas, 1983).

Psychometric Properties

Quite often the evidence provided by Bienvenu (1970) concerning the
split-half reliability (.93) of the MCI has been cited as sufficient justifica-
tion for the assumed high reliability and validity of the total inventory.
Recent reports have confirmed the high internal consistency reliability of
the MCI, with Cronbach's alphas of .94 (Costa, 1981; Peters, 1981) and
.95 (Schumm & Jackson, 1980; Schumm, Race, Morris, Anderson, Griffin, McCutchen, & Benigas, 1981). The test-retest reliability of the MCI
also appears to be quite high over five-week (r = .92; Schumm & Jackson, 1980) and two-month periods (r = .94; Rappaport, 1976). Likewise, one would initially get the impression from previous research that
the validity of the MCI was well established since the MCI has been found
to be substantially and significantly correlated with the Primary Communication Inventory (Collins, 1971, 1977; Guerney, 1977, p. 343) and a
host of marital adjustment tests (Collins, 1977; Dean & Lucas, 1978;
Elliott, 1982; Gruber, 1974; Jessee, 1978; Jessee & Guerney, 1981;
Joanning, 1982; Lee, 1979; Matteson, 1974; Murphy & Mendelson,
1973a; Rappaport, 1971; Ross, 1981), including Spanier's (1976; Spanier & Thompson, 1982; see also Spanier and Filsinger, Chapter 8, this
volume) Dyadic Adjustment Scale (Costa, 1981; Hansen, 1979;
Lumpkin, 1981). However, evidence is mixed regarding observational
measures of communication effectiveness, where some positive (Murphy
& Mendelson, 1973b), some negative (Campbell, 1974), and some non-
significant (Garland, 1981; Hansen, 1979; Joanning, 1982[1]; Schaffer,
1981) correlations have been found.

Even though Bienvenu (1970) clearly assumed that his inventory assessed different aspects of the communication process, few have questioned the dimensionality of the MCI, assuming that it was a unidimensional measure of communication, using only the total score for all 46 items as their dependent variable or outcome measure. Such an assumption appears to be quite reasonable given the high internal consistency reliability of the MCI; however, high internal consistency reliability—especially among instruments with many items—does not always guarantee unidimensionality (Green, Lissitz, & Mulaik, 1977). Surprised at the failure of the short 19-item version of the MCI (Bienvenu, 1970) to correlate substantially with a measure of perceptual accuracy (Fuhs, 1975), the senior author decided to check out the assumption of unidimensionality and undertook a further analysis of Fuhs's data, which indicated that the short MCI contained at least two dimensions, labeled *relationship hostility* and *self-disclosure* (Schumm, Figley, & Jurich, 1979). Essentially the same items appeared in subsequent studies based on the complete version of the MCI, as factors labeled *aversive disclosure* and *self-disclosure* (Schumm & Jackson, 1980) and *aversive communication* and *self-disclosure* (Schumm, Race, et al., 1981). In the latter two studies, factors labeled as *regard, empathy,* and *discussion* were also found; another factor labeled *conflict management* was found in the Schumm and Jackson (1980) study.

In a more recent analysis by Schumm, Anderson, et al. (1983), a canonical correlation of MCI scales with the regard, empathy, and congruence scales of an abbreviated version of the Barrett-Lennard (1962) Relationship Inventory (RI) suggested that a substantial component of the MCI was highly correlated with regard as measured by the RI. Regard in the RI appears to be much more akin to marital adjustment than to styles of marital communication per se. Moreover, in the Schumm, Race, et al. (1981) and Schumm and Jackson (1980) factor analyses of the total MCI, the primary factor in each analysis was the regard subscale rather than any of the scales more closely related to communication patterns. The possibility that the total MCI score represents marital adjustment more ✳ than marital communication, an idea suggested by both Murstein (1978) and Garland (1981), deserves further consideration.

However, even if the regard scale in the MCI is not a valid measure of communication (and that can be disputed if one interprets the items as indicators of communication positiveness rather than general supportiveness), the other scales are also moderately reliable (Table 10.1) and appear to have some degree of construct validity, as suggested by a study in which self-disclosure anxiety was found to be a function of self-esteem and aversive communication (Schumm, Figley, & Fuhs, 1981). Since the

TABLE 10.1   Reliabilities of Marital Communication Inventory Scales[a]

	Reliability Coefficients by Source[b]		
Scales	Schumm, Figley, and Fuhs, 1981	Schumm and Jackson, 1980	Schumm, Race, et al.,[c] 1981
Regard	–	.92 (.87)	–
	–	.97 (.92)	.88
Empathy	–	.75 (.45)	–
	–	.89 (.89)	.76
Self-disclosure (anxiety)	.68	.79 (.53)	–
	.75	.85 (.70)	.73
Discussion	–	.92 (.79)	–
	–	.95 (.56)	.86
Aversive Communication	.78	.78 (.81)	–
	.75	.83 (.87)	.75
Conflict Management	–	.76 (.64)	–
	–	.82 (.73)	–

a. Specific items included in the scales vary slightly between studies; use of items from the Schumm, Race, et al. (1981) study is recommended since that study involved the largest sample of subjects.
b. Data in the first row for each scale pertain to husbands; data in the second row pertain to wives. Blanks indicate either that items for that scale were not administered or, in the case of conflict management and the Schumm, Race, et al. (1981) study, that the scale was not determined to be a factor. Figures in parentheses for the Schumm and Jackson (1980) study are test-retest reliability r's.
c. Data from wives (N = 212) only.

MCI does appear to be correlated with marital social desirability as measured by an abbreviated version of Edmonds's (1967) Marital Conventionalization Scale (Schumm, Race, et al., 1981), it may be desirable to administer at least an abbreviated version of Edmonds's scale as a control variable (Schumm, Hess, Bollman, & Jurich, 1981).

It must be recognized that the face validity of the MCI items represents both a strength and a possible weakness for the inventory. The items vary widely in content, measuring perceptions of *spouse's* attitudes and behavior, as well as the *subject's* self-perceived attitudes and behaviors. The disadvantage is that the total MCI score is a composite of very different types of perceptions weighted in unequal numbers. The advantage is that an examination of individual items within the MCI can yield an extremely rich analysis of very precise attitudes or complaints of clients about their marital relationship. In that respect, the MCI is a much better tool for actual intervention with couples than it is a highly structured and refined research instrument. It should also be noted that the MCI does not attempt to assess interactional patterns (such as hidden agendas, interpersonal power struggles, and problems with balancing intimacy and individuality) that are often not within the immediate awareness of couples, yet are very important to therapists in diagnosing and understanding the underlying dynamics of marital difficulties.

Overview

Content and Availability

The Marital Communication Inventory consists of 46 questions[2] requiring the spouse to describe some aspect of marriage in terms of relative frequency in four categories (usually, sometimes, seldom, and never). There are separate forms for husbands and wives. Each contains an introductory page with directions and an explanation of the test, as well as a page on which the respondent can indicate age, spouse's age, length of present marriage, religious preference of self and spouse, main source of family income, and ages of male and female children. The 46 questions are on a single page with spaces beside each item for the respondent to check his or her answers. The questions themselves, apart from the standard form, are available in Schumm, Race, et al. (1981).

Administration

The administration of the inventory is extremely easy. The client needs only a pencil and the appropriate (male or female) form. The inventory requires only a seventh-grade reading level (Bienvenu, 1970, p. 27), for which it has received the praise of O'Leary and Turkewitz (1978a), and may be completed by the average client in less than 30 minutes. However, the small size of the print and the close proximity of the spaces for answers on some of the adjacent items may require enlargement when the inventory is given to persons with poor eyesight. Occasionally, a respondent will complain that there is no "always" category to balance the "never" category among the alternative responses. Our guess is that the "always" response was omitted to reduce social desirability effects that might induce some clients to report that ideal communication behaviors "always" occur in their marriage. However, the use of "never" for the negatively worded items might have the same relationship to social desirability. Family specialists who consider the imbalance of response categories to be a major difficulty may wish to contact Family Life Publications for permission to modify the categories accordingly (see Instrument Source Note, at chapter opening).

Scoring the inventory is also simple. Items 1, 2, 6, 8, 10, 12, 14, 15, 17, 18, 21, 23, 26, 28, 30, 32, 35, 37, 39, 40, 41, 43, and 46 are scored 3 points for "usually," 2 points for "sometimes," 1 point for "seldom," and no points for "never." The remaining items are scored 3 points for

TABLE 10.2   Means and Standard Deviation for MCI Scales
             in Several Experimental Groups

Study		Pretest	Posttest	Follow-Up
			Test[a]	
Collins, 1977	H:	85.13 (16.70)	93.92 (12.08)	—
	W:	86.96 (15.19)	97.50 (16.07)	—
Dode, 1979	H:	87.96 (15.67)	92.15 (15.62)	96.19 (14.16)
	W:	92.81 (17.56)	98.04 (16.58)	97.44 (12.80)
Schumm and	H:	93.4 (22.5)	98.6 (21.5)	—
Jackson, 1980	W:	92.9 (25.3)	96.3 (28.7)	—
Costa, 1981	All:	136.68 (—)	149.54 (—)	147.75 (—)
Jessee and	All:	86.03 (—)[b]	99.75 (—)	—
Guerney, 1981				
Joanning, 1982	H:	88.8 (17.5)	101.5 (10.3)	101.4 (8.9)
	W:	97.2 (14.8)	105.9 (10.6)	106.4 (9.9)

a. Mean scores are followed in parentheses by standard deviations when available
from the study.
b. Figures for the Relationship Enhancement treatment group only.

"never," 2 points for "seldom," 1 point for "sometimes," and no points
for "usually." Such a scoring procedure will yield total scores ranging
between zero and 138. Some researchers (for example, see Costa, 1981,
in Table 10.2) have used a scoring scheme with scores for each question
running from 1 to 4 rather than 0 to 3; the scoring makes no difference as
long as one is aware that most of the mean scores reported in the literature are based on the 0 to 3 scoring scheme. For example, Costa's (1981)
results would translate into scores of 93.55, 100.60, and 100.66 for pre-,
post-, and follow-up tests. In such situations, the standard deviations remain the same, regardless of how the items are scored.

Interpretation

Unfortunately, the MCI has not been standardized, even though Bienvenu (1978) has reported data from 410 couples given the MCI between
1971 and 1973 with mean scores ranging from 99.52 to 104.36 and standard deviations ranging between 15.80 and 18.83. For the 212 wives in
Schumm, Anderson, et al. (1983) the mean and standard deviation for
the MCI were 102.17 and 18.81, respectively. Lee (1979) also found
similar figures of 104.0 and 16.6 for his subjects. Examples of scores from
program evaluations are not uncommon, and a few are presented in Table 10.2. Typically, improvements in total MCI scores after treatment
range between 5 and 15 points.

While an average gain of 10 points in a sample of 25 clients would probably be *statistically* significant, the question of substantive improvement is probably more important to the clinician and client. Our thinking is that the increase must represent at least one-half point per item on the average in order to be of *substantive* significance, although allowance may be made for items in which no improvement is possible (as when the client scores 3 on an item at pretest). Accordingly, we would like to see an average increase of 23 points on the total inventory in order to have much confidence that our intervention substantially changed most clients' perceptions of their marital relationships and communication patterns. Lower levels of increase might suggest either that only a portion of clients experienced substantial change or that for many clients the intervention may have influenced only certain components of the total MCI.

Uses in Clinical Situations

Inasmuch as reviews indicate that communication training appears to be the *sine qua non* of effective marital therapy (Gurman & Kniskern, 1981; O'Leary & Turkewitz, 1978b), and that improvements in marital communication are important criteria for evaluating the effectiveness of marital therapy (Beck, 1976), the high degree of interest by clinicians in the MCI as a potential assessment tool becomes obvious. Indeed, the MCI scales feature characteristics of special appeal and importance to clinicians. They match many of the dimensions of change associated with the problems and outcomes seen by practitioners (Beck, 1976; Cromwell et al., 1976; Schiavi et al., 1979), are a reliable and valid as many other measures in common use, and are convenient to purchase, administer, and score, as well as flexible enough to be used with a wider variety of populations than many other instruments (Beck, 1976; Fisher, 1976; Cromwell et al., 1976).

Whether one's primary intention is to clarify treatment goals, isolate successful therapeutic strategies, or evaluate the effectiveness of one's program, the MCI, and especially its apparent subscales (Table 10.1), can provide a practical, inexpensive, and readily available assessment package. For example, the *self-disclosure* scale can give a quick assessment of spouses' comfort in expressing their feelings to one another. The *empathy* scale can provide a measure of each spouse's perceptions about the willingness or ability of the other to listen attentively. The *regard* scale can assess perceptions of the level of positive communication or general supportiveness received from one's partner and may be an indirect measure of how much a spouse feels his or her messages and personhood are valued by the other. The *aversive communication* scale can assess perceived levels of hostility and conflict associated with one's spouse, an indication of the extent to which aversive control strategies may be in operation in the marriage. The *discussion* scale can assess the spouses' perceived amount of shared couple communication. Along with one's clinical impressions, these scales can be used in part or in combination to suggest intervention strategies and treatment goals, and as critical outcome measures. A hypothetical example may help to illustrate more clearly and concretely these uses of the MCI.

Hypothetical Example

Mr. and Mrs. A appear for marital therapy with the presenting problem of wanting to improve their marriage. The two years of the couple's marriage have been stormy, with two separations lasting two and three months, respectively. On both occasions, Mrs. A had left Mr. A to return to her parents' home, feeling at the time that Mr. A did not really care about her. Despite energetic and frequent attempts to convince his wife of his sincerity, Mr. A remains frustrated by his wife's mistrust. Mr. A reports that early in the marriage he had been unattentive toward Mrs. A, spending many evenings out with his male friends. However, since their first separation he believes that he has been earnestly making himself available to his wife and is spending far less time with his friends. The couple's relationship is further stressed by the fact that Mrs. A's parents have never liked Mr. A and have repeatedly communicated their feelings to their daughter.

Initial therapy sessions are characterized by Mrs. A's blaming accusations, which are vague, yet emotional. Mr. A responds generally with apologetic assurances that he truly cares and wants their marriage to succeed. The therapist's initial clinical impression is that the couple is having difficulty establishing a couple identity. That impression is based on the fact that the couple have been together two years and yet have not been able to develop a sense of trust with one another. The instrusiveness of Mrs. A's parents also seems to be an obstacle to the couple's ability to develop a solid nucleus for their marriage.

The MCI subscales had been administered to the couple prior to their initial session as part of a routine battery of self-report measures. The results confirmed several of the therapist's initial clinical impressions and also provided additional information. Both Mr. and Mrs. A scored high on the regard scale, indicating that each perceived that the other showed affection, encouragement, respect, and support with some frequency. Similarly, each spouse perceived the other as willing to listen to what he or she has to say and as able to understand his or her feelings. Thus, when Mrs. A was asked some *specific* questions about her husband's communicative behaviors, she responded that he did show support, affection, and understanding, in spite of her more general and vague reports in the therapy sessions that he did not care for her. And despite Mrs. A's blaming, accusatory comments during the sessions, Mr. A likewise perceived his wife as frequently showing him support, affection, and understanding. The regard and empathy scales suggest that the couple do indeed have some relational strengths upon which to establish an enduring relationship, but that certain communicational deficits may be obstructing their relationship development.

The aversive communication scale revealed that Mrs. A did not perceive Mr. A as nagging, insulting, or irritating, but that, consistent with the therapist's clinical observation, Mr. A did perceive his wife in this manner. Both spouses' discussion scores revealed that both felt that mutual discussion occurred infrequently in their relationship. Intimate matters, pleasant events, or common interests were not frequently discussed together. Subsequent questioning during therapy about this lack of discussion revealed that much of the couple's time together was spent napping or watching television. Finally, Mrs. A's self-disclosure score revealed that she perceived herself as tending to keep her true feelings to herself and not feeling comfortable with letting her husband know how she felt when he had done things to annoy her. Thus, while Mrs. A was clearly able to criticize Mr. A in some situations, she was apparently quite reserved about directly expressing her specific feelings to him.

By using initial clinical impressions, results from the MCI subscales, and information derived from clarifying discrepancies between clinical impressions and scale scores, it is possible for the therapist to devise intervention strategies tailored to a couple's strengths and deficits. The fact that Mr. and Mrs. A each perceived the other as capable of regard and empathy could be reinforced whenever conflicts or feelings of mistrust might arise. Mrs. A could be encouraged to revise the aversive qualities in her communications and helped to be more self-disclosing of her underlying feelings. Her nagging about her husband's lack of interest could be reframed as her way of "making contact" with her husband and expressing her desire for greater intimacy. Finally, both spouses' low discussion scores suggest the value of giving the couple homework assignments that would increase the amount of time spent in interaction with one another. For example, the couple could be instructed to turn off the television for 30 minutes each evening at a predetermined time and discuss the day's events with each other.

The effectiveness of the interventions used with Mr. and Mrs. A and the couple's progress in eliminating their communicational deficits could be evaluated by administering the MCI subscales again following the completion of therapy. Changes in areas previously seen as problematic to the couple would be of particular interest. In the present case, these areas would include Mr. A's perceptions about his wife's aversive communication,

Mrs. A's own perceptions of her self-disclosure, and both spouses' perceptions about the amount of discussion shared between them.

Critique

In contrast to current usage, we would recommend using the subscales of the MCI rather than the MCI total score. For rigorous program evaluation, we think the total MCI score is of ambiguous interpretation and provides far less information than the subscales. However, while the subscales are useful for measuring certain concepts, there are single items in the MCI that deserve more attention. For example, item 22, "Does your husband say one thing but mean another?" would appear to tap congruence, an important dimension of the interpersonal relationship (Barrett-Lennard, 1962). We would hope that clinicians would supplement the MCI items with items from other scales, original or borrowed.

The MCI stands virtually alone in terms of the specificity of its items. Its closest competitor is the Primary Communication Inventory (PCI; Navran, 1967), which shares several virtually identical items (1, 4, 11, 15, 20, and 21) with the MCI (43, 37, 41, 38, 40, and 35). Other inventories may measure related concepts: For example, the RI measures regard, but the RI's regard items are cast at a much more global level (for instance, "My husband cares for me" [RI] versus "Does he pay you compliments and say nice things to you?" [MCI]). One measure, the Interpersonal Communication Skills Inventory (Boyd & Roach, 1977), is nearly as specific as the MCI, but requires a much more sophisticated vocabulary for the client, using terms such as "check out," "attend," "document," and "reflect back my meaning." Such terms are familiar to former participants in the Minnesota Couples Communication Program (Wampler, 1982), but are probably not easily understood, especially at pretest, by most clients. We think that other instruments, such as the Interpersonal Relationship Scale (Guerney, 1977, pp. 349-354) and the Family Life Questionnaire (Guerney, 1977, pp. 344-349), which have been correlated with the MCI (Collins, 1971; Costa, 1981; Ross, 1981), assess a more general impression of marital interaction rather than the specific frequencies of certain marital interactions assessed by some of the MCI items. Accordingly, the MCI scales may be more appropriate for studies in which self-report data are to be correlated with behavioral observations.

Fit into Assessment Packages

It is our opinion that the MCI subscales can be a very useful *part* of a larger assessment package that includes measures of marital satisfaction and global measures of some of the same concepts evaluated more concretely by the MCI, as well as some important specific concepts not tapped by the MCI scales. Some of the possible instruments might include those discussed elsewhere in this volume, the Barrett-Lennard Relationship Inventory or some of its abbreviated versions that have proven useful (Schumm, Bollman, & Jurich, 1981; Schumm, Jurich, & Bollman, 1980; Schumm, Benigas, et al., 1983), the Dyadic Trust Scale (Larzelere & Huston, 1980), or the PAIR instrument (Schaefer & Olson, 1981).

Of course, the validity of all these self-report measures rests, to a large extent, on the assumption that client perceptions are important even if they do not exactly correspond to reality as perceived by the therapist or others outside of the marital relationship. Further improvement can be made as well, we think, by adding scales associated with some of the communication patterns observed by Gottman (1979), such as mind reading, nonverbal negative communication, metacommunication, and cross complaining, with additional items added to assess more of the specific facets of a couple's problem-solving and conflict-resolution strategies.

(Appendix begins on page 202)

APPENDIX

FORM F

A MARITAL COMMUNICATION INVENTORY

Developed by

MILLARD J. BIENVENU, SR.

This inventory offers you an opportunity to make an objective study of the degree and patterns of communication in your marital relationship. It will enable you and your husband to better understand each other. We believe you will find it both interesting and helpful to make this study.

DIRECTIONS

1. Please answer each question as quickly as you can according to the way you feel *at the moment* (not the way you usually feel or felt last week).

2. Please do not consult your husband while completing this inventory. You may discuss it with him after both of you have completed it. Remember that counseling value of this form will be lost if you change *any* answer during or after this discussion.

3. Honest answers are *very* necessary. Please be as frank as possible. Your answers are confidential. Your name is not required.

4. Use the following examples for practice. Put a check ($\sqrt{}$) in *one* of the four blanks on the right to show how the question applies to your marriage.

	USUALLY	SOME-TIMES	SELDOM	NEVER
Does your husband like to talk about himself?				
Does he let you know when he is displeased?				

5. Read each question carefully. If you cannot give the exact answer to a question, answer the best you can but be sure to answer each one. There are no right or wrong answers. Answer according to the way *you* feel *at the present time.*

(continued)

APPENDIX Continued

	USUALLY	SOME-TIMES	SELDOM	NEVER
1 Do you and your husband discuss the manner in which the family income should be spent?				
2 Does he discuss his work and interests with you?				
3. Do you have a tendency to keep your feelings to yourself?				
4 Is your husband's tone of voice irritating?				
5. Does he have a tendency to say things which would be better left unsaid?				
6. Are your mealtime conversations easy and pleasant?				
7. Do you find it necessary to keep after him about his faults?				
8. Does he seem to understand your feelings?				
9. Does your husband nag you?				
10. Does he listen to what you have to say?				
11. Does it upset you to a great extent when your husband is angry with you?				
12. Does he pay you compliments and say nice things to you?				
13. Is it hard to understand your husband's feelings and attitudes?				
14 Is he affectionate toward you?				
15. Does he let you finish talking before responding to what you are saying?				
16. Do you and your husband remain silent for long periods when you are angry with one another?				
17. Does he allow you to pursue your own interests and activities even if they are different from his?				
18. Does he try to lift your spirits when you are depressed or discouraged?				
19. Do you fail to express disagreement with him because you are afraid he will get angry?				
20. Does your husband complain that you don't understand him?				
21. Do you let your husband know when you are displeased with him?				
22 Do you feel he says one thing but really means another?				
23. Do you help him understand you by saying how you think, feel, and believe?				
24. Do you and your husband find it hard to disagree with one another without losing your tempers?				

(continued)

APPENDIX Continued

		USUALLY	SOME-TIMES	SELDOM	NEVER
25.	Do the two of you argue a lot over money?	___	___	___	___
26.	When a problem arises that needs to be solved are you and your husband able to discuss it together (in a calm manner)?	___	___	___	___
27.	Do you find it difficult to express your true feelings to him?	___	___	___	___
28.	Does he offer you cooperation, encouragement and emotional support in your role (duties) as a wife?	___	___	___	___
29.	Does your husband insult you when angry with you?	___	___	___	___
30.	Do you and your husband engage in outside interests and activities together?	___	___	___	___
31.	Does your husband accuse you of not listening to what he says?	___	___	___	___
32.	Does he let you know that you are important to him?	___	___	___	___
33.	Is it easier to confide in a friend rather than your husband?	___	___	___	___
34.	Does he confide in others rather than in you?	___	___	___	___
35.	Do you feel that in most matters your husband knows what you are trying to say?	___	___	___	___
36.	Does he monopolize the conversation very much?	___	___	___	___
37.	Do you and your husband talk about things which are of interest to both of you?	___	___	___	___
38.	Does your husband sulk or pout very much?	___	___	___	___
39.	Do you discuss intimate matters with him?	___	___	___	___
40.	Do you and your husband discuss your personal problems with each other?	___	___	___	___
41.	Can your husband tell what kind of day you have had without asking?	___	___	___	___
42.	Does he fail to express feelings of respect and admiration for you?	___	___	___	___
43.	Do you and your husband talk over pleasant things that happen during the day?	___	___	___	___
44.	Do you hesitate to discuss certain things with your husband because you are afraid he might hurt your feelings?	___	___	___	___
45.	Do you pretend you are listening to him when actually you are not really listening?	___	___	___	___
46.	Do the two of you ever sit down just to talk things over?	___	___	___	___

(continued)

APPENDIX Continued

PLEASE MAKE SURE YOU HAVE ANSWERED ALL THE QUESTIONS

THE FOLLOWING WILL HELP YOUR COUNSELOR BETTER UNDER-
STAND THE INFORMATION YOU HAVE GIVEN HIM:

Your Age_____ Husband's Age_____ Length of Present Marriage_____

Your Religious Preference_____ Your Husband's Preference_____

Have You Ever Been Married, Divorced, or Widowed Before?   Yes   No
                                                          (Circle One)

If Yes, Please Explain _____

Your Education_____Occupation_____

Husband's Education_____His Occupation_____

THE MAIN SOURCE OF FAMILY INCOME IS: _____

(Choose one of the following)

    a) Savings and Investments.

    b) Profits and Fees from a Business or Profession.

    c) Salary, Commissions or Regular Income Paid on a Monthly or Semi-
       Monthly Basis.

    d) Wages; Hourly Wages, Piece Work, or Weekly Pay Check.

    e) Odd Jobs or Seasonal Work.

    f) Social Security, Welfare or Unemployment Insurance.

YOUR CHILDREN: Ages of Boys_____ Ages of Girls_____

THE MAIN FAULT OF AMERICAN HUSBANDS IS _____

Notes

1. Joanning (1982) found positive correlations at post-test and follow-up between the MCI and an observational measure of marital communication; however, the correlations, though large, were not statistically significant, given his small sample size.

2. The MCI has sometimes been identified as a 48-item inventory (e.g., Joanning, 1982). The additional two items are part of a set of instructions explaining to the respondent how to complete the inventory and are usually not scored with the other 46 items since the two are essentially practice items only.

3. Item 41, "Can your husband/wife tell what kind of day you have had without asking?" is somewhat controversial in its coding in that some therapists feel that one should *not* expect others to be able to read our minds without at least some verbal communication to confirm interpretations and perceptions derived from nonverbal cues.

References

Barrett-Lennard, G. T. Dimensions of therapist response as causal factors in therapeutic change. *Psychological Monographs*, 1962, 76(43, Whole No. 562).

Beaver, W. A. Conjoint and pseudo-disjunctive treatment in communication skills for relationship improvement with marital couples (Doctoral dissertation, Marquette University, 1978), *Dissertation Abstracts International*, 1978, 39, 3361A.

Beck, D. F. Research findings on the outcomes of marital counseling. In D. H. Olson (Ed.), *Treating relationships*. Lake Mills, IA: Graphic, 1976.

Bienvenu, M. J., Sr. Measurement of marital communication. *Family Coordinator*, 1970, 19, 26-31.

Bienvenu, M. J., Sr. A measurement of premarital counseling. *Family Coordinator*, 1975, 24, 65-68.

Bienvenu, M. J., Sr. *A counselor's guide to accompany a Marital Communication Inventory*. Saluda, NC: Family Life, 1978.

Boyd, L. A., & Roach, A. J. Interpersonal communication skills differentiating more satisfying from less satisfying marital relationships. *Journal of Counseling Psychology*, 1977, 24, 540-542.

Campbell, E. E. The effects of the Couple Communication training on married couples in the child rearing years: a field experiment (Doctoral dissertation, Arizona State University, 1974). *Dissertation Abstracts International*, 1974, 35, 1942A-1943A.

Collins, J. D. *The effects of the conjugal relationship modification method on marital communication and adjustment*. Unpublished doctoral dissertation, Pennsylvania State University, 1971.

Collins, J. D. Experimental evaluation of a six-month conjugal therapy and relationship enhancement program. In B. G. Guerney, Jr. (Ed.), *Relationship enhancement*. San Francisco: Jossey-Bass, 1977.

Costa, L. A. The effects of a Marriage Encounter program on marital communication, dyadic adjustment, and the quality of the interpersonal relationship (Doctoral dissertation, University of Colorado—Boulder, 1981). *Dissertation Abstracts* International, 1981, 42, 1850A.

Cromwell, R. E., Olson, D. H., & Fournier, D. G. Diagnosis and evaluation in marital and family counseling. In D. H. Olson (Ed.), *Treating relationships*. Lake Mills, IA: Graphic, 1976.

Dean, D. G., & Lucas, W. L. Whose marital adjustment—hers, his, or theirs? *Psychological Reports*, 1978, 43, 978.

Dode, I. L. An evaluation of the Minnesota Couples Communication Program: A structured educational enrichment experience (Doctoral dissertation, Arizona State University, 1979). *Dissertation Abstracts International*, 1979, 40, 1211A.

Edmonds, V. H. Marital conventionalization: Definition and measurement. *Journal of Marriage and the Family*, 1967, 29, 681-688.

Elliott, M. W. Communication and empathy in marital adjustment. *Home Economics Research Journal*, 1982, 11(1), 77-88.

Fisher, L. Dimensions of family assessment: A critical review. *Journal of Marriage and Family Counseling*, 1976, *2*, 367-382.

Fuhs, N. N. *Marital communication as a predictor of marital perceptual accuracy*. Unpublished master's thesis, Purdue University, 1975.

Garland, D. R. Training married couples in listening skills: Effects on behavior, preceptual accuracy, and marital adjustment. *Family Relations*, 1981, *30*, 297-308.

Geiss, S. K., & O'Leary, D. Therapist ratings of frequency and severity of marital problems: Implications for research. *Journal of Marital and Family Therapy*, 1981, *7*, 515-520.

Gottman, J. M. *Marital interaction: Experimental investigations*. New York: Academic, 1979.

Green, S. B., Lissitz, R. W., & Mulaik, S. A. Limitations of coefficient alpha as an index of test unidimensionality. *Educational and Psychological Measurement*, 1977, *37*, 827-838.

Gruber, G. R. The relationship of self-concept and adjustment to gains achieved in the Conjugal Relationship Enhancement Program (Doctoral dissertation, Pennsylvania State University, 1973), *Dissertation Abstracts International*, 1974, *34*, 6770A-6771A.

Guerney, B. G., Jr. (Ed.), *Relationship enhancement*. San Francisco: Jossey-Bass, 1977.

Gurman, A. S. Couples facilitative communication skill as a dimension of marital therapy outcome. *Journal of Marriage and Family Counseling*, 1975, *1*, 163-174.

Gurman, A. S., & Kniskern, D. P. Family therapy outcome research: Knowns and unknowns. In A. S. Gurman & D. P. Kniskern (Eds.), *Handbook of family therapy*. New York: Brunner/Mazel, 1981.

Hansen, D. A. Sex-role stereotyping, marital adjustment, and marital communication (Doctoral dissertation, University of Utah, 1979). *Dissertation Abstracts International*, 1979, *40*, 1894B.

Jessee, R. E. A comparison of gestalt relationship awareness facilitation and conjugal relationship enhancement programs (Doctoral dissertation, Pennsylvania State University, 1978). *Dissertation Abstracts International*, 1978, *39*, 649B.

Jessee, R. E., & Guerney, B. G., Jr. A comparison of gestalt and relationship enhancement treatments with married couples. *American Journal of Family Therapy*, 1981, *9*(3), 31-41.

Joanning, H. The long-term effects of the Couple Communication Program. *Journal of Marital and Family Therapy*, 1982, *8*, 463-468.

Larzelere, R. E., & Huston, T. L. The dyadic trust scale: Toward understanding interpersonal trust in close relationships. *Journal of Marriage and the Family*, 1980, *42*, 595-604.

Lee, P. A. The relationship between marital communication and marital adjustment over the family life cycle. (Doctoral dissertation, Florida State University, 1979). *Dissertation Abstracts International*, 1979, *40*, 6998A.

Lumpkin, W. C. The relationships of marital communication and marital adjustment with self-esteem and self-actualization (Doctoral dissertation, University of New Orleans, 1981). *Dissertation Abstracts International*, 1981, *42*, 2883A.

Matteson, R. Adolescent self-esteem, family communication, and marital satisfaction. *Journal of Psychology*, 1974, *86*, 35-47.

Montgomery, B. M. The form and function of quality communication in marriage. *Family Relations*, 1981, *30*, 21-30.

Murphy, D. C., & Mendelson, L. A. Communication and adjustment in marriage: Investigating the relationship. *Family Process*, 1973, *12*, 317-326. (a)

Murphy, D. C., & Mendelson, L. A. Use of the observational method in the study of live marital communication. *Journal of Marriage and the Family*, 1973, *35*, 356-363. (b)

Murstein, B. I. Marital Communication Inventory. In O. K. Buros (Ed.), *The eighth mental measurements yearbook* (Vol. 1). Highland Park, NJ: Gryphon, 1978.

Navran, L. Communication and adjustment in marriage. *Family Process*, 1967, *6*, 173-184.

O'Leary, K. D., & Turkewitz, H. Methodological errors in marital and child treatment research. *Journal of Consulting and Clinical Psychology*, 1978, *46*, 747-758. (a)

O'Leary, K. D., & Turkewitz, H. Marital therapy from a behavioral perspective. In T. J. Paolino & B. S. McCrady (Eds.), *Marriage and marital therapy*. New York: Brunner/Mazel, 1978. (b)

Peters, M. L. Short-range and long-range effects of a marriage enrichment as an adult learning project using a marriage workbook (Doctoral dissertation, Auburn University, 1981). *Dissertation Abstracts International*, 1981, *42*, 2442A.

Powers, W. G., & Hutchinson, K. The measurement of communication apprehension in the marriage relationship. *Journal of Marriage and the Family,* 1979, *41,* 89-95.

Rappaport, A. F. *Effects of an intensive conjugal relationship modification program.* Unpublished doctoral dissertation, Pennsylvania State University, 1971.

Rappaport, A. F. Conjugal Relationship Enhancement Program. In D. H. Olson (Ed.), *Treating relationships.* Lake Mills, IA: Graphic, 1976.

Ross, R. E. Comparative effectiveness of relationship enhancement and therapist-preferred therapy on marital adjustment (Doctoral dissertation, Pennsylvania State University, 1981). *Dissertation Abstracts International,* 1981, *42,* 4610A.

Schaefer, M. T., & Olson, D. H. Assessing intimacy: The PAIR inventory. *Journal of Marital and Family Therapy,* 1981, *7,* 47-60.

Schaffer, M. An evaluation of the Minnesota Couple Communication Program upon communication of married couples (Doctoral dissertation, University of Southern Mississippi). *Dissertation Abstracts International,* 1981, *41,* 4643B.

Schiavi, R. C., Derogatis, L. R., Kuriansky, J., O'Connor, D., & Sharpe, L. The assessment of sexual function and marital interaction. *Journal of Sex and Marital Therapy,* 1979, *5,* 169-224.

Schumm, W. R., Theory and measurement in marital communication training programs. *Family Relations.* 1983, *32,* 3-11.

Schumm, W. R., Anderson, S. A., Race, G. S., Morris, J. E., Griffin, C. L., McCutchen, M. B., & Benigas, J. E., Construct validity of the Marital Communication Inventory. *Journal of Sex and Marital Therapy,* 1983, *9,* 153-162.

Schumm, W. R., Benigas, J. E., McCutchen, M. B., Griffin, C. L., Anderson, S. A., Morris, J. E., & Race, G. S. Measuring empathy, regard, and congruence in the marital relationship. *Journal of Social Psychology,* 1983, *119,* 141-142.

Schumm, W. R., Bollman, S. R., & Jurich, A. P. The dimensionality of an abbreviated version of the Relationship Inventory: An urban replication with married couples. *Psychological Reports,* 1981, *48,* 51-56.

Schumm, W. R., Figley, C. R., & Fuhs, N. N. Predicting self-disclosure anxiety in the marital relationship. *Journal of Psychology,* 1981, *107,* 273-279.

Schumm, W. R., Figley, C. R., & Jurich, A. P. The dimensionality of the Marital Communication Inventory: A preliminary factor analytic study. *Psychological Reports,* 1979, *45,* 123-128.

Schumm, W. R., Hess, J. L., Bollman, S. R., & Jurich, A. P. Marital conventionalization revisited. *Psychological Reports,* 1981, *49,* 607-615.

Schumm, W. R., & Jackson, R. W. Marital communication or marital adjustment? A brief report on the Marital Communication Inventory. *Psychological Reports,* 1980, *46,* 441-442.

Schumm, W. R., Jurich, A. P., & Bollman, S. R. Dimensionality of an abbreviated Relationship Inventory for couples. *Journal of Psychology,* 1980, *105,* 225-230.

Schumm, W. R., Race, G. S., Morris, J. E., Anderson, S. A., Griffin, C. L., McCutchen, M. B., & Benigas, J. E. Dimensionality of the Marital Communication Inventory and marital conventionalization: A third report. *Psychological Reports,* 1981, *48,* 163-171.

Selby, J. E. Marital adjustment and marital communication of doctoral students and their wives (Doctoral dissertation, University of Missouri—Columbia, 1972). *Dissertation Abstracts International,* 1973, *33,* 5502A-5503A.

Spanier, G. B. Measuring dyadic adjustment: New scales for assessing the quality of marriage and similar dyads. *Journal of Marriage and the Family,* 1976, *38,* 15-38.

Spanier, G. B., & Thompson, L. A confirmatory analysis of the Dyadic Adjustment Scale. *Journal of Marriage and the Family,* 1982, *44,* 731-738.

Sprenkle, D. H., & Fisher, B. L. An empirical assessment of the goals of family therapy. *Journal of Marital and Family Therapy,* 1980, *6,* 131-139.

Straus, M. A., & Brown, B. W. *Family measurement techniques.* (rev. ed.). Minneapolis: University of Minnesota Press, 1978.

Wampler, K. S. The effectiveness of the Minnesota Couple Communication Program: A review of research. *Journal of Marital and Family Therapy,* 1982, *8,* 345-355.

CHAPTER 11

The Marital Agendas Protocol

CLIFFORD I. NOTARIUS
NELLY A. VANZETTI
Catholic University of America

The Marital Agendas Protocol (MAP) is a five-item questionnaire designed to aid marital therapists in evaluating client couples' presenting problems and in assessing the effectiveness of therapy. A completed MAP provides the clinician with: (1) the areas of marital conflict that each spouse feels are problematic in the relationship; (2) the spouses' perceptions about their partners' views of these problem areas; (3) spouses' views about who is primarily responsible for unresolved disagreements in each identified problem area; (4) each spouse's expectancies for being able to resolve disagreements in each problem area; and (5) each spouse's beliefs about how important it is to resolve disagreements in the surveyed problem areas.

An important assumption underlying MAP is that problem or conflict resolution is a major determinant of marital satisfaction. This assumption is supported by several interactional studies of distressed and nondistressed couples (for example, Gottman, Markman, & Notarius, 1977; Margolin & Wampold, 1981) and by the emphasis on effective problem solving in varied approaches to marital therapy (for example, Ables & Brandsma, 1977; Jacobson & Margolin, 1979; Nadelson, 1978). In addition, traditional measures of marital adjustment have typically included questions assessing the couple's level of agreement and disagreement on potential relationship problem areas (for example, see Locke & Wallace, 1959; Spanier, 1976).

The following section describes the development and theoretical rationale of MAP in greater detail. Subsequent sections will present empirical support for MAP, discuss research findings using the instrument, and provide suggestions for MAP's use in marital therapy. A case example will be presented to help illustrate MAP's clinical utility. Finally, a commen-

---

Instrument Source Note: A copy of MAP is available from Clifford I. Notarius, Department of Psychology, Catholic University of America, Washington, D.C. 20064.

tary section will discuss MAP's relationship to other available assessment devices for marital and family therapists.

Development of the Marital Agendas Protocol

As behavioral marital therapy approaches encountered couples who were resistent to change, behavioral therapy programs began to incorporate treatment strategies that extended well beyond traditional behavioral approaches (Weiss, 1980). The strategic therapies (for example, Haley, 1976; Watzlawick, Weakland, & Fisch, 1974; Madanes, 1981) have had a large impact on the evolution of behavioral marital treatments and have led to integrative models combining behavioral and systems therapy strategies (see Birchler & Spinks, 1980; Weiss, 1980). A second influence helping to reshape behavioral marital therapy has been the application of cognitive variables and processes to improve our understanding of intimate conflict (Doherty, 1981a, 1981b) and to increase the range of strategies available in behavioral marital therapy (Baucom, Note 1). The application of cognitive processes to marriage and marital therapy occurred against the backdrop of exciting developments within cognitive behavior therapy. Among the most notable of these developments was Bandura's (1977) self-efficacy theory, which was proposed as a unifying theory of behavior change. Out of this attention to cognitive processes, and particularly self-efficacy theory, MAP developed.

Bandura defines an efficacy expectancy as a person's belief about his or her ability to perform a given behavior. In the scheme of person → behavior → outcome, efficacy expectancies are the beliefs a person holds about his or her ability to behave in a specific way. These can be distinguished from outcome expectancies, which refer to the person's beliefs about the payoffs expected from performance of the behavior. Efficacy theory hypothesizes that psychotherapy will be effective to the extent that therapeutic interventions enhance a person's efficacy expectancies. According to the model, efficacy is enhanced more by enactive therapeutic strategies, such as participant modeling, than by verbal persuasion techniques, such as insight therapy (Bandura, 1977). Bandura (1982) has summarized a thorough research program on efficacy expectancies, persuasively demonstrating that self-efficacy expectancies: (1) are potent predictors of behavior—efficacy expectancies appear to be better predictors of future behavior than is the past behavior in the same situation; (2) determine how much effort people will expend attempting to overcome an obstacle; (3) influence the phenomenological impact of negative outcomes; and (4) relate to the level of emotional arousal experienced in dealing with a stressor. Clearly, each of these characteristics is relevant, if not essential, to successful therapeutic outcomes. The potency of efficacy expectancies to predict behavior (item 2, above) is a highly desirable characteristic of the construct and it makes its measurement a useful index of a client's mastery of new behaviors and hence a useful index of therapeutic progress. Further, it provides a clear, concise index of the client's tolerance for failure and persistence in the face of obstacles (items 1 and 3), thus giving the clinician valuable insight into how the client will deal with the therapeutic process.

Given the demonstrated utility of the efficacy construct for understanding mastery behavior in individuals and the increasing attention to the operation of cognitive processes in marriage (see Doherty, 1981a, 1981b), we began to develop MAP as an assessment tool to measure efficacy expectancies in marriage. As a first step it was necessary to translate the individually oriented construct of self-efficacy into a measurable operation focused on the functioning of the marital relationship (for example, "What are *we* capable of doing about x in situation y?"). Since effective problem solving is an essential component of marital satisfaction, we focused the assessment of marital or relational efficacy on spouses' beliefs about their ability to resolve problem discussions. Doherty (1981b, p. 35) offered a similar conceptualization of the efficacy construct applied to marriage, defining efficacy as the "individual's expectation for the couple or family as a group to engage in effective problem-solving activity." Extrapolating from Bandura's model, problem solving in relationships where partners have high relational efficacy is expected to be characterized by persistence, greater resistance to frustration, and less disappointment in the face of conflict or failure. Combining these characteristics with the power of efficacy expectancies to predict behavior, the couple with high relational efficacy is expected to be more successful at conflict resolution and therefore to be more satisfied with the marriage than the couple with low relational efficacy.

Operationalizing Relational Efficacy

To provide a context for understanding the relational efficacy construct, we embedded an operationalization of efficacy within a broader assessment measure tapping spouses' perceptions of relationship problems. For this purpose we used the problem inventory (Gottman, Notarius, Gonso, & Markman, 1976) format, which asks spouses to consider separately ten common marital agendas: money, communication, in-laws, sex, religion, recreation, friends, alcohol and drugs, children, and jealousy. This format requires spouses to address their beliefs about relational efficacy within each agenda area in keeping with Bandura's proposition that efficacy expectancies are situationally specific and cannot be generalized. Thus relational efficacy is assessed by asking spouses to consider each agenda area and to indicate: "If ten disagreements arose in this area, how many would you be capable of resolving to your mutual satisfaction?" Along with the measure of relational efficacy, spouses are also asked to rate the perceived severity of each agenda area (MAP question 1) and to rate how they believe their partners will respond to this question (MAP question 2). These two ratings, of self and of partner, permit analysis of discrepancies between the spouses' views on problems in the marriage—a useful index since other discrepancy scores have been found to be related to marital satisfaction (for example, see Murstein & Beck, 1972). Additional MAP questions ask spouses to rate how important each agenda area is to their current feelings about their relationship[1] and to indicate whom they feel is primarily responsible for unresolved disagreements in each area: self, spouse, or both. This latter question taps the spouses' attributions of blame for the problems in the marriage; specifically, it addresses attributions of blame for failures in dealing with problems. We wondered whether distressed and nondistressed couples would differ in these attributions and, if so, how. Recent papers by Bernal and Baker (1979) and Doherty (1981a, 1981b) would suggest that distressed couples would make more individual attributions of blame (blaming spouse or self) than nondistressed couples, who would make more dyadic attributions (both are responsible). Much of the literature on marital and family therapy also emphasizes helping couples or families view problems as relational and not individual.

Empirical Support for MAP

In this section we review some basic evidence pertaining to the validity and utility of MAP. In the later discussion of clinical application, we will present some additional findings that may help the marital therapist understand and intervene in the distressed marriage.

Two studies were conducted to initiate evaluation of the validity of MAP (Notarius & Vanzetti, Note 2).[2] In both studies, volunteer couples were recruited to complete questionnaire packets consisting of MAP, the Locke-Wallace Marital Adjustment Test (MAT; Locke & Wallace, 1959), and either the Marlowe-Crowne Index of Social Desirability (Crowne & Marlowe, 1960) or the Primary Communication Inventory (Navran, 1967) and the Spouse Observation Checklist (Wills, Weiss, & Patterson, 1974).

Correlational analyses were completed to assess criterion validity for MAP; specifically, did MAP discriminate between distressed and nondistressed couples? Spouses' relational efficacy ratings for each of the ten marital agendas were summed to yield an overall measure of relational efficacy for each spouse. This sum was then correlated with the spouses' MAT scores. In both studies, with independent samples of 51 and 36 couples, respectively, the analysis revealed that relational efficacy was significantly related to marital satisfaction (the average correlation between marital satisfaction and relational efficacy was .57) Further, relational efficacy was negatively related to spouse's perceptions of displeasing behaviors emitted by their partners, both for husbands ($r = -.43$) and wives ($r = -.36$). Wives' relational efficacy was also positively related to their perceptions of pleasing behaviors from their husbands ($r = .32$). Finally, relational efficacy was related to a self-report measure of communication for wives ($r = .41$) but not for husbands.[3]

To assess the influence of social desirability on responses to relational efficacy and to the MAT, scores on these questionnaires were correlated with the Marlowe-Crowne. Neither husbands' nor wives' relational efficacy was correlated with this measure. Husbands' scores on the MAT showed a slight tendency to be influenced by a social desirability set ($r = .23$), while wives' MAT scores were not correlated with the Marlowe-Crowne.

As another index of criterion validity, the respondents' ratings of severity of the ten problem areas were summed to yield a problem intensity score. This intensity score showed a strong relationship with marital satisfaction ($r = -.70$ for husbands; $r = -.80$ for wives). The problem intensity score was not related to the Marlowe-Crowne for husbands or wives. Respondents' estimates of how their partners would rate the severity of each problem area revealed a similar pattern. This item showed strong correlations with the MAT in both husbands ($r = -.74$) and wives ($r = -.82$). Responses to this question were not correlated with the Marlowe-Crowne in either spouse.

Comparison of the problem intensity ratings each spouse made for him- or herself with the ratings he or she made predicting partner's responses yielded three discrepancy indices: (1) actual similarity, the relationship between a spouse's self-ratings and partner's self-ratings of problem intensity; (2) perceived similarity, the relationship between a spouse's self-rating of problem intensity and the same spouse's prediction of how partner will rate the problem areas; and (3) prediction accuracy, the relationship between a spouse's prediction of how his or her partner will rate the problem areas and the partner's actual problem intensity ratings. Discrepancy scores were obtained for each of these indices by taking the absolute value of the difference between the two relevant standardized intensity ratings for each problem area and summing these over the ten problem areas. Each of these discrepancy indices was significantly related to marital satisfaction; the strongest association emerged between actual similarity and the MAT, $r = -.67$.

Finally, an overall index of "blaming other" attributions for unresolved disagreements revealed a strong relationship with marital satisfaction (for husbands, $r = -.55$; for wives, $r = -.39$) and with relational efficacy (for husbands, $r = -.42$; for wives, $r = -.36$). The sum totals of "blaming self" attributions (for example, "I am primarily responsible for unresolved disagreements") and "dyadic" attributions (for example, "We are both equally responsible for unresolved disagreements") were not related to either relational efficacy or the MAT. Thus only blaming one's spouse appears related to marital satisfaction. Contrary to expectations, dyadic attributions do not characterize nondistressed couples more than distressed couples. Instead, the tendency to blame one's partner for unresolved problems is the only type of attribution that is found to characterize distressed couples more than nondistressed couples, and this tendency is related to marital satisfaction and relational efficacy.

Using MAP in Applied Settings

Like most assessment instruments, MAP can be used in a variety of ways for a variety of purposes. Also like most assessment strategies, the skills of the assessor are probably as important as the instrument itself. We will offer some suggestions and illustrations of how we have used MAP, present a hypothetical case history demonstrating MAP's role in assessment, treatment, and evaluation, and discuss adapting MAP to fit the individualized needs of therapists and their clients.

Assessment Overview

Thus far, we have used MAP exclusively with couples seeking marital or relationship therapy. Typically, each partner independently completes MAP either before or during the first session. After obtaining a brief accounting of the reasons the couple is seeking therapy at this time, we request that the couple arrive at a joint ranking of the top three problem areas in their relationship. MAP is returned to the partners with no directive to either conceal or disclose their individual responses. This interactive task helps to reveal the couple's problem discussion style, identify the top problem areas in the relationship, and assess the similarity or divergence in the couple's conceptualizations of relationship problems. For example, as the couple attempts to arrive at their joint ranking of the top problem areas, the therapist observes: (1) the level of agreement or disagreement between spouses in the problem areas defined as most salient, (2) the process by which agreement on the top three areas is reached (for example, does one partner consistently yield to the views of the other; do the partners "trade" problem areas—"Let's call your problem area number 1, mine number 2, and both of our's number 3, otherwise we'll never agree"; are the partners able to arrive at agreement?), (3) the willingness of partners to share their respective ratings and the curiosity of each spouse to see his or her partner's form, and (4) the outcome of the task (for example, are partners surprised that they view problems similarly or differently; does the decision-making process bring spouses closer or are they pushed apart by their differences?).

Once the couple has agreed on the top three problem areas, the therapist often uses these as a window onto the couple's typical pattern of problem onset, resolution, and outcome. Thus we have the couple provide us with play-by-play descriptions of one or more recent encounters that illustrate each of the identified major problem areas. Therapists actively direct the play-by-plays to gather information about (1) partners' behaviors and feelings prior to the onset of the problem encounter (What kind of day were you having? How were you feeling? What were you thinking? What were you doing just before the problem encounter started?); (2) what exactly happened in the problem encounter (How did it start? What happened next? What did you do then?); (3) partners' behaviors and feelings at the end of the problem encounter (How did your encounter end? How did each of you feel at the end of it? What did each of you do after it ended? What were each of you thinking at the end of it?); and (4) the similarity of the problem encounter being described to others about the same issue and to others about different issues. The therapist's primary goal is to have the problem encounter "make sense" to him or her and to understand the reasonableness of the couple's feelings, thoughts, and actions. In addition, the therapist can begin to demonstrate to the couple that complex problem encounters that seem overwhelming can be restructured with the therapist's help to provide new understanding of typical conflicts. This restructuring often contributes to resolution of existing problems and provides a framework for constructively confronting future conflicts. Obviously, this assessment procedure goes far beyond MAP's "numbers"; MAP provides a convenient, not an exclusive, vehicle for collecting this information and structuring the therapy session.

Between sessions, completed MAP questionnaires are reviewed and discussed to further the therapist's understanding of the couple's functioning. The magnitude of each problem intensity rating helps identify the sentiment surrounding the marital agendas. Inspection of the couple's three discrepancy indices helps establish the level of mutual understanding characterizing the couple. These comparisons can be therapeutically useful, as an example may help illustrate. One wife rated the sex agenda as very problematic and predicted that her husband would rate it similarly. The husband in fact also rated the sex agenda as very problematic for himself, but predicted that his wife would rate this area very low. When the husband learned that his wife saw a sexual agenda in their relationship and recognized that she understood his concern about this problem area, he was less desperate about the relationship and more

hopeful that therapy might offer them something. We might conceptual-
ize the pattern of discrepancy scores as operationalizing an important
aspect of the objectification process in marriage (see Weiss, 1978). Objectification refers to marital partners' abilities to identify situational variables influencing the relationship, to made discriminations in behavior
exchange, and to communicate effectively (Weiss, 1978). As objectification is mastered by the couple, we would expect there to be a decrease in
the actual similarity index (indicating greater agreement between partners' problem intensity ratings). A couple able to objectify problems in the
relationship should produce a lower actual similarity index than a couple
unable to objectify relational problems. Thus monitoring this discrepancy
index during the course of therapy many provide a useful assessment of
one aspect of the objectification process.

Examining the relational efficacy scores contributes information
about how helpless the partners feel about solving disagreements in each
problem area. Couples with low relational efficacy across all problem
areas are likely to have a generalized sense of despair about their relationship and are likely to benefit from a different therapeutic approach
than might be used with a couple who feel efficacious in all but one or two
problem areas. The latter couple may or may not have better skills to
draw upon as therapy confronts the problematic agendas, but they generally will not need the same level of support from the therapy that the
former couple requires. Examining the areas in which a partner feels his
or her spouse is primarily responsible for unresolved disagreements gives
the clinician insight into the level and nature of blame operating in the
relationship. Reattribution interventions (Baucom, Note 1) may be use-
fully focused on those problem areas where each spouse believes his or
her partner is primarily responsible for unresolved conflicts. Each of the
above hypotheses about the couple should be tempered by ratings of
problem importance. An agenda rated as highly important by a spouse is
likely to be more influential in the relationship than a problem area rated
low in importance. Agenda areas that are highly important to one spouse
who feels unable to resolve disagreements in this area but that are unimportant to the partner are worth pinpointing for therapeutic attention.

Hypothetical Case

The data we will report are taken from a couple who completed the
questionnaire survey. We offer some suggestions for how we might use
MAP's information with the caution that confirming evidence from the
couple is absent. Thus the example parallels the situation wherein a couple completes MAP prior to a first session and in which responses to MAP
might be used to plan for a first session with a couple.

TABLE 11.1 Hypothetical Couple's Response to MAP

Marital Agenda Area	Problem Intensity Ratings[a]		Prediction of Partner's Response[b]		Relational Efficacy[c]		Who Is Responsible	
	H	W	H	W	H	W	H	W
Money	0	20	0	20	8	9	B	S
Communication	50	45	50	30	4	7	B	S
In-laws	0	70	70	10	3	4	S	S
Sex	60	30	70	40	1	4	M	B
Religion	0	0	0	0	8	9	M	B
Recreation	60	0	70	0	8	6	M	B
Friends	60	10	50	0	3	7	S	B
Alcohol and drugs	0	0	0	10	8	9	B	B
Children	0	10	0	25	8	8	B	B
Jealousy	0	60	40	85	2	5	S	B
	230	245	350	220	53	68		

a. Ratings range from 0, which indicates area not at all a salient problem, to 100, which indicates area is a severe problem in the marriage.
b. As in the previous question, ratings range from 0 to 100 to indicate identified spouse's estimate of how partner will respond to the problem intensity rating.
c. Ratings of 0 to 10 in response to "If ten disagreements arose in this area, how many would you be capable of resolving to your mutual satisfaction?"
d. B = both, M = me, and S = spouse in response to "Who do you think is primarily responsible for unresolved disagreements in this problem area?"

The couple, Steven and Barbara, have been married 21 years and have two children. Steven is 47 years old and Barbara is 44 years old. His score on the MAT was 62; hers was 73. Their responses to MAP are presented in Table 11.1.

Examination of the problem intensity ratings reveals that Steven identifies four problem areas of moderate severity—communication, sex, recreation, and friends. Barbara identifies two problems of moderate severity—in-laws and jealousy—and two problems of lesser severity—communication and sex. Only on the communication agenda do Steven and Barbara approach agreement on the salient problems facing the relationship. Comparison of the spouses' prediction accuracy indices reveals an index of 310 for Barbara predicting Steven's problem intensity ratings, and a prediction accuracy index of 205 for Steven predicting Barbara's ratings. From these responses, we would entertain the hypothesis that Barbara is much less aware of how Steven views problems in the relationship than Steven is aware of Barbara's feelings about problems.

The couple is in greater agreement about the problem areas most likely to lead to unresolved disagreements. The relational efficacy ratings reveal that unresolved disagreements are most likely in the areas of in-

laws, sex, and jealousy, with Steven also feeling that friends and communication issues are likely to lead to disagreements. These ratings, along
with each partner's belief that his or her spouse is primarily responsible
for unresolved disagreements targets the in-laws area as particularly important and sensitive. During assessment with the couple we would want
to come to understand Steven and Barbara's discrepant problem intensity ratings for this area as well as their accurate perceptions of each other's ratings here. It appears that the couple has defined this problem area
as Barbara's, but that she holds Steven responsible for their difficulties in
dealing with this agenda. During the assessment, we would also want to
understand the in-laws problem in the context of a 21-year marriage. In
consideration of the developmental stages facing all marriages, establishing a workable relationship with in-laws is a relatively early task. The fact
that in-laws has been and continues to be a problem in this marriage of 21
years deserves exploration. Finally, the therapist would explore hypotheses for the low efficacy ratings; these might include: (1) poor skills, (2)
perception of the problem as unimportant, (3) insufficient effort spent at
problem solving, (4) impact of negative outcomes, (5) experience of high
levels of emotional arousal, and/or (6) influence of irrational relationship
beliefs (Eidelson & Epstein, 1982).

The pattern of ratings on the recreation area can also be informative
and therapeutically useful with this couple. Steven identifies recreation
as a problem and predicts that Barbara will also find this area problematic. Steven also believes that he is responsible for unresolved disagreements in this area. Barbara, however, does not report recreation as a
problem area, is unaware that Steven sees it as such, and does not believe that he is responsible for unresolved disagreements. Barbara is,
however, aware that they resolve somewhat fewer disagreements in this
area than in others. Open discussion of Steven and Barbara's respective
ratings in this area may go a significant way toward helping the couple to
recognize and deal with the recreation agenda more effectively.

The sex problem area follows a pattern similar to that of the recreation
area, with Steven feeling unable to resolve disagreements, feeling responsible for this fact, and believing that Barbara sees the problem area
as far more severe than she actually does. Barbara recognizes that Steven
will view this agenda as more severe than she does, but her intensity
rating is fairly low, suggesting either that she is downplaying the importance of this area or that she does not find it problematic. If the latter is the
case, this information would be quite potent for Steven, who erroneously
believes that Barbara experiences sex as a more severe problem than he
himself does. Both Steven and Barbara's awareness that they are unable
to resolve many disagreements in this area suggests that it would be useful to explore the couple's satisfaction with their sexual relationship.

Yet another pattern of problem definition is presented by the spouses' respective ratings of the jealousy area. Barbara identifies jealousy as a problem in the marriage and predicts that Steven sees jealousy as an even more severe problem. Steven accurately recognizes Barbara's sentiments about jealousy, but he indicates that this is not at all a problem in the marriage. He believes that they are capable of resolving very few of their disagreements in this area and he blames Barbara for this outcome. We begin to speculate that Barbara is jealous of some aspect of Steven's behavior and that he believes she should not feel as she does. Another possibility is that Steven has developed a pattern of not accommodating Barbara's requests for change in this area; he is comfortable with this arrangement, while Barbara feels that he is disturbed by it. Whatever additional assessment may reveal, this pattern of responses to MAP provides helpful clues about how the couple construes these marital agendas. The reader might want to consider the pattern of responses to the friends agenda and formulate his or her own hypotheses for how this agenda affects Steven and Barbara's relationship.

The summed scores are also informative with this couple. Steven appears to believe that Barbara will rate the agenda areas more severely than he will (Steven's summed Q.2 versus his summed Q.1: 350 versus 230), whereas Barbara believes that she and Steven will view the overall problem severity about equally. Steven feels less able to resolve disagreements (sum efficacy 53 versus Barbara's 68) and believes that either he or Barbara is responsible for unresolved disagreements, whereas Barbara, overall, believes that they are both responsible for unresolved disagreements.

Ultimately, MAP's specific use with each couple must depend on the therapist. As we mentioned earlier, we have found it useful to bring MAP into the therapy session and to have the couple agree on the top three problem areas facing the marriage. We are also likely to ask what goals they hope to accomplish in therapy and how these goals relate to the identified problem areas. Most important from these procedures is the opportunity to observe the couple's interaction. Through this and the process of therapy, our hunches about the couple formulated on the basis of MAP responses are tested, refined, and adjusted. As the therapy proceeds, it may be useful to administer MAP, particularly the relational efficacy question, after each session in order to evaluate therapy and to assist the therapist in understanding the change process. Whether or not relational efficacy is an effective measure of therapeutic progress must await further research. Theoretically, this construct could give a therapist information about when the change process begins and how it progresses. This information can complement clinical observation of the couple's behavior in the therapy sessions to give the clinician an excellent sense of the clinical indicators of therapeutic progress.

It should be clear that we do not believe that the information garnered from MAP can be revealed only through this instrument. Skillful interviewing and use of other marital assessment instruments may yield the same information as MAP or perhaps, to some, a more useful analysis of the couple. MAP was developed to provide an inexpensive marital assessment tool to be considered among the expanding range of assessment alternatives available to the marital therapist. Any more persuasive promotions or cautions about MAP must await continued research. Nevertheless, MAP's ease of administration and its relationship to the MAT, the PCI, and the SOC argue in favor of MAP. With particular regard to the SOC, Vincent (Note 3) has discussed the difficulties present in soliciting some couples' cooperation in completing the SOC as part of their therapy assessment and the hesitancy of some therapists to use the SOC. Given the moderate correlation between MAP and the displeases scores from the SOC, therapists might want to consider using MAP as part of their assessment plan.

Commentary

Although the relational efficacy formulation is a recent development, marital problem solving has usually been assessed in various ways as part of several standard instruments for measuring marital adjustment. Locke and Wallace's (1959) MAT requires spouses to rate the extent of agreement or disagreement on eight common areas of relational functioning (such as friends, finances, and sex) along a six-point scale ranging from "always agree" to "always disagree." Spanier's (1976) Dyadic Adjustment Scale (DAS) extends the same basic extent-of-agreement question to 15 marital areas. Relational efficacy assessment is subtly different from these extent-of agreement-questions in that it is intended to yield a more refined, differentiated index of problem solving. Both types of assessment, however, reflect the importance clinicians and researchers have placed on the contribution that effective problem solving makes to marital adjustment.

A potential advantage of MAP's format is that it may provide a useful measure of therapeutic outcome as well as a measure to monitor the process of therapeutic change. The MAT and DAS cast most questions in the context of past behavior, making these instruments relatively insensitive to change. The MAP, instead, frames questions in terms of expectancies for future behavior. Given the power of expectancies in predicting behavior (Bandura, 1982), MAP should be sensitive to changes in respondents' capabilities for solving relationship problems. These changes are hypothesized to reflect therapeutic effectiveness, and the sum of these expectancies to reflect marital satisfaction. In practice, we find that the MAP provides more useful diagnostic information than the DAS or the MAT. Also, since MAP easily can be used weekly to monitor the therapy process, it may have more utility than the MAT. However, if the therapist wishes to compare a particular couple's general level of distress with "average" levels of distress reported in research and treatment studies, then either the MAT or the DAS should also be administered, since these questionnaires are the most widely used and reported.

MAP's focus on identifying and detailing spouses' expectancies for problem solving in several specific problem areas comes at the expense of not providing information on all criteria believed to contribute to marital adjustment (such as degree of commitment to the relationship). This information can be gathered by utilizing other available assessment devices or through the clinical interview. Indeed, a comprehensive assessment of marriage would necessitate more information than is provided by MAP. Another area not directly addressed by MAP is that of the functional or positive aspects of the marriage. If the therapist desired to know if and to what extent positive behaviors are exchanged between the spouses, MAP could not provide that information. In this case, the clinician might elect to administer the SOC, which is designed specifically to provide information on the perception of behavior exchange between spouses (see Chapter 4, this volume).

Another dimension not addressed by MAP is information provided by objective external observation of a couple's interactions. Several observational coding schemes for classifying behavior in interactions currently exist (for example, MICS and CISS; see Chapters 5 and 6, this volume). These provide an outsider's measure of the actual behavioral events in the relationship. MAP, like any self-report instrument, taps the phenomenological reality of the couple, which may or may not be synonymous with the external reality of events in the relationship. This personal reality is certainly important in understanding a marriage (see Robinson & Price, 1980; Williams, 1979; Floyd & Markman, Note 4), but its relationship to a couple's actual behavior is unknown.

A related issue is the relationship between objectively measurable problem-solving skills and relational efficacy expectancies. It should not be assumed that efficacy expectancies necessarily reflect skill level. Low relational efficacy *might* reflect a lack of skills (that is, the couple cannot resolve conflicts because they do not have the skills necessary to do so); they know they cannot resolve conflicts from past experience. Low efficacy might also, however, be present when the necessary skills are available but the couple gives up too quickly when faced with a conflict situation. Possession of skills does not imply ease of their application, particularly in the area of marital conflict, where two people are engaged in an interactive system. For example, a spouse might hold the belief that conflict should never be present in a "good marriage" and, although the skills are available for effective problem resolution, as the intensity of the first stages of conflict resolution rises, the spouse backs away from resolution. Similarly, overemphasis on failures, the experience of uncomfortably high levels of arousal, and/or the perception of the agenda area as unimportant could prohibit effective utilization of skills and lead to low efficacy. High efficacy might be related to good skills (that is, the couple can resolve conflicts because they have the requisite skills), but it also might be present at lower skill levels. The couple with high efficacy and moderate to poor skills may simply persist long enough in their attempts to problem solve that they are eventually successful. Alternatively, the couple with high efficacy and poor skills may be characteristic of the conflict-avoiding couple or the "united-front" couple, who tend to self-report a problem-free relationship and operate to reduce quickly, at all costs, the experience of conflict in the relationship.

One implication of this formulation concerns the relationship of therapeutic interventions to efficacy. If skills are not necessarily related to efficacy, there is no reason to assume that teaching these skills will produce enhanced efficacy expectancies. Instead, if relational efficacy expectancies are the mechanism of change in marital therapy, then we may profit from focusing study on a range of therapeutic interventions and processes that operate to enhance relational efficacy. By assessing and monitoring relational efficacy throughout an intervention, the observant therapist may uncover those aspects of therapy that are most potent in producing change in couples. Over time this kind of study would contribute answers to the question of what therapeutic procedures are effective with what types of couples presenting with what specific problems. These important empirical agendas notwithstanding, assessment of relational efficacy should provide the clinician with, at worst, a good predictor of a couple's performance in problem-solving situations and, at best, a sensitive index of therapeutic process and progress.

In closing, we would like to express our hope that use of MAP be considered by therapists of varying theoretical orientations. Although MAP was developed within a social learning context, the assessment information obtained should be useful to a broad range of clinicians insofar as problem identification is an assessment agenda shared by all marital therapists. Furthermore, MAP avoids many of the problems typically voiced against other assessment instruments developed by behavioral marital therapists. For example, many therapists have been reluctant to use the SOC routinely (see Chapter 4) because it is difficult to solicit the couple's cooperation to keep the daily records and because it is an intrusive procedure (Vincent, Note 3). Other instruments such as the Areas of Change (AC) Questionnaire (Weiss, Hops, & Patterson, 1973; see Chapter 16) can provide information similar to that provided by MAP, but they may require couples to provide information about which they are unaware. For example, with the

Areas of Change Questionnaire, spouses may not be readily able to provide accurate information about which behaviors they feel should be increased or decreased to improve the relationship; some spouses do not think in terms of behavior exchange and its effect on the relationship. While helping spouses to achieve this specificity may be a goal of some therapists, the fact that some couples may not be able to do this at the start of therapy makes the use of the AC Questionnaire problematic as an initial assessment device for clinicians of varying orientations.

Finally, while empirical support is not yet available, MAP may provide assessment information directly relevant to therapists of varying theoretical orientations. For example, the couple with very high problem intensity ratings in multiple areas and very low relational efficacy scores may be extremely resistant to initial change efforts and may be most responsive to a paradoxical intervention strategy. Clinical experience with MAP will ultimately determine its utility. We would welcome information from those who use MAP in their practice of marital and family therapy.

Summary

The Marital Agendas Protocol is a new self-report assessment device designed to (1) pinpoint marital problem areas currently salient in a relationship, (2) examine the level of shared understanding of these problem areas, (3) measure relational efficacy, which is defined as spouses' expectancies about the couple's ability to resolve disagreements in each problem area, and (4) identify the problem areas in which each spouse feels it is important to resolve disagreements.

Initial data gathered on MAP demonstrate that it is related to the Locke-Wallace MAT, the Primary Communication Inventory, and the Spouse Observation Checklist, supporting MAP's validity. The strengths of the instrument are that it is low cost; it operationalizes relational efficacy, which may prove to be a useful measure of therapeutic change and a powerful predictor of problem-solving behavior; it provides a convenient structure for observing marital interaction during assessment; and it can be easily tailored to fit a wide range of assessment situations in clinical settings. MAP's weaknesses are that it is a new instrument lacking extensive norms for comparing couples; it currently lacks sufficient data to evaluate its utility as a measure of therapeutic change; and it bears an unknown relationship to actual behavior.

At this time, MAP should be considered a flexible idiographic relationship assessment tool that can be used in a variety of settings. It is appropriate for use with married and unmarried couples and for assessing the marital relationship in family therapy settings. As part of a larger assessment package, MAP may contribute substantially to a comprehensive evaluation of a marital relationship.

MARITAL AGENDAS PROTOCOL

Instructions: Please read each question carefully and record your answers in the spaces provided. Please do not leave any questions blank.

NAME OR ID NUMBER: _____ SEX: M ____ F ____ DATE _____

Question 1a: Consider the list below of marital issues that all marriages must face. Please rate how much of a problem each area currently is in your relationship by writing in a number from 0 (not at all a problem) to 100 (a severe problem). For example, if children were somewhat of a problem you might enter 25 below "children". If children were no problem in your relationship, you might enter a 0 below "children". If children were a severe problem, you might enter 100. If you wish to add other areas not included in our list, please do so in the blank spaces provided. Be sure to rate all areas.

MONEY	COMMUNICATION	IN-LAWS	SEX	RELIGION	RECREATION

FRIENDS	ALCOHOL & DRUGS	CHILDREN	JEALOUSY

Question 1b: How do you predict your spouse will respond to question 1? Enter ratings using the same 0 to 100 scale to indicate how you believe your spouse will respond to question 1. If you added areas to question 1, please add these same areas again and rate each according to how you think your spouse would rate them.

MONEY	COMMUNICATION	IN-LAWS	SEX	RELIGION	RECREATION

FRIENDS	ALCOHOL & DRUGS	CHILDREN	JEALOUSY

Question 2: Out of every ten disagreements in each marital area below, how many do you believe you and your spouse resolve to your mutual satisfaction? Enter a number from 0 to 10 in each of the boxes below. If you added areas, please add them again and rate them also.

MONEY	COMMUNICATION	IN-LAWS	SEX	RELIGION	RECREATION

FRIENDS	ALCOHOL & DRUGS	CHILDREN	JEALOUSY

Question 3: Who do you feel is responsible for unresolved disagreements in each of the marital areas? Below each area, write "me" if you think that you yourself are primarily responsible for unresolved disagreements, write "partner" if you feel your partner is primarily responsible, or write "both" if you feel you and your partner are equally responsible for unresolved disagreements. Again, if you added areas to the previous questions, please enter these in the spaces provided and rate them also.

MONEY	COMMUNICATION	IN-LAWS	SEX	RELIGION	RECREATION

FRIENDS	ALCOHOL & DRUGS	CHILDREN	JEALOUSY

Notes

1. The perceived importance of an agenda area may be a significant modifier of other MAP questions. For example, the significance of an agenda area to a spouse who indicates low relational efficacy for that agenda and who also views the area as unimportant may be much less than for another spouse who has similarly low relational efficacy for the area but who considers the area very important.

2. The second study was part of a larger master's research project conducted by Suzanne Meeks.

3. Two additional relational efficacy indices were also computed and correlated with the MAT. An average efficacy measure computed on the three most salient agenda areas identified by a spouse and a weighted efficacy measure representing the sum of each relational efficacy rating weighted by respondents' certainty of their answers on a scale from 0 (not at all certain) to 100 (very certain) both yielded correlations similar to the summed relational efficacy measure. Therefore, at this time, we would recommend using the summed relational efficacy index.

Reference Notes

1. Baucom, D. H. *Cognitive behavioral strategies in the treatment of marital discord.* Paper presented at the meeting of the Association for Advancement of Behavior Therapy, Toronto, November 1981.

2. Notarius, C., & Vanzetti, N. *Marital Agendas Protocol: Development and validation.* Manuscript in preparation, 1983.

3. Vincent, J. P. *Assessment of learned behaviors: A clinical approach.* Paper presented at the meeting of the American Psychological Association, Washington, D.C., August 1982.

4. Floyd, F., & Markman, H. *Observational biases in spouse observation: Toward a cognitive/behavioral model of marriage.* Manuscript submitted for publication, 1982.

References

Ables, B. S., & Brandsma, J. M. *Therapy for couples.* San Francisco: Jossey-Bass, 1977.

Abramson, L. Y., Seligman, M. E. P., & Teasdale, J. D. Learned helplessness in humans: Critique and reformulation. *Journal of Abnormal Psychology,* 1978, *87,* 49-74.

Bandura, A. Self-efficacy: Toward a unifying theory of behavior change. *Psychological Review,* 1977, *84,* 191-215.

Bandura, A. Self-efficacy mechanism in human agency. *American Psychologist,* 1982, *37,* 122-147.

Bernal, G., & Baker, J. Toward a metacommunicational framework of couple interactions. *Family Process,* 1979, *18,* 293-302.

Birchler, G. R., & Spinks, S. H. Behavioral-systems marital and family therapy: Integration and clinical application. *American Journal of Family Therapy,* 1980, *8,* 6-28.

Crowne, D. P. & Marlowe, D. A new scale of social desirability independent of psychopathology. *Journal of Consulting Psychology,* 1960, *24,* 349-554.

Doherty, W. J. Cognitive processes in intimate conflict: I. Extending attribution theory. *American Journal of Family Therapy,* 1981, *9,* 3-13. (a)

Doherty. W. J. Cognitive processes in intimate conflict: II. Efficacy and learned helplessness. *American Journal of Family Therapy,* 1981, *9,* 35-44. (b)

Eidelson, R. J., & Epstein, N. Cognition and relationship maladjustment: Development of a measure of dysfunctional relationship beliefs. *Journal of Consulting and Clinical Psychology,* 1982, *50,* 715-720.

Gottman, J., Markman, H., & Notarius, C. The topography of marital conflict: A sequential analysis of verbal and nonverbal behavior. *Journal of Marriage and the Family,* 1977, *39,* 461-477.

Gottman, J., Notarius, C., Gonso, J., & Markman, H. *A couples guide to communication.* Champaign, IL: Research Press, 1976.

Haley, J. *Problem solving therapy.* San Francisco: Jossey-Bass, 1976.

Jacobson, N. S., & Margolin, G. *Marital therapy: Strategies based on social learning and behavior exchange principles.* New York: Brunner/Mazel, 1979.

Kanner, A. D., Coyne, J. C., Schaefer, C., & Lazarus, R. S. Comparison of two modes of stress measurement: Daily hassles and uplifts versus major life events. *Journal of Behavioral Medicine,* 1981, *4,* 1-39.

Locke, H. J., & Wallace, K. M. Short marital adjustment and prediction tests: Their reliability and validity. *Marriage and Family Living,* 1959, *2,* 251-255.

Madanes, C. *Strategic family therapy.* San Francisco: Jossey-Bass, 1981.

Margolin, G., & Wampold, B. E. Sequential analysis of conflict and accord in distressed and nondistressed marital partners. *Journal of Consulting and Clinical Psychology,* 1981, *49,* 554-567.

Murstein, B. I., & Beck, G. D. Person perception, marriage adjustment, and social desirability. *Journal of Consulting and Clinical Psychology,* 1972, *39,* 396-403.

Nadelson, C. C. Marital therapy from a psychoanalytic perspective. In T. J. Paolino & B. S. McCrady (Eds.), *Marriage and marital therapy: Psychoanalytic, behavioral, and systems theory perspectives.* New York: Brunner/Mazel, 1978.

Navran, L. Communication and adjustment in marriage. *Family Process,* 1967, *6,* 173-180.

Robinson, E. A., & Price, M. G. Pleasurable behavior in marital interaction: An observational study. *Journal of Consulting and Clinical Psychology,* 1980, *48,* 117-118.

Spanier, G. B. Measuring dyadic adjustment: New scales for assessing the quality of marriage and similar dyads. *Journal of Marriage and the Family,* 1976, *38,* 15-28.

Watzlawick, P., Weakland, J., & Fisch, R. *Change: Principles of problem formation and problem resolution.* New York: Norton, 1974.

Weiss, R. L. The conceptualization of marriage from a behavioral perspective. In T. J. Paolino & B. S. McCrady (Eds.), *Marriage and marital therapy: Psychoanalytic, behavioral, and systems theory perspectives.* New York: Brunner/Mazel, 1978.

Weiss, R. L. A systems behavioral approach to marital therapy. In J. P. Vincent (Ed.), *Advances in family intervention, assessment and theory* (Vol. 1.), Greenwich, CT: JAI, 1980.

Weiss, R. L. The new kid on the block: Behavioral systems approach. In E. E. Filsinger & R. A. Lewis (Eds.), *Assessing marriage: New behavioral approaches.* Beverly Hills, CA: Sage, 1981.

Weiss, R. L., Hops, H., & Patterson, G. R. A framework for conceptualizing marital conflict, a technology for altering it, some data for evaluating it. In L. A. Hamerlynck, L. C. Handy, & E. J. Mash (Eds.), *Behavior change: Methodology, concepts and practice.* Champaign, IL: Research Press, 1973.

Williams, A. M. The quantity and quality of marital interaction related to marital satisfaction: A behavioral analysis. *Journal of Applied Behavior Analysis,* 1979, *12,* 665-678.

Wills, T. A., Weiss, R. L., & Patterson, G. R. a behavioral analysis of the determinants of marital satisfaction. *Journal of Consulting and Clinical Psychology,* 1974, *42,* 802-811.

CHAPTER 12

Assessing Marital and Premarital Relationships: The PREPARE-ENRICH Inventories

DAVID G. FOURNIER
Oklahoma State University

DAVID H. OLSON
JOAN M. DRUCKMAN
University of Minnesota

Since the rate of marital dissolution in the United States reached historic highs in the middle 1970s, greater effort has been placed on the development and evaluation of preventative intervention strategies, such as programs in preparation for marriage and marriage enrichment. Given that each year nearly 200,000 marriages end prior to the couples' second anniversaries and that over 40 percent of all first marriages are expected to end in divorce, it is not surprising that new approaches to preparation and enrichment are being pursued vigorously. Each year over 2 million adults and 1 million children must cope with the life-restructuring events associated with marital dissolution.

The above statistics verify that many couples experience serious marital conflicts early in their relationships. These findings also suggest that few engaged couples successfully anticipate the conflicts that will be encountered in their marriages. In addition, it appears that most couples do not have the communication skills necessary to resolve conflicts when they do occur. These concerns underscore the need to better assist couples preparing for marriage and to provide follow-up programs that will enable married couples to enrich and maintain their relationships.

The impetus for the development of the PREPARE-ENRICH Inventories has been the lack of assessment tools specifically designed to provide

Instrument Source Note: The manual and materials for PREPARE-ENRICH are available from PREPARE-ENRICH, Inc., P.O. Box 190, Minneapolis, Minnesota 55440.

systematic and objective assessments of both *personal* and *relationship* issues for couples. PREPARE and PREPARE-MC help *engaged* couples identify issues unique to their own relationships so that they may begin more realistic assessment of their upcoming marriages. ENRICH is intended to assist *married* couples in focusing on their marital strengths and to summarize topic areas that are most troublesome for further pursuit in counseling or enrichment programs.

The PREPARE-ENRICH Inventories provide diagnostic information relevant to the needs for: (1) an objective *global diagnosis* providing a quick overview of couple strengths and weaknesses compared to other couples in similar stages; (2) an objective *specific diagnosis* of marital topics representing unique couple concerns or used to verify other counselor insights about the couple; (3) a *description* of the couple system and insight into the contributions made by each individual subsystem to the dyad; (4) a *provocative tool* for use in counseling to illustrate certain couple issues or to stimulate discussion of important topics; and (5) an objective procedure to illustrate couple progress over time or to *evaluate* the effectiveness of counseling interventions or educational programs. PRE-PARE-ENRICH scores highlight individuals and couples in an objective manner and can be used in a variety of ways.

Inventory Development

Historical Context

The PREPARE-ENRICH Inventories have evolved from a variety of research studies designed to assess premarital attitudes and to evaluate marriage preparation programs. While these projects began 14 years ago with the Pre-Marital Attitude Scale (PMAS) by Olson and Gravatt (1968), the primary impetus came during the fall of 1976, when a large research team headed by David H. Olson began a series of evaluation studies on marriage preparation programs (Druckman, Fournier, Robinson, & Olson, Note 1; Olson & Norem, Note 2). In an attempt to utilize the most reliable tools available for assessing outcomes, a major search was undertaken to review and evaluate existing premarital assessment instruments. Although this evaluative effort is well documented (Fournier, 1979), the highlights will be summarized.

Literally hundreds of measurement techniques exist to assess aspects of marital and family life (Cromwell, Olson, & Fournier, 1976; Straus & Brown, 1977). However, most techniques lack a number of desirable measurement characteristics and few were designed specifically for use with couples. Fourteen instruments judged to be relevant for couples were evaluated according to the following characteristics: *length of instrument* (too long/short); *appropriateness of content* (coverage and relevance); *reliability and validity of scores; appropriateness of response format* (limited or vague); *ease of administration; scoring systems; clinical utility of results; assessment of social desirability; appropriateness of normative group;* and other methodological concerns, such as *system focus of measure* (individual or relationship), *system level responding* (individual or couple), and *self-report versus observational* assessments, were also considered. In short, of the techniques evaluated, only two appeared useful as self-report measures in outcome research on marriage preparation and early marriage adjustment. A more detailed analysis of these two techniques revealed other difficulties and led to the decision of the research team to develop a new instrument called PREPARE (Fournier, 1979; Olson, Fournier, & Druckman, 1982).

PREPARE (The Pre-Marital Personal and Relationship Evaluation) was the original PREPARE-ENRICH Inventory and is developmentally linked with the PMAS (Pre-Marital Attitude Scale, 1968), IRI (Interpersonal Relationship Inventory, 1970), and IRAS (Interpersonal Relationship Attitude Scale, 1976) developed by Olson and colleagues and reproduced in Fournier (1979). PREPARE (1977) was originally developed for research and evaluation. However, those who used PREPARE in the context of applied research remarked that the technique might fill an important need for professionals working with engaged couples and encouraged the authors to refine the instrument for broader application. During 1977 and 1978, a major validation study on PREPARE with over 1000 engaged couples was completed. In addition, reactions and evaluative comments were received from over 200 counselors, clergy, and specialists who had used PREPARE with at least one couple (Fournier, 1979). PREPARE'S clinical utility was highly rated by practitioners and the instrument met acceptable levels of reliability and validity. However, additional improvements were identified and in 1979 PREPARE was modified. These refinements increased the utility of PREPARE in clinical practice and eventually led to the development of PREPARE-MC (Marriage with Children Edition; 1981) for engaged couples who have at least one child from a former relationship. Later in 1981, ENRICH (Evaluating and Nurturing Relationship Issues, Communication and Happiness) was developed for use with married couples seeking marriage counseling and/or enrichment. The inventories, which share similar formats and a rigorous developmental history, provide a package of assessment procedures suitable for a variety of clinical and educational applications. In addition, the computer-generated results are similar enough in style and content that learning administration and interpretation for one instrument is usually sufficient for effective use of all three inventories.

This developmental review has focused primarily on the historical context of the three PREPARE-ENRICH inventories. The next section will cover several psychometric aspects of the inventories. Since these summaries are by necessity brief, readers are referred to Fournier (1979) for complete coverage of the technical and developmental aspects of PREPARE and to the *Counselor's Manual* (Olson et al., 1982) for complete documentation of the clinical procedures and formats.

Psychometric Properties

Content Validity

The content of the PREPARE-ENRICH Inventories was specifically selected to represent a diverse range of topic areas most relevant to marital and premarital relationships. Rather than making assessments of individual or intrapsychic characteristics, most items reflect couple issues that require respondents to reflect on their relationship. These items were specifically developed to identify interpersonal processes that become problematic for many couples. Representative articles on relationship conflicts were reviewed and various conflicts were identified and categorized. Table 12.1 represents a summary of the most commonly mentioned problems in the research literature and the PREPARE-ENRICH categories used to tap those areas. This table indicates the important linkage between existing research and the rationale for category selection and item development.

The above procedure was followed to maximize face or content validity. Items and categories were also submitted for review by practitioners who rated the relevance of the inventory for engaged and married couples. Experience with the instrument has also identified an interesting "educational" effect associated with simply taking the inventory. Couples report that a shared exposure to new ideas about marriage often stimulates discussion and increases awareness about relationship strengths and weaknesses (Druckman et al., Note 1).

Construct Validity

The issue of construct validity was also addressed during initial development and refinement of the PREPARE-ENRICH Inventories (Fournier, 1979). The methodological procedures included: (1) correlational analysis of the relationship between PREPARE-ENRICH scale scores and over 100 previously established scales assessing individual and marital topics; and (2) factor analysis on the entire scale, each category separately, and each category combined with an assessment of social desirability. While the main findings will be summarized briefly, the original reference contains a detailed description of the methodological procedures and all relevant findings (Fournier, 1979).

One goal of construct validity is to assess the relationship between new measures and existing measures that are consistent with theoreti-

TABLE 12.1   Most Common Conflicts from a Cross Section of Marital
              Studies and Corresponding PREPARE-ENRICH Categories

Common Conflict Issues	Number of Times Each Conflict Was Mentioned[a]	PREPARE-ENRICH Categories
Intrapersonal issues		
Personality	13	Personality Issues[b]
Personal habits/health	13	Personality Issues[b]
Incompatible background	11	Religious Orientation[b]
Interests/values	15	Leisure Activities[b]
Expectations	2	Realistic Expectations[c]
	–	Marital Satisfaction[d]
Idealization, social desirability	1	Idealistic Distortion[b]
Interpersonal issues		
Communication	9	Communication[b]
Sex	14	Sexual Relationship[b]
Commitment	2	Marital Cohesion[d]
Marital roles	9	Equalitarian Roles[b]
Arguments	7	Conflict Resolution[b]
External issues		
Relatives	9	Family and Friends[b]
Friends	8	Family and Friends[b]
Children	8	Children and Marriage[b]
Money	11	Financial Management[b]
Work	10	Financial Management[b]

a. Fournier, Springer, and Olson (Note 3); Hobart (1958); Hunt and Hunt (1977); Kitson and Sussman (Note 4); Mace (1972); Microys and Bader (Note 5); Rappoport (1963); Raush, Goodrich, and Campbell (1963); Sager (1976); Stahmann and Hiebert (1977).
b. All three inventories.
c. PREPARE-MC only.
d. ENRICH only.

cally derived hypotheses relevant to the construct. All twelve scales are significantly correlated with the Locke-Wallace Marital Adjustment Scale. In addition, significant relationships were established between PREPARE-ENRICH scales and existing measures of relationship conflict, esteem, communication, empathy, equalitarianism, assertiveness, temperament, cohesion, and independence, among others (Fournier, 1979).

Factor analysis attempts to establish the degree of interrelatedness of a set of items and the extent to which a set of empirically related items can be explained by theoretically relevant ideas. Since PREPARE has twelve categories, factor analysis on the full scale should reveal twelve significant factors that mirror the titles of the scale categories. Results revealed eleven unique factors, with the categories Personality Issues and Communication merging to account for the discrepancy. Intrascale factor analysis revealed that most categories contained only one significant factor verifying a predominant unidimensional structure for each scale. Finally, each scale was factored along with social desirability to assess the degree of separation or independence between scales and socially conventional response sets. Again, most scales revealed a two-factor solution, with items from social desirability and the PREPARE scale loading on separate factors. Although the results were generally positive, and number of weaknesses were identified and subsequently addressed in the 1979 revised edition of the PREPARE Inventory.

Score Characteristics

PREPARE-ENRICH is a comprehensive, computer-processed procedure with a variety of components specially designed to meet common needs. The *Summary Analysis* portion of the computer results lists each of the derived scores that are part of PREPARE-ENRICH. These include: 48 individual (percentile and revised) scores and 68 couple scores on PREPARE, and 54 individual scores and 80 couple scores on ENRICH. In addition, each computerized printout has 7-10 pages of item listings that help identify a couple's unique pattern of similarities and differences. The *Summary Analysis* page and other sections will be discussed in more detail later in this chapter. Table 12.2 presents score norms and reliability estimates for PREPARE-ENRICH.

Table 12.2 lists the categories within PREPARE-ENRICH and details the number of items per category, the overall mean and dispersion of scores, and two types of reliability. These figures come from nationwide samples of 5718 and 1344 individuals, respectively, for PREPARE and ENRICH. While the PREPARE sample represents a good cross section of engaged individuals, only the ENRICH sample was derived from probability sampling.

The data indicate that the majority of scales have a full range of results (theoretical range is 10-50) and were normally distributed around the mean. PREPARE-ENRICH raw scores are converted into percentile scores so that each individual can be compared relative to national norms. Percentile scores range from 0 to 100 and represent the percentage of persons who score lower than the respondent. *Individual percentile scores* are calculated for both male and female partners for each of the 12 content categories in PREPARE and 14 categories in ENRICH.

An important methodological feature of the PREPARE-ENRICH Inventories is the assessment of social desirability (modified marital conventionalization scale; Edmonds, 1967) and the subsequent correction of individual percentile scores. While it is generally believed that engaged couples tend to be extremely idealistic in their views of marriage, most

TABLE 12.2   Statistical Summary of PREPARE-ENRICH Norms and Reliability

PREPARE-ENRICH Categories	Number of Items	Descriptive Statistics - Raw Scores						Reliability Estimates			
		PREPARE (N = 5718)			ENRICH (N = 1344)			PREPARE		ENRICH	
		$\bar{X}$	SD	Range	$\bar{X}$	SD	Range	(N = 5718) Alpha	(N = 36) Retest	(N = 1344) Alpha	(N = 115) Retest
Idealistic Distortion	15 (PREPARE) 5 (ENRICH)	229.3	67.9	0-388	13.7	4.6	5-25	.88	.79	.92	.92
Realistic Expectations (PREPARE)	10	32.5	6.5	10-50	—	—	—	.75	.82	—	—
Marital Satisfaction (ENRICH)	10	—	—	—	37.2	6.7	10-50	—	—	.81	.86
Personality Issues	10	36.0	6.9	10-50	34.5	6.2	16-49	.74	.78	.73	.81
Communication	10	38.0	6.1	13-50	34.5	6.5	14-50	.70	.79	.68	.90
Conflict Resolution	10	37.6	6.0	14-50	33.9	6.1	11-50	.72	.76	.75	.90
Financial Management	10	35.6	5.7	11-50	37.4	6.6	12-50	.67	.81	.74	.88
Leisure Activities	10	38.7	5.2	14-50	34.4	4.1	21-47	.51	.79	.76	.77
Sexual Relationship	10	37.9	4.7	17-50	37.4	6.8	14-50	.50	.64	.48	.92
Children and Marriage	10	37.8	4.5	20-50	38.3	5.7	19-50	.49	.74	.77	.89
Family and Friends	10	38.2	6.2	13-50	38.0	5.8	15-50	.70	.73	.72	.82
Equalitarian Roles	10	36.1	6.8	12-50	28.5	5.6	13-48	.77	.83	.71	.90
Religious Orientation	10	35.7	6.9	10-50	39.5	6.4	13-50	.82	.93	.77	.89
Marital Cohesion (ENRICH)	5	—	—	—	—	—	—	—	—	.76	.75
Marital Adaptability (ENRICH)	5	—	—	—	—	—	—	—	—	.80	.72

premarital assessment tools neglect this vital concern. In PREPARE-EN-RICH not only is social desirability (called Idealistic Distortion) measured, but formulas are used to adjust each individual's percentile score to account for the response bias of trying to create an "impossibly good impression" (Edmonds, 1967) of their relationship. The *individual revised scores* adjust each category percentile score according to: (1) each individual's relative amount of Idealistic Distortion and (2) the empirical relationship between each scale and social desirability. For example, scales highly associated with social desirability are corrected more radically than scales with less association. The presentation of both actual percentile and revised percentile scores provides valuable information about the extent to which social desirability has affected the validity of an individual's scores.

Couple scores provide a summary of the convergent and/or divergent opinions that couples have about their relationships. Information is provided that identifies: (1) differences or disagreements in partner responses, (2) potentially negative agreements in partner responses, (3) indecisive responses, and (4) similar responses or agreements that appear to be positive for the relationship. This *Item Summary* on the computer printout allows the clinician to preview quickly the frequency of potentially problematic responses and the PREPARE-ENRICH categories that represent relationship strengths or areas in need of improvement.

The *Positive Couple Agreement Score,* available for each category, is the final couple score presented and reflects the percentage of items in which both partners responded in a positive manner. When these scores are compared to the *National Couple Averages,* one can compare any given couple to all other couples in the normative sample to help identify possible *Strength* and *Work Areas.* Empirical formulas are used to facilitate couple comparison and each computer printout lists tentative couple descriptions to be considered in each category. Computer identification of *Strength* and *Work Areas* are *not* intended as final judgments but rather as initial assessments to be explored and verified or modified in discussion with couples.

Scale Reliability

Reliability coefficients are intended to estimate the consistency or accuracy of measurement and to determine the stability of measures over time. While many statistical procedures are available to estimate reliability, Cronbach's coefficient alpha (internal consistency) and retest reliability (stability over time) are the most commonly used techniques. Coefficient alpha is based on intrascale communality and provides a good assessment of which items contribute most directly to derived scale scores. Since most scales tap characteristics that do not shift significantly during short periods of time, retest reliability compares a person's scale scores after short intervals of time. Alpha is considered to be a minimum-likelihood estimate (reliability probably higher, but not lower), while the retest method is considered to be a maximum-likelihood estimate (reliability probably lower; Nunnally, 1967).

Table 12.2 lists representative reliability estimates from research on PREPARE-ENRICH. Alpha coefficients range from .49 on Children and Marriage to .88 on Idealistic Distortion for PREPARE and .48 on Sexual Relationship to .92 on Idealistic Distortion for ENRICH. Retest reliability estimates are generally higher, with a range of .64 to .93. In general, these reliabilities are sufficient for research purposes and to determine the general tendency of persons to be similar to or different from normative expectations. Since PREPARE-ENRICH was primarily designed as a discussion tool and secondarily to determine general comparability between couples, these reliabilities meet minimum requirements. However, the reliabilities are *not* high enough to determine whether couples should be denied marriage or required to seek counseling without other sources of information. PREPARE-ENRICH was not developed as a predictive test and should not be used in this capacity.

PREPARE-ENRICH Materials and Procedures

The PREPARE-ENRICH Inventories are part of a comprehensive package of materials and procedures designed to meet the needs of professionals engaged in marriage preparation, marriage enrichment, and marriage counseling. Inventories are flexible diagnostic and discussion tools and can be used in group settings with 50 or more couples as well as with a single couple in private sessions. In addition to the item booklets for PREPARE, PREPARE-MC, and ENRICH, numerous other printed and computer-generated documents have been developed to facilitate use of the inventories, including a recently revised *Counselor's Manual* (Olson et al., 1982).

Overview of Materials

Item booklets. The PREPARE-ENRICH Inventories are 8-page booklets that contain 125 items pertaining to marital issues. The items relate to the individual, the partner, and/or the relationship rather than to marriage in general. All items (excluding the final 10 on ENRICH) are answered on a 5-point Likert-type scale: (1) strongly agree; (2) moderately agree; (3) neither agree nor disagree; (4) moderately disagree; and (5) strongly disagree. The extended 5-point response format allows for variation and never forces couples to agree or disagree with strongly worded items. These choices are clearly displayed at the top of each page of the booklet and on the specially designed computer answer sheet. Items from the PREPARE-ENRICH categories are randomly distributed throughout the inventory and have both positive and negative slants to reduce possible response bias. Clear instructions are provided on the front page of the booklet and are designed to reduce anxiety and to encourage respondents to reflect carefully on the statements. Follow-up studies indicate that couples learn a great deal about themselves and their relationships merely by responding to the statements (Druckman et al., Note 1).

Answer sheets. PREPARE-ENRICH answer sheets are specially printed documents designed to be optically scanned for computer processing. Each sheet is color coded according to inventory and must be used with the proper item booklet (PREPARE—brown, PREPARE-MC—burgandy, ENRICH—blue). The front page of each answer sheet contains 19 demographic and contextual questions and a special identification section using number codes for the couple and for the counselor. This allows complete confidentiality during the computer processing stage and helps reassure couples who may have questions about how their forms are identified. The back of the answer sheet is the same for each inventory and contains 125 clearly numbered groups of 5 circles to facilitate recording of couple responses. Each respondent is asked to fill in the *one* circle that best corresponds to his or her point of view about each item. The computer answer sheets are filled in with a pencil. Answer sheets are replaced free with each couple processed at the PREPARE-ENRICH computer facilities.

Computer printout. PREPARE-ENRICH scoring includes a 15-20 page computer printout specially designed to highlight individual and couple scores, national norm scores, and clearly labeled listings of each person's responses to all inventory items. In addition, other sections have been designed to identify unique aspects of each couple's relationship and to help facilitate discussion. Table 12.3 summarizes the sections of the computer printout. Visual examples will be provided later in this chapter.

Couple feedback and prediction form. Each computer printout includes a set of couple feedback forms designed to facilitate the process of discussing results with the couple. Each form contains: (1) a statement to couples highlighting the importance of preparing for marriage and the anticipated benefits for their relationship; (2) a brief bibliography of readings related to marriage preparation, enrichment, and communication; (3) a section designed to have each partner predict the three PREPARE-ENRICH categories that represent couple Strength areas and also to identify three couple Work areas that may need more discussion; and (4) a section for couples to record actual PREPARE-ENRICH scores to allow comparison with their earlier predictions. Couples can be asked to choose strong and weak areas individually or as a couple; this task can be

TABLE 12.3   Components of the PREPARE-ENRICH
              Computer Printout

Title	Description/Purpose	Length
Cover page	Identifies inventory used, couple ID, user ID, and date.	1 page
Background page	Summarizes 18 couple demographics.	1 page
Summary analysis	Summarizes all individual scores, couple scores, and item scores; individual scores (54 for ENRICH, 48 PREPARE), couple scores (80 for ENRICH, 68 for PREPARE).	1 page
Couple profile	Provides a visual chart of couple scores.	1 page
Expanded couple profile	Provides summary of key scores for each category plus a tentative relationship description to be explored with couple.	2 pages
Item summary: Issues for discussion	Provides comprehensive listing of items by content category and indicates how each partner responded to the item.	8-10 pages
Couple feedback sheets	Provides a condensed summary that can be given to couples.	1-2 pages

given as a "homework assignment" until the results are returned or at the beginning of the first feedback session. In general, the primary purpose of this form is to help identify topics in need of discussion from the viewpoint of the couple and to provide them with a document that can be kept and used in the future to discuss marital issues.

Counselor feedback form. Also returned with each computer-processed inventory is a specially printed counselor feedback form. This form is designed to help the counselor organize results and to make choices about issues most in need of discussion. Since PREPARE-ENRICH results are extensive, it became necessary to develop a strategy to help counselors maximize topic selection. The main sections of the counselor feedback form include: (1) recording of Idealistic Distortion; (2) worksheet for determining most likely Strength and Work areas for each couple; (3) worksheet to determine how accurate each partner was in predicting strong and weak areas; (4) worksheet to record descriptions of three couple Strength areas; (5) worksheet to record descriptions of three couple Work areas and space for writing key items or topics unique to each couple; and (6) space to record any other notes about relationship issues to discuss. The counselor feedback form is included as a part of each scoring but is an optional tool and may be used differently by each counselor, depending on the situation.

Hypothetical Example (ENRICH)

Presenting Problem and Background

The computer profile of an actual couple on the ENRICH Inventory will be used to illustrate several key aspects of the diagnostic capabilities of the inventories. The example couple went to a private counselor for marriage counseling and reported general unhappiness and growing resentment. The wife is considered by both partners as most dissatisfied; however, both have "considered divorce." Both partners are in their mid 30s and are college graduates. The marriage is the second for the wife (two children from first marriage) and the first for the husband. The marriage has lasted five years and they have had one child. Both partners came from intact families sharing the same religious preference. Both partners are Caucasian. The wife was first-born in her family, while he was second in his family. They currently reside in a small town; however, he grew up in a large city, while she is originally from a similar small town. The husband earns $20,000-$30,000 per year as a full-time laborer; the wife has some professional training and is currently not employed.

The descriptive information presented above was taken directly from the ENRICH computer printout. Page 2 of each printout fully documents each partner's responses to 18 questions on the front of each answer sheet. Marital history, family background, important demographics, work history, and marital impressions combine to provided information helpful in beginning to form a *context* for interpretation and intervention.

Summary Analysis

Table 12.4 is a reproduction of the ENRICH Summary Analysis for the example couple and closely approximates page 3 of the computer printout. Category titles are listed along with all individual percentile (PCT) and revised (REV) scores, item summary scores, and the positive couple agreement scores and norms. This page lists all scores and provides an overview of the couple and their relative standing with other couples. Most scores receive clearer documentation in subsequent sections of the printout.

The results in Table 12.4 are fairly representative of couples seeking marriage counseling. Both partners provide a highly realistic point of view (Idealistic Distortion score) and seem to have extensive complaints and unhappiness. Individual percentile scores and extremely low, particularly for the wife, who is in the lowest 10 percent on nearly every category. These scores indicate lack of adjustment or predominantly negative

TABLE 12.4 Summary Analysis Page from ENRICH Computer Printout

E N R I C H   S U M M A R Y   A N A L Y S I S

ENRICH CATEGORIES	INDIVIDUAL SCORE TRENDS				ITEM SUMMARY					PERCENT POSITIVE COUPLE AGREEMENT	
	MALE PARTNER		FEMALE PARTNER		DISAGREE	NEG	UNDECIDED	AGREE	POS	COUPLE POSITIVE AGREEMENT	NATIONAL COUPLE AVERAGES
	PCT	REV	PCT	REV							
********************											
IDEALISTIC DISTORTION	** 29.**		** 12.**								
********************											
MARITAL SATISFACTION	10.	10.	10.	10.	2	7	1	0	0	0.	34.
PERSONALITY ISSUES	8.	7.	15.	14.	3	6	1	0	0	0.	46.
COMMUNICATION	48.	43.	18.	17.	4	3	0	3	3	30.	34.
CONFLICT RESOLUTION	9.	8.	11.	10.	4	6	0	0	0	0.	30.
FINANCIAL MANAGEMENT	19.	17.	9.	8.	4	5	0	1	1	10.	44.
LEISURE ACTIVITIES	17.	16.	17.	16.	3	4	0	3	3	30.	35.
SEXUAL RELATIONSHIP	8.	7.	14.	13.	2	5	1	2	2	20.	47.
CHILDREN AND MARRIAGE	10.	10.	8.	7.	2	6	1	1	1	10.	47.
FAMILY AND FRIENDS	31.	29.	13.	12.	5	1	2	2	2	20.	47.
**EQUALITARIAN ROLES	66.	65.	92.	91.	4	0	1	5	5	50.	44.
**RELIGIOUS ORIENTATION	10.	10.	6.	5.	2	0	4	4	4	40.	56.
**MARITAL COHESION	46.	43.	42.	41.	4	0	0	1	1	20.	54.
**MARITAL ADAPTABILITY	82.	80.	66.	65.	3	0	0	2	2	40.	47.
NORMS BASED ON 1200 COUPLES					AVERAGE COUPLE POSITIVE AGREEMENT					21.	43.

INDIVIDUAL PERCENT SCORES *PCT* RANGE FROM 0 TO 100 AND AVERAGE 50. REVISED SCORES *REV* ADJUST PCT SCORES BASED ON A PERSONS TENDENCY TO DESCRIBE THEIR RELATIONSHIP IN AN OVERLY IDEALISTIC MANNER. ITEM SUMMARY IS BASED ON 10 ITEMS PER CATEGORY AND MATCHES ITEMS LISTED IN THE ISSUES FOR DISCUSSION SECTION. THE POSITIVE COUPLE AGREEMENT SCORE IS PERCENT POSITIVE AGREEMENT ON 10 ITEMS. ** CATEGORIES ARE SPECIALLY SCORED.

feelings about the relationship. The Item Summary indicates that only 24 of 120 items are considered positive couple agreement items. Most items are negative agreements or disagreements. These figures, when computed as an average positive couple agreement (21 percent), are less than half the national average (43 percent) and underscore the seriousness of the situation.

It is highly recommended that counselors identify a couple's strong points as well as weak points and balance the discussion of these to avoid excessive defensive reactions from the couple. In marriage counseling, it is generally observed that couples often focus on the negative and tend to overlook the aspects of their relationship that are successful. ENRICH highlights potential strength or agreement areas and can be utilized to help remind the couple that not all things are negative. Conversely, engaged couples tend to focus on the positive and overlook potential negative relationship areas. Thus the same strategy of balancing potential strengths and weaknesses is recommended for PREPARE users.

The final four categories in ENRICH require special interpretation of individual revised scores and positive couple agreement. In the categories of Religious Orientation and Equalitarian Roles, extreme scores represent different *value orientations* or preferred *styles of behavior* rather than personal satisfaction. High scorers on Equalitarian Roles want to share roles, decision making, and household responsibilities equally, while low scorers value traditional husband-wife roles and areas of responsibility. High scorers on Religious Orientation have traditional beliefs about practicing religion, while low scorers have more individualistic interpretations. In either category, it is more important to examine congruence of scores than absolute score values. Positive couple agreement is determined by total agreement and does not consider absolute score values.

In the categories of Cohesion and Adaptability, very high scores (Cohesion = too much togetherness; Adaptability = chaotic) may be just as problematic as very low scores (Cohesion = too much apartness; Adaptability = too rigid). Moderate scores in the 30-70 percent range would reflect potentially more functional levels of cohesiveness or adaptability (Olson, Sprenkle, & Russell, 1979).

Brief Interpretive Summary for Example Couple

The PREPARE-ENRICH computer printout contains a two-page Expanded Couple Profile to help counselors make choices about couple strengths and weaknesses. Although space limitations preclude reproduction of these pages, the basic information provided in the Expanded Couple Profile is included in the following discussion. The couple presented in Table 12.4 will be referred to as Tom and Mary.

Marital Satisfaction (Probable Couple Work Area)

Tom and Mary both have revised scores of 10 percent, indicating a high level of dissatisfaction with the marriage. The positive couple agreement score of 0 percent means that not one of the ten category items were answered in a manner reflecting positive adjustment.

Personality Issues (Probable Couple Work Area)

Tom and Mary both have Revised Scores near the tenth percentile, indicating very low approval of the personality traits and behaviors of the other partner. Mutual concern about personal issues is also reflected in the positive couple agreement score of 0 percent.

Communication (Some Strength and Work Issues)

Tom's revised score of 43 percent suggests that he has a few concerns about his ability to talk with Mary, although he could be described as generally satisfied. Mary's score of 17 percent suggests a high level of misunderstanding and an inability to say clearly what is on her mind. The positive couple agreement score is a moderately low 30 percent, with four disagreement items and three items of negative agreement.

Conflict Resolution (Probable Couple Work Area)

Tom and Mary both have scores around the tenth percentile, demonstrating serious concerns about the way arguments are resolved. Neither partner feels understood and both tend to blame each other for their problems. The positive couple agreement score of 0 percent reinforces the need to work out more satisfactory solutions to their problems.

Financial Management (Probable Couple Work Area)

Tom's score of 17 percent and Mary's score of 8 percent are both in the lower percentiles, suggesting serious dissatisfaction about how money is handled. Priorities for spending and decisions about who is responsible for making purchases are problems that need to be addressed. The positive couple agreement score of 10 percent verifies Finances as a primary couple Work area.

Leisure Activities (Some Strength and Work Issues)

Tom and Mary both have scores of 16 percent, suggesting concern about not spending enough time together and some incompatibility regarding types of activities that each enjoys. The positive couple agreement score of 30 percent means that some issues in the Leisure section may be used as strong points to begin focusing on positive aspects of their marriage.

Sexual Relationship (Probable Couple Work Area)

Tom and Mary both have very low revised scores (7 percent and 13 percent), suggesting considerable concern about how affection is expressed and concern about an unsatisfactory sexual relationship. In addition, both are concerned about family planning decisions. The positive couple agreement of 20 percent is much lower than the norm and validates the need for considerable work.

Children and Marriage

Tom and Mary both have very low revised scores, suggesting concern about commitment to the children and important disagreements about discipline and child-rearing decisions. Both partners agree that problems with the children have led to marital difficulties. The positive couple agreement score of 10 percent is much below average.

Family and Friends (Probable Couple Work Area)

Tom's revised score of 29 percent suggests that he may be experiencing discomfort with in-law relationships, dislikes some of Mary's friends, and resents the time that she spends with them. Mary's score of 12 percent denotes that she has severe dissatisfaction with Tom's relatives and thinks that he is overly involved with his family. Their positive agreement score (20 percent) is well below the norm.

Equalitarian Roles

Mary's revised score (91 percent) demonstrates an extremely equalitarian position desiring shared roles, joint decision making, and equal household assignments. Tom's revised score (65 percent) is also equalitarian, although considerably less than Mary's. Tom generally values equality, but believes that the husband should have more power in making decisions and that the wife should be more responsible for running the household.

Religious Orientation

Tom and Mary both have low revised scores (10 percent and 5 percent), meaning that they are less traditional in their religious beliefs and may question the role of religion in their lives. Four items have indecisive responses, which tend to lower revised scores.

Marital Cohesion

Tom and Mary both have cohesion revised scores in the moderate range (34 percent and 41 percent), suggesting that there is some balance between togetherness and apartness. However, the 20 percent positive couple agreement score suggests high levels of disagreement about cohesiveness in the marriage. Couple satisfaction or dissatisfaction in this area should be explored.

Marital Adaptability

Tom's score (80 percent) indicates that the relationship is often too changeable, overly chaotic, and/or has difficulty maintaining stability. Mary's score (65 percent) shows a slightly different view in that most issues are perceived as chaotic or changeable, with some rigidity on decision making. The positive couple agreement score is close to the norm; however, they have three items with different perceptions that need to be explored.

The above couple description can be quickly determined by using the Expanded Couple Profile and the Issues for Discussion section. Table 12.5 is a duplication of the Issues for Discussion section, illustrating the item listings available for two of the categories identified as Couple Work Areas, Marital Satisfaction, and Conflict Resolution. This section provides detailed item analysis and usually covers about 8-10 pages of the computer printout.

As shown in Table 12.5, male and female responses (M = Male, F = Female) are compared and placed into one of four types. Each PRE-PARE-ENRICH category is presented separately, with clearly labeled item listings for a detailed summary revealing similarities and differences in responses. When the general interpretations from the Expanded Couple Profile are combined with the Item Breakdowns, considerable detail can be added to the diagnosis. In addition, any item has the potential to lead to an entire area of couple discussion. The counselor feedback form was designed to facilitate the description process and to reduce interpretation time.

Limitations

The primary limitations of the PREPARE-ENRICH Inventories involve availability, the necessity of computer processing, and some empir-

TABLE 12.5 Issues for Discussion from ENRICH Computer Printout

ISSUES FOR DISCUSSION — ITEM BREAKDOWN

1 STRONGLY AGREE	2 MODERATELY AGREE	3 NEITHER AGREE NOR DISAGREE	4 MODERATELY DISAGREE	5 STRONGLY DISAGREE

DISAGREEMENT ITEMS: COUPLE DISAGREES BY 2 OR MORE POINTS ON AN ITEM.

SPECIAL FOCUS ITEMS: BOTH INDIVIDUALS HAVE RESPONSES TO
POTENTIAL ISSUES AN ITEM THAT MAY BE PROBLEMATIC FOR THEM.

INDECISION ITEMS: EITHER OR BOTH INDIVIDUALS HAVE NOT YET MADE A CLEAR DECISION ON THE ITEM.

AGREEMENT ITEMS: COUPLES AGREE WITH EACH OTHER IN A POSITIVE WAY.

RESULTS FOR COUPLE # 6

MARITAL SATISFACTION

POSITIVE COUPLE AGREEMENT ITEMS

DISAGREEMENT OR DIFFERENCE ITEMS
052. M= 4.   F= 1. I am unhappy with our financial position and the way money is handled.
099. M= 2.   F= 4. I am dissatisfied about relationships with parents, in-laws or friends.

POTENTIAL ISSUES FOR DISCUSSION

014. M= 2. F= 2. I am not very pleased with the personal habits or personality of my partner.
019. M= 4. F= 5. I am very happy with how we handle household tasks and responsibilities.
032. M= 2. F= 1. I am not very happy with our communication - partner does not understand me.
036. M= 4. F= 5. I am very happy about how we make decisions and resolve conflicts.
053. M= 4. F= 4. I am very happy with management of leisure time and time spent together.
082. M= 4. F= 4. I am very pleased with how we express affection and relate sexually.
088. M= 2. F= 1. I am not very happy about the way we handle our parenting responsibilities.

COUPLE INDECISION ITEMS
113. M= 4. F= 3. I feel very good about how we practice our religious beliefs and values.

CONFLICT RESOLUTION

POSITIVE COUPLE AGREEMENT ITEMS

DISAGREEMENT OR DIFFERENCE ITEMS

004. M= 4. F= 1. In order to end an argument, I usually give up too quickly.
058. M= 2. F= 5. When we have a problem, I can always tell my partner what is bothering me.
074. M= 4. F= 2. I would do anything to avoid conflict with my partner.
112. M= 2. F= 5. When we argue, I usually end up feeling that the problem was all my fault.

POTENTIAL ISSUES FOR DISCUSSION

010. M= 2. F= 1. We have very different ideas about the best way to solve disagreements.
039. M= 4. F= 5. When discussing problems, I usually feel that my partner understands me.
071. M= 2. F= 1. Sometimes we have serious disputes over unimportant issues.
079. M= 1. F= 1. At times I feel our arguments go on and never seem to be resolved.
083. M= 4. F= 5. When we disagree, we openly share our feelings then resolve our problems.
096. M= 2. F= 2. I usually feel that my partner does not take our disagreements seriously.

COUPLE INDECISION ITEMS

ical concerns that require further attention. Although the inventories have been in use since 1976, materials have only recently been available on a wide scale. Current policy limits the availability of materials to persons with clinical or pastoral training in marriage counseling. In some cases, attendance at a one-day work-shop to learn how to use and interpret the instrument is also required. This training was required to ensure that the results were limited to their intended purposes and not used to predict couple happiness or to block an impending marriage. Ensuring proper use of the inventories remains a high priority of the developers.

Since the computer printout is such a vital aspect of the PREPARE-ENRICH Inventories, there is no self-scoring component available. The reliance on an external agent to process the results is a factor that many counselors find difficult to incorporate into their practices. This limitation is less critical for individuals who may choose to stagger appointments over two-week periods or who may choose to discuss other issues not requiring the printout. The use of sophisticated computer-processing facilities has strengths and limitations that must be evaluated within the context of clinical goals and diagnostic situations.

Several empirical aspects of the PREPARE-ENRICH Inventories need to be addressed in future revisions. These include: (1) establishment of higher reliability coefficients for some of the weaker scales; (2) greater precision in the process used to calculate and report revised (REV) scores; and (3) more flexible procedures for handling missing data.

PREPARE-ENRICH scale reliabilities range from a low of .49 to a high of .88. As previously mentioned, these are sufficient for research purposes and can be used to determine differences that exist between individuals and sample norms. The reliabilities are not high enough for predictive testing. While this was not an intended purpose of PREPARE-ENRICH, it is conceivable that some users may be tempted to use the results as evidence to deny a couple's wish to marry. Higher reliabilities are needed to limit the negative impact of potential misuses of the inventories.

Increasing reliabilities is somewhat problematic with the inventories. Since the goal of assessment was to include a broad and representative exposure to issues important to marriage, the range of topics required reduces the potential homogeneity of items within a scale. Slightly reworded phrases may increase the reliability, yet would add little to increasing the range of coverage of marital issues. Adding five items to each scale would also increase reliability, yet would add considerable time to the assessment. Although it is essential that reliabilities be increased, it is important not to do so at the expense of covering a wide range of marital concerns.

The revised scores on PREPARE-ENRICH are carefully constructed to reflect the effect of social desirability on scale scores. It is an essential assessment, but could stand further empirical testing. At times, the formulas do not appear to correct the score as dramatically as they should. Persons with a high level of social desirability, Idealistic Distortion, often will have extremely high percentile scores even after correction. Thus a person who is honest and carefully reflecting on PREPARE-ENRICH items may be penalized when compared to a person who is presenting an impossibly good image of his or her relationship. Reducing penalties for realistic assessments should be a priority in future refinements of the revised score calculations.

Handling of missing data is always a problem in assessment. With the PREPARE-ENRICH Inventories, missing responses are automatically recoded to the "neither agree nor disagree" response category. This procedure allows practitioners the opportunity to assess whether the item was deliberately avoided, was accidentally overlooked, or could not be answered. Most items would be listed in the Couple Indecision section and could be discussed with the couple directly. While the process of couple discussion may not be affected, the empirical scores can be changed. Persons with an unusually high number of undecided responses tend to score very low. The Item Summary section of the Summary Analysis page gives a clear indication of indecision. It is essential that users determine whether indecision is the result of lack of discussion about the topic, irrelevance of the item, or some other factor that may reflect response tendencies.

Conclusion

The PREPARE-ENRICH Inventories were designed for relationship diagnosis and contain procedures that are both methodologically sound and conceptually consistent with theoretical notions about marital systems. The combination of objective computer processing, relevant item content, and exhaustive couple response summaries provides a solid basis for descriptions of personal and couple issues. Couples find the procedures to be meaningful to their relationships and usually look forward to receiving and discussing the computer-processed results. Counselors enjoy the flexibility and comprehensiveness of the information and the range of diagnostic situations suitable for evaluation with the inventories. Hours of interview time can be condensed by using the inventories to identify the areas most likely in need of attention.

In summary, the PREPARE-ENRICH Inventories have been used successfully with thousands of couples. Norms are regularly updated to ensure an adequate and representative sample for marriage preparation and marriage counseling or enrichment. Follow-up studies of counselors using the PREPARE-ENRICH Inventories indicate that many couples are profoundly affected by the procedures and that counselors are highly satisfied with the overall usefulness and clarity of the materials (Olson et al., 1982).

Reference Notes

1. Druckman, J. M., Fournier, D. G., Robinson, B., & Olson, D. H. *Effectiveness of five types of pre-marital preparation programs.* Unpublished technical report, Department of Family Social Science, University of Minnesota,—St. Paul, 1979.

2. Olson, D. H., & Norem, R. *Evaluation of five pre-marital programs.* Unpublished Manuscript, Department of Family Social Science, University of Minnesota, 1977.

3. Fournier, D. G., Springer, J. S., & Olson, D. H. *Conflict and commitment in seven stages of marital and premarital relationships.* Unpublished technical report, Department of Family Social Science, University of Minnesota—St. Paul, 1978.

4. Kitson, G. C., & Sussman, M. B. *Marital complaints, demographic characteristics and symptoms of mental distress among the divorcing.* Paper presented at the meeting of the Midwest Sociological Society, Minneapolis, April 1977.

5. Microys, G., & Bader, E. *Do premarriage programs really help?* Unpublished Manuscript, Department of Family and Community Medicine, University of Toronto, 1977.

6. Fournier, D. G. *A framework for the evaluation of a systemic diagnostic battery.* Paper prepared for the preconference workshop on Family Therapy Assessment, annual meeting of the National Council on Family Relations, Washington, D.C., 1982.

References

Bodin, A. M. Conjoint family assessment. In P. McReynolds (Ed.), *Advances in psychological assessment.* Palo Alto, CA: Science and Behavior, 1968.

Cromwell, R. E., & Kenney, B. P. Diagnosing marital and family systems: A training model. *Family Coordinator,* 1979, *28,* 101-108.

Cromwell, R. E., Olson, D. E., & Fournier, D. G. Tools and techniques for diagnosis in marital and family therapy. *Family Process,* 1976, *15,* 1-49.

Cromwell, R. E., & Peterson, G. W. Multisystem-multimethod assessment: A framework. In E. E. Filsinger & R. A. Lewis (Eds.), *Assessing marriage: New behavioral approaches.* Beverly Hills, CA: Sage, 1981.

Edmonds, V. H. Marital conventionalization: Definition and measurement. *Journal of Marriage and the Family,* 1967, *29,* 681-688.

Fournier, D. G. Validation of PREPARE: A premarital counseling inventory (Doctoral dissertation). *Dissertation Abstracts International,* 1979, *40,* 2385-2386B.

Hobart, C. W. Disillusionment in marriage and romanticism. *Marriage and Family Living,* 1958, *20,* 156-162.

Hunt, M., & Hunt, B. *The divorce experience.* New York: McGraw-Hill, 1977.

Mace, D. R. *Getting ready for marriage.* Nashville: Abingdon, 1972.

Nunnally, J. C. *Psychometric theory.* New York: McGraw-Hill, 1967.

Olson, D. H., Fournier, D. G. & Druckman, J. M. *Counselor's manual for PREPARE-ENRICH* (rev. ed.). Minneapolis: PREPARE-ENRICH, Inc., 1982.

Olson, D. H., & Gravatt, A. E. Attitude change in a functional marriage course. *Family Coordinator,* 1968, *17,* 99-104.

Olson, D. H., Sprenkle, D. H., & Russell, C. S. Circumplex model of marital and family system I: Cohesion and adaptability dimensions, family types, and clinical applications. *Family Process,* 1979, *18,* 3-28.

Rappoport, R. Normal crises, family structure and mental health. *Family Process,* 1963, *2,* 68-80.

Raush, H. L., Goodrich, W., & Campbell, J. Adaptation to the first years of marriage. *Psychiatry,* 1963, *26,* 368-380.

Sager, C. J. *Marriage contracts and couple therapy: Hidden forces in intimate relationships.* New York: Brunner-Mazel, 1976.

Stahmann, R. F., & Hiebert, W. J. Premarital counseling: Process and content. In R. F. Stahmann & W. J. Hiebert (Eds.), *Klemer's counseling in marital and sexual problems: A clinician's handbook* (2nd ed.). Baltimore: Williams & Wilkins, 1977.

Straus, M. A. & Brown, B. W. *Family measurement techniques* (rev. ed.). Minneapolis: University of Minnesota Press, 1977.

PART IV

FAMILY QUESTIONNAIRES

This part of the volume continues the presentations of self-report assessment devices. Those included in this section focus on the whole family, as opposed to the marital orientation emphasized in Part III. Systems-oriented therapists may be especially comfortable with this part of the volume. In Chapter 13, Moos and Moos discuss the Family Environment Scale (FES), as well as several other instruments in their package of assessment of social ecologies in which people live. The FES offers the advantages of standardization and rules for interpretation.

An assessment technique compatible with modern family stress theory is presented by McCubbin and Patterson in Chapter 14. The Family Inventory of Life Events and Changes (FILE) represents an important development in understanding the stressful events families face. As McCubbin and Patterson state, family members may not be fully aware of the stress that "everyday" events, such as an eldest child going away to college, may pose for them.

Chapter 15 is a presentation of the Family Adaptability and Cohesion Evaluation Scales (FACES-II). Olson and Portner discuss the Circumplex Model of family functioning. Their scheme is immensely intuitive, and in developing a family typology they touch the core impulses involved in such designations as "enmeshed," "chaotic," and "rigid," which therapists have long used to discuss distressed family systems.

Margolin and Fernandez (Chapter 16) provide a wrap-up of self-report techniques for marital and family assessment. They try to provide an answer to a critical question: Does the use of formal assessment provide enough useful information over and above that obtained by therapist insight to justify the expenditures involved? Their chapter also contains a discussion of the assessment of children's perception of family life.

CHAPTER *13*

Clinical Applications of the Family Environment Scale

RUDOLF H. MOOS
BERNICE S. MOOS

Stanford University and
Veterans Administration Medical Center

Background and Rationale

The Family Environment Scale (FES) is one of a set of nine Social Climate Scales that measures the social environments of educational (classrooms and student living groups), psychiatric (hospital-based and community-based treatment programs), correctional, and work and family settings (Moos, 1974). The scales measure three underlying domains of factors that characterize such settings: the quality of interpersonal rela- *①* tionships (relationship domain), the emphasis on personal growth goals *②* (personal growth or goal orientation domain), and the degree of structure *③* and openness to change (system maintenance and change domain).

The FES is composed of ten subscales that tap individuals' perceptions of the social-environmental characteristics of their families. The scale has three parallel forms: (1) the Real Form (Form R) measures people's perceptions of their families of origin or orientation; (2) the Ideal Form (Form I) measures people's conceptions of their ideal or preferred family environments; (3) the Expectations Form (Form E) taps expectations about family settings (such as an adolescent child's expectations of a new foster family). Brief descriptions and item examples for each of the ten FES subscales are given in Table 13.1.

Authors' Note: Preparation of this chapter was supported by NIAAA Grant AA02863 and Veterans Administration Medical Research Funds. Portions of the material are adapted from Fuhr, Moos, and Dishotsky (1981) and Moos and Fuhr (1982).

Instrument Source Note: The *FES Manual* and copies of the scale, answer sheets, scoring stencil, and profile sheets are available from Consulting Psychologists Press, 577 College Avenue, Palo Alto, California 94306.

TABLE 13.1   Family Environment Scale Subscale Descriptions

Relationship Dimensions

(1) Cohesion

Commitment, help, and support family members provide for one another: "Family members really help and support one another."

(2) Expressiveness

How much family members are encouraged to act openly and to express their feelings directly: "Family members often keep their feelings to themselves."

(3) Conflict

The amount of openly expressed anger, aggression, and conflict among family members: "We fight a lot in our family."

Personal Growth Dimensions

(4) Independence

The extent to which family members are assertive, self-sufficient, and make their own decisions: "We think things out for ourselves in our family."

(5) Achievement orientation

The extent to which activities (e.g., school and work) are cast into an achievement-oriented or competitive framework: "We feel it is important to be the best at whatever you do."

(6) Intellectual-cultural orientation

The degree of interest in political, social, intellectual, and cultural activities: "We often talk about political and social issues."

(7) Active-recreational orientation

The extent of participation in social and recreational activities: "Friends often come over for dinner or to visit."

(8) Moral-religious emphasis

The emphasis on ethical and religious issues and values: "Family members attend church, synagogue, or Sunday school fairly often."

System Maintenance Dimensions

(9) Organization

The importance of clear organization and structure in planning family activities and responsibilities: "Activities in our family are pretty carefully planned."

(10) Control

The extent to which set rules and procedures are used to run family: "There is a strong emphasis on following rules in our family."

The relationship dimensions are measured by the cohesion, expressiveness, and conflict subscales. These subscales assess family commitment and support, the extent to which family members act openly and express their feelings directly, and the amount of openly expressed anger and conflict among them.

The personal growth or goal orientation dimensions assess the extent to which the family environment emphasizes assertiveness and self-sufficiency (independence), the extent to which such activities as school and work are cast into an achievement-oriented or competitive framework (achievement orientation), the degree of interest in cultural (intellectual-cultural orientation) and recreational (active-recreational orientation) activities, and the emphasis on ethical and religious issues (moral-religious emphasis). The system maintenance and change dimensions assess the importance of clear organization and structure in planning family activities and responsibilities (organization) and the extent to which set rules and procedures are used to run family life (control).

Scale Development

We employed interview and observational methods to gain a naturalistic understanding of the social environments of families and to obtain an initial pool of questionnaire items. The choice and wording of items was guided by the formulation of the three domains of social-environmental dimensions. Each item had to identify an aspect of the family environment that could reflect the emphasis on interpersonal relationships (such as the degree of cohesion), on an area of personal growth (such as the degree of achievement or moral-religious emphasis), or on the organizational structure of the family (such as the degree of organization). For instance, an emphasis on cohesion is inferred from the following items: "Family members really help and support one another" and "There is a feeling of togetherness in our family." An emphasis on achievement is inferred from these items: "We feel it is important to be the best in whatever we do" and "Getting ahead in life is very important in our family." An emphasis on organization is inferred from such items as: "Activities in our family are carefully planned" and "We are generally very neat and orderly."

Information gathered from members of 285 families on an initial 206-item form (A) of the FES was used to develop the 90-item Form R (Real). Five psychometric criteria were used to select the 90 true/false items and 10 subscales of the FES. These criteria enabled us to develop dimensions composed of items that are highly related to each other (internal consistency), to control for acquiescence response set, and to identify dimensions that discriminate among families and are only moderately intercorrelated (for more details, see Moos & Moos, 1981).

Normative Samples and Psychometric Properties

Normative Samples

Normative data on the FES Form R subscales have been collected for 1125 normal and 500 distressed families. The sample of normal families is composed of families from varied areas of the United States, single-parent and multigenerational families, families drawn from ethnic minority groups, and families of all age groups (newly married families, families with preschool and adolescent children, families whose children have left home, and families composed of older adults). The normal family sample includes a group of 294 families drawn randomly from specified census tracts in several counties in California. The fact that the FES subscale means and standard deviations for this group are similar to those for the rest of the sample indicates that the overall norms are representative of the range of normal families.

The sample of distressed families is composed of families drawn from a psychiatrically oriented family clinic and a probation and parole department, families of alcohol abusers and of psychiatric patients, and families in which an adolescent or younger child was in a crisis situation, had run away from home, was identified as delinquent, or was being placed into a foster home. As expected, when compared to normal families, distressed families are lower on cohesion, expressiveness, independence, and intellectual and recreational orientation and higher on conflict and control. These differences are still evident after statistical controls are instituted for socioeconomic and family background characteristics such as age and education of adult partners and number of children. The subscale means and standard deviations for the normal and distressed family samples are provided in the FES Manual (Moos & Moos, 1981). The manual also includes normative information for families of different sizes, families with one spouse over the age of 60, single-parent families, and black and Hispanic families.

Psychometric Properties

Information about the psychometric properties of the FES subscales is provided in the manual (Moos & Moos, 1981). In brief, the ten subscales have adequate internal consistencies (ranging from .61 to .78), relatively high average item-subscale correlations (ranging from .27 to .44), and good 2-month test-retest reliabilities (ranging from .68 to .86). The subscale scores are quite stable over 4-month (ranging from .54 to .91) and 12-month (ranging from .52 to .89) intervals, but they are also sensitive to changes such as those that may occur during family therapy. The intercorrelations of the ten subscales average around .20, indicating that they measure distinct though somewhat related aspects of the social environments of families.

Other psychometric and statistical information includes 4-month and 12-month FES profile stabilities (they are relatively high), and data on the relationships between FES subscale scores and such background factors as family size and partners' age and education (there are low to moderate relationships), on gender differences in perceptions of family environments (there are relatively few), and on parent/child differences (on average, adolescent children tend to see less emphasis on cohesion, expressiveness, independence, and religious orientation and more emphasis on conflict and achievement than do their parents). A comparison of the subscale means and standard deviations of a group of parents and adolescent children from the same families is provided in the *FES Manual*.

The Family Incongruence Score

There is considerable variation in the degree of agreement between family members about their family environment. In some families, husbands and wives or parents and children show very high agreement, while in others they show substantial disagreement. Therefore, we developed a Family Incongruence Score to tap the extent of disagreement among family members. This Incongruence Score makes it possible to focus on such questions as: Do disturbed or separated families show more disagreement among family members than normal or intact families? Is there more incongruence among single-parent than among two-parent families? Does the degree of disagreement among family members change during treatment? Directions for calculating the Family Incongruence Score and comparing it to scores obtained in the normative sample are provided in the manual.

Special Forms of the FES

There are two special forms of the FES, the Ideal Form (Form I) and the Expectations Form (Form E). These two forms are parallel to Form R; that is, each of the 90 items in Form I and Form E is parallel to an item in Form R. The answer sheets and scoring keys for the three forms are identical.

The Ideal Form

The Ideal Form focuses on how individuals conceive of an ideal family setting. This form was developed to measure the goals and value orientations of family members. Form I can be used with Form R to identify areas in which individuals feel that change should occur. Knowledge of the discrepancies between perceptions of the actual and the preferred family environment can help in planning changes in specific areas of family functioning. In addition, Form I may be used to assess the value orientations or value changes that occur among family members over time (such as during treatment). The Ideal Form has been completed by 417 individuals in 281 families. The subscale means and standard deviations are provided in the *FES Manual.*

The Expectations Form

The Expectations Form (Form E) assesses individuals' expectations about family settings. Form E can be useful in premarital counseling to facilitate discussions between prospective spouses about what they expect their family milieu to be like. It can also characterize clients' and counselors' expectations of what a family will be like after the completion of family therapy.

Test Administration and Scoring

The FES Form R items are printed in a reusable booklet designed to be used with a separate answer sheet. Occasionally respondents may be unable to use the separate answer sheet, in which case they may be instructed to mark their answers beside each item in the booklet. The responses can then be transcribed onto answer sheets to facilitate scoring. An examiner can give simple clarifications of word meanings on request, but care should be taken not to influence the direction of the individual's response. Indecisive respondents may be assisted by comments such as "Answer true if you think it is true most of the time" (or "true of most of the members of your family on most days").

Scoring is a simple clerical task using the plastic overlay template provided. Items are arranged so that each column of responses constitutes one of the subscales. The scorer simply counts the number of Xs showing through the template in each column and enters the total in a box at the bottom of the answer sheet. An average score is then calculated for all the members of each family for each subscale. Individual subscale scores or family averages can be converted to standard scores using a table provided in the *FES Manual.* Individual and family profiles that display these standard scores may be generated.

Applications to Clinical Situations

The FES can be used to describe or contrast the social environments of different families, to compare individual family members' perceptions with each other, and to contrast actual and preferred family milieus (for example, see Moos & Moos, 1981). To facilitate the interpretation of the FES, we have recently developed a clinically applicable typology of family environments based on data obtained from a representative community sample of families. In essence, we developed a set of classification rules that are relatively parsimonious and can be applied without the use of a computer or other complex scoring method. FES profiles are classified into family types using a hierarchical set of rules; a profile is assigned to the first applicable family type. Families are grouped according to their most salient characteristics, considering their personal growth orientation first, their relationship orientation next, and their system maintenance characteristics last. The procedure led us to identify seven family types: independence oriented, achievement oriented, moral-religious oriented (structured and unstructured types), intellectual-cultural oriented, support oriented, conflict oriented, and disorganized. The classification rules and mean FES profiles for each of these types are provided elsewhere (Billings & Moos, 1982).

The FES has been used extensively to assess and facilitate change in family settings. For instance, Eichel (1978) employed the scale to help nurses obtain systematic information on their patients' families. By conducting a case-by-case analysis of individual FES profiles and of the congruence of perceptions among family members, Panio (Note 1) showed how an understanding of family functioning can be helpful in treating addiction problems. To illustrate such applications, we provide examples of the utility of the FES in formulating case descriptions and in facilitating the process of family therapy.

Formulating Clinical Case Descriptions

We have used the FES together with two other Social Climate Scales to help develop a social-ecological perspective of the personal and social problems faced by an adolescent girl and her family (Moos & Fuhr, 1982). In this example, we show how such a perspective can provide clinicians with a valuable conceptual framework and sensitize them to environmental factors that tend to remain unrecognized even though they may have an important influence.[1]

The Presenting Problem

Beth was a 15-year-old only child whose parents were in their late 40s. Mr. B had a managerial job in an aerospace firm and Mrs. B was a medical social worker in a large hospital setting. Beth entered individual counseling on her parents' insistence after her academic performance had deteriorated markedly and she had dropped out of school and subsequently become moody and depressed. The therapist found it difficult to develop a relationship and to talk with Beth. Moreover, Beth provided ambiguous information about her school experiences and about the extent to which her problems were academic or social. What precisely had caused her to drop out? What was her life like outside the classroom? Were her parents contributing to the problem? In two two-hour sessions with the family at their home, we employed semistructured interviews and structured questionnaires to obtain answers to these questions.

Beth's classrooms. What caused Beth to drop out of school? To focus on this question, we used the Classroom Environment Scale (Moos & Trickett, 1974) to obtain Beth's description of her classes. Although Beth named history as her favorite subject, she felt that students disliked the class and ignored the teacher, that they were unfriendly to each other and to her, and that class activities were confused and disorganized. She reported that students had almost no say about how class time was spent and that there was little emphasis on innovative teaching methods or unusual class projects. In conjunction with her descriptions of her other classes, the results suggested that the primary problem for Beth was her lack of interaction with her peers (low affiliation) rather than an inability to relate to the teacher (her perceptions of teacher support and teacher control were quite close to her ideal) or a lack of academic orientation (she felt that the emphasis on task orientation in her classes was about right). Since Beth previously had shown above-average academic performance, this information indicated that her problems lay more in the interpersonal than the academic arena.

A basic deficit in Beth's social life was highlighted by the finding that she spent much of her time alone. We learned that Beth generally ate dinner by herself because her parents both worked overtime regularly and came home late. She rarely engaged in social telephone calls, had no close friends, and did both her homework and her part of the housework alone. Beth spent a considerable amount of time in solitary activities (such as reading, photography, and playing the piano) and passive pursuits (such as watching television). Why did Beth spend so much time alone? We thought that information on the social milieu of her family would help to provide an answer.

The social environment of the family. Beth and her parents independently evaluated their family on the ten dimensions of the FES (see Figure 13.1). Beth gave a moderately but consistently more negative assessment. She described her family as very low on cohesion, answering only one of nine questions on the cohesion subscale in a positive direction. In contrast, Beth's parents perceived a moderate amount of cohesion. Moreover, although Beth's parents felt that there were few disagreements or open expressions of anger and aggression, Beth felt that family members fought a lot, lost their tempers, and often criticized each other (conflict).

Beth gave the family a very low score on recreational orientation. She reported that most weekends and evenings were spent at home, that nobody was active in sports, that friends did not come to visit often, and

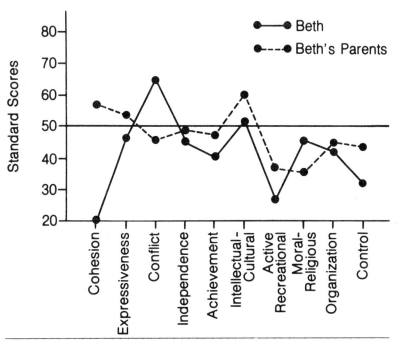

Figure 13.1   Actual Family Environment as Perceived by Beth B and Her Parents

that family members rarely attended movies or plays. Beth's parents generally agreed with her appraisal, although their ratings were somewhat higher. In addition, they reported an almost total lack of participation in joint social and recreational activities during the past month. These results suggested that Beth's lack of involvement in social activities with her peers might reflect the fact that she had not learned appropriate social and interpersonal skills from her parents.

Beth also felt that the degree of control in the family was quite low. For example, she stated: "We can do whatever we want to in our family" (true), "There are very few rules to follow in our family" (true), and "You can't get away with much in our family" (false). In conjunction with her perceptions of low family cohesion, this indicates that Beth felt that her parents neither supported nor controlled her adequately. With respect to the other areas, Beth and her parents tended to agree on the amount of family concern with intellectual pursuits (slightly above average), independence (above average), and achievement and religious issues (slightly below average).

In order to identify the extent to which Beth and her parents agreed

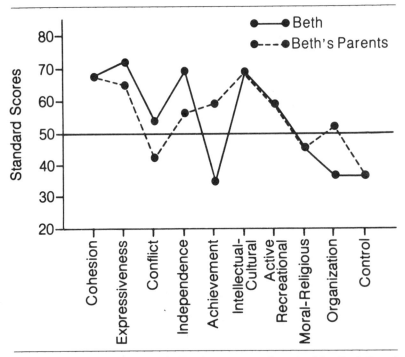

Figure 13.2   Preferred Family Environment as Perceived by Beth B and Her Parents

about the type of family setting they wanted, we asked them to complete the Ideal Form (Form I) of the FES. Figure 13.2 shows that their perceptions of an ideal family milieu were congruent in most areas. For example, Beth and her parents wanted a close-knit expressive family unit with relatively little conflict and considerable emphasis on independence and intellectual and recreational pursuits. However, Beth's parents wanted to emphasize achievement much more strongly than Beth did. A comparison of Beth's perceptions of her actual (Figure 13.1) and preferred (Figure 13.2) family milieu helps to clarify the extent and focus of her dissatisfaction. Beth wanted to see substantial increases in cohesion, expressiveness, independence, and both cultural and recreational orientation.

Mr. and Mrs. B's work settings. The FES results left us with some questions. Beth and her parents agreed in wanting a more cohesive, recreationally oriented family milieu. Why were they not able to create such a setting? Since both Beth's parents were employed in demanding professional jobs, we wondered whether factors in their work milieu might be implicated. We therefore asked Mr. and Mrs. B to use the Work Environment Scale (WES; Moos, 1981) to describe their work settings. Mr. B was a manager in an aerospace firm and was responsible for most of the financial transactions and for supervising data collection, personnel, accounting, customer relations, and plant security. The WES results showed that Mr. B liked and was very committed to his job, primarily because of his positive relationships with his coworkers and supervisors and the stimulation of daily challenges and problems. He also felt that task orientation was above average and that there was considerable time urgency and pressure to work hard and meet deadlines.

Mrs. B was employed as a medical social worker in a busy hospital setting. On a typical day, she interacted with between 20 and 40 patients. Mrs. B cared about her patients and felt responsible for their welfare. The WES results showed that she was enthusiastic and committed to her job and felt she was encouraged to make her own decisions. She saw the work setting as clear and well organized and was satisfied with the amount of help provided by her supervisor. However, Mrs. B also perceived a considerable amount of time urgency and work pressure in her job situation. For instance, she almost never missed work, since she felt that no one else would take care of her patients adequately while she was gone.

A social-ecological interpretation. A relatively clear picture of Beth's situation emerged from the foregoing information. Mr. and Mrs. B were highly committed to and satisfied with their jobs and described their relationship to each other quite favorably. They both worked hard, enjoyed substantial responsibility, and were interested in pursuing their professional careers and obtaining higher-level managerial positions. In contrast, Beth was very critical of both home and school. Although the family status quo was satisfactory for Mr. and Mrs. B in view of their demanding and rewarding work environments, it did not meet Beth's needs for parental support or the sense of belongingness that emerges from shared participation in family activities. Considering that Beth enjoyed reading for pleasure and liked to engage in intellectual and cultural pursuits, and recalling that the major differences between her real and ideal class descriptions involved affiliation, we concluded that her school problems derived primarily from interpersonal and social rather than academic factors.

Beth's "school problems" seemed to have their roots in her relationship to her parents. Beth's parents worked long and demanding hours and did not have sufficient time to understand or fulfill her emotional needs adequately. Moreover, Beth's parents were dedicated to achievement in their own careers and strongly pressured their daughter to do well academically and to make plans for college and a career. While Beth also desired these goals, she harbored deep anger toward her parents for valuing their professional activities more than her emotional needs. The mixture of resentment and rejection aroused by this situation had a detrimental influence on Beth's motivation and performance in school. Beth felt that her parents had rejected her in favor of their careers; she retaliated by rejecting school as a means of hurting her parents and attracting attention from them. These problems were exacerbated by the fact that Beth's parents had never shown her how to relate comfortably and warmly with others, nor how to plan and enjoy casual social activities with her peers.

Most important, neither Beth nor her therapist, who tended to view the problem in person-centered terms, had been able to "diagnose" the situation. Beth had not conceptualized her problem as rooted in her family relationships, primarily because she felt guilty about placing her needs above those of her parents. Beth's parents did not realize that her problems were due in part to their abiding commitment to their respective careers. The therapist had focused attention on Beth's feelings about school and academic performance and neglected to explore contributing environmental factors. The new information we developed led the therapist to discover that a series of recent events had upset a previously workable equilibrium that Beth's parents had established between the pressures of family and work activities.

Although Beth and her parents had moderately serious problems, it was clear that they did care about each other and were amenable to making necessary changes. Our formulation of the situation pointed to the need for family therapy due to the family-related nature of the problem. Moreover, we thought that family therapy would probably be effective because joint meetings could help to mitigate Beth's feelings of rejection and enhance family cohesion and expressiveness, and because Beth and her parents basically agreed about the features of their ideal family milieu. In addition, since Beth's parents were unaware of the depth of her feelings, it seemed that feedback of the FES results jointly to all three family members would serve to define the problem more clearly and initiate discussions about potential changes. The desire of all three family members to engage in intellectual and recreational pursuits could then be used to encourage their joint participation in some highly valued activities and provide an important step toward increasing family cohesion and togetherness. The therapist initiated joint family sessions and was able to use these ideas to effect positive changes in the family environment and subsequently in Beth's mood and academic performance.

Assessment and Feedback in
Ongoing Family Therapy

Over the past six years, the FES has been used as an adjunct to ongoing family therapy in two local outpatient clinics. Typically, the Real and Ideal Forms of the FES are administered early in therapy and the Real Form is given again both at the end of therapy and several months later.

We provide a case example here to illustrate how the FES can describe the social milieu of a family in treatment and how such information can facilitate the therapeutic process and evaluate progress in therapy (for more details, see Fuhr, Moos, & Dishotsky, 1981).

The Cartwright Family

John and Mary Cartwright were in their late twenties and had been married for two years. Mrs. Cartwright had a nine-year-old daughter (Shirley) from a brief previous marriage. Mrs. Cartwright was in close contact with her three older brothers, who were frequent guests and lived in the Cartwrights' home for several weeks at a time. Mrs. Cartwright initially sought individual therapy during the breakup of her first marriage a few years ago. At that time, she had problems centering around relationships with men, difficulty in expressing her feelings, lack of self-confidence, and excessive drinking under stress.

Subsequently, Mr. and Mrs. Cartwright entered therapy to discuss her drinking problem and explore a lack of warmth in their relationship. Mrs. Cartwright's drinking was often triggered by her brothers' demeaning and antagonistic behavior. Rather than expressing her feelings, she suppressed her anger and drank heavily until she blew up in a violent rage. Managing their daughter Shirley's behavior was also problematic, since neither parent was effective in setting limits for her. Mr. and Mrs. Cartwright did not approve of Shirley's friends, and both complained that she never complied with their requests. According to the therapist, Mrs. Cartwright undercut her husband's attempts to discipline Shirley, thereby weakening his authority.

The Cartwright's also complained of a chaotic family life. During a typical day, Mrs. Cartwright would get up late and rush to work. She and her husband would arrive home late for dinner, with Mrs. Cartwright behind schedule in preparing it, but her husband refusing to help. Mrs. Cartwright's daughter often had an unwelcome friend visiting, which added to the tension. Consequently, much of the Cartwrights' time together was occupied by ineffective efforts to organize their family activities. Mr. Cartwright, who was a law student, would often react to the disorder by withdrawing to the library or elsewhere outside the home.

The FES profiles of the Cartwright family. After several counseling sessions, the therapist explained to the Cartwrights that he wanted to explore the issues of togetherness, expression of feelings, organization, and control in their family by using the FES. He asked Mr. and Mrs. Cartwright to fill out the FES in three ways. They each gave their impressions of the current family environment (Form R). Since Mrs. Cartwright's brothers had a significant impact on the family, the Cartwrights also used Form R to describe

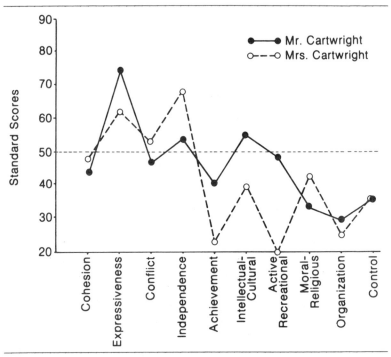

Figure 13.3   Pretherapy Family Environment for the Cartwright Family

what the family was like when her brothers were present. They then used Form I to indicate how they saw an ideal family environment.

The picture of the family provided by the FES (Figure 13.3) was very similar to the therapist's impressions. The combination of moderate to high expressiveness and independence, and low organization and control defined a family with relatively little commitment or sense of togetherness. For example, Mr. and Mrs. Cartwright both felt that they did not get enough attention, that neither volunteered to help carry out daily chores, that they put little energy into family activities, and that they were often just killing time at home. They also agreed that family activities were not carefully planned, that they were not neat and orderly, that duties were not clearly defined, and that there were few rules to follow or set ways of doing things. Mrs. Cartwright also perceived little or no family participation in recreational activities, although Mr. Cartwright disagreed. This came as a surprise to the therapist, who thought that the couple was the center of an active social life.

The adverse influence of Mrs. Cartwright's brothers was clearly shown by the Cartwrights' description of the family milieu when the brothers were present. Both agreed that cohesion and expressiveness were much lower (one to two standard deviations below average), while conflict was much higher (more than one standard deviation above average). Both indicated that they kept their feelings to themselves when Mrs. Cartwright's brothers were present, and found it hard to "blow off steam" constructively, to discuss personal problems, or to complain and stand up for their rights. The brothers were not on sufficiently intimate terms with Mr. Cartwright to permit usual family interaction patterns to be maintained. They were seen as intruders who disrupted the family environment.

Feedback of FES information to the Cartwright family. To illustrate how feedback of FES results can be used in ongoing therapy, we turn to Figure 13.4, which shows the Cartwrights' ideal family milieu (Form I). The dashed line at zero represents no difference between real and ideal scores. A positive score indicates a higher ideal score than real score; for example, both Mr. and Mrs. Cartwright saw a need for more cohesion. The Cartwrights agreed on the amount of change they needed to make in most areas, although Mrs. Cartwright wanted much more family organization than her husband did. The therapist's first step in feedback was to point out this consensus to the Cartwrights: They both wanted more cohesion, less conflict, and more cultural and recreational activities. The couple found this feedback encouraging, because they had not been aware of the high congruence in their value systems.

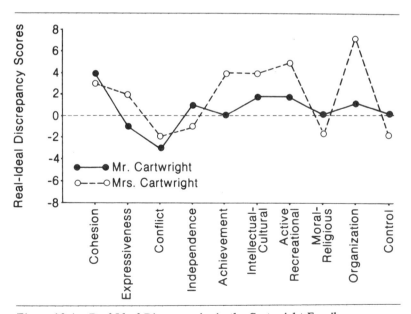

Figure 13.4   Real-Ideal Discrepancies in the Cartwright Family

Mr. and Mrs. Cartwright found it most useful to consider several dimensions in tandem in planning changes. For example, in discussing the items on the FES conflict and organization subscales, Mr. Cartwright realized that his lack of assistance in housework, compounded by the family's scheduling problems and poor planning of activities, significantly contributed to the tension and conflict. Mr. Cartwright was surprised to learn of the pervasive negative effects of family disorganization on his wife's feelings toward him. This problem was solved by a joint decision to obtain part-time household help. Similarly, the couple realized that their problems in setting limits with Shirley, reflected on the FES control subscale, also eroded their feelings of togetherness. This led to intensive discussion of how Mrs. Cartwright undercut her husband's authority and ventilation of his feelings about this issue.

Feedback of the FES scores with and without Mrs. Cartwright's brothers at home strongly underscored their deleterious effect on the couple's relationship. The Cartwrights had to move to a new home at this time, and they decided to use this event to create a new social as well as physical environment for themselves. The move helped them to institute an abrupt change in relating to Mrs. Cartwrights's brothers and to develop more control over the friends Shirley brought home.

The outcome of therapy for the Cartwright family. Mr. and Mrs. Cartwright completed the Real FES for both the nuclear and the extended (with brothers) family three months later to allow us to track progress in therapy. Improvements were substantial, as was expected from the relatively high agreement on goals. The Cartwrights described their relationship much more favorably; cohesion and organization were higher, whereas conflict was somewhat lower (see Figure 13.5). In addition, participation in cultural and recreational activities increased, although Mr. and Mrs. Cartwright both felt that more change was needed in these areas.

Mr. Cartwright had learned from discussions in therapy that a greater degree of neatness and order and a clearer definition of duties could improve his relationship to his wife. Mrs. Cartwright indicated that the house was neater and that tasks were more equitably allocated. The system of control in the family did not change substantially; both Mr. and Mrs. Cartwright wanted and still had a family emphasizing flexible rules and democratic decision making. However, their move to a new neighborhood enabled them to institute more control over Shirley's friends. Because Mrs. Cartwright's brothers visited less frequently, their disruptive effects became clearer and she was able to deal with them in a much more forthright and assertive manner.

Use of the FES with the Cartwrights aided the therapist in assessing and changing the family system. The FES highlighted Mr. Cartwright's contribution to the family's disorganization, and showed how disorder

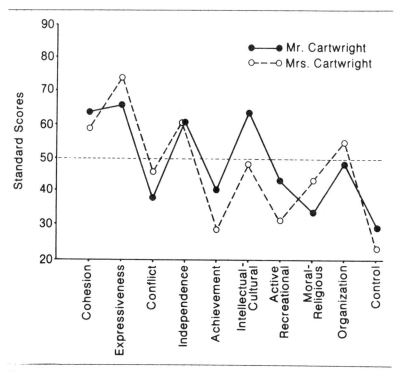

Figure 13.5   Posttherapy Family Environment for the Cartwright Family

and low control undermined the Cartwrights' affection for each other. The scale revealed that lack of shared recreational pursuits was a severe problem for Mrs. Cartwright, and emphasized that activities with her brothers divided the couple. Most important, the FES brought out a high level of agreement between Mr. and Mrs. Cartwright's perceptions of their relationship and their desired directions for change. Follow-up administration showed that they were able to work together to decrease conflict and to increase cohesion, recreation, and organization.

Applications to Program Evaluation

In order to provide ideas about applications of the FES to program evaluation, we present a selective overview of some relevant work here. Brief descriptions of these and other projects are given in an annotated bibliography (Moos, Clayton, & Max, 1979) as well as in the *FES Manual* (Moos & Moos, 1981) and other sources (Cronkite, Moos, & Finney, in press; Moos & Moos, in press).

The Outcome of
Family-Oriented Treatment

Several studies have found the FES to be sensitive to changes that may occur in family environments during treatment. For example, in a study of an eight-week treatment program intended to change delinquent behavior by changing the family system, Christensen (1976) found that a treated group perceived more cohesion and less conflict after the program, whereas there were no changes among individuals in an untreated control group. Bader (1976) studied experimental and control group families before, immediately after, and two months after a one-week multiple-family-therapy-family workshop. The families in the experimental group showed significant increases in cohesion, expressiveness, and independence immediately after the workshop, as well as additional increases in these areas at the two-month follow-up interval. The control group did not change significantly over time on any of the FES subscales.

In an evaluation of the effects of behaviorally oriented parent training groups, Karoly and Rosenthal (1977) found that parents in a treatment group showed an increase in their perceptions of family cohesion and support, while parents in a control group did not perceive significant changes in their families. Finally, Druckman (1979) evaluated the effects of a family-oriented treatment program for juvenile offenders. She found that families who completed family therapy, as well as those who dropped out (some of whom entered other types of treatment), obtained higher posttest than pretest scores on several of the FES dimensions. Compared to the dropouts, families who completed treatment had higher pretest scores on the intellectual-cultural orientation subscale, suggesting that they may have been receptive to treatment oriented around discussion and self-understanding. However, recidivism rates did not decrease as a result of treatment completion. The only difference between recidivist and nonrecidivist families was the recidivists were extremely cohesive, which the author suggests may be dysfunctional.

The Outcome of
Treatment for Alcoholism

We have used the FES to assess the families of alcoholic patients and to predict the outcome of treatment for alcoholism. In one study, recovered and relapsed alcoholic patients were followed two years after residential treatment and compared to sociodemographically matched normal-drinking community controls. There were no differences in the family environments of recovered patients and of community controls. However, the family environments of the relapsed patients showed more conflict and less cohesion, expressiveness, organization, and congruence between the spouses than those of the other two groups (Moos, Finney, & Chan, 1981). A longitudinal analysis showed that the more cohesive and supportive the family (as indexed by high cohesion and recreational orientation and low family conflict), the better the prognosis for the alcoholic family member (Finney, Moos, & Newborn, 1980).

Family Environment and
Individual Adaptation

The FES has been used to examine the relationships between characteristics of family environments and role and social functioning among both adults and children. For instance, Dimond (1979) examined the links among family environment factors, adaptation to chronic illness (morale and change in social functioning), and medical status in hemodialysis patients. Family cohesion and expressiveness were associated with higher morale, even while controlling for the number of medical problems a patient had during the six-month data collection period. Cohesion was also associated with better ability to maintain social functioning after the onset of dialysis. The emphasis on cohesion and expressiveness has also been found to facilitate self-care ability and adaptive behavior among mentally retarded adults in foster family homes (Willer & Intagliata, 1981). On the other hand, families that place more emphasis on organization and control are less likely to experience the deinstitutionalization of a family member as a crisis event (Willer, Intagliata, & Atkinson, 1981).

The reliance on effective coping responses to life stressors seems to promote positive interaction among family members and thus results in more cohesive family environments; in contrast, an increased frequency of life stressors has been related to more negative family environments. Spouses located in family environments that are high in conflict and low in cohesion tend to be less instrumental and to report more anxiety, depression, and physical symptoms (Boss, 1980; Finney, Moos, Cronkite, & Gamble, in press; Maynard, Maynard, McCubbin, & Shao, 1980). Work-setting factors can moderate these relationships (Billings & Moos, in press), as can the congruence between personal dispositions and the characteristics of family and work settings. In one study, for instance, independent women who were not in autonomous environments tended to be depressed; dependent women in autonomous environments also tended to be depressed (Wetzel, 1978). Taken together, these and related findings indicate that the FES taps important characteristics of the family environment that affect the adaptation of family members.

Summary

The FES is a standardized scale that provides an efficient way to gather data about family settings and develop a broader understanding about the current environmental factors that influence clients. It is applicable to many kinds of families, including single-parent families and ethnic minority families. The scale can be used to describe the social environment of a family, to compare individual family members' perceptions, and to identify the congruence between actual and preferred family settings. More generally, it can help to compare and contrast families, to formulate clinical case descriptions, to guide and monitor the progress of therapy, and to examine the connections between family environments and individual adaptation. The structured, easily understandable format of the scale makes it particularly suitable for use as a screening tool. Also, although it may be preferable in some instances, the clinician need not be present during the assessment; a paraprofessional can obtain the information and answer typical questions.

The FES provides a conceptual framework of three domains of social-environmental factors that can help train family counselors and clarify some of the salient aspects of family interaction (Cromwell & Keeney, 1979; Waters, 1979). The conceptual congruence between these domains and the domains tapped by our other social-environmental measures makes it possible to obtain an integrated perspective on an individual's overall social environment. Such a perspective can foster a more comprehensive understanding of the interconnections between the family and other important settings in clients' lives.

Note

1. Names and details given in our examples are altered to protect the anonymity of the families involved.

Reference Note

1. Panio, A. *Assessing the families of drug abusers utilizing the Family Environment Scale.* Paper presented at the National Drug Abuse Conference, San Francisco, 1977.

References

Bader, E. *Redecisions in family therapy: A study of change in an intensive family therapy workshop.* Unpublished doctoral dissertation, California School of Professional Psychology, San Francisco, 1976.

Billings, A., & Moos, R. Family environments and adaptation: A clinically applicable typology. *American Journal of Family Therapy,* 1982, *10,* 26-38.

Billings, A., & Moos, R. Social support and functioning among community and clinical groups: A panel model. *Journal of Behavioral Medicine,* in press.

Boss, P. The relationship of psychological father presence, wife's personal qualities, and wife/family dysfunction in families of missing fathers. *Journal of Marriage and the Family*, 1980, *42*, 541-549.

Christensen, B. *A family systems treatment program for families of delinquent adolescent boys.* Unpublished doctoral dissertation, Department of Sociology, Brigham Young University, 1976.

Cromwell, R., & Keeney, B. Diagnosing marital and family systems: A training model. *Family Coordinator*, 1979, *28*, 101-108.

Cronkite, R., Moos, R., & Finney, J. The context of adaptation: An integrative perspective on community and treatment environments. In W. A. O'Connor & B. Lubin (Eds.), *Ecological models: Applications to clinical and community mental health.* New York: John Wiley, in press.

Dimond, M. Social support and adaptation to chronic illness: The case of maintenance hemodialysis. *Research in Nursing and Health*, 1979, *2*, 101-108.

Druckman, J. A family oriented policy and treatment program for juvenile status offenders. *Journal of Marriage and the Family*, 1979, *41*, 627-636.

Eichel, E. Assessment with a family focus. *Journal of Psychiatric Nursing and Mental Health Services*, 1978, *16*, 11-15.

Finney, J., Moos, R., Cronkite, R., & Gamble, W. A conceptual model of the functioning of married persons with impaired partners: Spouses of alcoholic patients. *Journal of Marriage and the Family*, in press.

Finney, J., Moos, R., & Mewborn, C. Posttreatment experiences and treatment outcome of alcoholic patients six months and two years after hospitalization. *Journal of Consulting and Clinical Psychology*, 1980, *48*, 17-29.

Fuhr, R., Moos, R., & Dishotsky, N. Use of family assessment and feedback in ongoing family therapy. *American Journal of Family Therapy*, 1981, *9*, 24-36.

Karoly, P., & Rosenthal, M. Training parents in behavior modification: Effects on perceptions of family interaction and deviant child behavior. *Behavior Therapy*, 1977, *8*, 406-410.

Maynard, P., Maynard, N., McCubbin, H., & Shao, D. Family life in the police profession: Coping patterns wives employ in managing job stress and the family environment. *Family Relations*, 1980, *29*, 494-501.

Moos, R. *The Social Climate Scales: An overview.* Palo Alto, CA: Consulting Psychologists Press, 1974.

Moos, R. *Work Environment Scale manual.* Palo Alto, CA: Consulting Psychologists Press, 1981.

Moos, R., Clayton, J., & Max, W. *The Social Climate Scales: An annotated bibliography.* Palo Alto, CA: Consulting Psychologists Press, 1979.

Moos, R., Finney, J., & Chan, D. The process of recovery from alcoholism: I. Comparing alcoholic patients and matched community controls. *Journal of Studies on Alcohol*, 1981, *42*, 383-402.

Moos, R., & Fuhr, R. The clinical use of social-ecological concepts: The case of an adolescent girl. *American Journal of Orthopsychiatry*, 1982, *52*, 111-122.

Moos, R., & Moos, B. *Family Environment Scale manual.* Palo Alto, CA: Consulting Psychologists Press, 1981.

Moos, R., & Moos, B. Adaptation and the quality of life in work and family settings. *Journal of Community Psychology*, in press.

Moos, R., & Trickett, E. *Classroom Environment Scale manual.* Palo Alto, CA: Consulting Psychologists Press, 1974.

Waters, J. The Family Environment Scale as an instructional aid for studying the family. *Teaching of Psychology*, 1979, *6*, 162-164.

Wetzel, J. Depression and dependence upon unsustaining environments. *Clinical Social Work Journal*, 1978, *6*, 75-89.

Willer, B., & Intagliata, J. Social-environmental factors as predictors of adjustment of deinstitutionalized mentally retarded adults. *American Journal of Mental Deficiency*, 1981, *86*, 252-259.

Willer, B., Intagliata, J., & Atkinson, A. Deinstitutionalization as a crisis event for families of mentally retarded persons. *Mental Retardation*, 1981, *19*, 28-29.

CHAPTER 14

Stress: The Family Inventory of Life Events and Changes

HAMILTON I. McCUBBIN
JOAN M. PATTERSON
University of Minnesota

Everything was going so well. I got the job I wanted, where I wanted it, and with the salary we had dreamed of. My wife was looking forward to the educational opportunity she had waited for. The move went smoothly. But six months later, my wife was diagnosed as having cancer! Even though the move was something we had all wanted, we experienced stress, a lot of stress. The long-term effects of a rapid succession of changes had taken their toll. While we had everything going for us, the impact of the changes . . . new career . . . new community . . . new home . . . all piled up and the result was a major illness in the family. Stress researchers say that what my family experienced and the illness that followed were not as uncommon as we may think. Stress, and family stress in particular, can have a negative impact upon family members.

The impact of cumulative life changes upon the health of individuals has been a major topic of research in the past decade. The concepts of life stress and strains have received increased attention in both the popular media and the scientific literature. Family stress, as conceptualized in this chapter, emerges out of three bodies of scientific research: psychobiological stress theory, individual and family development theory, and family stress theory. In the last 25 years, there has been a proliferation of research guided, in part, by the following hypothesis: Stress, arising from

Authors' Note: The authors would like to thank Dr. Richard Sauer, Director, Agricultural Experiment Station, who supported this project. Additionally, we would like to thank Dr. David Olson, Andrea Larsen, Howard Barnes, Mark Wilson, and Marla Muxen, who contributed in a major way to the analysis of data and findings that were included in this investigation. This project was funded by the Agricultural Experiment Station, Family Stress and Coping Project, University of Minnesota.

Instrument Source Note: Materials related to the FILE are available from Dr. Hamilton McCubbin, Family Social Science, 290 McNeal Hall, St. Paul, Minnesota 55108.

an accumulation of life events and strains, plays a role in the etiology of various somatic and psychiatric disorders.

This concept of "cumulative life changes" has been applied only recently in a systematic manner to the study of family stress and of family behavior in response to stressful conditions. The purposes of this chapter are, first, to clarify the meaning of stressors, strain, stress, and their impact on family life; and second, to demonstrate the value of evaluating family stress as a clinical procedure in determining a family's vulnerability and resilience.

Rationale

Psychobiological Stress Research

Cannon (1929) is credited with early experimental work showing that stimuli (such as life events) associated with emotional arousal cause changes in physiological processes. Meyer (cited in Leif, 1948), used a "life chart" in medical diagnosis and demonstrated the relationship between ordinary life events and illness. In explaining this relationship, it has been pointed out that the human body attempts to maintain homeostasis. Any life change that upsets the body's steady state calls for readjustment. Excessive changes tax the body's capacity for readjustment and thereby produce stress. Thus life events are conceived of as stressors that require change in the individual's ongoing life pattern (Holmes & Rahe, 1967). Stress is the organism's physiological and psychological response to these stressors, particularly when there is a perceived imbalance between environmental demands (life change) and the individual's capability to meet these demands.

Most of the research showing a positive relationship between life events and illness has used an instrument, developed by Holmes and Rahe (1967), that lists 43 events of a family, personal, occupational, and financial nature that require some change or readjustment. In the earliest version, the Schedule of Recent Experience (Hawkins, Davies, & Holmes, 1957), an individual's score was the number of events experienced in a given time period (usually six months to two years). Subsequently, proportional weights were assigned to each event based on the relative amount of readjustment (in terms of intensity and length of time) required by an individual experiencing each event. An individual's score was the sum of the weights associated with each event experienced. This scale and modifications of it have been used in numerous prospective and retrospective studies over the past decade. Positive relationships have been found between the magnitude of life changes and various criterion correlates such as heart disease, fractures, childhood leukemia, pregnancy, beginning of prison terms, poor teacher performance, low college grade-point average, and college foot-

ball players' injuries (Holmes & Masuda, 1974). But the value of this instrument in the study of married individuals and as an index of family stress has
not been established.

Development Theory

Most individuals can recall a time of major transition in their lives when
they moved from a stable, predictable role, through a period of uncertainty characterized by trial and error behavior into a new period of stability with a changed, now predictable role set. The transitions from college
to first job and from single status to being married are two normative
transitions experienced by many persons. Such transitions, while normal, are nonetheless upsetting life events marked by psychological and
interpersonal conflicts and confusion.

Within the context of family life, transitions have an added impact.
Because families function as a total unit, even a seemingly minor event
experienced by one member, such as entering school for the first time, or
becoming an adolescent, or assuming new job responsibilities, may trigger other changes in the family unit. Or a transition may require a sweep-
ing reorganization of the family unit and its social network. For example,
in the case of divorce, the family unit will struggle with the loss of a member, loss of social status, loss of income, and the need to reestablish the
family in a new community of friendships. A transition may be long anticipated and even rehearsed in advance, as in the case of parents who prepare for their first child, an event may be untimely and unexpected, as in
the case of a wife becoming pregnant at age 40.

Most of these life changes are normal in that they are likely to happen
in a family unit over the life course. Their significant common denomina-
tor is that they encompass a transition period often marked by feelings of
uncertainty, anxiety, a sense of loss, and intrafamily conflict as the family
unit tries to adjust and eventually adapt to the situation. This transition
period involves processes of adjustment, reorganization, consolidation,
and adaptation (McCubbin & Patterson, 1982, 1983). Families are called
upon to change established patterns of behavior and bring stability to the
family unit, both in terms of family relationships among members and in
terms of the family's relationship to the community. Yet, although such
transitions may be universally experienced, it is only recently that careful
attention has been paid to their content and process.

Family members change over time. Erickson (1976) views each life
stage as a key psychosocial crisis, which is not a threat or catastrophe but
"a turning point, a crucial period of increased vulnerability and height-
ened potential." The way in which an individual family member resolves
the crisis can either enhance or weaken his or her ability to master crises
in subsequent stages. When viewed from a family perspective, one can

observe how well the developmental tasks of individual members "cog-wheel" so as to move each other along or, conversely, to retard or slow down the resolution of the psychosocial crises.

The family unit changes over the life cycle. By keying on the oldest child in the family unit, Duvall (1977) divided the family cycle into eight stages: married couple without children, childbearing, preschool age, school age, teenage, launching, middle age, and aging family. Just as individuals have their own developmental tasks, the family unit is called upon to respond to normative family demands across the life cycle. These responsibilities are defined as growth opportunities that arise at each of the stages in the family cycle. Meeting these growth opportunities successfully leads to approval and success with later tasks, whereas failure to meet these challenges contributes to familial unhappiness, disapproval, and difficulty with later family developmental tasks.

Family transitional events such as marriage, parenthood, launching children, and retirement call for family reorganization and adaptation as both new demands and new opportunities are imposed on the family unit.

While both men and women progress through individual and family unit developmental stages and tasks, the timing and meaning of these tasks may be very different for each. From a family perspective, these gender differences may create an additional source of family stress. Riegel (1975) attempted to delineate such gender differences over the life cycle by noting the differences in the influences of psychosocial and biological factors upon each sex. For example, he views the birth of children as having a powerful biological effect upon mother and primarily a social effect upon father.

Family Stress Theory

Within the family field, a considerable body of theory and research has evolved independently of the psychobiological and developmental stress research briefly summarized above. Beginning with the early work of Hill (1949), who studied the stressors of war separation and reunion, family scholars have primarily focused their research efforts on nonnormative or situational stressors in an effort to understand why it is that families faced with a single event such as a loss, illness, or separation vary in their ability to adjust or adapt to the situation. The theoretical model most often used to explain this variability is the ABCX family crisis model (Hill, 1958), which states that

> A (the stressor event)—interacting with B (the family's crisis meeting resources)—interacting with C (the definition the family makes of the event)—produce X (the crisis) (Hill, 1958, p. 141).

In this model, Hill defined a "stressor" as a situation for which the family has had little or no prior preparation and a "crisis" as any sharp or decisive change for which old patterns of behavior are inadequate. These definitions are analogous to those used in life events research to define stressors and stress, respectively. Hill further described stressors in terms of their hardships, which he operationalized as the number of additional changes that were required by the stressor event. This concept of hardships corresponds to the weights or life change units assigned to life events in psychobiological stress research.

Building upon this ABCX model, McCubbin and Patterson (1982, 1983) advanced the concept of family pile-up of normative and nonnormative life events and family strains to explain why some families are vulnerable to the impact of any single stressor and may lack the regenerative power or the resilience to recover and adapt to a family crisis. If a family's resources (to cope with stressors) are already depleted, overtaxed, or exhausted from dealing with other life changes (both normative and situational), the family unit may be unable to make further adjustments when confronted with additional social or interpersonal stressors. In other words, family life changes and strains are additive and may push the family unit to its limit. At this point, one would anticipate some negative consequence for the family system and/or for its members.

We have advanced a Double ABCX Model to describe family adjustment and adaptation to stressors or family crises. In Hill's original model, the "A" factor was the stressor event. In the Double ABCX Model, the "A" factor has been relabeled *family demands* and includes: (1) the *stressor,* defined as a life event (normative or nonnormative) experienced by the family unit at a discrete point in time that produces change in the family social system; (2) *family hardships,* defined as those demands on the family unit specifically associated with the stressor event (for example, increasing financial debts when a parent loses a job); and (3) *prior strains,* defined as the residuals of family tension that linger from unresolved prior stressors or that are inherent in ongoing family roles such as being a parent or spouse (Pearlin & Schooler, 1978). When a new stressor is experienced by a family unit, these prior strains are exacerbated and families become aware of them as demands in and of themselves. For example, marital conflict may intensify when parents disagree about how to manage the care of a child recently diagnosed to have a chronic illness. Unlike stressor events that occur at a specific point in time, prior strains may not have a definite onset and emerge more insidiously in the family. Just as their onset is unclear, the resolution of strains is often also unclear to families, and they have difficulty with this aspect of demands.

Demands on the family produce internal tension that calls for management (Antonovsky, 1979). When this tension is not overcome, stress emerges. *Family stress* (as distinct from stressor) is defined as a state that arises from an actual or perceived demand-capability imbalance in the family's functioning and calls for adjustment or adaptive behavior. Concomitantly, *distress* is defined as stress that is perceived as unpleasant or undesirable by the members in the family unit.

This systematic effort to develop and improve our understanding of family behavior in response to stress underscores the importance of the pile-up of family life stressors and strains as an important factor in predicting family adjustment and adaptation to change over the family life cycle. This linkage (stress and adjustment) is predicated on understanding the family as a "system" in terms of the interconnectedness of its members. What affects one person in the family affects the others to some degree. Change in any one part of the system requires some readjustment by the whole family system and by its members. Life events and strains, which are experienced by the family as a whole or by any one member, when added together, will have a powerful impact upon the stability of the family unit. Specifically, behavioral scientists have hypothesized that the pile-up of life changes and strains occurring within a brief period of time (for example, one year) has a high probability of disrupting the family's unity and contributing to deterioration in the family unit and the emotional and physical well-being of its members.

Development and Psychometric Properties

The Family Inventory of Life Events and Changes (FILE; McCubbin, Patterson, & Wilson, 1981; see Appendix) is a 71-item self-report instrument designed to record normative and nonnormative family demands—stressors, hardships, prior strains—a family unit may experience within a year.

As a *family* life change inventory, all events and strains experienced by any member of the family are recorded, since, from a family systems theoretical perspective, what happens to any one member affects the other members to some degree. Families usually are dealing with several stressors and strains simultaneously and FILE provides an index of this pile-up, which in turn is an index of a family's vulnerability to crisis. FILE is an operational measure of both the "a" and the "aA" factors of the Double ABCX Model of family stress. The questionnaire is to be completed by adult family members (together or separately), a single parent, or a cohabiting couple (together or separately). There are alternative procedures, described below, for calculating a family stress score based on who completes the questionnaire.

The initial selection of family stressor and strain items was guided, in part, by those life changes appearing on other individual life change inventories (Coddington, 1972; Dohrenwend, Krasnoff, Askenasy, &

Dohrenwend, 1978; Holmes & Rahe, 1967). In addition, situational and developmental changes experienced by families at different stages of the life cycle were included. These items were derived from clinical and research experience of the investigators, and from a careful review of family stress research from the previous decade (McCubbin, Joy, Cauble, Comeau, Patterson, & Needle, 1980). Each item was worded to reflect a change in a family member or a change in family relationships. The change may be either positive or negative.

The first version of FILE (Form A; McCubbin, Wilson, & Patterson, 1979) consisted of 171 items, which were conceptually grouped into 8 categories: family development, work, management, health, finances, social activities, law, and extended family relationships. This extensive inventory has been used in the study of rural farm and nonfarm families, and families faced with childhood chronic illness such as cystic fibrosis, myelomeninogocele, or cerebral palsy.

However, in our efforts to adapt this inventory for use in prevention-oriented settings (family practice clinics, pediatric clinics, family life education centers, and the like) and in clinical counseling, we reduced FILE (Form C; McCubbin, Patterson, & Wilson, 1981) to 71 items, grouped by factor analysis into nine subscales:

(1) *Intra-Family Strains* (17 items): Focuses upon sources of tension and conflict between family members and upon parenting strains and the increased difficulty in enacting the parenting role (Cronbach alpha = .72).

(2) *Marital Strains* (4 items): Focuses upon the strains associated with the marital role arising from sexual or separation issues (Cronbach alpha = .16).

(3) *Pregnancy and Childbearing Strains* (4 items): Relates to pregnancy difficulties or adding a new member to the family unit (Cronbach alpha = .24).

(4) *Finance and Business Strains* (12 items): Focuses upon sources of increased strain on a family's money supply and sources of strain arising from a family-owned business or investments (Cronbach alpha = .60).

(5) *Work-Family Transitions and Strains* (10 items): Focuses upon strains associated with a member moving in and out of the work force and upon intrafamily demands related to work difficulties (Cronbach alpha = .55).

(6) *Illness and Family Care Strains* (8 items): Focuses on family demands associated with injury or illness to a family member or friend or problems with child care, and strains associated with having a chronically ill member or a relative/member requiring more help or care (Cronbach alpha = .56).

(7) *Family Losses* (6 items): Focuses upon demands due to the loss of a family member or a friend, or to a breakdown in relationships (Cronbach alpha = .34).

(8) *Family Transitions In and Out* (5 items): Associated with family

members moving out or moving back into the family or a member
beginning a major involvement outside the family unit (Cronbach
alpha = .52).
  (9) *Family Legal Strains* (5 items): Focuses upon a family member's
      violation of the law or mores (Cronbach alpha = .62).
 (10) *Family Pile-Up* (71 items): Focuses upon the total number of family
      demands associated with stressors and strains in the nine areas of
      family life (Cronbach alpha = .81).

Validity

Factor analyses were completed on data obtained on two independent samples of husbands and wives (N = 1330 and N = 1410) representing all stages of the family life cycle. The results revealed the same
factor structure of nine subscales (McCubbin & Patterson, 1981; Olson,
McCubbin, Barnes, Larsen, Muxen, & Wilson, 1982). One of the major
difficulties in using factor analysis with life change inventories designed to
focus upon a wide range of events and strains over the life span is in the
low frequency of occurrence of specific events. However, we retained
certain infrequently occurring life events, such as "a child member died,"
because of the major impact such stressors have on families, making
them, therefore, essential to understanding families under stress. Thus
items included in FILE represent a balance of empirical findings with our
conceptual framework. Stress items that would normally have dropped
out of the final structure due to low loadings were maintained as part
of FILE.

Several tests of validity have been reported for FILE (McCubbin &
Patterson, 1981). Specifically, total pile-up of family life stressors and
strains was significantly and inversely correlated with measures of
changes in the health status (for example, pulmonary functioning) of children with cystic fibrosis (Patterson & McCubbin, in press). A greater
number of family stressors and strains in a 12-month period was associated with a subsequent decline in the children's pulmonary functioning as
recorded during two clinic visits that occurred three to six months later.
Additionally, the pile-up of family stressors and strains was correlated
significantly with measures of family functioning: (1) family cohesion,
−.24; (2) independence of family members, −.16; (3) family organization, −.14; and (4) family conflict, −.23.

Reliabilities

The internal reliabilities were reported above as part of the description
of each of the subscales. The total index of Family Pile-Up is reliable with
a Cronbach alpha of .81. Select subscales of FILE had respectable reliabilities—Intra-Family Strains, Finance and Business Strains, and Family Legal Strains. However, it is important to exercise caution in the use of
any of the other subscales as *independent* measures of family stress; the

TABLE 14.1   Pearson's Correlations on Test-Retest Reliability
              for FILE (N = 125)

FILE Subscales	Correlations
Intra-Family Strains	.73
Marital Strains	.68
Pregnancy and Childbearing Strains	.84
Finance and Business Strains	.64
Work-Family Transitions and Strains	.80
Illness and Family Care Strains	.66
Family Losses	.71
Family Transitions In and Out	.72
Family Legal Strains	.83
Family Pile-Up	.80

internal reliabilities of these subscales are relatively low due to the wide variance in the frequency of occurrence of some family life events and hence the relative instability of these groupings of items.

Test-retest reliabilities have been established for FILE. The data presented in Table 14.1 reveal relatively stable responses across a period of four to five weeks when FILE was administered to the same subjects (Olson et al., 1982). If we consider that some life stressors and strains could have emerged during the one-month period, suggesting that there were changes in the families of the respondents, the test-retest reliabilities take on added significance as indices of stable responses across time.

Administration and Scoring Procedures

The Family Inventory of Life Events and Changes is designed to be administered to either one or both adult members of the family unit. Preferably, couples should complete the inventory separately, and both scores used to determine the level of family stress. The respondent is asked to record (that is, check yes or no) the life events and strains that happened to any member of the family unit and to the family as a group during the past year. *Family* is defined as a group of two or more persons living together who are related by blood, marriage, or adoption. This includes persons who live with you and to whom you have a long-term commitment.

FILE may be scored five ways, depending upon the purpose and ultimate use of the statistical information in research and/or counseling. Descriptions of the five possible scores follows.

Family life events score. FILE is completed by adult family members together. This score is computed by giving each of the yes responses a score of 1. The yes responses are summed to arrive at a score for each of the subscales and the total pile-up scale.

Family-couple life events score. FILE is completed separately by each partner. A family-couple score is computed by examining the two completed instruments simultaneously one item at a time. If either or both partner recorded yes on an item, the family-couple score would be a yes and would be given a score of 1. This is done for each of the items; the items are then summed for each subscale and the total pile-up scale. This scoring procedure is based on the assumption that partners may actually observe and/or experience different family life events or strains by virtue of differences in the ways each experiences family life. Therefore, each member's observations and responses would be treated as a valid record of family stressors and strains.

Family-couple discrepancy scores. FILE is completed separately by each partner. By scoring the independent responses of each member of the couple together, we can determine the number of discrepancies or differences between the male partner's record and the female partner's record of stressors and strains. Each discrepancy (that is, one member recorded yes and the other no) is given a score of 1 and summed for both the subscales and the total pile-up scale. It is important to note that the scores derived through this procedure are indices of "differences" in couple observations and experiences and can be viewed as possible areas of couple miscommunication or separation, as well as over- or understatements of family stress. These scores are not normally viewed as indices of how much stress or distress the family may be experiencing. However, the differences in couple observations, particularly around sensitive areas of family life, such as intrafamily strains, are extremely valuable in stimulating meaningful interaction in the counseling interview.

The two remaining procedures for calculating family stress scores are based on a methodology developed by Holmes and Rahe (1967) in which each life event and strain is assigned a standard weight that indicates the relative magnitude and intensity of the event or strain. Standardized family weights have been assigned to each of the items in FILE. These weights indicate the relative "stressfulness" of items, that is, the degree of social readjustment an average family will make in its usual pattern of life as a result of experiencing each event or strain. The standardized weights for the 71 FILE items are presented in Table 14.2.

Family readjustment score. FILE is completed by adult family members together. This score is computed by assigning the standard weight for each life event and strain that the respondent(s) recorded as yes (that is, it happened during the past year). Then the standard weights are added up to give a family readjustment score for the subscales and the total pile-up scale.

Family-couple readjustment score. FILE is completed separately by each partner. Following the same procedure described for family-couple

1. Increase of husband/father's time away from family	46
2. Increase of wife/mother's time away from family	51
3. A member appears to have emotional problems	58
4. A member appears to depend on alcohol or drugs	66
5. Increase in conflict between husband and wife	53
6. Increase in arguments between parent(s) and child	45
7. Increase in conflict among children in the family	48
8. Increased difficulty in managing teenage child(ren)	55
9. Increased difficulty managing school-age children (6-12 yrs.)	39
10. Increased difficulty managing toddler(s) (1-2 yrs.)	36
11. Increased difficulty managing preschool children (2-6 yrs.)	36
12. Increased difficulty managing infant(s) (0-1 yr.)	35
13. Increase in the amount of "outside activities" which the child(ren) are involved in	25
14. Increased disagreement about a member's friends or activities	35
15. Increase in the number of problems or issues which don't get resolved	43
16. Increase in the number of tasks or chores which don't get done	35
17. Increased conflict with in-laws or relatives	40
18. Spouse/parent was separated or divorced	79
19. Spouse/parent has an "affair"	68
20. Increased difficulty in resolving issues with a former or separated spouse	47
21. Increased difficulty with sexual relationship between husband and wife	58
22. Spouse had unwanted or difficult pregnancy	45
23. An unmarried member became pregnant	65
24. A member had an abortion	50
25. A member gave birth to or adopted a child	50
26. Took out a loan or refinanced a loan to cover increased expenses	29
27. Went on welfare	55
28. Change in conditions (economic, political, weather) which hurts the family business	41
29. Change in agriculture market, stock market, or land values which hurts family investments and/or income	43
30. A member started a new business	50
31. Purchased or built a home	41
32. A member purchased a car or other major item	19
33. Increased financial debts due to overuse of credit cards	31
34. Increased strain on family "money" for medical/dental expenses	23
35. Increased strain on family "money" for food, clothing, energy, home care	21
36. Increased strain on family "money" for child(ren)'s education	22

(continued)

TABLE 14.2 Continued

37. Delay in receiving child support or alimony payments	41
38. A member changed to a new job/career	40
39. A member lost or quit a job	55
40. A member retired from work	48
41. A member started or returned to work	41
42. A member stopped working for extended period (e.g., laid off, leave of absence, strike)	51
43. Decrease in satisfaction with job/career	45
44. A member had increased difficulty with people at work	32
45. A member was promoted at work or given more responsibilities	40
46. Family moved to a new home or apartment	43
47. A child/adolescent member changed to a new school	24
48. Parent/spouse became seriously ill or injured	44
49. Child became seriously ill or injured	35
50. Close relative or friend of the family became seriously ill	44
51. A member became physically disabled or chronically ill	73
52. Increased difficulty managing a chronically ill or disabled member	58
53. Member or close relative was committed to an institution or nursing home	44
54. Increased responsibility to provide direct care or financial help to husband's and/or wife's parent(s)	47
55. Experienced difficulty in arranging for satisfactory child care	40
56. A parent/spouse died	98
57. A child member died	99
58. Death of husband's or wife's parent or close relative	48
59. Close friend of the family died	47
60. Married son or daughter was separated or divorced	58
61. A member "broke up" a relationship with a close friend	35
62. A member was married	42
63. Young adult member left home	43
64. A young adult member began college (or post-high school training)	28
65. A member moved back home or a new person moved into the household	42
66. A parent/spouse started school (or training program) after being away from school for a long time	38
67. A member went to jail or juvenile detention	68
68. A member was picked up by police or arrested	57
69. Physical or sexual abuse or violence in the home	75
70. A member ran away from home	61
71. A member dropped out of school or was suspended from school	38

life events scores, each item recorded yes by either or both partners is assigned the appropriate standardized weight (see Table 14.2). These weights are summed to obtain subscale scores and the total pile-up family-couple readjustment score.

Given our interest in counseling families regarding stress and our instinctual feeling that family life events and strains are not all "equal" in demand (that is, the death of a spouse is more stressful than conflict with in-laws), we will emphasize the use of the last two scoring procedures throughout the remainder of this chapter.

Comparing Family Scores:
Family Norms

Family research on development, transitions, and stress have pointed to the obvious fact that stressful life events and strains are in part a function of at what stage of the family life cycle a family may be. For example, the probability of a family experiencing the death of a member increases as the family moves into the later stages of the family cycle. Therefore, it would be advantageous if the norms for family stress were established by stage of the family cycle, rather than developed for all families in a total group. Through the use of data obtained on 1140 couples, or 2280 married individuals, who were representative of seven stages of the family life cycle, we were able to calculate normative data so that families completing FILE could be compared with other families at their respective stages of development (Olson, McCubbin, Barnes, Larsen, Muxen, & Wilson, 1983). The seven stages of the family cycle and the norms for each stage (based on family-couple readjustment scores) are presented in Table 14.3.

TABLE 14.3   Comparative Norms for Family Pile-Up over the Family Cycle

		Stress Level[a]		
Family Stage	Mean	Low	Moderate	High
(I) Couple	478	0-210	211-719	720+
(II) Preschool	530	0-220	221-839	840+
(III) School age	500	0-265	266-734	735+
(IV) Adolescent	545	0-240	241-849	850+
(V) Launching	635	0-320	321-949	950+
(VI) Empty nest	425	0-160	161-689	690+
(VII) Retirement	395	0- 75	76-699	700+

a. Cut-off scores for low, moderate, and high stress levels were determined by the mean and one standard deviation above the mean (high stress) and one standard deviation below the mean (low stress). Cut-off scores were rounded off to even numbers.

Interpretation of Family Stress Scores

Understandably, families are most concerned about the demands that are placed on them and whether the pile-up of stressors and strains may be too much or abnormal. Therefore, the total pile-up score should be given the most consideration in counseling families. Families are encouraged to compare their scores with the norms outlined in Table 14.3. Specifically, an individual family score, when compared with the norms (for the appropriate family stage of development), provides a means of classifying the family into the high-stress, moderate-stress, or low-stress group.

High-stress score. A high-stress family score indicates that a family unit has experienced an unusual number of stressors and strains that presumably have taxed the family's psychological and interpersonal resources (morale, hope, money, stability, esteem, and so on). It is not uncommon for families to feel "out of control" or exhausted in the face of high demands even though they may not seek professional counseling or assistance. High-stress families are considered vulnerable to future stressors and strains, are prone to experience sudden tension and conflicts, seemingly without provocation, and are less able to recover from the impact of problems or difficulties. Their problem-solving abilities may be hampered, leaving them with a feeling that there are many loose ends and unresolved conflicts. While some families under this level of stress may feel comfortable and organized, eventually such excessive demands usually take their toll, particularly if there are insufficient resources to reduce the demands to a more manageable level.

Moderate-stress scores. These families fall within the normal range of stressors and strains and are typically viewed as nonproblematic. However, since families vary in their ability to manage stress, many families may struggle with this level of demand, particularly if they lack adequate coping resources. Families who are struggling are particularly vulnerable to the impact of any additional stressor or strain and even a seemingly minor event may trigger a crisis—"the straw that broke the camel's back."

Low-stress scores. In most cases, these families would appear to be unburdened by life changes and strains. They face an unusually low number of demands. Life may appear uneventful, even possibly mundane. While there is a general feeling of comfort or maybe relief, these families may also be poised to seek stimulating life experiences and strains.

Interpretation of these scores to families must be treated with care and sensitivity to their feelings and concerns. It is not generally helpful to alarm a family as to the stressfulness of their circumstances on the basis of scores either below or above the normal range. Rather, the emphasis of interpreting scores would be better focused upon: (1) the family's vulnerability to future stressful life events or strains; (2) the family's use of important psychological, interpersonal, and tangible resources and strengths that may be exhausted in the near future; (3) specific stressors and specific strains that may need their attention; (4) the family's coping skills and abilities in managing these demands (that is, what they are doing to help themselves); (5) the family's feelings about their circumstances and difficulties; and (6) the family's problem-solving ability to resolve or eliminate some of the more manageable demands.

Family Stress Case Study

Janet Dahl visited the family counseling clinic in early January to discuss the problems she and her husband had with their oldest daughter, Jennifer (age 16), who was not eating properly. Both Janet and her husband, Bill, had read about adolescent children with anorexia nervosa and were convinced that this was Jennifer's problem. Mrs. Dahl, who is 41 years of age, the same age as Bill, was very apprehensive about seeking help, but felt that this was the best thing to do for their daughter. After getting a basic family history, the counselor asked the whole family to attend the second session.

In the second intake interview, everyone came with the exception of the oldest son, Steve (age 19), who had recently moved to another state to begin college. The youngest daughter, Natalie (age 12), also came, bringing the total number present to four. There was considerable tension in the family, based, in part, on the belief that only Jennifer needed to come, for she had the problem. Mr. Dahl was agitated at being there and angry at Janet for arranging this. While in the waiting room, both parents were asked to complete the Family Inventory of Life Events and Changes, separately. Janet and Bill were informed that both questionnaires would be considered by the counselor, although neither parent's responses would be revealed unless they chose to share this information with each other after the session.

The Dahl Family Stress Summary

The results from Janet's and Bill's completion of FILE revealed some important information about the family's life stressors and strains. The results of the scoring, summarized in Table 14.4, indicated that the total family life change units were extremely high for the Dahl family, exceeding the norms for families at their stage of the life cycle and indicating that this family was experiencing a pile-up of stressors and strains. Second, the stressors and strains appeared to be clustered into two areas of family functioning, namely, Finance and Business Strains and Intra-Family strains.

TABLE 14.4   Dahl Family Stress Profile

Family Stage	Normal Range	Family Score
(I) Couple	211-719	
(II) Preschool	221-839	
(III) School age	266-839	
(IV) Adolescent	241-849	965
(V) Launching	321-949	
(VI) Empty nest	161-689	
(VII) Retirement	76-699	

Clinical Summary

NAME: Dahl Family   FAMILY STAGE: (V) Launching

This family's pile-up score is above the midrange and into the high stress level. There is a need to examine the areas of family life most stressed by the situation and discuss with the family their feelings about the demands they face, focusing on specific stressors and strains.

Specifically, the Dahl family not only struggled with their apprehensions and concerns about Jennifer, but were faced with a host of demands that appeared to hurt the family unit and chip away at its stability. The stressors and strains most emphasized were as follows:

Intra-Family Strains
    Increase in arguments between parent(s) and child(ren)
    Increase in the number of problems or issues which don't get resolved
    Increased disagreement about a member's friends or activities
    A member appears to have emotional problems
    Increase in conflict between husband and wife
    Increase of wife/mother's time away from family
    Increase in the number of tasks or chores which don't get done
    Increased difficulty with sexual relationship between husband and wife
Finance and Business Strains
    Increased strain on family money for child(ren)'s education
    Took out a loan or refinanced a loan to cover increased expenses
    Increased strain on family money for food, clothing, energy, home care
Work-Family Transitions and Strains
    Decrease in satisfaction with job/career
    A member changed to a new job/career
    A young adult member began college (or post-high school training)

The general results (comparison of total stress scores with norms) were shared with all family members. The counselor emphasized that many things were happening to the Dahl family that would help explain how difficult things must be for them.

Bill and Janet Dahl did not seem totally surprised by the results. They did, however, seize the opportunity to raise some issues with the counselor that concerned them. They wanted to know what specifically pushed their family score so high.

An awareness of their high-stress score was a sufficient stimulus for Mr. Dahl to carry the discussion. He wanted to talk about how sad everyone had been since Steve, the oldest son, left for college. This is when it all began—when Jennifer started to act differently, would not eat, and would not listen to anyone. Jennifer spoke up. She did not feel that she had a problem. She was close to Steve and felt so down with him gone that she didn't want to eat. She felt everyone was picking on her, as if they were angry with her, and so she became stubborn.

There seemed to be a general agreement that Steve's departure was very important to everyone, yet no one wanted to share their feelings and felt afraid to express this sadness. The mother seemed to become more involved with her new job, wanting to be successful at it. She felt this helped her to cope with Steve's leaving home. Natalie resented her mother's working and felt left out of everything. Mr. Dahl also felt very depressed and felt that he was not close to his wife: "She seemed distant and not interested in me and our relationship."

Both parents agreed that one important motive for their both working was to make certain they had enough money to support Steve's education and to prepare for Jennifer's college education as well. They were frustrated with their financial situation and angry that college loans were not available to them.

As the family discussed their specific stressors, it became apparent that Jennifer alone did not have the problem; they all did. They experienced two major changes in Steve's transition to college and Mrs. Dahl's return to the work force. It was hard for everyone, even though these changes were expected and necessary. The family chose to end the counseling with the expectation that they needed time to adjust and wanted to support each other now that they had an understanding of the situation. The counselor asked that they contact the agency in a month to let the counselor know how they were doing.

Assessment of FILE

The Family Inventory of Life Events and Changes (FILE) provides the clinician and the family life educator with a brief but meaningful index of the pile-up of stressors and strains in a family. In this respect, it is extremely useful as an initial screening test to evaluate what demands have been placed on a family unit during the past 12 months. As noted in the case of the Dahl family, using FILE, the counselor was able to (1) identify some of the major stressors and daily hassles that chip away at the family's flexibility and resiliency; (2) foster the family's own awareness of what stressors, strains, and hardships they have been struggling with; and (3) encourage the family to look at all these demands and the impact they may have on the family unit. These data were made available to the family and the counselor with an investment of 10-15 minutes of family and counselor time.

An index of pile-up offers the psychodynamic therapist a snapshot of recent stressors and strains that could be used as a stimulus for discussing the history of family members and the total family unit (see Napier, 1978). An expanded version of FILE has a chronic strain index (that is, a select number of events that occurred longer ago than the past year but that probably still carry a residue of strain), which could be used by a psychodynamic therapist to identify historical events influencing current behavior of client families.

In situations in which a family is not committed to long-term counseling or therapy and a single visit or two is all one can reasonably expect, the brief assessment of family stressors and strains can be helpful. While the information can be alarming to the family, particularly if they are prone to deny the existence of any problems or difficulties, the information can serve as a catalyst for family self-evaluation and a motivating force for continuing in the therapeutic setting. It is equally true, as in the case of the Dahl family, that families may come to terms with their problems and needs and seek to address their solutions on their own. The brief encounter around stressors and strains can be helpful to those seeking assistance as well as to families seeking general health education and enrichment.

Any inventory that attempts to document family life stressors and strains will fall short of many clinical expectations and goals. First of all, an inventory would not be able to cover all possible stressors and strains. The original version of the Family Inventory of Life Events and Changes (McCubbin et al., 1979) has 171 items, and is still used in research investigations. However, the "stress" of completing such a lengthy inventory must also be taken into consideration. Understandably, from the point of view of the client, a request to complete a comprehensive family life inventory, if such existed, would be too demanding if not an alienating task.

Second, even though standard weights have been assigned to indicate the intensity of each stressor or strain, it does not capture any given family's unique perspective and feelings. Consequently, even though a family falls within the normal range of stressors and strains, it may feel burdened by the pile-up of stressors and strains. This subjective perception of the family deserves attention in the counseling setting so family members can discuss their feelings about specific stressful events, such as the Dahl family's need to speak about Steve's departure and their grieving.

It is important to emphasize how FILE can be used as a tool in individual, marital, or family counseling and therapy rather than as a definitive index of all family stressors and strains. It is reasonable to assume that FILE includes several important indices of family strain, such as marital conflict and parent-child conflict, that can serve as signals of other stressors and strains not mentioned in FILE. Therefore, counselors could explore and help families to identify some of the antecedent stressors and strains that contributed to family distress. It would be helpful (as we have found) to ask families to list five or ten additional stressors and strains not mentioned in FILE so as to tailor the inventory to fit a specific family. Families have appreciated the opportunity to expand upon the list and in doing so inform the counselor of other issues and concerns that deserve attention. Some of the more important stressors and strains likely to emerge are sudden and unexpected losses that occurred many years ago, as well as those repeated blows such as racial or sexual discrimination or changes at work that create uncertainty and undermine the family members' esteem and the family's stability.

FILE as Part of Family Assessment

Family life educators and family counselors have emphasized the use of FILE as part of a battery of family assessment tools. Specifically, we have underscored the use of FILE in conjunction with tools designed to assess family coping and family resources. In the Double ABCX Model of family stress (McCubbin & Patterson, 1982, 1983) we have emphasized the balance between family demands and family resources as an important index of family adaptation to stress. Therefore, it follows that we should help families to evaluate the resources they can use in resisting the impact of stressors and in fostering their ability to recover from a crisis. In Figure 14.1, we attempt to portray this concept of family balance and to indicate the educational and clinical value of evaluating what resources families have to work with. Certainly, other clinical tools in this volume can and have been used. For example, the Family Adaptability and Cohesion Evaluation Scale (Olson, Portner, & Bell, 1982; see also Chapter 16, this volume) is extremely helpful in evaluating the role of family cohesion and adaptability in buffering the impact of stressors and strains. This line of reasoning can be applied to other family measures such as the Family Environment Scales (Moos, 1974; see also Chapter 13), which could be useful in defining family resources. The Family Inventory of Resources for Management (McCubbin, Comeau, & Harkins, 1981), designed to assess esteem and communication, mastery and health, social support, and financial well-being, may also be used.

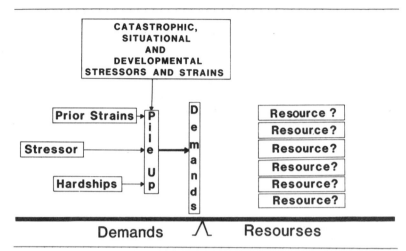

Figure 14.1   Balancing Family Demands with Family Resources

It is also helpful to evaluate family coping behaviors and strategies, given the important role that coping plays in the management of stress. The several family-oriented assessment tools developed as part of the Family Stress and Coping Project at the University of Minnesota may be used to assess family resistance and resiliency. The inventories include: (1) F-COPES (Family Crisis Oriented Personal Evaluation Scales; Mc-Cubbin, Larsen, & Olson, 1982), used in the study of family coping with transitions; (2) CHIP (Coping Health Inventory for Parents; McCubbin, McCubbin, Cauble, & Nevin, 1981), designed to assess parental efforts to cope with handicapped or chronically ill children; (3) DECS (Dual Employed Coping Scales; Skinner & McCubbin, 1982), used in the assessment of families managing the demands of dual wage earners; and (4) A-COPE (Adolescent Coping Orientation for Problem Experiences; Patterson, McCubbin, & Needle, 1982), designed to assess an adolescent's efforts to cope with personal and family demands.

Summary

Family stress has been and will continue to be an important issue for both family life educators interested in prevention and family therapists committed to helping families help themselves. The Family Inventory of Life Events and Changes has been introduced as one tool to assess briefly, but accurately, family stressors and strains. We have outlined the conceptual framework for the development of the instrument and the role such a tool can play in assessment and in the clinical process. It is important to underscore the value of such a tool in helping families to evaluate themselves and as a guide in counseling. However, it is also important to call attention to the limitations of any self-report instrument, and to the limited number of stressors and strains actually evaluated. Above all, we would like to encourage the specific use of FILE as an instrument in the hands of qualified clinicians and family life or health educators. Families benefit most from a sudden awareness of stressors and strains (through using FILE) when their concerns and apprehensions are dealt with by individuals interested in and sensitive to their struggles.

APPENDIX

University of Minnesota
Family Social Science
290 McNeal Hall
St. Paul, MN 55108
Medical Education and Research
Association of
Gillette Children's Hospital

Family Health Program
• FORM C
1981
© H. McCubbin

IID
GID
FID

FILE

Family Inventory of Life Events and Changes

Hamilton I. McCubbin   Joan M. Patterson   Lance R. Wilson

PURPOSE

Over their life cycle, all families experience many changes as a result of normal growth and development of members and due to external circumstances. The following list of family life changes can happen in a family at any time. Because family members are connected to each other in some way, a life change for any one member affects all the other persons in the family to some degree.

> "FAMILY" means a group of two or more persons living together who are related by blood, marriage or adoption. This includes persons who live with you *and* to whom you have a long term commitment.

DIRECTIONS

"DID THE CHANGE HAPPEN IN YOUR FAMILY?"
Please read each family life change and decide whether it happened to any member of your family—**including you.**

• DURING THE LAST YEAR
First, decide if it happened any time **during** the last 12 months and check YES or NO.

	During Last 12 Months Yes No
	☐ ☐

FAMILY LIFE CHANGES	DID THE CHANGE HAPPEN IN YOUR FAMILY? During Last 12 Months		FAMILY LIFE CHANGES	DID THE CHANGE HAPPEN IN YOUR FAMILY? During Last 12 Months	
	Yes	No		Yes	No
I. INTRA-FAMILY STRAINS			12. Increased difficulty in managing infant(s) (1-2½ yrs.)	☐	☐
1. Increase of husband father's time away from family	☐	☐	13. Increase in the amount of "outside activities" which the child(ren) are involved in	☐	☐
2. Increase of wife mother's time away from family	☐	☐	14. Increased disagreement about a member's friends or activities	☐	☐
3. A member appears to have emotional problems	☐	☐	15. Increase in the number of problems or issues which don't get resolved	☐	☐
4. A member appears to depend on alcohol or drugs	☐	☐	16. Increase in the number of tasks or chores which don't get done	☐	☐
5. Increase in conflict between husband and wife	☐	☐	17. Increased conflict with in-laws or relatives	☐	☐
6. Increase in arguments between parent(s) and child(ren)	☐	☐	**II. MARITAL STRAINS**		
7. Increase in conflict among children in the family	☐	☐	18. Spouse/parent was separated or divorced	☐	☐
8. Increased difficulty in managing teenage child(ren)	☐	☐	19. Spouse/parent has an "affair"	☐	☐
9. Increased difficulty in managing school age child(ren) (6-12 yrs.)	☐	☐	20. Increased difficulty in resolving issues with a "former" or separated spouse	☐	☐
10. Increased difficulty in managing preschool age child(ren) (2½-6 yrs.)	☐	☐	21. Increased difficulty with sexual relationship between husband and wife	☐	☐
11. Increased difficulty in managing toddler(s) (1-2½ yrs.)	☐	☐			

Please turn over and complete ♦

(continued)

APPENDIX Continued

FAMILY LIFE CHANGES	DID THE CHANGE HAPPEN IN YOUR FAMILY? During Last 12 Months		FAMILY LIFE CHANGES	DID THE CHANGE HAPPEN IN YOUR FAMILY? During Last 12 Months	
	Yes	No		Yes	No
III. PREGNANCY AND CHILDBEARING STRAINS			**VI. ILLNESS AND FAMILY "CARE" STRAINS**		
22. Spouse had unwanted or difficult pregnancy	☐	☐	48. Parent/spouse became seriously ill or injured	☐	☐
23. An unmarried member became pregnant	☐	☐	49. Child became seriously ill or injured	☐	☐
24. A member had an abortion	☐	☐	50. Close relative or friend of the family became seriously ill	☐	☐
25. A member gave birth to or adopted a child	☐	☐	51. A member became physically disabled or chronically ill	☐	☐
IV. FINANCE AND BUSINESS STRAINS			52. Increased difficulty in managing a chronically ill or disabled member	☐	☐
26. Took out a loan or refinanced a loan to cover increased expenses	☐	☐	53. Member or close relative was committed to an institution or nursing home	☐	☐
27. Went on welfare	☐	☐	54. Increased responsibility to provide direct care or financial help to husband's and/or wife's parent(s)	☐	☐
28. Change in conditions (economic, political, weather) which hurts the family business	☐	☐	55. Experienced difficulty in arranging for satisfactory child care	☐	☐
29. Change in Agriculture Market, Stock Market, or Land Values which hurts family investments and/or income	☐	☐	**VII. LOSSES**		
30. A member started a new business	☐	☐	56. A parent/spouse died	☐	☐
31. Purchased or built a home	☐	☐	57. A child member died	☐	☐
32. A member purchased a car or other major item	☐	☐	58. Death of husband's or wife's parent or close relative	☐	☐
33. Increasing financial debts due to over-use of credit cards	☐	☐	59. Close friend of the family died	☐	☐
34. Increased strain on family "money" for medical/dental expenses	☐	☐	60. Married son or daughter was separated or divorced	☐	☐
35. Increased strain on family "money" for food, clothing, energy, home care	☐	☐	61. A member "broke up" a relationship with a close friend	☐	☐
36. Increased strain on family "money" for child(ren)'s education	☐	☐	**VIII. TRANSITIONS "IN AND OUT"**		
37. Delay in receiving child support or alimony payments	☐	☐	62. A member was married	☐	☐
V. WORK-FAMILY TRANSITIONS AND STRAINS			63. Young adult member left home	☐	☐
38. A member changed to a new job/career	☐	☐	64. A young adult member began college (or post high school training)	☐	☐
39. A member lost or quit a job	☐	☐	65. A member moved back home or a new person moved into the household	☐	☐
40. A member retired from work	☐	☐	66. A parent/spouse started school (or training program) after being away from school for a long time	☐	☐
41. A member started or returned to work	☐	☐	**IX. FAMILY LEGAL VIOLATIONS**		
42. A member stopped working for extended period (e.g., laid off, leave of absence, strike)	☐	☐	67. A member went to jail or juvenile detention	☐	☐
43. Decrease in satisfaction with job/career	☐	☐	68. A member was picked up by police or arrested	☐	☐
44. A member had increased difficulty with people at work	☐	☐	69. Physical or sexual abuse or violence in the home	☐	☐
45. A member was promoted at work or given more responsibilities	☐	☐	70. A member ran away from home	☐	☐
46. Family moved to a new home/apartment	☐	☐	71. A member dropped out of school or was suspended from school	☐	☐
47. A child/adolescent member changed to a new school	☐	☐			

References

Antonovsky, A. *Health, stress and coping.* San Francisco: Jossey-Bass, 1979.

Cannon, W. B. *Bodily changes in pain, hunger, fear and rage.* New York: D. Appleton, 1929.

Coddington, R. D. The significance of life events as an etiologic factor in the diseases of children II: A study of a normal population. *Journal of Psychosomatic Research,* 1972, *16,* 205-213.

Dohrenwend, B. S., Krasnoff, L., Askenasy, A. R., & Dohrenwend, B. P. Exemplification of a method for scaling life events: The PERI life event scale. *Journal of Health and Social Behavior,* 1978, *19*(2), 205-229.

Duvall, E. *Marriage and family development*. Philadelphia: J. B. Lippincott, 1977.

Erikson, E. (Ed.). *Adulthood*. New York: Norton, 1976.

Hawkins, N. G., Davies, R., & Holmes, T. H. Evidence of psychosocial factors in the development of pulmonary tuberculosis. *American Review of Tubercular and Pulmonary Disease*, 1957, *75*(5), 768-780.

Hill, R. *Families under stress*. New York: Harper & Row, 1949.

Hill, R. Generic features of families under stress. *Social Casework*, 1958, *49*, 139-150.

Holmes, T. H., & Masuda, M. Life change and illness susceptibility. In B. S. Dohrenwend & B. P. Dohrenwend (Eds.), *Stressful life events: Their nature and effects*. New York: John Wiley, 1974.

Holmes, T. H., & Rahe, R. The social readjustment rating scale. *Journal of Psychosomatic Research*, 1967, *11*, 213-218.

Lief, A. (Ed.). *The commonsense psychiatry of Dr. Adolf Meyer*. New York: McGraw-Hill, 1948.

McCubbin, H. I., Comeau, J., & Harkins, J. FIRM—Family Inventory of Resources for Management. In H. I. McCubbin & J. Patterson, *Systematic assessment of family stress, resources, and coping: Tools for research, education, and clinical intervention*. St. Paul: Family Social Science, University of Minnesota, 1981.

McCubbin, H. I., Joy, C., Cauble, A. E., Comeau, J., Patterson, J., & Needle, R. Family stress and coping: A decade review. *Journal of Marriage and the Family*, 1980, *42*, 855-872.

McCubbin, H. I., Larsen A., & Olson, D. H. *Family crisis oriented personal evaluation scales (F-COPES)*. St. Paul: Family Social Science, University of Minnesota, 1982.

McCubbin, H. I., McCubbin, M., Cauble, A. E., & Nevin, R. *Coping health inventory for parents (CHIP)*. St. Paul: Family Social Science, University of Minnesota, 1981.

McCubbin, H. I., & Patterson, J. *Systematic assessment of family stress, resources and coping: Tools for research, education and clinical intervention*. St. Paul: Family Social Science, University of Minnesota, 1981.

McCubbin, H. I., & Patterson, J. Family adaption to crises. In H. McCubbin, A. E. Cauble, & J. Patterson (Eds.), *Family stress, coping and social support*. Springfield, IL: Charles C Thomas, 1982.

McCubbin, H. I., & Patterson, J. Family stress and adaptation to crises: A double ABCX model of family behavior. In H. I. McCubbin, M. Sussman, & J. Patterson (Eds.), *Advances and developments in family stress theory and research*. New York: Haworth, 1983.

McCubbin, H. I., Patterson, J., & Wilson, L. *Family inventory of life events and changes (FILE) Form C*. St. Paul: Family Social Science, University of Minnesota, 1981.

McCubbin, H. I., Wilson, L., & Patterson, J. *Family inventory of life events and changes (FILE) Form A*. St. Paul: Family Social Science, University of Minnesota, 1979.

Moos, R. H. *Family environment scales and preliminary manual*. Palo Alto, CA: Consulting Psychologists Press, 1974.

Napier, A. Y. *The family crucible*. New York: Harper, 1978.

Olson, D. H., McCubbin, H. I., Barnes, H., Larsen, A., Muxen, M., & Wilson, M. *Family inventories: Inventories used in a national survey of families across the family life cycle*. St. Paul: Family Social Science, University of Minnesota, 1982.

Olson, D. H., McCubbin, H. I., Barnes, H., Larsen, A., Muxen, M., & Wilson, M. *Families: What Makes Them Work*. Beverly Hills, CA: Sage, 1983.

Olson, D. H., Portner, J., & Bell, R. *The family adaptability and cohesion evaluation scales (FACES)*. St. Paul: Family Social Science, University of Minnesota, 1982.

Patterson, J., & McCubbin, H. I. The impact of family life events and changes on the health of a chronically ill child. *Family Relations*, in press.

Patterson, J., McCubbin, H. I., & Needle, R. *Adolescent coping orientation for problem experiences (A-COPE)*. St. Paul: Family Social Science, University of Minnesota, 1982.

Pearlin, L. I., & Schooler, C. The structure of coping. *Journal of Health and Social Behavior*, 1978, *19*, 2-21.

Riegel, K. F. Adult life crises: A dialectic interpretation of development. In N. Datan & L. H. Ginsberg (Eds.), *Life-span developmental psychology*. New York: Academic, 1975.

Skinner, D., & McCubbin, H. I. *Dual employed coping scales (DECS)*. St. Paul: Family Social Science, University of Minnesota, 1982.

CHAPTER *15*

Family Adaptability
and Cohesion Evaluation Scales

DAVID H. OLSON
JOYCE PORTNER
University of Minnesota

In spite of their divergent orientations, family therapists and family theorists do agree on some issues. One discovery is that the conceptual clustering of concepts from the family theory and family therapy literatures both revealed two central dimensions of family behavior: *cohesion* and *adaptability*.

Family cohesion and adaptability are the two primary dimensions integrated in the Circumplex Model as formulated by Olson, Russell, and Sprenkle (1979, 1980; Olson, Sprenkle, & Russell, in press). *Family communication* is the third dimension in the Circumplex Model and it facilitates movement on the other two dimensions. A separate scale for assessing parent-adolescent communication is described elsewhere (Olson, Portner, & Bell, 1982). Also, a separate scale on marital communication is included in the ENRICH Inventory, which is also described in Chapter 12.

FACES II, a modification of the original FACES (Family Adaptability and Cohesion Evaluation Scores), was developed to assess empirically the two central dimensions of cohesion and adaptability in the Circumplex Model.

Family cohesion assesses the degree to which family members are separated from or connected to their family. Family cohesion is defined as *the emotional bonding that family members have toward one another*. Within the Circumplex Model, specific concepts used to diagnose and measure the cohesion dimension are: emotional bonding, boundaries, coalitions, time space, friends, decision making, and interests and recreation.

Instrument Source Note: Copies of the FACES II manual may be purchased from Dr. David Olson, Family Social Science, 290 McNeal Hall, University of Minnesota, St. Paul, Minnesota 55108. The manual includes the FACES II items, answer sheet, norms and cutting points, and other related information.

Family adaptability has to do with the extent to which the family system is flexible and able to change. Family adaptability is defined as *the ability of a marital or family system to change its power structure, role relationships, and relationship rules in response to situational and developmental stress.* Specific concepts used to diagnose and measure the adaptability dimension are: family power (assertiveness, control, discipline), negotiation style, role relationships, and relationship rules.

Within the Circumplex Model, there are four levels of family cohesion, ranging from extreme low cohesion (disengaged) to extreme high cohesion (enmeshed). The two moderate or balanced levels of cohesion have been labeled separated and connected. There are also four levels of family adaptability, ranging from extreme low adaptability (rigid) to extreme high adaptability (chaotic). The two moderate or balanced levels of adaptability have been labeled flexible and structured (see Figure 15.1).

By combining the 4 levels of the cohesion and 4 levels of the adaptability dimensions, 16 distinct types of marital and family systems are identified. Of these 16 types, 4 are moderate *(balanced types)* on both the cohesion and adaptability dimensions; 8 are extreme on one dimension and moderate on the other *(midrange types)*; and 4 are extreme on both dimensions *(extreme types).*

FACES II enables the researcher or clinician to place individual families or groups of families within the Circumplex Model. This assists in further understanding the dynamics of particular kinds of families and setting treatment goals and program objectives.

FACES II was designed so that individual family members can describe how they *perceive* their family. The reading level is about seventh grade, so that children as young as 12 can understand the items. It is assumed that all family members will not see their family system in the same way and, therefore, it is important to have as many family members take FACES II as possible.

An additional feature of FACES II is that it's designed so that it can be given twice—once for how family members currently see their family, (perceived) and once for how they would like it to be (ideal). By comparing both the *perceived* and the *ideal* for each family member it is possible to assess the level of *satisfaction* with the current family system. It also provides information regarding how each individual would like to see the family system change. Comparing the perceived and ideal across all the family members provides a rather comprehensive picture of their family system.

Theoretically, the perceived-ideal discrepancy is valuable since it provides a measure of *family satisfaction* with the current family system. This relates to a newly developed alternative hypothesis regarding extreme types in the Circumplex Model, which makes the model *less value biased.* This hypothesis states that extreme types will function well as long

TABLE 15.1 FACES II: Factor Analysis

Family Cohesion	*FACTOR I* *Loadings*
Emotional Bonding	
(+) 1. Family members are supportive of each other during difficult times.	.47
(+) 17. Family members feel very close to each other.	.56
Family Boundaries	
(−) 3. It is easier to discuss problems with people outside the family than with other family members.	.54
(−) 19. Family members feel closer to people outside the family than to other family members.	.58
Coalitions	
(−) 9. In our family, everyone goes his/her own way.	.58
(−) 29. Family members pair up rather than do things as a total family	.43
Time	
(+) 7. Our family does things together.	.61
(+) 23. Family members like to spend their free time with each other.	.61
Space	
(−) 5. Our family gathers together in the same room.	.47
(+) 25. Family members avoid each other at home.	.51
Friends	
(+) 11. Family members know each other's close friends.	.35
(+) 27. We approve of each other's friends.	.35
Decision Making	
(+) 13. Family members consult other family members on their decisions.	.34
(+) 21. Family members go along with what the family decides to do.	.47
Interests and Recreation	
(−) 15. We have difficulty thinking of things to do as a family.	.48
(+) 30. Family members share interests and hobbies with each other.	.51

(continued)

TABLE 15.1   Continued

Family Adaptability	FACTOR II Loadings
Assertiveness	
(+) 2. In our family, it is easy for everyone to express his/her opinion.	.52
(+) 14. Family members say what they want.	.39
(−) 28. Family members are afraid to say what is on their minds.	.26
Leadership (Control)	
(+) 4. Each family member has input in major family decisions.	.55
(+) 16. In solving problems, the children's suggestions are followed.	.46
Discipline	
(+) 6. Children have a say in their discipline.	.49
(+) 18. Discipline is fair in our family.	.22
Negotiation	
(+) 8. Family members discuss problems and feel good about the solutions.	.48
(+) 20. Our family tries new ways of dealing with problems.	.44
(+) 26. When problems arise, we compromise.	
Roles	
(+) 10. We shift household responsibilities from person to person.	.24
(+) 22. In our family, everyone shares responsibilities.	.39
Rules	
(−) 12. It is hard to know what the rules are in our family.	.10
(−) 24. It is difficult to get a rule changed in our family.	.19

as *all* family members like it that way (Olson et al., 1980, in press; Olson & Killorin, 1980). This is particularly relevant for cultural groups that have norms that support family behavior at the extremes (for example, rigidly enmeshed patterns in Mormon, Orthodox Jewish, and Amish families).

Development

The original FACES was developed in 1979 by Olson, Bell, and Portner. This one hundred eleven item self-report scale was constructed specifically to measure the two major dimensions in the Circumplex Model. Two populations were used to develop this instrument: 410 young adults to assess the empirical validity and 35 marriage and family counselors to assess the clinical validity of the scale. The instrument was then used in a study of 210 parent/adolescent triads. The alpha reliability of family cohesion was .83 and .75 for family adaptability.

Portner (1981) compared 55 families (parent and one adolescent) in family therapy with a matched control group of 117 nonproblem families. She compared the two groups using FACES and the Inventory of Parent-Adolescent Conflict (IPAC). As hypothesized, nonclinic families were more likely to fall into the balanced areas of the Circumplex Model on cohesion and adaptability than the clinic families (58 percent and 42 percent, respectively). Clinic families tended to be more toward the chaotic disengaged extreme (30 percent), with fewer nonclinic families at that extreme (12 percent).

Bell (1982) also utilized FACES and the IPAC to study 33 families with runaways and compared them with the same 117 nonproblem families used in the Portner (1981) study. As hypothesized, he found significantly more nonproblem families as described by the mothers and adolescents (but not the fathers) in the balanced area compared to the runaway families. Conversely, he found more runaway families at the midrange and extreme levels than nonproblem families. Also, significantly more runaway families (29 percent) were disengaged than were nonproblem families (7 percent). A higher percentage of runaway families (23 percent) were also more chaotic compared to nonproblem families (7 percent).

FACES II was developed in order to overcome some of the limitations with the original FACES. More specifically, one goal was to develop a shorter instrument with simple sentences so that it could be used with children and those with limited reading ability. Also, the number of double negatives was reduced and a revised 5-point response scale was developed. The individual autonomy (independence) scale was dropped from cohesion because it was considered more an individual characteristic rather than a family system characteristic. All of the other concepts related to the two dimensions were retained.

During the initial development of FACES II (spring 1981), 464 adults responded to 91 items. The average age of respondents was 30.5 years. The 91 items covered the 15 content areas of cohesion and adaptability with 6 items per content area, some of which were moderate items from the original FACES. On the basis of the factor analysis and reliability (alpha) analysis, the initial scale was reduced to 50 items.

To assess construct validity, factor analysis was done separately for the cohesion and adaptability items. Although there were 13 factors for cohesion and 9 factors for adaptability, the first 4 factors for each dimension accounted for about 75 percent of the variance. For the reduced scale of 50 items, the Cronbach alpha reliability figure for cohesion was .91; for adaptability, it was .80.

A test-retest reliability study was conducted in fall 1981, using the 50-item version. The time lapse between the first and second administration of FACES II was four to five weeks. Respondents were 124 university and high school students who were *not* currently enrolled in a family studies course. The average age was 19.2 years. They were asked to describe their "family of origin." The test-retest reliability for the total 50-item FACES II scale was .84; it was .83 for cohesion and .80 for adaptability.

The 50 items of the initial FACES II were administered to 2498 individuals in a cross-section study by Olson, McCubbin, Barnes, Larsen, Muxen, and Wilson (1983). This study included couples across the life cycle from young couples to retired couples. Adolescents in these families also completed FACES II. On the basis of further factor analysis and reliability checks, the 50-item scale was reduced to 30 items, with 2-3 items for each of the 14 content areas.

Validity and Reliability

The *final version* of FACES II consists of a 30-item scale containing 16 cohesion items and 14 adaptability items. There are 2 items for each of the following 8 concepts related to the cohesion dimension: emotional bonding, family boundaries, coalitions, time, space, friends, decision making, and interests and recreation. There are 2 or 3 items for each of the 6 concepts related to the adaptability dimension: assertiveness, leadership, discipline, negotiation, roles, and rules.

Construct validity was assessed by factor analysis of the data from the Olson et al. (1983) study on a sample of 2498 (N = 2082 parents, 416 adolescents). When the factor analysis solution was restricted to 2 factors, the 30 items loaded as indicated in Table 15.1. Cohesion items loaded most heavily on Factor I and adaptability items loaded mainly on Factor II.

Discriminant and predictive validity was established using the national survey data from the Olson et al. (1983) study. A discriminant analysis was used to distinguish between balanced and extreme families on the Circumplex Model. A predictive analysis was then done using the other couple and family variables to see how well they could predict the balanced from extreme families. Accuracy of predictions made by stage using couple data was as follows: childless couple stage, 100 percent; families with young children, 82 percent; families with adolescents, 82 percent; older couples, 86 percent. In summary, FACES II seemed to demonstrate discriminant and predictive validity clearly.

To assess the internal consistency reliability of the scale, Cronbach's alpha was computed separately for the two random halves of the sample and replicated again with the total sample of family members (N = 2498). The reliability based on the total sample was .87 for cohesion, .78 for adaptability, and .90 for the total scale. Test-retest reliability was established for the 50-item version and was .83 for cohesion, .80 for adaptability, and .84 for the entire FACES II.

FACES II is designed to be easily administered and quickly hand-scored. Scoring is done directly on the answer sheet. National norms and cutting points are designed so that the scores can be plotted directly into the Circumplex Model (see Figure 15.2). The cutting points for the four levels of cohesion and adaptability are indicated on Figure 15.2. Because of the similarity of the male and female responses, they were combined for both parents and adolescents. There are, however, separate cutting points for parents and adolescents.

The norms on FACES II are based on the parents and adolescents that participated in the Olson et al. (1983) study. Using only cases where there were complete data for all 30 items, a total of 2082 parents and 416 adoles-

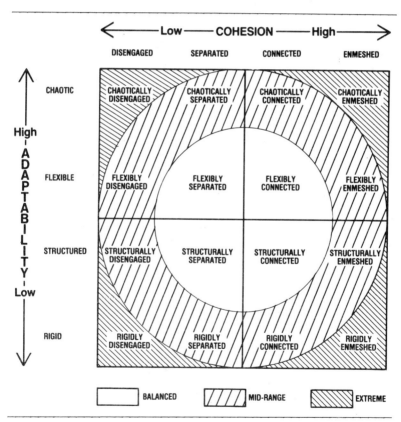

Figure 15.1   Circumplex Model: Sixteen Types of Marital and Family Systems

C O H E S I O N

	DISENGAGED PARENTS (56.9 or below) ADOLES. (47.9 or below)	SEPARATED PARENTS (57.0-65.0) ADOLES. (48.0-56.0)	CONNECTED PARENTS (65.1-73.0) ADOLES. (56.1-64.0)	ENMESHED PARENTS (73.1 and above) ADOLES. (64.1 and above)
CHAOTIC PARENTS 56.1 or above ADOLES. 52.1 or above				
FLEXIBLE PARENTS 50.1-56.0 ADOLES. 45.1-52.0				
STRUCTURED PARENTS 44.0-50.0 ADOLES. 38.0-45.0				
RIGID PARENTS 43.9 or below ADOLES. 37.9 or below				

ADAPTABILITY

NAME: _____
FAMILY MEMBER: _____
SEX: _____ AGE: _____
DATE: _____
EVALUATION: _____ (Pre/Post/FU)

TOTAL COHESION: _____
TOTAL ADAPTABILITY: _____
FAMILY TYPE: _____

In plotting the couple or family's cohesion and adaptability scores
into the Circumplex Model, try to mark the specific location within
the particular type that most accurately reflects the actual scores.

	Parents (n=2,030)		Adolescents (n=416)	
	$\bar{X}$	SD	$\bar{X}$	SD
Cohesion	64.9	8.4	56.3	9.2
Adaptability	49.9	6.6	45.4	7.9

Figure 15.2 FACES II Cutting Points

cents were used as the normative sample. Because the mean scores, standard deviations, and ranges for males and females were similar, they were combined. However, because there were such differences in the means for parents and adolescents, they were kept as separate groups.

The lack of agreement between family members was rather striking. On family cohesion, the correlation between husbands and wives was .46, .46 for husbands and adolescents, and .39 between wives and adolescents. On family adaptability, the husband-wife correlation was .32, for husband and adolescents it was .31, and for wives and adolescents it was only .21. This lack of agreement raises the validity issue of who's report is most valid. But, more important, it demonstrates the importance of obtaining FACES assessments from as many family members as possible to gain a comprehensive picture of the family system.

Significant differences were found in the Olson et al. (1983) study between stages of the family life cycle. Wives tended to rate cohesion significantly higher across all stages than did husbands. Cohesion was rated significantly higher by both husbands and wives in the early stages and later stages of the life cycle, reaching the lowest point during the adolescent stage. On adaptability, wives also perceived significantly more than husbands. While both spouses perceived greater adaptability in the early and later stages, the dip in the adolescent stage was not as great as with cohesion.

For more details and materials on FACES II, a complete manual can be purchased by writing the first author: Dr. David Olson, Family Social Science, University of Minnesota, St. Paul MN 55108. The manual includes the FACES II items, the answer sheet, the norms and cutting points and other related information.

Uses in Clinical Situations

FACES II can serve several evaluative functions in a clinical setting. It may assist in diagnosis, establishing treatment goals, measuring change during treatment, and evaluating final effects of treatment (pre, post, follow-up comparison).

In diagnosis, FACES II can help the clinician focus on understanding the dynamics of that family system rather than focusing on only the presenting problem. Graphing the total cohesion and total adaptability scores for each family member gives a global perspective of *how each family member experiences* his or her family. Because of the lack of agreement between family members previously described, it is even more important to obtain data from as many family members as possible.

In using FACES II in clinical and research settings, it is valuable to administer it twice in order to assess both the *perceived* and the *ideal* descriptions from as many family members as possible. By comparing the perceived-ideal discrepancies for each person, it is possible to assess each individual's level of *satisfaction* with his or her current family system. No norms are needed for the ideal, since the individual's ideal description serves as his or her own norm base.

An important new theoretical hypothesis (Olson et al., 1980, 1982) on the Circumplex Model demonstrates the importance of the *family satisfaction* dimension. This alternative hypothesis states that families extreme on both dimensions will function well as long as *all* individuals like it that way. The perceived *vs.* ideal discrepancy on the family satisfaction scale provides a method for assessing how individuals feel about their current family system.

Differences between family members' perceptions and ideals may illuminate problem areas. For example, while spouses may both perceive the level of family cohesion to be enmeshed, one may ideally like it that way while the other might prefer it at the other extreme, that is, disengaged. One spouse is, therefore, more satisfied with the high level of cohesion. On the other hand, because the second spouse wants more independence (less cohesion), his or her level of satisfaction will be much lower. In other words, while this couple may agree on how they perceive their relationship, they disagree on how they want it to be and their ideal descriptions provide possible therapeutic goals.

Discrepancies between family members help to illuminate the complexity of a marital and family system. Differences in their perceptions and ideals can create more confusion and difficulties in a family. Any similarity, whether in the perceived description or in desired ideal, can be interpreted by the therapist as a relationship strength.

FACES II can also be used to describe one's *family of origin*. This type of information can be particularly valuable therapeutically. Comparisons can be made between an individual's description of his or her current family (perceived), preferences (ideal), and family of origin (past).

Many families also like to know how they compare to other families. Although the therapist needs to be cautious in "proscribing normality," utilizing the FACES II norms may be of help in defining societally acceptable limits and in pointing out that there are other families that are similar. It should also be emphasized that it is more important that the family members are satisfied with the kind of family system they have (low discrepancy between perceived and ideal) than that they have a specific type of family system. In other words, there is no one best system for all families.

Olson et al's. (1983) recent study indicates that there are different types of family systems that are perceived as functional at different stages of the life cycle. For example, couples perceive greater cohesiveness early in their marriages and families with adolescents seem to experience less cohesion and greater independence. The therapist may thus find it help-ful during diagnosis to check out the appropriateness of individual family members, perceived and ideal levels for their stage in the family life cycle.

Following from the diagnosis, treatment goals can be derived and treatment strategy selected. The description of each member's ideal for his or her family can provide useful information about possible directions for change. Focus on the family system dynamics does not mean that the presenting problem should be ignored. In developing a treatment strat-egy, the therapist should recognize that the presenting problem is where the pain is focused and should take into account both the family system dynamics and the presenting problem.

FACES II can be administered several times, if desired, during treat-ment in order for both the therapist and the clients to get a sense of the change that has occurred. It is strongly suggested that FACES II be ad-ministered at least before and after treatment in order to assess the imme-diate effectiveness of the treatment program. A follow-up administration of FACES II at 3-6 months may also give some indication of the lasting effect of treatment, recognizing that other intervening factors could have an effect.

FACES II may be used in several types of intervention settings, includ-ing traditional marriage/family therapy, marriage/family enrichment groups, and group therapy programs. The clinician needs to make a deci-sion, on a case-by-case basis, as to how much of the Circumplex Model to explain to the clients so that they understand the FACES results. In an educational/intervention-type setting, a considerable amount of the de-tail of the Circumplex Model can be incorporated. For example, a popu-larized accounting of the Circumplex Model is part of the *Understanding Us* program, which focuses on family enrichment (Carnes, 1981). FACES II and the Circumplex Model are also being used in a group ther-apy program for families with chemical dependency members.

One specific advantage of using FACES II and the Circumplex Model in a group setting is that families can understand themselves better by seeing how other types of families operate. They can learn advantages and disadvantages of their own and other family types. They can observe a range of family types and may even try to experience some of these different patterns of relating in their own family. For example, a woman in an enmeshed relationship may have yearned for the freedom of a more disengaged relationship, but discovered by observing a disengaged cou-ple just how isolating and lonely a disengaged relationship can be. Hav-ing seen this, she may opt for attempts to modify her own relationship to a connected or structured level. Similarly, the husband in a disengaged relationship, yearning for enmeshment, may discover just how stifling and restrictive an enmeshed relationship is. In this way, a group setting can help couples/families expand their awareness of alternative types of relating in their own family.

Family Assessment Using FACES II

The Jones family was referred to a family counseling center because of drug use by the 15-year-old son, Mark. While the mother (Mary) came with high expectations that their son would be helped, the father (Harry) came reluctantly. All three family members took FACES II twice, once for how they "perceived" their family and a second time for how they would "ideally" like it to be. The results from that assessment are summarized in Figure 15.3.

First of all, it is apparent that while the parents generally agreed that they perceived their family as "structurally separated," their son felt that it was "rigidly enmeshed." Ideally, Mark wanted the family to be "flexibly disengaged" so the rules would be more flexible and he could also have more freedom and time away from the family (disengaged). Because of the high perceived-ideal discrepancy for Mark, it is clear that he was *not* very satisfied with the current family system.

On the other hand, Mary and Harry were more satisfied with the current family system. Mary was more satisfied than Harry, as the smaller discrepancy between her perceived and her ideal indicated. While the parents both would *ideally* have liked the family to be more connected, Mark wanted it to be less connected (disengaged). While Mary and Mark wanted the family to be more flexible, Harry wanted more rigidity.

Part of the treatment process was focused on sharing with the family their different perceptions and ideals, and the current levels of satisfaction for each member. The family then began working together with the therapist to decide what type of family system they could agree on and to try to develop it together. This helped provide goals and direction for the treatment process.

Insiders' and Outsiders' Reports

While FACES II provides information on family members' (the "insiders") perceptions of reality, clinicians or researchers (the "outsiders") can also observe the family's behavior from a different perspective. Because these two sources of information often differ (Olson, 1977), it is valuable to obtain both perspectives to obtain a more comprehensive picture of the family system and subsystems.

The outsiders' perspective on the family's reality regarding family cohesion and family adaptability could be obtained through use of the Clinical Rating Scale (Olson & Killorin, 1980), based on the Circumplex Model. The Clinical Rating Scale (CRS) contains six subscales for family

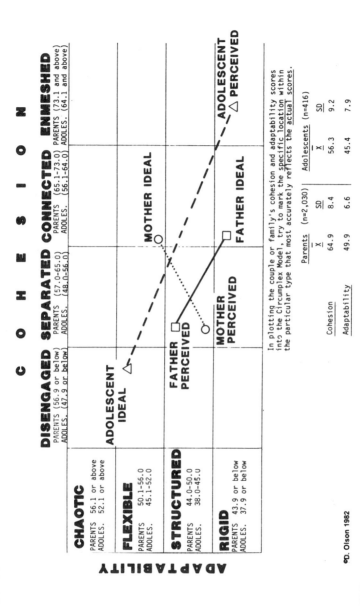

Figure 15.3   FACES II Family Profile

311

adaptability and six subscales for family cohesion that are very similar to those assessed by FACES II. The CRS can be used by therapists in evaluating or assessing families before, during, and after treatment.

Advantages and Limitations

FACES II provides a wealth of self-report information from family members on the important dimensions of family cohesion and adaptability. These two dimensions were found to be important to both family theorists and therapists alike, and they are the two central dimensions integrated into the Circumplex Model.

FACES II is a simple and efficient method that provides data on how family members perceive their current family system (perceived), how they would like it to be (ideal), and their levels of satisfaction with that system (discrepancy between the perceived-ideal). It can also be used to describe members' families of origin. A Couple Version is also available for younger and older couples without children in the home.

FACES II has high levels of reliability (test-retest and internal consistency), high levels of validity (construct, discriminant, and predictive) and has national norms based on "normal" families across the family life cycle.

FACES II is designed for both clinical assessment and research evaluation. Clinically, it can be used for diagnostic assessment, for treatment planning, and for assessment of change in family counseling and educational programs. In family therapy and education programs, it can be used to increase family members' awareness of various types of family systems in addition to their own. This information can be used to expand their potential choices and give direction for the type of relationship they would like to have for themselves.

One of the inherent limitations of any self-report instrument is that it can only provide an "insider" perspective. This limitation can, however, be overcome by also obtaining an "outsider's" perspective on the family system. This can be done using the Clinical Rating Scale developed to parallel the FACES II instrument conceptually.

While FACES II can provide a *global perspective* on an entire family system, it fails to take into account the various dyadic and triadic combinations. Likewise, it does not enable one to assess individual exceptions adequately, as in the case of a disengaged father in an otherwise enmeshed family system. It is hoped that future versions of FACES will be more able to tap this level of complexity.

APPENDIX

FACES II ITEMS

by
David H. Olson, Joyce Portner, and Richard Bell

1. Family members are supportive of each other during difficult times.
2. In our family, it is easy for everyone to express his/her opinion.
3. It is easier to discuss problems with people outside the family than with other family members.
4. Each family members has input in major family decisions.
5. Our family gathers together in the same room.
6. Children have a say in their discipline.
7. Our family does things together.
8. Family members discuss problems and feel good about the solutions.
9. In our family, everyone goes his/her own way.
10. We shift household responsbilities from person to person.
11. Family members know each other's close friends.
12. It is hard to know what the rules are in our family.
13. Family members consult other family members on their decisions.
14. Family members say what they want.
15. We have difficulty thinking of things to do as a family.
16. In solving problems, the children's suggestions are followed.
17. Family members feel very close to each other.
18. Discipline is fair in our family.
19. Family members feel closer to people outside the family than to other family members.
20. Our family tries new ways of dealing with problems.
21. Family members go along with what the family decides to do.
22. In our family, everyone shares responsibilities.
23. Family members like to spend their free time with each other.
24. It is difficult to get a rule changed in our family.
25. Family membes avoid each other at home.
26. When problems arise, we compromise.
27. We approve of each other's friends.
28. Family members are afraid to say what is on their minds.
29. Family members pair up rather than do things as a total family.
30. Family members share interests and hobbies with each other.

©D. Olson 1982   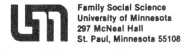   Family Social Science
University of Minnesota
297 McNeal Hall
St. Paul, Minnesota 55108

(continued)

APPENDIX Continued

FACES II: Couple Form

by
David H. Olson, Joyce Portner, and Richard Bell

1. We are supportive of each other during difficult times.
2. In our relationship, it is easy for both of use to express our opinion.
3. It is easier to discuss problems with people outside the marriage than with my partner.
4. We each have input regarding major family decisions.
5. We spend time together when we are home.
6. We are flexible in how we handle differences.
7. We do things together.
8. We discuss problems and feel good about the solutions.
9. In our marriage, we each go our own way.
10. We shift household responsibilities between us.
11. We know each other's close friends.
12. It is hard to know what the rules are in our relationship.
13. We consult each other on personal decisions.
14. We freely say what we want.
15. We have difficulty thinking of things to do together.
16. We have a good balance of leadership in our family.
17. We feel very close to each other.
18. We operate on the principle of fairness in our marriage.
19. I feel closer to people outside the marriage than to my partner.
20. We try new ways of dealing with problems.
21. I go along with what my partner decides to do.
22. In our marriage, we share responsibilities.
23. We like to spend our free time with each other.
24. It is difficult to get a rule change in our relationship.
25. We avoid each other at home.
26. When problems arise, we compromise.
27. We approve of each other's friends.
28. We are afraid to say what is on their minds.
29. We tend to do more things separately.
30. We share interests and hobbies with each other.

Family Social Science
University of Minnesota
297 McNeal Hall
St. Paul, Minnesota 55108

References

Bell, R. Q. *Parent/adolescent relationships in families with runaways: Interaction types and the Circumplex Model.* Unpublished doctoral dissertation, Family Social Science, University of Minnesota, 1982.

Carnes, P. *Understanding us.* Minneapolis: Interpersonal Communication Programs, 1981.

Olson, D. H. Insiders' and outsiders' views of relationships: Research strategies. In G. Levinger & H. Rauch (Eds.), *Close relationships.* Amherst: University of Massachusetts Press, 1977.

Olson, D. H., & Killorin, E. *Clinical rating scale for the Circumplex Model.* St. Paul: Family Social Science, University of Minnesota, 1980.

Olson, D. H., McCubbin, H., Barnes, H., Larsen, A., Muxen, M., & Wilson, M. *Families: What makes them work.* Beverly Hills, CA: Sage, 1983.

Olson, D. H., Portner, J., & Bell, R. *FACES II: Family Adaptability and Cohesion Evaluation Scales.* St. Paul: Family Social Science, University of Minnesota, 1982.

Olson, D. H., Russell, C. S., & Sprenkle, D. H. Circumplex Model of marital and family systems II: Empirical studies and clinical intervention. In J. Vincent (Ed.), *Advances in family intervention, assessment and theory.* Greenwich, CT: JAI, 1979.

Olson, D. H., Russell, C. S., & Sprenkle, D. H. Marital and family therapy: A decade review. *Journal of Marriage and the Family,* 1980, *42,* 973-993.

Olson, D. H., Sprenkle, D. H., & Russell, C. S. Circumplex Model of marital and family systems I: Cohesion and adaptability dimensions, family types, and clinical applications. *Family Process,* 1979, *18,* 3-28.

Olson, D. H., Sprenkle, D. H., & Russell, C. S. Circumplex Model of marital and family systems VI: Theoretical update. *Family Process,* in press.

Portner, J. *Parent/adolescent relationships: Interaction types and the Circumplex Model.* Unpublished doctoral dissertation, Family Social Science, University of Minnesota, 1981.

CHAPTER 16

Other Marriage and Family Questionnaires

GAYLA MARGOLIN
VIVIAN FERNANDEZ
University of Southern California

Much like newscasters who wrap up their broadcast of the day's featured events by highlighting the remaining noteworthy news, our aim here is to highlight important developments in the world of marital and family assessment. Our purpose in writing this chapter is to call attention to self-report inventories, other than those already presented, that assist clinicians who work with couples and families. In this process of winnowing out self-report instruments that benefit marital and family therapists, it quickly became clear that our task involved highly subjective discriminations. Despite considerable evidence regarding the reliability and validity of certain instruments, there is little empirical evidence that the inclusion of a specific assessment instrument does indeed improve the effectiveness of the clinician's decision making. In other words, it is difficult if not impossible to ascertain that the course of therapy would be less rewarding or less efficient had a particular instrument not been included.

Thus the task we defined for ourselves in preparing this chapter was to determine what would be gained through the use of questionnaire data that go beyond what normally is obtained through direct interactions with the couple. When marital or family therapy is specifically requested, there is no need to verify, through self-report questionnaires, that the couple or family is in fact experiencing distress. As pointed out elsewhere (for example, see Jacobson, Elwood, & Dallas, 1981; Snyder, Wills, & Keiser, 1981), the diagnostic objective in such instances involves a more precise determination of the extent and sources of the marital distress. In identifying instruments that contribute to this diagnostic objective, we used the following four criteria:

(1) Does the instrument give us perspective on the intensity of the problem? Although not always a consideration in the choice of an inter-

vention, degree of distress takes on importance when there are large discrepancies between the two spouses or when the intensity of distress on the self-report questionnaires differs from what was observed in the therapy session. The fact that standardized instruments offer a way to quantify levels of distress can be of value to the clinician. Besides simply translating marital satisfaction into numerical values, we can use normative information for a given measure to assess how a spouse compares to other distressed spouses, other nondistressed spouses, and, in general, to determine what constitutes meaningful differences in satisfaction levels. Instruments that quantify level of dissatisfaction also offer a way to compare the experiences and perceptions of the two partners.

(2) Does the instrument help us plan an intervention? There are three major ways that self-report questionnaires can help in treatment planning. First, and perhaps most typically, through questionnaires the therapist can discover what the problems are and thus determine appropriate targets for intervention. For self-report questionnaires to contribute to this process, they must do more than confirm the obvious, that the couple is dissatisfied with their communication, for example. The questionnaire data must provide a more systematic and wide-ranging assessment of conflict areas than can be accomplished through an interview.

Second, questionnaire data can assist the therapist in identifying what factors affect the problematic behavior. Changing problem behaviors requires knowing what variables influence the occurrence versus nonoccurrence of those behaviors. Couples sometimes are well aware of these variables and can accurately identify them in an interview. Other times couples need to engage in a systematic evaluation of their relationship to determine what factors influence their subjective feelings. If one-time questionnaires do not serve this function, couples can report on the same question at repeated intervals so that the therapist can carefully analyze behavior-environment relationships.

Third, continued assessment over the course of therapy serves as feedback to the therapist regarding what intervention strategies work. In one way or another, all family therapists assess the family's progress since the last session and then use that information to plan the next intervention. However, the more structured and consistent the assessment procedures, the easier it becomes to recognize the correspondence between specific therapeutic interventions and overall progress.

(3) Is the instrument a cost-efficient way to collect information? Even if questionnaires do not provide data that are qualitatively different from what eventually would be obtained through an interview, the questionnaire format typically provides a more rapid overview of the situation. If the use of questionnaires accelerates a therapist's initial orientation to a

particular couple, then more therapy time can be directed to areas that require extensive exploration.

(4) Does the use of self-report questionnaires provide a safe medium for disclosing important information? Spouses vary considerably in the degree to which they feel comfortable articulating thoughts and feelings in the therapy session as opposed to communicating the same information in a written format. Since marital therapy often is conducted conjointly, highly sensitive information may be difficult to disclose for fear of hurting the spouse or incurring reprisals. Self-report questionnaires may be a safe way to convey such information. There is a parallel advantage from the therapist's perspective: By offering spouses a means of expressing their anger, hurt, and disappointments to the therapist, self-report questionnaires may reduce the amount of blaming that occurs in the therapy session.

The review that follows examines a variety of assessment procedures that we believe meet one or more of the above criteria. Rather than present an all-inclusive listing, our intention was to describe representative instruments. Although there are a variety of types of self-report procedures, our emphasis is limited to standardized questionnaires administered verbally or in written form to one or more family members.

Self-Report Questionnaires

As has been illustrated in Chapters 8 through 15, self-report questionnaires elicit information about how family members view themselves, one another, and the relationships among them. Questionnaires typically are given at the beginning of therapy to obtain a wide variety of information with dispatch and ease. The same questionnaires may be administered again at points during therapy and after therapy has ended to assess change and the overall effects of therapy. While a number of the questionnaires already reviewed (such as the Dyadic Adjustment Scale, Chapter 8) were designed to assess the overall quality of relationships, many of the questionnaires presented below tend to have more focused objectives of asssessing one particular dimension of interaction.

Closeness Versus Distance

Interactions that occur among family members generally communicate a desire for increased intimacy or decreased intimacy (Alexander & Parsons, 1982). The interactional fabric of families typically includes both types of interpersonal functions, that is, some behaviors that pull the interactants together, some that push them apart, and some that contain both functions, creating the classic "double-bind" situation. However, based on the cumulative impact of interactions, a predominant message of closeness or distance may be revealed in the behavior of each family member to every other family member. The following questionnaires either assess family members' subjective experiences of closeness versus distance or assess the occurrence of specific actions that reflect this dimension.

The *Inventory of Family Feelings* (IFF) by Lowman (1980, 1981; Fineberg & Lowman, 1975) is a self-administered inventory that examines the overall degree of attachment between each pair of family members. The format of the IFF requires the respondent to answer "agree," "disagree," or "neutral" to items that assess how the respondent feels about each other family member (for example, "I feel close to this family member") as well as how the respondent perceives others feel about him or her (for example, "This family member doesn't pay a lot of attention to me"). Items are worded so that the inventory can be completed by any family member with a sixth-grade education. In mapping a family's pattern of positive and negative feelings, the inventory provides (1) individual scores, or how each family member rates every other member; (2) dyad scores, or the average of two members' feelings toward each other; (3) response scores, or the average of all scores that an individual gives to all other members of his or her family; and (4) reception scores, or the average of all scores given to one member by the others as a group.

Thus far there have been three validation studies of the IFF (Lowman, 1980). Overall, these studies show that families and couples in treatment score less positively than do control families. As anticipated, the most negative affect displayed in the treatment families centered on and emanated from the identified child patient. IFF affect scores, in addition, correlate negatively with level of psychopathology on the MMPI and correlate positively with observers' ratings of affect on Leary's Circumplex Model.

Summary IFF data for a treatment family are presented in Figure 16.1 in the form of a Dyadic Relationships Graph. In reference to this figure, Lowman (1981, p. 66) suggests:

> It appears that the father received the lowest Reception Score on responses from the others. As portrayed (in the Figure), the dyadic relationships in the family can be characterized as being allied within generations, the parents and the two girls having the most positive relationships and the other relationships being typically less positive. The one exception to this is the moderately positive relationship between the mother and the younger daughter.

As this example illustrates, the particular advantage of the IFF is found in its comparison among family members. By quantifying and comparing the strength of affective connections that characterize each dyad, the IFF identifies coalitions and alliances in the family. The strength of intragenerational versus cross-generational alliances are readily observed. Further-

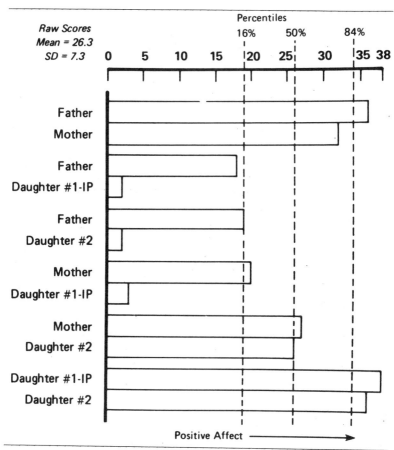

Figure 16.1   IFF Dyadic Relationships Graph

SOURCE: Reprinted from Joseph Lowman, "Love, Hate, and the Family: Measures of Emotion," pp. 57-77 in E. E. Filsinger and R. A. Lewis (Eds.), *Assessing Marriage: New Behavioral Approaches.* Copyright 1981, Sage Publications, Inc.

more, the comparison within each dyad reveals the extent of perceived equity or inequity of positive affect between any two family members. Information about the structure of family alliances, as provided by the IFF, is particularly useful for interventions that attempt to restructure the entire family system and to alter patterns of transaction within that system.

As its title suggests, the *Personal Assessment of Intimacy in Relationships* (PAIR) is designed to assess intimacy, which, according to its authors, Schaefer and Olson (Note 1, 1981; Olson & Schaefer, n.d.), is closely linked to the "separateness-togetherness" dimension of cohesion. Based on Olson's (Note 2) conceptual definition of intimacy, the PAIR identifies and assesses five areas of intimacy: emotional, social, sexual, intellectual, and recreational. The PAIR measures each spouse's expected degree of intimacy in each area, that is, what the individual would like from the relationship, versus the realized degree of intimacy, or what they are actually receiving. Rather than assume any ideal or absolute level of intimacy, spouses' scores are interpreted in terms of the differences between perceived and expected intimacy as well as the differences between the two partners.

The PAIR originated as a 7-scale, 350-item inventory but was later reduced to 75 items on the basis of the factor loading and discriminative validity of individual items. Psychometric testing of the 75-item scale showed that each scale was significantly correlated with the Locke-Wallace Marital Adjustment Scale (range = .44 to .60) and with the cohesion and expressiveness scales of the Moos Family Environment Scale (range = .20 to .48). To make administration of the PAIR as efficient as possible, the 75-item version underwent another reduction resulting in 36 items, again based on the criteria of high loading on the expected factor, low loadings on other factors, and response endorsement close to a 50/50 split. Two scales that appeared in the original version, aesthetic and spiritual intimacy, were dropped due to their failure to meet the psychometric criteria. In addition to the items that loaded onto the five remaining intimacy scales, items from Edmond's Conventionality Scale have been included to measure the extent to which the spouse gives socially desirable responses.

The final version of the PAIR contains six items for each scale including the conventionality scale. The respondent uses a five-point rating to indicate the extent to which she or he agrees versus disagrees with each item when viewing the relationship as "it is now" and then as she or he "would like it to be." Representative items include "I often feel distant from my partner" (emotional intimacy), "We enjoy spending time with other couples" (social intimacy), "I feel our sexual activity is just routine" (sexual intimacy), "My partner helps me clarify my thoughts" (intellectual intimacy), and "We enjoy the same recreational activities" (recreational intimacy). The subscales have fairly normal distributions, with scores ranging from a minimum of 6 to a maximun of 96.

As illustrated in Figure 16.2, the PAIR offers a graphic representation of the degree of perceived and expected intimacy in each of the five areas for each spouse. For this particular couple, the wife exhibits substantial discrepancies between expected and perceived scores across all five intimacy scales, while the husband exhibits discrepancies in two scales. Altogether there are two areas in which both spouses feel deprived, intellectual and sexual intimacy, and that are readily identified as targets for therapy. Based on this profile, it is obvious that the wife desires far more widespread changes than does the husband, which constitutes another issue for therapy. Since both spouses' conventionality scores are within

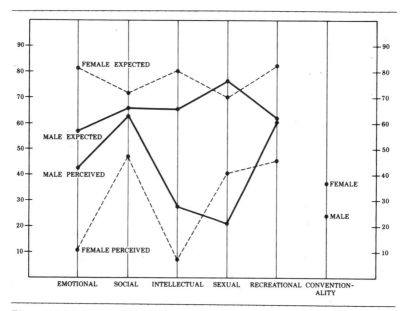

Figure 16.2   Summary of PAIR Scores

SOURCE: From "Assessing Intimacy: The PAIR Inventory," by M. T. Schaefer and D. H. Olson. Reprinted from Vol. 7, No. 1 of the *Journal of Marital and Family Therapy.* Copyright 1981 by the American Association for Marriage and Family Therapy. Reprinted by permission.

one standard deviation of the mean, there does not appear to be any distortion due to social desirability factors.

In addition to substantiating what the couple already knows about the strengths and weaknesses of their marriage, the PAIR offers an objective measure of unmet expectations and needs that may be difficult for spouses to articulate. The comparison between current preceptions and overall expectations helps spouses look beyond what is currently wrong with their marriage, thus facilitating the specification of treatment goals.

Another measure of intimacy that is strongly associated with the PAIR ($r = +.77$) is found in the *Waring Intimacy Questionnaire* (WIQ; Waring, Note 3; Waring, Weisz, & McElrath, Note 4). The WIQ, a 90-item true-false questionnaire, examines 8 component scales in an overall measurement of intimacy: (1) conflict resolution, or the ease with which differences of opinion are resolved; (2) affection, or the degree to which feelings of emotional closeness are expressed by the couple; (3) cohesion, or a feeling of commitment to the marriage; (4) sexuality, or the degree to which sexual needs are communicated and fulfilled by the marriage; (5) identity, or the couple's level of self-confidence and self-esteem; (6) compatibility, or the degree to which the couple is able to work and play together comfortably; (7) autonomy, or the success with which the couple gains independence from their families of origin and from their own offspring; and (8) expressiveness, or the degree to which thoughts, beliefs, attitudes, and feelings are shared within the marriage. WIQ data from both spouses are compiled in an intimacy profile that portrays the eight dimensions for each partner, identifies areas where there is a discrepancy in the wife's and the husband's preceived intimacy, and measures overall intimacy in the marriage (taking into account a social desirability score).

The 90-item WIQ is the final product of what was originally a 496-item questionnaire. Items initially were removed due to their content ambiguity, sex bias, or social desirability bias. Items were consequently chosen based on their high correlation with the total scale score and their low correlations with irrelevant scales. The final 90-item questionnaire is scored to provide separate scale profiles for each spouse. Comparing the profiles of the two spouses may reveal consensus in their perceptions of relationship problems or strengths (for example, an adequate sexual relationship as reflected in high sexuality scores for each), or may reveal discrepancies between the spouses (for example, a high cohesion score for husband versus a low cohesion score for wife, indicating varying levels of commitment to the marriage). Pretreatment to posttreatment comparisons have suggested that the WIQ is a sensitive tool for measuring treatment effects (Waring & Russell, 1980).

A more behavioral measure of closeness versus distance is found in the *Marital Status Inventory* (MSI; Weiss & Cerreto, 1980), which assesses precisely what steps each spouse has taken toward the dissolution of the marriage. Compared to the other instruments, which tend to measure the overall strength of a couple's emotional ties, this measure focuses directly on the types of distancing actions that already have been taken by each partner. In developing this scale, Weiss and Cerreto (1980, p. 80) worked from the assumption that "the termination of marriages unfolds as a series of discrete acts." Their objectives were to choose items that represented the sequential unfolding of steps toward divorce, to measure the extent to which the items form a unidimension scale, and to provide an instrument that would inform clinicians of the dissolution potential of a marriage.

The MSI contains 14 true-false items that range from vague thoughts of divorce (for example, "I have considered divorce or separation a few times . . . "), to specific thoughts (for example, "I have considered who would get the kids . . . "), to overt behavior (for example, "I have discussed the issue seriously and at length with my spouse"), to behaviors initiating divorce procedures (for example, "I have contacted a lawyer"). Empirical investigation of this scale has led to changes from the prior scaling of several items; yet the coefficient of scalability was a high .87. While there was a strong correlation between the MSI and the Locke-Wallace Marital Adjustment Inventory for a sample of couples who received parent training ($r = -.73$ for husband and $-.72$ for wives), there was not a strong correlation for couples receiving marital therapy. Thus the findings suggest that, for couples in therapy, marital satisfaction and marital stability are independent dimensions and must be assessed separately.

The information provided by the MSI regarding each spouse's progressive steps in the direction of divorce is often difficult to obtain simply through interviews. Certain questions (such as, Do thoughts of divorce occur to you more frequently than once per week?) can be uncomfortable to discuss and tend to interfere with other objectives of the interview such as generating an optimistic, collaborative therapeutic atmosphere. While obviating the need for direct inquiry regarding each separate step in the direction of divorce, this instrument alerts the therapist if one or both partners has engaged in distancing types of actions. For spouses who have taken a number of steps toward separation, this instrument may serve to stimulate discussion about where the relationship is headed, regardless of whether or not they receive therapy. More generally, this instrument may prove extremely valuable if further research indicates that progression to a particular stage on the scale precludes successful couples therapy and warrants divorce counseling instead.

A comparison of these four instruments demonstrates that there are different ways to measure the closeness versus distance dimension of relationships. The IFF offers a way to measure the strength of positive affect in general; the PAIR and the WIQ define and examine multiple dimensions of intimacy. Finally, the MSI measures distancing actions that have been taken by each spouse. The MSI, which evolved from a tradition of comprehensive behaviorally oriented assessment, is generally administered as part of a larger assessment package (Jacobson & Margolin, 1979; Weiss & Margolin, 1977). The PAIR, in contrast, has been used singly to gather information and provide feedback to couples. As suggested by the high correlation between the WIQ and PAIR, these two measures are quite similar. The PAIR, however, has been validated primarily on a large sample of nonclinical couples as they began an enrichment weekend. The WIQ has been used with couples in which there were psychiatric problems and/or problems of physical illness. Each of the four measures amasses information regarding closeness versus distance more systematically, comprehensively, and efficiently than could be done in the interview. Yet the capabilities of these scales to predict long-range patterns of closeness versus distance still remain to be demonstrated.

Change

A number of self-report questionnaires ask the couple to report what general areas of marital interaction are sources of tension. The *Areas of Change Questionnaire* (AC; Weiss, Hops, & Patterson, 1973; Weiss & Birchler, Note 5), in contrast, is more clearly oriented toward delineating specific treatment goals. This questionnaire assesses what specific behaviors each spouse wants changed, whether that behavior is to be accelerated or decelerated, and whether the behavior is to be changed a little or a lot. The instrument also asks each spouse to predict what types of changes the partner desires. Thus use of this instrument helps not only to pinpoint major relationship problems but also to determine whether the couple's communication regarding these problems is clear.

The AC made up of two parts containing identical listings of 34 items reflecting specific issues for a couple. Part I instructs the respondent to indicate whether she or he wants the partner to increase, decrease, or not change the rate of each behavior (for example, "I want my partner to pay attention to my sexual needs"). Part II asks the respondent to indicate whether an increase, decrease, or no change would be pleasing to the partner (for example, "It would please my partner if I paid more attention to his or her sexual needs"). Desired change is indicated in both sections along a 7-point Likert scale from "much less" (-3) to "no change" (0) to "much more" $(+3)$.

The AC has been found to discriminate between distressed and non-distressed couples (Birchler & Webb, 1977), to have high internal consistency, and to correlate highly with the Locke-Wallace Marital Adjustment Scale (Weiss et al., 1973). Based on use of this instrument in several treatment outcome studies, overall AC scores have been shown to be a sensitive index of pretreatment to posttreatment change (Margolin & Weiss, 1978; Weiss; et al., 1973). It has been suggested that the AC "provides a statement by each spouse regarding the particular behaviors which are occuring at either an insufficient or an excessive frequency" (Jacobson et al., 1981, p. 471). However, in a recent examination of the AC, Margolin, Talovic, and Weinstein (Note 6) found generally low correlations between the AC and the Spouse Observation Checklist (see Chapter 4). Thus, despite the specificity of the AC, it can no longer be assumed that the AC is an accurate index of behavioral frequencies. Margolin et al. (Note 6) also examined the perceptual accuracy component of the AC, that is, are spouses aware of what types of changes and how much change is desired of them? Based on their results, distressed rather than nondistressed spouses exhibit more perceptual accuracy, indicating that distressed couples are likely to air their marital complaints more frequently and openly than do nondistressed couples.

Although summary AC scores are strongly related to other measures of global marital adjustment, the usefulness of this measure transcends its summary score. It provides a comprehensive indexing of marital complaints, much more extensive than could be obtained in a single interview session. This characteristic, plus its ease of administration, makes the AC a good measure for repeated assessments during the course of therapy to determine what areas still are troublesome. The AC also provides clinically important information regarding specific sources of misperception. As suggested by Margolin et al. (Note 6) there is tremendous therapeutic advantage in finding out, for example, that both spouses actually want to increase their frequency of sexual intercourse although neither knows this of the other. Such instances of agreement over desired change represent mutual goals for the couple. Instances of disagreement, on the other hand, direct the therapist to difficulties in the couple's communication process as well as to specific content areas that are conflictual. Finally, due to its specific behavioral format, the AC is likely to be less susceptible to social desirability factors than instruments with more value-laden and global questions.

Another behaviorally oriented instrument is Stuart and Stuart's (1973) *Marital Pre-Counseling Inventory* (MPI). This questionnaire directs spouses' attention to what currently is going on in their relationship and to what they would like to be going on. Stuart and Stuart describe three purposes of the MPI: (1) it provides clients with socialization into therapy by directing their observations to positive elements of their own and their spouses' behaviors; (2) it provides highly organized, comprehensive data relevant to therapeutic goals; and (3) it provides the therapist and couple with a periodic evaluation of therapeutic progress. The inventory consists of 13 separate sections. As part of these, spouses evaluate their own behavior, one another's behavior, shared and individual interests, decision making, communication, sexual interaction, and general satisfaction. In each section, the respondent is asked to describe the current relationship patterns (for example, "Whose responsibility do you think it usually is now to make the following decisions?"). Then the respondent is to reconsider each area and indicate how decisions should be made. In assessing areas of change, the MPI directs attention to how a change in one's own behavior, rather than the partner's behavior, could improve the relationship (for example, "How do you think a change in your own behavior could improve your experience in these or any other areas of your sexual experience?").

Stuart and Stuart provide some data on the validity of the MPI. Comparing pretreatment and posttreatment scores on the MPI for 400 couples, they found: (1) substantial reductions in the discrepancy scores for the Decision Making scale (that is, spouses reported more congruence between how they perceived decisions to be made and how they wanted decisions to be made); and (2) increases in the General Satisfaction section (that is, from mean pretreatment satisfaction ratings of 38 percent for women and 30 percent for men to mean posttreatment ratings of 81 percent for both sexes).

As illustrated by both the AC and the MPI, measurements that focus on desired changes are particularly useful in treatment planning. These instruments direct spouses' attention and the therapist's attention to behaviorally specific treatment goals. They also serve as vehicles for helping spouses to think of change in specific, as opposed to global, terms.

Conflict

Through previously described instruments, such as the AC or the Dyadic Adjustment Scale (see Chapter 8), it is possible to assess the extent to which couples disagree about certain topics and to *infer* how well they resolve conflict. However, instruments of overall marital satisfaction do not directly assess the way that spouses handle conflict or the manner in which they express anger.

The *Conflicts Tactics Scale* (CT), by Straus (1979), was designed to fill this void by assessing, through questionnaire procedures, a variety of techniques that might be employed during a family conflict. According to Straus (1979, p. 77), while it is possible for these techniques to be assessed in an open-ended format, "in practice, the way people deal with conflict is so much a part of the unrealized, 'taken for granted,' ongoing pattern of life that much will be missed unless the respondent is specifically asked." The CT assesses three primary modes of dealing with conflict: (1) reasoning, or an intellectual approach through the use of rational discussion, argument, and reasoning; (2) verbal aggression, or the use of verbal and nonverbal acts that symbolically hurt the other; and (3) violence, or the use of physical force against another. The scale has been designed to measure conflict among all family members. To measure marital conflict, the scale examines both husband-to-wife and wife-to-husband actions. Other possible administrations examine parent-to-child, child-to-parent, and sibling-to-sibling conflict.

The original form (A) of the CT contains 14 items, while the revised form (N), which has been used in a large national survey, contains 19 items. In this later version, items range from "Discussed the issue calmly" (reasoning), to "Insulted or swore at the other" (verbal/symbolic agression), to "Threw something at the other one" (violence). There are six possible response categories, ranging from "never" to "more than 20 times," indicating the number of times each action occured during the past year. Each respondent indicates how often she or he engaged in the behavior during the past year, how often the partner engaged in the behavior during the past year, and whether or not the behavior ever had occurred in the history of the relationship. These questions can be administered in either an interview or a questionnaire format.

The three subscales have been standardized on a 0 to 100 scale indicating each respondent's percentage score vis-à-vis the total possible score. Percentile norms derived from a sample of 2143 families are available for husband-wife, wife-husband, child-child, father-child, and mother-child scores. Alpha coeffcients of reliability indicate high consistency for the verbal aggression and violence scales, but somewhat lower consistency for the reasoning scale. Moderate validity for these scales has been demonstrated by comparing CT scores as reported by each spouse, and also as reported by students for their parents (Straus, 1974, 1979).

Although used primarily for research, as opposed to clinical purposes, the CT can be of assistance to the clinician who wishes to assess a family's history of violence or to evaluate a family for child abuse or spouse abuse. The inventory may direct the clinician's attention to trouble spots in a given family that go beyond the presenting problem (such as spouse tensions in a child referral). In view of the extensive population studied for norming this instrument, the CT is particularly useful for examining whether a couple or family is similar to or deviant from a representative cross section of the population.

The *Conflict Inventory* (Margolin, Note 7), another measure for assessing how spouses handle conflict, was designed more explicitly for use in marital therapy. The CI is a newly developed self-report instrument that assesses spouses' views of how they respond to disagreements. The CI contains 26 items that span aggressive ("Insult your partner or call him/her names"), withdrawing ("Try to hide the tension you feel and act as though nothing is happening"), and problem-solving strategies ("State your position clearly"). Spouses answer the following five questions for each of the items: (1) How often do you exhibit the following behavior? (2) How often you like to exhibit the following behavior? (3) How often does your partner exhibit the behavior? (4) How often would you like your partner to exhibit the behavior? and (5) How often would your partner like you to exhibit each behavior? Indices of perceptual accuracy are obtained by matching responses between the two partners ("How often I do each behavior" in comparison to "How often my partner thinks I do each behavior"). The degree of discrepancy between desired and actual frequency of behavior is measured by matching responses within each spouse's questionnaire.

Preliminary data from spouses' ratings of one another indicate consistency in the three factors: .85 for Problem Solving, .89 for Withdrawal, and .91 for Aggression. Investigations of the CI are currently under way to determine (1) its correspondence with the CT and the Dyadic Adjustment Scale; (2) the extent to which discrepancies between desired and actual conflict behaviors correspond to overall adjustment; and (3) the extent to which the 26 items are endorsed in normal and distressed samples.

For the clinician, the CI offers a way to assess each spouse's perception of how conflict currently is handled and how she or he would like it to be handled. As such, differences in spouses' idealized perspectives are readily apparent (for example, husband rates it desirable to "suggest having sex to make up after an argument," while wife rates it undesirable). Spouses' preferred modes of conflict resolution also point out potential clashes between the spouses' values and the therapist's own ideas about how a couple should resolve conflict. Although CI items have content validity, in that they describe actions commonly reported by couples, evaluations regarding the utility of this instrument await further empirical investigation.

Sexual Interest Activity

With the increasing numbers of referrals specifically for sexual therapy, assessment devices that focus on sexual functioning and sexual satisfaction are needed. One widely used self-report inventory that meets this specific need is the *Sexual Interaction Inventory* (SII), by LoPiccolo and Steger (1974). The SII was designed for purposes of treatment planning and measuring treatment outcome when a couple's presenting complaints center around sexual issues. Since there are no objective standards for "normal" sexual behaviors, the SII measures dysfunction in terms of the discrepancy between actual and ideal behaviors. The SII examines 17 heterosexual behaviors, ranging from "seeing the partner nude" to "having intercourse with both of them having an orgasm." For each behavior, spouses independently rate how often it currently occurs, how often they would like it to occur, how pleasant they find the behavior, how pleasant they think the spouse finds it, and how pleasant the activity ideally should be for oneself and for the spouse. By summing across behaviors, the SII can be scored on five scales for each partner, that is, Frequency Dissatisfaction, Self-Acceptance, Mate Acceptance, Pleasure Mean, and Perceptual Accuracy; the SII also contains an overall summary scale.

Data on the SII summarized by LoPiccolo and Steger (1974) indicate high test-retest reliability and high internal consistency for each of the scales. Of the 11 SII scales, 9 discriminate sexually dysfunctional client couples from normals; all 11 scales appear to be reactive to a full course of sex therapy. Similar to the IFF and the PAIR, SII results are plotted on a graph for easy interpretation. The scores are plotted in respect to standard score means and standard deviations for each scale, which have been derived from a sample of 124 couples. A couple's profile contains both the husband's and the wife's scaled scores, making it easy to compare the two spouses. The manual that accompanies the SII (LoPiccolo & Steger, Note 8) offers interpretations for single-scale and multiple-scale profiles that aid in diagnostic determinations and in formulating treatment plans. For example, for scale 2 (Self-Acceptance-Male), part of the interpretation reads: "This scale compares the male's current pleasure with his desired pleasure. . . . This scale should be interpreted configurally with scale 3. If scale 2 and scale 3 are both elevated above 70, the male gets little pleasure from sex and wants to change. If scale 2 is elevated but scale 3 is not, the male has unrealistic expectations or low self-esteem" (LoPiccolo & Steger, Note 8, p. 4). The SII interpretation guide helps identify good and poor treatment risks, points out when comunication training is needed, and indicates what additional assessment questions should be pursued before deciding upon a treatment plan.

Communication

As emphasis on communication per se can be investigated through the *Primary Communication Inventory* (PCI; Navran, 1967), the *Personal Report of Spouse Communication Apprehension* (PRSCA; Powers & Hutchinson, 1979), or the *Marital Communication Inventory* (MCI; Bienvenu, 1970; see Chapter 10), to name a few examples. The PCI contains 25 items, 18 of which focus on verbal communication (for example, "Do you and your spouse use words which have a special meaning not understood by outsiders?") and 7 of which are related to nonverbal communication ("Does your spouse explain or express himself to you through a glance or gesture?"). Each question is answered on a 5-point Likert scale ranging from "very frequently" to "never." Norms for happily and unhappily married couples are available for the PCI. The MCI similarly asks spouses to rate one another ("usually" to "never") on 48 items related to patterns, characteristics, and styles of communication (see Chapter 10). In contrast to the MCI and the PCI, which focus on the spouse's behavior, the PRSCA asks spouses to comment on their own behaviors. This scale specifically examines communication apprehension, or the extent to which one's fear of communicating outweighs the prospect of gain from interaction. Respondents respond on a Likert scale ("strongly agree" to "strongly disagree") to such items as "I feel tense and nervous while communicating when my spouse is in a bad mood" and "I feel no apprehension at verbalizing my immediate reaction to my spouse." While lacking norms comparing distressed and nondistressed couples, high scorers on the PRSCA report greater marital satisfaction than do low scorers.

As a supplement to unstructured interviewing procedures, each of these instruments directs attention to specific facets of communication. In addition, discussion surrounding the inventories between the spouses may help identify ways that spouses misperceive one another and may stimulate their own thinking about how to be more effective communicators.

Children's Reports of Family Interaction

As indicated by what we have reviewed thus far, there are far more inventories to assess marital interaction than to assess the interaction of all family members including the children. Similarly, while there are a preponderance of questionnaires that use parental reports to assess the child as the identified patient (see Achenbach, 1978; Achenbach & Edelbrock, 1979; Becker, 1960; Kohn, 1977; Lessing, Williams, & Revelle, 1981; Quary, 1977), there are fewer questionnaires that rely on the child as the reporter, or that assess parent-child relationships. As part of this review of self-report questionnaires regarding family interaction, we want to draw attention to questionnaires designed explicitly for children to assess parent-child relations. Although few in numbers, these questionnaires highlight the fact that children's perceptions serve as a valuable resource in understanding family interaction.

The *Adolescent Form of the Family Communication Inventory* (A-FCI; Bienvenu, 1969) was developed to assess the patterns and characteristics in communication from parents to adolescents. The A-FCI contains 36 items for adolescents to rate their parents in terms of general characteristics (such as critical, sarcastic, trusting, understanding), as well as specific behaviors (such as parents pay compliments to child, parents consider child's opinion in making decisions). Adolescents respond to each item by checking one of three possible responses: "usually," "sometimes," and "never." The instrument requires a seventh-grade reading level and is best suited for adolescents ages 13 and older. According to Bienvenu (1969, p. 121), the A-FCI helps the adolescent in "focusing in on his relationship with his parents in a way that he had not done before. Furthermore, the non-verbal client is often better able to communicate his feelings and attitudes through this technique." In addition to stimulating discussion in family therapy sessions, the A-FCI can be used to pinpoint specific problem areas in parent-adolescent communication.

The *Parent Perception Inventory* (PPI; Hazzard, Christensen, & Margolin, in press) is a measurement of children's reports of important positive and negative parental behaviors. Compared to the A-FCI, the PPI covers other areas in addition to communication, and is to be used with younger children. The PPI contains 18 questions, reflecting 9 positive response classes (positive reinforcement, comfort, talk time, involvement in decision making, time together, positive evaluation, allowing independence, assistance, and nonverbal affection) and 9 negative classes of responses (privilege removal, criticism, command, physical punishment, yelling, threatening, time-out, nagging, and ignoring). The PPI is administered by reading the description and examplars of each behavioral class (for example, for criticism, the question reads, "How often does your mother tell you you're no good, tell you that you messed up or didn't do something right, or criticize you?"). The child then responds by circling a phrase on a 5-point scale ranging from "never" to "a lot." The entire scale is administered for one parent and then is repeated for the second parent.

The PPI was designed to be used for comparing children's perceptions of their parents at pretherapy and posttherapy, that is, to measure whether or not children view the parents as acting differently as a function of therapy. It was designed to be especially sensitive to a behaviorally oriented parent-training approach in which the parents are taught specific child-management skills. Its usefulness for this purpose, however, still is being examined. Data on the PPI, unrelated to this treatment outcome question, have indicated that: (1) children of nondistressed compared to distressed families report fewer negative behaviors from the mother; (2) children of nondistressed compared to distressed families indicate greater similarity in the behavior of their two parents; and (3) PPI scores are related to children's self-concept scores.

Two well-known objective scales used primarily for research purposes are *Bronfenbrenner's Parental Behavior Questionnaire* (BPB; Siegelman, 1965) and Schaefer's *Child Report Questionnaire* (CRQ; Schaefer, 1965). Although their length is a problem, both instruments assess important dimensions of parent-child interaction and can be used to note perceived strengths and deficiencies of the parent-child relationship. Schaefer's scale was developed around the two orthogonal dimensions of love versus hostility and autonomy versus control. These abstract dimensions then were translated into 26 categories of observable parental behavior (for instance, hostility was translated into irritability, negative evaluation, and rejection). The complete inventory contains a 10-item scale for each of the 26 separate categories. Sample items for irritability, for example, are "Loses her/his temper with me when I don't help around the house" and "Gets cross and nervous when I'm noisy inside the house." Internal consistency reliabilities for the 4 abstract scales are high (range [2] .66 to .84). Approximately half of the 26 scales differentiate normal from delinquent boys. As opposed to the 260 items of Schaefer's scale, Siegelman used the BPB, which consisted of 45 statements concerning parental behavior. The BPB measures 15 variables that represent 3 basic factors: loving, punishing, and demanding. Both of these scales can be used to see how the child's relationship is different with the mother and the father, as well as how different children within the same family perceive each parent.

There are, in addition, two projective-type scales that deserve our attention. The first is the *Family Relations Test* (FRT; Bene & Anthony, 1957) which was designed to measure the direction and intensity of the child's feelings toward the various members of his or her family and also to measure the child's perceptions of how the family members view him or her. FRT procedures create a playful situation: There are 20 paper doll figures representing various people from young children to grandparents. As the first step in the FRT, the child chooses figures that represent members of his or her own family. Each family figure, plus a "Nobody" figure, is then attached to a boxlike base that has a slit on top. The child is then given cards that contain messages and is instructed to put each card into the figure for whom the message best fits.

There are two versions of the FRT, one for older children and one for younger children. The form for younger children (ages 8 and younger) measures positive feelings coming from the child (for example, "[child's name] likes to play with you"), positive feelings going toward the child (for example, "You make [child's name] feel happy. Who makes [child's name] feel happy?"), as well as negative feelings going in both directions. Besides being worded differently, the form for older children differentiates between mild versus strong positive and negative feelings (for example, "This person in the family nags sometimes" [mild] versus "Sometimes I think I would be happier if this person was not in our family" [strong]). The form for older children also involves specific items for parental overindulgence and overprotection (for example, "This is the person in the family that mother makes too big a fuss about"). Summing the number of items for each category that have been distributed to each family member offers an indication of the relative psychological importance of various family members, the ratio of positive to negative feelings associated with each family member, and the amount of perceived reciprocity (outgoing versus incoming) in those feelings.

Overall, the FRT helps children to express perceptions and reactions of which they are aware, but that may be difficult to articulate without the structure and concreteness of this task. The test manual provides considerable information about the interpretation of FRT responses and offers many examples of children in inpatient and outpatient treatment. Unfortunately, however, there are no normative data on well-adjusted children. As an indication of validity of the FRT, data from parents regarding their feelings toward the child compare favorably with children's test results on incoming feelings.

Finally, the *Roberts Apperception Test for Children* (RATC) (McArthur & Roberts, 1982) is a new instrument to assess children's perceptions of common interpersonal situations. In contrast to other inventories, which directly assess children's perceptions of their own family, this instrument elicits children's thoughts, concerns, conflicts, and coping styles in a less personalized family-oriented situation. Similar in format to the Thematic Apperception Test and to the Children's Apperception Test, in the RATC children are presented with stimulus cards and asked to make up a story about each picture. The RATC, however, differs from other projective tests in that it was designed specifically for children ages 6 through 15, and children are depicted in each scene. Each card represents important interpersonal themes such as parental conflict, parental affection, parental support, maternal limit setting, peer conflict, and sibling rivalries. The objective scoring system for the RATC provides (1) a profile matrix, which contains eight adaptive scales (such as support, limit setting, and resolution) and five clinical scales (such as anxiety, regression, and aggression), as well as (2) an interpersonal matrix, which summarizes the relationship between particular themes and interactions with a particular person (for example, the relationship between aggression and a father figure). As with any projective test, interpretations of the RATC are not straightforward. However, in view of the age-normed profiles based on 200 well-adjusted children, it is possible to determine when a child's score on a particular scale is statistically deviant. Based on the child's profile, inferences can be made about the child's overall level of functioning as well as about the nature of his or her relationships with key figures.

As illustrated by this brief review of child measures, there are a number of ways to obtain children's impressions of the family structure and, more specifically, of parent-child or child-child relationships. The A-FCI and the PPI were designed specifically to be used in family therapy. While the emphasis of the A-FCI is on stimulating discussion in the therapy setting, the purpose of the PPI is to measure treatment outcome. For a more comprehensive picture of how children feel they are treated by their parents, the BPB or the CRQ are good choices. Their utility in the clinical situation, however, has not yet been demonstrated. The FRT and the RATC, on the other hand, have been designed primarily for situations in which the child is the identified patient. Use of these instruments may reveal important issues in the broader family context and thus may alert the therapist when family therapy, as opposed to individual child therapy, is needed.

The reliability of children's reports is, of course, an issue when using any of these measures. Due to the power structure of families, children typically have more to fear than adults in accurately revealing their perceptions of other family members. For this reason, it is important for the therapist to let the child know under what circumstances information will be told to the parents. Sometimes simply filling out the questionnaires helps children to organize their thoughts so that they can better articulate their ideas in the therapy session. At other times the questionnaires foster private communications between the therapist and child that then can be brought back into the family therapy session. In either case, by using what is learned from these questionnaires, the therapist communicates to the child that his or her opinions play an important part in what occurs in family therapy.

Conclusions

We have reviewed a number of self-report instruments that can be of assistance in the difficult job of conducting marital and family therapy. With the exception of behaviorally oriented therapies, marital and family therapy has developed with little emphasis on structured assessment. Our intention was to suggest ways that structured assessment could be better integrated into marital and family therapy.

The focus was on questionnaires that provide a standardized format for eliciting and interpreting family members' self-reports. This type of measurement, of course, is subject to numerous sources of error, such as inaccuracy, inconsistency, response biases, social desirability biases, and so on. Nonetheless, the majority of the information we rely on in marital and family therapy is subject to the same problems. In view of the fact that marital and family therapists generally do not have direct access to important transactions that occur in the marital and family systems, we need to rely on the self-report of family members. Similarly, in view of the fact that emotions, passions, attitudes, opinions, and other nonobservable dimensions constitute the raw material for marital and family therapy, self-report is our only way to tap into these spheres. Whether or not to accept self-report as a valid data base is thus a moot issue. It is our hope that we have provided ideas about how to introduce greater systematization and comprehension into such reports.

Reference Notes

1. Schaefer, M. T., & Olson, D. H. *Diagnosing intimacy: The PAIR Inventory.* Paper presented at the National Council on Family Relations, San Diego, October 1977.

2. Olson, D. H. *Communication and intimacy.* Unpublished manuscript, University of Minnesota, 1977.

3. Waring, E. M. *Waring Intimacy Questionnaire, Form 90.* Unpublished booklet. Available from E. M. Waring, Victoria Hospital, Department of Psychiatry, 375 South Street, London, Ontario, N6A465.

4. Waring, E. M., Weisz, G., & McElrath, D. *The measurement of intimacy in marriage by questionnaire.* Unpublished manuscript, University of South Carolina, undated.

5. Weiss, R. L., & Birchler, G. R. *Areas of change.* Unpublished manuscript, University of Oregon, 1975.

6. Margolin, G., Talovic, S., & Weinstein, C. *The Areas of Change Questionnaire: A practical approach to marital assessment.* Manuscript submitted for publication, 1982.

7. Margolin, G. *Conflict Inventory.* Unpublished manuscript, University of Southern California, 1980.

8. LoPiccolo, J., & Steger, J. C. *Sexual Interaction Inventory (SII) scoring and interpretation manual.* Unpublished manuscript, State University of New York at Stony Brook, undated.

References

Achenbach, T. M. The Child Behavior Profile: I. Boys aged 6 through 11. *Journal of Consulting and Clinical Psychology,* 1978, *46,* 478-488.

Achenbach, T. M., & Edelbrock, C. S. The Child Behavior Profile: II. Boys aged 12-16 and girls aged 6-11 and 12-16. *Journal of Consulting and Clinical Psychology,* 1979, *47,* 223-233.

Alexander, J., & Parsons, B. V. *Functional family therapy.* Monterey, CA: Brooks/Cole, 1982.

Becker, W. C. The relationship of factors in parental ratings of self and each other to the behavior of kindergarten children as rated by mothers, fathers and teachers. *Journal of Consulting Psychology,* 1960, *24,* 507-527.

Bene, E., & Anthony, J. *Manual for the Family Relations Test.* London: National Foundation for Educational Research in England & Wales, 1957.

Bienvenu, M. J. Measurement of parent-adolescent communication. *Family Coordinator,* 1969, *17,* 117-121.

Bienvenu, M. J. Measurement of marital communication. *Family Coordinator,* 1970, *18,* 26-31.

Birchler, G. R., & Webb, L. J. Discriminating interaction in behavior in happy and unhappy marriages. *Journal of Consulting and Clinical Psychology,* 1977, *45,* 494-495.

Fineberg, B. L., & Lowman, J. Affect and status dimensions of marital adjustment. *Journal of Marriage and the Family,* 1975, *37,* 155-160.

Hazzard, A., Christensen, A., & Margolin, G. Children's perceptions of parental behaviors. *Journal of Abnormal Child Psychology,* in press.

Jacobson, N. S., Ellwood, R., & Dallas, M. The behavioral assessment of marital dysfunction. In D. H. Barlow (Ed.), *Behavioral assessment of adult disorders.* New York: Gilford, 1981.

Jacobson, N. S., & Margolin, G. *Marital therapy: Strategies based on social learning and behavior exchange principles.* New York: Brunner/Mazel, 1979.

Kohn, M. The Kohn Social Competence Scale and Kohn Symptom Checklist for the preschool child: A follow-up report. *Journal of Abnormal Child Psychology,* 1977, *5,* 249-263.

Lessing, E. E., Williams, V., & Revelle, W. Parallel forms of the IJR Behavior Checklist for Parents, Teachers and Clinicians. *Journal of Consulting and Clinical Psychology,* 1981, *49,* 34-50.

LoPiccolo, J., & Steger, J. C. The Sexual Interaction Inventory: A new instrument for assessment of sexual dysfunction. *Archives of Sexual Behavior,* 1974, *3,* 585-595.

Lowman, J. Measurement of family affective structure. *Journal of Personality Assessment,* 1980, *44,* 130-141.

Lowman, J. Love, hate, and the family: Measures of emotion. In E. E. Filsinger & R. A. Lewis (Eds.), *Assessing marriage: New behavioral approaches.* Beverly Hills, CA: Sage, 1981.

Margolin, G., & Weiss, R. L. Comparative evaluation of therapeutic components associated with behavioral marital treatment. *Journal of Consulting and Clinical Psychology,* 1978, *46,* 1476-1486.

McArthur, D. S., & Roberts, G. E. *Roberts Apperception Test for Children—Manual.* Los Angeles: Western Psychological Services, 1982.

Navran, L. Communication and adjustment in marriage. *Family Process,* 1967, *6,* 173-184.

Olson, D. H., & Schaefer, M. T. *PAIR: Personal Assessment of Intimacy in Relationships—Procedure manual.* St. Paul: Family Social Science, University of Minnesota, n.d.

Powers, W. G., & Hutchinson, K. The measurement of communication apprehension in the marriage relationship. *Journal of Marriage and the Family,* 1979, *41,* 89-95.

Quay, H. C. Measuring dimensions of deviant behavior: The Behavior Problem Checklist. *Journal of Abnormal Child Psychology,* 1977, *5,* 277-287.

Schaefer, E. S. Children's reports of parental behavior: An inventory. *Child Development,* 1965, *36,* 413-424.

Schaefer, M. T., & Olson, D. H. Assessing intimacy: The PAIR Inventory. *Journal of Marital and Family Therapy,* 1981, *7,* 47-60.

Siegelman, M. Evaluation of Bronfenbrenner's questionnaire for children concerning parental behavior. *Child Development,* 1965, *36,* 163-174.

Snyder, D. K., Wills, R. M., & Keiser, T. W. Empirical validation of the Marital Satisfaction Inventory: An actuarial approach. *Journal of Consulting and Clinical Psychology,* 1981, *49,* 262-268.

Straus, M. A. Leveling civility and violence in the family. *Journal of Marriage and the Family,* 1974, *36,* 13-29.

Straus, M. A. Measuring intrafamily conflict and violence: The Conflict Tactics (CT) Scales. *Journal of Marriage and the Family,* 1979, *41,* 75-88.

Stuart, R. B., & Stuart, F. *Marital Pre-Counseling Inventory.* Champaign, IL: Research Press, 1973.

Waring, E. M., & Russell, L. Cognitive family therapy: An outcome study. *Journal of Sex and Marital Therapy,* 1980, *6.*

Weiss, R. L., & Cerreto, M. S. The Marital Status Inventory: Development of a measure of dissolution potential. *American Journal of Family Therapy,* 1980, *8,* 80-85.

Weiss, R. L., Hops, H., & Patterson, G. R. A framework for conceptualizing marital conflict, a technology for altering it, some data for evaluating it. In L. A. Hamerlynck, L. C. Handy, & E. J. Mash (Eds.), *Behavior change: Methodology, concepts and practice.* Champaign, IL: Research Press, 1973.

Weiss, R. L., & Margolin, G. Marital conflict and accord. In A. R. Ciminero, K. S. Calhoun, & H. E. Adams (Eds.), *Handbook for behavioral assessment.* New York: John Wiley, 1977.

About the Authors

Stephen A. Anderson is Assistant Professor and Clinical Faculty Member in the Marital and Family Therapy Training Program, Department of Human Development and Family Relations, University of Connecticut. He is a Clinical Member of the American Association for Marriage and Family Therapy. His areas of interest include family stress and coping, normative transitions over the family life cycle, assessment and uses of family myths in family therapy, and evaluation of clinical outcome in marital and family therapy.

Ralph E. Chavez is a graduate research assistant in medical psychology at Southern Illinois University—Carbondale. His areas of interest are marital and sex therapy and research, and psychosomatic medicine, both research and treatment.

Rand D. Conger is Associate Professor and Department Head of Human Development and Family Ecology at the University of Illinois—Urbana. His principal research and teaching interests are in the areas of parent-child interaction, adolescent development, and observational assessment of social process. His work has appeared in several professional journals and edited volumes.

Joan M. Druckman, Ph.D., is a practicing licensed psychologist in the state of California and is a faculty member of the California Graduate School of Marital and Family Therapy in San Rafael, California. She is a coauthor of the PREPARE and ENRICH premarital and marital assessment inventories. Her current research interests include marital and family assessment and family treatment evaluation.

Erik E. Filsinger is Assistant Professor of Family Studies in Home Economics at Arizona State University. He has published numerous scholarly articles and is coeditor, with R. A. Lewis, of *Assessing Marriage: New Behavioral Approaches* (Sage, 1981). He is currently an Associate Editor for the *Journal of Marriage and the Family.*

David G. Fournier is Associate Professor of Family Relations and Child Development and Faculty Associate of the Family Study Center at Oklahoma State University. He is author or coauthor of several diagnostic techniques and has published evaluative reviews of marriage and family assessment. He is currently President of the Oklahoma Council on Family Relations and Treasurer of the Oklahoma Association for Marriage and Family Therapy. He received his B.A. and M.A. in psychology from the University of Missouri—Kansas City and his Ph.D. in family social science from the University of Minnesota in 1979.

John M. Gottman is Professor of Psychology at the University of Illinois—Urbana-Champaign. He received his Ph.D. in 1971 from the University of Wisconsin—Madison. He is the recipient of a Research Scientist Development Award from the National Institute of Mental Health for 1979-1984. His specialty areas include clinical and developmental psychology, and his research interests are in the areas of marital interaction and children's friendships and acquaintanceships.

Charles L. Griffin is an Instructor in the Department of Family and Child Development, Kansas State University, and a member of the American Association for Marriage and Family Therapists and of the National Council on Family Relations. His research interests include clinical practice and the assessment of outcome in marriage and family therapy.

Stephen N. Haynes is Professor of Psychology at Southern Illinois University—Carbondale. He has published numerous papers and books in the areas of marital distress, behavioral assessment, and medical psychology.

Alletta Hudgens is employed as a Family Therapist at Abbott-Northwestern Hospital in Minneapolis, Minnesota, and is also in private practice. She has taught courses in women's issues and sex roles at the University of Minnesota.

Michael Kearney is currently working as a marriage and family therapist in the Twin Cities area. He is a Ph.D. candidate in the Department of Family Social Science at the University of Minnesota, St. Paul.

Hamilton I. McCubbin is Professor and Head of the Department of Family Social Science, University of Minnesota. He is a member of the Native Hawaiian Education Executive Committee and is Vice-President of Publications, National Council of Family Relations. He is also on the editorial boards of several scholarly journals, including the *Journal of Marriage and the Family* and the *Journal of Family Relations*. His intellectual pursuits include research and writing on family stress, coping, and social support; family adaptation to life change events; and family coping with cerebral palsy, myelomeninogocele, and cystic fibrosis. He is author or coauthor of *Family Separation and Reunion* (1974), *Families in the Military System* (1976), *Family Stress, Coping and Social Support* (1982), and *Families: What Makes Them Work* (1983).

Gayla Margolin is Assistant Professor of Psychology at the University of Southern California. She is coauthor of *Marital Therapy: Strategies Based on Social Learning and Behavior Exchange Principles.* Her scholarly and applied interests are in marital and family assessment and therapy, with a particular focus on marital conflict.

Howard J. Markman is Associate Professor of Psychology and Director of Clinical Psychology Training at the University of Denver. His research interests are in the etiology and prevention of marital distress. He is currently conducting a longitudinal study of 150 couples, starting before marriage and continuing through the early stages of family development.

Bernice S. Moos is a statistician and computer programmer in the Department of Psychiatry and Behavioral Sciences at the Stanford University and Veterans Administration Medical Centers. During the past decade she has engaged in a program of research on alcoholism and alcohol abuse, and has focused primarily on assessing the characteristics of families and their impacts.

Rudolf H. Moos is Research Career Scientist and Professor in the Department of Psychiatry and Behavioral Sciences at the Stanford University and Veterans Administration Medical Centers, where he also directs the Social Ecology Laboratory. He is particularly interested in the conceptualization of social environments and their determinants and effects. He has been involved in a program of research to assess the stress and resource characteristics of family settings and how they are related to the outcome of treatment for alcoholism and for depression.

Clifford I. Notarius is Associate Professor of Psychology at the Catholic University of America in Washington, D.C.

David H. Olson is Professor of Family Social Science at the University of Minnesota. He is Associate Editor and on the editorial board of several professional family journals, including *Journal of Marriage and the Family, Family Process, International Journal of Family Therapy, Journal of Marriage and Family Therapy, American Journal of Family Therapy,* and *Family System Medicine.* He has published the following books: *Treating Relationships, Power in Families,* five volumes of the *Inventory of Marriage and Family Literature,* and *Family Studies Review Yearbook,* Volume 1. The primary goal of his work is to bridge research, theory, and practice.

Joan M. Patterson is a Research Associate in the Department of Family Social Science, University of Minnesota. She is coeditor of *Social Stress and the Family* and *Family Stress, Coping and Social Support.* She is also coauthor of a manual of assessment tools for measuring stress and coping and of several manuscripts advancing a theoretical framework (Double ABCX) for understanding variation in family response to stress.

Barbara Ann Perry is a counselor in private practice in Eugene, Oregon. She holds a courtesy appointment at the University of Oregon, where she is affiliated with the Oregon Marital Studies Program.

Joyce Portner is Program Director in the Department of Continuing Education in Social Work, University of Minnesota. She also has a marriage and family therapy practice with the Family Consultation Center in Minneapolis.

Walter R. Schumm is Assistant Professor in the Department of Family and Child Development, Kansas State University. His research interests include research methodology in family studies and relationships between marital quality and personal values and attitudes.

Douglas K. Snyder is Associate Professor of Psychology at the University of Kentucky—Lexington. His clinical and research interests lie primarily in marital assessment and therapy. He serves as a Consulting Editor for the *American Journal of Family Therapy* and the *Merrill-Palmer Quarterly Journal of Developmental Psychology*. He is the recipient of a three-year research grant from the National Institute of Mental Health to identify predictors of couples' response to marital therapy.

Graham B. Spanier is Vice Provost for Undergraduate Studies and Professor of Sociology and Psychiatry at the State University of New York—Stony Brook. His primary interests are in the quality and stability of marital relationships and in family demography. His most recent book is *The Child in the Family*, coauthored with Jay Belsky and Richard Lerner. He is now preparing a book summarizing a longitudinal study of the transition from marriage to divorce to remarriage.

Kendra J. Summers, while completing a doctoral degree in clinical psychology at the University of Oregon, has been active in the field of marital research, focusing on both the analysis of couples' interactions and the potential impact of video playback on spouses. She completed a B.A. in psychology and an M.S. in human development and the family at the University of Nebraska.

Nelly A. Vanzetti is completing her doctoral studies in clinical psychology at Catholic University in Washington, D.C.

Robert L. Weiss is Professor of Psychology and Director of the Oregon Marital Studies Program at the University of Oregon. He has been active in marital research and theory since 1967.